MEDIA POWER IN POLITICS

MEDIA POWER IN POLITICS
Second Edition

Doris A. Graber
University of Illinois at Chicago

A Division of Congressional Quarterly Inc.
1414 22nd Street N.W., Washington, D.C. 20037

Library of Congress Cataloging-in-Publication Data

Media power in politics.

    1. Mass media—Political aspects—United States.
2. Mass media—Social aspects—United States.
I. Graber, Doris A. (Doris Appel), 1923-
HN90.M3M43   1990   302.23   89-15925
ISBN 0-87187-515-2

To Emily, Lauren, Brittany, and Spencer
who need the power of knowledge
to master their world

CONTENTS

PREFACE

The media's role in U.S. politics has always fascinated and concerned political observers. Research based on scientific analysis, previously hampered by the lack of adequate theories and research tools, is now booming. It is therefore becoming increasingly difficult for students of the interplay of media and politics to master the wealth of new studies. The problem is particularly acute when courses combine a media and politics perspective with concentration on other facets of politics.

Media Power in Politics solves the problem. It allows students to familiarize themselves with some of the best literature in this rapidly expanding field without burdening them with an excessive amount of reading and numerous trips to the library's reserve reading room. As described fully in the Introduction, this volume is a collection of essays that may be used as primary reading for courses on mass media and politics, public opinion, political communication, and mass media and society. It is also suitable as supplementary reading in American government courses and in courses that focus on public policy formation. The book includes contributions by media professionals as well as scholars. The selections span several social science disciplines, thus giving students a chance to see problems from an interdisciplinary perspective.

Media Power in Politics is divided into six parts, prefaced by introductions that outline major areas of media impact. A brief commentary precedes each selection, highlighting its principal contributions and introducing its author or authors. The essays follow the original text in all essential matters. Deletions and editorial inserts are clearly marked. Footnotes have been renumbered when necessary to maintain unbroken sequences, but footnote styles have not been altered. Factual errors, such as erroneous dates and misspelled names, have been corrected.

The thirty-seven selections reprinted in this book represent the work of sixty-five authors. Many of them are nationally and internationally recognized scholars; others have just begun careers that promise to earn them distinction. I thank all of them for the contributions they have made to understanding media and for their willingness to allow me to include their work in this collection of readings. Thanks also are due to the many publishers who consented to the use of selections that originally appeared in their books and journals.

Preparation of a book of readings entails many tasks beyond selecting and editing the contents and writing introductory comments. I am grateful to the staff at CQ Press for handling these tasks ably and expeditiously as well as for performing the usual editorial functions. Special thanks are due to Joanne Daniels, director of CQ Press, Kerry Kern, production editor, and Margaret Seawell Benjaminson, project editor. Glenn Pinnau of the University of Illinois at Chicago provided excellent research and technical assistance. I am grateful for his extraordinary diligence and skill.

Doris A. Graber

INTRODUCTION

I s mass media power in politics a reality, an exaggeration, or a myth? No clear, definitive answers are in sight despite a great deal of research and informed speculation. Current investigations shed light on many factors that explain variations in media power. They suggest when, where, and why media power peaks and when it reaches bottom. In fact, the literature exploring media power has been expanding so rapidly that it is difficult for newcomers to the field to gain an overview of the substantive information and research approaches. A book of readings simplifies the task.

Media Power in Politics is designed to introduce the reader to the many ways in which questions about media power in politics have been asked and answered. The essays analyze mass media effects on the political system in general and on political subsystems—such as Congress, the executive branch, and organized lobbies and protest groups—in particular. They record numerous instances of interactions with the mass media that have brought about profound changes in the structure and functions of political institutions and groups. The nature and magnitude of such changes raise exceptionally provocative questions about the roles that a privately controlled profession—journalism—and the private mass media enterprise as a whole play and should play in the political process.

Each of the six sections into which the essays have been grouped illustrates the influence of mass media on an important facet of U.S. politics. Part 1 deals with mass media effects in general. The selections in Parts 2 through 5 explore the influence of mass media on political opinions and preferences, on presidential and congressional elections, on participants within and outside the political power structure, and on the formation and implementation of domestic and foreign public policies. Part 6 examines private and public efforts in the United States and abroad to control the impact of the mass media.

Several principles guided the choice of specific selections. Most important among these were the significance and quality of the research and its ability to shed light on diverse aspects of media power. This second edition includes several studies that compare media power in the United States with media power abroad because comparisons bring media effects into sharper focus. Similarly, this edition presents more writings by foreign authors than did the first because they approach the issue of media power from different perspectives. While a concerted effort was again made to include well-known media scholars from different social science disciplines, newcomers to the field and practitioners also have been given space. To offer as many approaches as possible, each author's work, with one minor exception, is represented by a single selection only.

Attractiveness and clarity of presentation and ease of reading also were major choice criteria. Several long-term and recent "classics" in the field have been retained to show its intellectual origins and contemporary milestones. Thirteen essays from the first edition appear, in slightly abbreviated form, in the current volume. For the twenty-four new selections, the goal has been to include the most recent and thought-provoking scholarship. The book, therefore, alerts readers to the latest developments in a rapidly growing, interdisciplinary area of study. It presents the work of political scientists, sociologists, communication researchers, and media practitioners.

To stimulate thinking about the processes for acquiring knowledge, along with thinking about substantive issues and public policies, several of the readings contain information about theories, research designs, and research methods. A number of essays explain and illustrate particularly well the procedures for content analysis. The introduction to Part 1 includes a brief description of this important media research technique. The footnotes and bibliographies in most selections provide ample leads to additional methodological explanations as well as other types of reading.

Readers should keep in mind that the excerpts were chosen with a specific purpose in mind: to assess the impact of the media on the political process. This was not necessarily the primary purpose of each of the authors. Therefore, the precise thrust of the original work cannot always be judged from the thrust of the excerpts presented here. Readers also must keep in mind that a price must be paid for trimming selections to hone the argument and accelerate its pace. Interesting methodological and factual details and arguments had to be omitted. The reward is a more succinct presentation of relevant information that allows the main arguments to emerge with greater clarity.

In addition to the six broad categories into which these essays have been divided, other groupings are possible. Readers wishing to focus on research trends, for example, will find selections 1.1, 1.2, 2.1, 2.4, 2.5, 3.1, and 5.3 particularly helpful. The essays also make it possible to compare various research techniques, including quantitative content analysis (1.4, 2.6, 3.6, 4.3, 4.7, 5.1, 5.2, and 5.6); qualitative content evaluation (2.3, 3.5, and 6.4); along with large- and small-scale surveys that use cross-sectional or panel approaches (1.6, 2.1, 2.4, 3.2, 3.4, 5.4, 5.5, 5.6, and 6.2). Other research techniques presented in the book are intensive interviews (2.5, 3.6, 4.2, 4.6, and 6.2) and experimental work (2.5).

The essays also can be used to study various aspects of the newsmaking process. All selections are relevant, but several address the topic explicitly (1.4, 2.3, 3.5, 4.2, 4.3, 4.7, 5.4, 5.6, 6.5, and 6.6). The study of news making raises questions about the implications of the television age for the quality of American democracy when public opinion, elections, and the influence of pressure groups have been altered by the medium. Many essays touch on these questions. In a few essays, these questions come close to being at the heart of the argument (1.3, 2.3, 2.4, 3.1, 3.5, and 6.4). The media's role in crises is explored in selections 4.5, 5.2, 5.3, and 6.3. Finally, one might establish a separate category for essays that present comparative analysis. Several essays offer comparisons among different countries or groups and comparisons among different types of media (1.4, 1.6, 4.3, 4.6, 6.3, 6.4, and 6.6).

Many essays illustrate concepts covered also in other sections. The boundaries between the six parts of the book are therefore flexible. For example, the essay by Adams and others (1.5) in Part 1, which addresses the study of media effects, can be supplemented by selections from Parts 4 and 5. The selections in Part 2 by Page, Shapiro, and Dempsey (2.4) and by Iyengar (2.5), which deal with agenda setting, are also relevant for media effects discussed in Part 1. Other essays relevant to Part 1 are the Paletz and Guthrie selection (4.3) in Part 4, which examines media impact on political actors, and four selections from Part 5, which addresses public policies (5.1, 5.3, 5.4, and 5.6). The McCombs and Shaw essay (2.1) focuses on agenda setting but does so in the context of a presidential election. It was placed in Part 2, which deals with shaping the political agenda, although it also contributes to Part 3, which deals with the impact of media on elections. Selections in Part 4, which report how the media treat specific political actors, can be supplemented with the Schram selection (3.5) in Part 3, on presidential elections, the Pritchard selection (5.1) in Part 5, on decision making by prosecutors, and the Luke essay (6.3) in Part 6, on the nuclear policies of several leaders. Other selections in Part 6, which discuss efforts to control media output, also shed light on the reciprocal influence of the media and the executive branch, Congress, and pressure groups covered in Part 4 (6.1, 6.2, 6.3, and 6.5).

Similarly, discussion of media impact on public policy is not limited to Part 5. Articles in other sections raise policy issues concerning the treatment of dissident groups (4.6, 4.7), the regulation of various economic sectors (6.1, 6.3, 6.5), and child abuse (2.2). All of these selections broaden the picture sketched out in Part 5.

The flexibility of *Media Power in Politics* springs from its rich content and from the variety of disciplinary viewpoints that are included. The importance of the issues raised by the media's role in contemporary politics and the fascination of exploring this new area in the study of politics have attracted many brilliant scholars. You are invited to sample their works in whatever order best suits your purposes.

1. PUTTING MASS MEDIA EFFECTS IN PERSPECTIVE

T his section puts research on mass media effects into historical and contextual perspective. Where have we been? Where are we going? In the first selection, Joseph T. Klapper summarizes pre-1960 theories and research about media effects. The main conclusion reached in his book— *the* classic work on media effects—is that the mass media function among and through multiple and intertwined mediating factors and influences. Most of the time, the media reinforce existing conditions rather than producing new ones. Their impact, therefore, is limited.

Denis McQuail updates the story of media effects research. His essay presents a broad overview of current theories, research, and knowledge about the influence of mass media on politics. He argues that the minimal effects myth of the 1960s has been exploded and that media research has entered a new phase, thanks to new theories and new research tools. Scholars now take a broader view of the scope and variety of possible effects. They realize the need to examine each type separately and the importance of studying the context in which effects occur.

In the next selection Walter Lippmann comments on the role presumably and actually played by the media in informing citizens. He notes the wide discrepancy between the role assigned to the media by democratic theory and the capabilities of the media in the real world. News is not truth. It is a tiny slice of reality removed from the context that gives it meaning. No study of the effects of news on public thinking would be complete without including at least a small portion of the wisdom of this modern political philosopher. His trenchant writings about public affairs spanned more than fifty years and continue to provide important insights into the media's impact on politics.

Walter C. Soderlund and Carmen Schmitt shed further light on the problem of conveying truth. The same situation reported by news media in various countries will give rise to very different images. The effects of the reporting will vary accordingly. Thus it is not the situation itself that influences thought and action but the image that emerges when the facts are reported.

The Soderlund and Schmitt essay is the first of several selections that provide details about content analysis as a research technique. Content analysis assesses the media stimulus that produced or failed to produce a

5

particular effect. The technique can be used informally, through reading or watching mass media stories and gleaning general impressions; or it can be used formally, through more elaborate procedures. In formal content analysis, researchers specify the features of the story that relate to their particular concerns. They then examine the story systematically to identify and record the presence or absence of these features. Soderlund and Schmitt, for example, recorded (*coded* is the technical term) whether stories about El Salvador were editorials, cartoons, or straight news stories and whether they appeared on the front or back page. They also noted to whom the stories were attributed, the specific issues and actors discussed, and whether the stories reflected positively or negatively on various political groups. Content analysis most commonly is done manually because categorizations often require complex judgments, but it also can be done through computer searches of texts that judge the frequency and verbal context of words designating key concepts.

During the early phases of media effects research, investigators usually looked only for changes in behavior. When behavior remained stable, they declared that there had been no effects. But when research was broadened to include effects other than behavior, such as changes in attitudes or knowledge, large new areas of effects came into view. The selection by William C. Adams and his coworkers demonstrates how difficult it is to anticipate all possible effects of a media stimulus. Much work remains to be done to conceptualize all conceivable media effects and to build adequate methods of discovery into research designs.

The final selection, by Laurence Parisot, raises yet another issue in the complex story of media effects. The influence of the media can be severely diminished if the audience lacks faith in journalists and journalism. Stories that normally would have a powerful impact may accomplish little if they lack credibility for the audience. The Parisot essay assesses credibility factors in five countries, permitting both cross-cultural and interinstitutional comparisons.

1.1

The Effectiveness of Mass Communication

Joseph T. Klapper

Editor's Note. What effect does published news have on society? Joseph T. Klapper addresses this question through a comprehensive examination of the findings of modern communications research during its formative years between 1940 and 1960. He evaluated more than one thousand studies to produce *The Effects of Mass Communication.*

Although Klapper warned that many important media effects might have escaped attention in the early studies, his findings were interpreted as demonstrating that media effects are minimal. The book had a profound impact on media studies, discouraging them for a number of years. As the selections presented here demonstrate, that interpretation of Klapper's work was unwarranted. He chronicled the complexities that media researchers face and the resulting disparities in their findings about the nature and magnitude of effects. Klapper's work remains a sound analysis of the implications of early effects research. His analysis is essential for understanding the directions of subsequent research on the effects of mass communication.

Klapper received his training as a sociologist at Columbia University. He served on the faculties of the University of Washington, Stanford, City College of New York, and Brooklyn Polytechnic Institute. He also held research positions in government and the private sector, including the directorship of social research for the Columbia Broadcasting System (CBS). This selection is from *The Effects of Mass Communication* (New York: Free Press, 1960).

Twenty years ago, writers who undertook to discuss mass communications typically felt obliged to define that then unfamiliar term. In the intervening years, conjecture and research upon the topic, particularly in reference to the *effects* of mass communication, have burgeoned. The literature has reached that stage of profusion and disarray, characteristic

of all proliferating disciplines, at which researchers and research administrators speak wistfully of establishing centers where the accumulating
data might be sifted and stored. The field has grown to the point at which
its practitioners are periodically asked by other researchers to attempt to
assess the cascade, to determine whither we are tumbling, to attempt to
assess, in short "what we know about the effects of mass communication."

What we know of course varies, depending on whether we are
discussing one type of effect or another. In regard to some points, the
evidence is remarkably consistent. In regard to others, the data contain
apparent anomalies or apparent outright contradictions. These characteristics of the data are by now well known, and they have given rise to a
widespread pessimism about the possibility of ever bringing any order to
the field.

The author acknowledges and will here briefly document the
pessimism, but he neither condones nor shares it. He will rather propose
that we have arrived at the brink of hope. More specifically, he will here
propose that we have reached the point at which certain empirical
generalizations may be tentatively formulated. A few such generalizations
will be presented, and it will be further proposed that they are capable of
ordering a good deal of the data, of resolving certain apparent anomalies,
and of indicating avenues for new and logically relevant research.

The Bases of Pessimism

The pessimism, at present, is widespread, and it exists both among
the interested lay public and within the research fraternity.

Some degree of pessimism, or even cynicism, is surely to be expected
from the lay public, whose questions we have failed to answer. Teachers,
preachers, parents, and legislators have asked us a thousand times over
these past fifteen years whether violence in the media produces delinquency, whether the escapist nature of much of the fare does not blind
people to reality, and just what the media can do to the political
persuasions of their audiences. To these questions we have not only failed
to provide definitive answers, but we have done something worse: we
have provided evidence in partial support of every hue of every view. We
have claimed, on the one hand, and on empirical grounds, that escapist
material provides its audience with blinders and with an unrealistic view
of life,[1] and, on the other hand, that it helps them meet life's real
problems.[2] We have hedged on the crime and violence question, typically
saying, "Well, probably there is no causative relationship, but there just
might be a triggering effect."[3] In reference to persuasion, we have
maintained that the media are after all not so terribly powerful,[4] and yet
we have reported their impressive successes in promoting such varied
phenomena as religious intolerance,[5] the sale of war bonds,[6] belief in the

American Way,[7] and disenchantment with Boy Scout activities.[8] It is surely no wonder that a bewildered public should regard with cynicism a research tradition which supplies, instead of definitive answers, a plethora of relevant but inconclusive and at times seemingly contradictory findings.

Considerable pessimism, of a different order, is also to be expected within the research fraternity itself. Such anomalous findings as have been cited above seemed to us at first to betoken merely the need of more penetrating and rigorous research. We shaped insights into hypotheses and eagerly set up research designs in quest of the additional variables which we were sure would bring order out of chaos and enable us to describe the process of effect with sufficient precision to diagnose and predict. But the variables emerged in such a cataract that we almost drowned. The relatively placid waters of "who says what to whom" [9] were early seen to be muddied by audience predispositions, "self-selection," and selective perception. More recent studies, both in the laboratory and the social world, documented the influence of a host of other variables including various aspects of contextual organization;[10] the audiences' image of the sources;[11] the simple passage of time;[12] the group orientation of the audience member and the degree to which he values group membership;[13] the activity of opinion leaders;[14] the social aspects of the situation during and after exposure to the media,[15] and the degree to which the audience member is forced to play a role;[16] the personality pattern of the audience member,[17] his social class, and the level of his frustrations;[18] the nature of the media in a free enterprise system;[19] and the availability of "social mechanism[s] for implementing action drives." [20] The list, if not endless, is at least overwhelming, and it continues to grow. Almost every aspect of the life of the audience member and the culture in which the communication occurs seems susceptible of relation to the process of communication effect. As early as 1948, Berelson, cogitating on what was then known, came to the accurate if perhaps moody conclusion that "some kinds of *communication* on some kinds of *issues,* brought to the attention of some kinds of *people* under some kinds of *conditions,* have some kinds of *effects.*" [21] It is surely no wonder that today, after another decade at the inexhaustible fount of variables, some researchers should feel that the formulation of any systematic description of what effects are how effected, and the predictive application of such principles, are goals which become the more distant as they are the more vigorously pursued.

But, as has been said, the present author takes no such pessimistic view. He rather proposes that we already know a good deal more about communication than we thought we did, and that we are on the verge of being able to proceed toward more abundant and more fruitful knowledge.

The Bases of Hope

This optimism is based on two phenomena. The first of these is a new orientation toward the study of communication effects which has recently become conspicuous in the literature. And the second phenomenon is the emergence, from this new approach, of a few tentative generalizations.

In describing the new approach, and in presenting the generalizations, the author submits rather than asserts. He hopes to be extremely suggestive, but he cannot yet be conclusive. And if these pages bespeak optimism, they also bespeak the tentativeness of exploratory rather than exhaustive thought. Explicit note will in fact be taken ... of wide areas to which the generalizations do not seem to apply, and warnings will be sounded against the pitfalls of regarding them as all-inclusive or axiomatic.

The "Phenomenistic" Approach

The new orientation, which has of course been hitherto and variously formulated, can perhaps be described, in a confessedly oversimplified way, as a shift away from the concept of "hypodermic effect" toward an approach which might be called "situational" or "functional." [22] Because of the specific, and for our purposes sometimes irrelevant, connotations attached to these two terms, we will here use a word coined by the present author in an earlier publication and refer to the approach as "phenomenistic." [23] Whatever it be called, it is in essence a shift *away* from the tendency to regard mass communication as a necessary and sufficient cause of audience effects, toward a view of the media as influences, working amid other influences, in a total situation. The old quest of specific effects stemming from the communication has given way to the observation of existing conditions or changes, followed by an inquiry into the factors, *including* mass communication, which produced those conditions and changes, and the roles which these factors played relative to each other. In short, attempts to assess a stimulus which was presumed to work alone have given way to an assessment of the role of that stimulus in a total observed phenomenon.

Examples of the new approach are becoming fairly numerous. The so-called Elmira[24] and Decatur[25] studies, for example, set out to determine the critical factors in various types of observed decisions, rather than to focus exclusively on whether media did or did not have effects. The Rileys and Maccoby focus on the varying functions which media serve for different sorts of children, rather than inquiring whether media do or do not affect them.[26] Some of the more laboratory-oriented researchers, in particular the Hovland school, have been conducting ingeniously designed controlled experiments in which the communication stimulus is a constant, and various extra-communication factors are the variables.[27]

This new approach, which views mass media as one among a series of factors working in patterned ways their wonders to perform, seems to the author already to have been extremely useful, and to have made possible a series of generalizations which will very shortly be advanced.

Before the generalizations are advanced, however, a few words of preliminary warning about the phenomenistic approach seem highly in order.... [I]f research is to provide socially meaningful answers to questions about the effects of mass communication, it must inquire into the relative prevalence of these different conditions under which mass communication has different effects. Unfortunately, communication research has not often addressed itself to such questions.... It may, however, be noted that if the phenomenistic approach thus tends to delay the provision of definitive answers, it does so in the interests of the eventual answers being the more meaningful.

It must be remembered that though mass communication seems usually to be a *contributory* cause of effects, it is often a major or necessary cause and in some instances a sufficient cause. The fact that its effect is often mediated, or that it often works among other influences, must not blind us to the fact that mass communication possesses qualities which distinguish it from other influences, and that by virtue of these qualities, it is likely to have characteristic effects....

...[T]he phenomenistic approach seems to the present author to offer good hope that the disarray of communications research findings may to some degree be ordered.... [T]he approach has in fact made possible a series of generalizations which will now be advanced. They are submitted very gingerly. They seem to the author at once extremely generic and quite immature; they seem on the one hand to involve little that has not been said, and on the other hand to be frightfully daring. They do seem, however, to be capable of relating a good deal of data about the processes, factors, and directions of communication effects, and of doing this in such a way that findings which hitherto appeared to be at best anomalous if not actually contradictory, begin to look like orderly variations on a few basic themes.

Emerging Generalizations

The generalizations will first be presented in their bare bones and without intervening comment.... Without further ado, then, it is tentatively proposed that:

1. Mass communication *ordinarily* does not serve as a necessary and sufficient cause of audience effects,[28] but rather functions among and through a nexus of mediating factors and influences.

2. These mediating factors are such that they typically render mass

communication a contributory agent, but not the sole cause, in a process of reinforcing the existing conditions. . . .

3. On such occasions as mass communication does function in the service of change, one of two conditions is likely to exist. Either:

a. the mediating factors will be found to be inoperative and the effect of the media will be found to be direct; *or*

b. the mediating factors, which normally favor reinforcement, will be found to be themselves impelling toward change.

4. There are certain residual situations in which mass communication seems to produce direct effects, or directly and of itself to serve certain psycho-physical functions.

5. The efficacy of mass communication, either as a contributory agent or as an agent of direct effect, is affected by various aspects of the media and communications themselves or of the communication situation (including, for example, aspects of textual organization, the nature of the source and medium, the existing climate of public opinion, and the like). . . .

Conclusions

It would seem desirable to conclude . . . with an evaluative note on the five generalizations. . . . What follows is . . . a purely subjective and personal offering. As in all previous such contexts, the author here submits rather than asserts.

On the positive side, the generalizations appear to have served three major functions.

First . . . the generalizations have permitted us in some measure to organize, or to "account for," a considerable number of communications research findings which have previously seemed discrete and anomalous. . . .

[T]his organization of existing data . . . permitted us to see gaps—to discover, for example, that certain presumed outcomes have to date been neither documented nor shown not to occur. This points to a second contribution: the generalizations seem capable of indicating avenues of needed research which are logically related to existing knowledge.

. . . [F]uture thought and research must inevitably change the generalizations themselves. As presently formulated, they constitute only a single tentative step forward, and it may reasonably be hoped that their refinement or emendation would enlarge rather than reduce the area of their applicability.

Finally, it is in the extent of the applicability of the generalizations, coupled with their present primitive nature, that the author finds particular basis for hope. Sketchy and imperfect as they are, these propositions regarding the process and direction of effect seem applicable to the effects of persuasive communications and to the effects of various kinds of non-persuasive media content upon a wide range of audience orientations and behavior patterns. Furthermore, the mediating variables to which the generalizations point—variables such as predispositions, group membership, personality patterns, and the like—seem to play essentially similar roles in all these various kinds of effects. Even if the generalizations turn out to be wholly in error, they seem nevertheless sufficiently useful and sufficiently applicable to justify the faith that *some* generalizations can in due time be made. And the author has indicated, from the outset, that he is "less concerned with insuring the viability of these generalizations than he is with indicating that the time for generalization is at hand."

For certainly these particular generalizations do not usher in the millennium. They are imperfect and underdeveloped, they are inadequate in scope, and in some senses they are dangerous.

They do not, for example, cover the residuum of direct effects, such as the creation of moods, except to note that such effects exist. They recognize, but in no way illuminate, the dynamism of the variety of effects stemming from such contextual and presentational variables as order, timing, camera angles, and the like. They are less easy to apply, and are conceivably inapplicable, to certain other broad areas of effect, such as the effect of the media upon each other, upon patterns of daily life, and upon cultural values as a whole. To be sure, we have spoken of cultural values as a mediating factor which in part determines media content, but certainly some sort of circular relationship must exist, and media content must in turn affect cultural values.

Such concepts suggest what is perhaps the greatest danger inherent both in these generalizations and in the approach to communications research from which they derive. And that danger . . . is the tendency to go overboard in blindly minimizing the effects and potentialities of mass communications. In reaping the fruits of the discovery that mass media function amid a nexus of other influences, we must not forget that the influences nevertheless differ. Mass media of communication possess various characteristics and capabilities distinct from those of peer groups or opinion leaders. They are, after all, media of *mass* communication, which daily address tremendous cross-sections of the population with a single voice. It is neither sociologically unimportant nor insignificant that the media have rendered it possible, as Wiebe (1952) has put it, for Americans from all social strata to laugh at the same joke, nor is it insignificant that total strangers, upon the first meeting, may share valid social expectations that small talk about Lucy and Desi, or about Betty Furness, will be mutually comprehensible. We must not lose sight of the particular characteristics of the media nor of the likelihood that of this particular character there may be engendered peculiar effects.

We must remember also that under conditions and in situations other than those described in this volume, the media of mass communication may well have effects which are quite different and possibly more dramatic or extensive than those which have here been documented.

For example, the research here cited which bears upon mass communication as an instrument of persuasion has typically dealt with non-crucial issues and has been pursued either in laboratories or in naturalistic situations within a relatively stable society. Little attention has here been given to the potentialities of persuasive mass communication at times of massive political upheaval or in situations of actual or imminent social unrest. . . .

Even within a relatively stable social situation, the media of mass communication may well exercise extensive social effects upon the masses by the indirect road of affecting the elite. Particular vehicles of mass communication (e.g., *The New York Times*) and other vehicles directed toward a more specialized audience (e.g., *The Wall Street Journal* or *U.S. News and World Report*) may reasonably be supposed to affect the decisions and behavior of policy-making elites. Individual business and political leaders may or may not be "opinion leaders" in the sense in which the term is used in communications research—i.e., they may or may not critically influence a handful of their peers. But their decisions and their consequent behavior in themselves affect society at large, and the mere fact of their taking a particular stand frequently serves to make that stand and the issue to which it pertains a topic of media reporting and debate, and a topic in regard to which personal influence, in the more restricted sense of the term, is exercised. The media may, in short, stimulate the elite to actions which affect the masses and which incidentally restimulate and so affect both the media and channels of interpersonal influence.

It has also been suggested that the classic studies of how voters make up their minds—e.g., Lazarsfeld, Berelson, and Gaudet (1948) and Berelson, Lazarsfeld, and McPhee (1954)—provide an incomplete picture of the total effects of mass communication because they concentrate only on effects which occur *during* the campaign itself. Lang and Lang (1959), for example, point out that although most of the voters observed in such studies apparently kept to a decision made before the campaign began, shifts in voting behavior sufficient to produce changes of administration do occur. They suggest that such changes take place slowly *between* the campaigns, as new issues arise and as images of the parties change or fail to change. Mass communication, they propose, makes these issues salient and builds the party images, and may thus exercise a much more extensive effect than is revealed in the classic voting studies. The Langs call for research designed to investigate the possibility of such effects and of various other types of effect which they believe mass communication may exercise upon political opinion.

Some elections, furthermore, may be more "critical" than others. Key (1955), for example, notes that there is "a category of elections," including those of 1896 and 1928, in which

> . . . voters are, at least from impressionistic evidence, unusually deeply concerned, in which the extent of electoral involvement is relatively quite high, and in which the decisive results of the voting reveal a sharp alteration of the pre-existing cleavage within the electorate. Moreover, and perhaps this is the truly differentiating characteristic of this sort of election, the realignment made manifest in the voting in such elections seems to persist for several succeeding elections.[29]

The elections on which the classic voting studies focus are not "critical" by these criteria, but are rather occasions on which previously manifested alignments held more or less stable. What role mass communication may play in determining voters' decisions before a "critical" election is not yet known.

Mass media may also have extensive but as yet undocumented effects of various non-political sorts. We have already alluded, for example, to the probable but unmapped interplay between the mass media and cultural values. To look more closely into one aspect of this matter, one might postulate that the media play a particularly important role in the socialization and acculturation of children. . . . But to what degree do the media structure, even for younger children, the society and the culture which they are entering? The influence of the media in these respects is no doubt modified by the influence of the family, of the school, and of peer groups; but the question of ultimate media effect is complicated, perhaps beyond the possibility of simplification, by the fact that the persons comprising these very sources of extra-media influence are themselves exposed to and affected by the media. . . .

One may also speculate on the possibility that some of the functions served by mass communication may, perhaps indirectly and perhaps only after a long period, have certain effects both upon the audience as individuals and upon integral elements of the social structure. We have noted, for example, that certain light media material, such as comic strips, serves certain audience members by providing a common ground for social discourse. It is interesting to speculate on what alternative systems of serving the same function may be thereby replaced, may be reduced in importance, or may simply fail to develop for lack of being needed. If no comic strips or other mass media material existed to serve the conversational needs of the adult males observed by Bogart (1955), might they and others like them perhaps be more actively interested in each other's real life goals and problems? Do mass media, by providing an easily available and common ground for chit-chat, perhaps reduce or retard the development of interest in one's fellow men? And to what degree, if any, has the serving of such functions by mass media affected the functions previously served by such institutions as the neighborhood bar and barber shop? . . .

The phenomenistic approach, which our generalizations suggest, also has its dangers and limitations. As we have noted, the identification of conditions under which mass communication has different effects is only a step in the direction of answering the basic questions about the incidence of such effects. If the influence of mass communication is to be described in socially meaningful terms, research must also inquire into the relative prevalence of the conditions under which the several effects occur.

The need of recognizing such limitations and of taking precautions against such dangers does not seem to the author, however, to compromise the usefulness of either the generalizations or the phenomenistic approach. The most fruitful path for communications research appears to him to be neither the path of abstract theorizing nor the path, which so many researchers have deserted, of seeking simple and direct effects of which mass communication is the sole and sufficient cause. The author sees far greater hope in the new approach which begins with the existing phenomenon—an observed change of opinions, for example—and which attempts to assess the roles of the several influences which produced it. He sees similar hope in the pursuit of logically related controlled experiments in which the multifarious extramedia factors being investigated are built into the research design. These are the paths which seem to him to have brought us to the point of tentative generalization and which seem likely to lead further toward the still distant goal of empirically-documented theory.

Notes

1. e.g., Arnheim, Rudolf (1944). "The World of the Daytime Serial," and Herzog, Herta (1944). "What Do We Really Know about Daytime Serial Listeners," in Lazarsfeld, Paul F. and Stanton, Frank N., eds., *Radio Research 1942-1943*, New York: Duell, Sloan and Pearce.
2. e.g., Warner, W. Lloyd and Henry, William E. (1948). "The Radio Day Time Serial: A Symbolic Analysis," *Genetic Psychology Monographs*, XXXVII, 3-71.
3. This is a typical conclusion of surveys of pertinent literature and comment, e.g., Bogart, Leo (1956). *The Age of Television*. New York: Frederick Ungar Publishing Company, pp. 258-74.
4. e.g., Lazarsfeld, Paul F. and Merton, Robert K. (1948). "Mass Communication, Popular Taste and Organized Social Action," in Bryson, Lyman, ed., *The Communication of Ideas*, New York: Harper and Brothers; Klapper, Joseph T. (1948). "Mass Media and the Engineering of Consent." *American Scholar*, XVII, 419-29.

5. Klapper, Joseph T. (1949). *The Effects of Mass Media*. New York: Bureau of Applied Social Research, Columbia University, pp. II-25, IV-52.

6. Merton, Robert K. (1946). *Mass Persuasion*. New York: Harper and Brothers.

7. The efficacy as well as the limitations of media in this regard are perhaps most exhaustively documented in the various unclassified evaluation reports of the United States Information Agency.

8. Kelley, Harold H. and Volkart, Edmund H. (1952). "The Resistance to Change of Group Anchored Attitudes," *American Sociological Review*, XVII, 453-65.

9. Lasswell proposed in 1946 (Smith, Bruce L.; Lasswell, Harold D.; and Casey, Ralph D. (1946). *Propaganda, Communication and Public Opinion*. Princeton: Princeton University Press, p. 121) that communications research might be described as an inquiry into, "*Who* says *what*, through what *channels* (media) of communication, *to whom*, (with) what . . . results." This now classic formulation was widely adopted as an organizational framework for courses and books of reading in communication research and greatly influenced research orientations as well.

10. Hovland, Carl I. (1954). "Effects of the Mass Media of Communication," in Lindzey, Gardiner, ed., *Handbook of Social Psychology*. Cambridge, Mass.: Addison-Wesley Publishing Company, Inc., II, 1062-103; Hovland, Carl I., et al. (1957). *The Order of Presentation in Persuasion*. New Haven: Yale University Press.

11. e.g., Merton (1946), p. 61 ff; Freeman, Howard E.; Weeks, H. Ashley; and Wertheimer, Walter I. (1955). "News Commentator Effect: A Study in Knowledge and Opinion Change," *Public Opinion Quarterly*, XIX, 209-15; Hovland, Carl I.; Janis, Irving L.; and Kelley, Harold H. (1953). *Communication and Persuasion*. New Haven: Yale University Press, Chapter ii, which summarizes a series of studies by Hovland, Weiss, and Kelman.

12. Hovland, Carl I.; Lumsdaine, Arthur A.; and Sheffield, Fred D. (1949). *Experiments on Mass Communication*, "Studies in Social Psychology in World War II." Vol. III. Princeton: Princeton University Press, in re "sleeper effects" and "temporal effects."

13. e.g., Kelley and Volkart (1952); Riley, John W. and Riley, Mathilda White (1959). "Mass Communication and the Social System," in Merton, Robert K.; Broom, Leonard; and Cottrell, Leonard S. Jr., eds.; *Sociology Today: Problems and Prospects*. New York: Basic Books; Ford, Joseph B. (1954). "The Primary Group in Mass Communication." *Sociology and Social Research*, XXXVIII, 3; Katz, Elihu and Lazarsfeld, Paul F. (1955). *Personal Influence: The Part Played by People in the Flow of Mass Communication*. Glencoe, Ill.: The Free Press, reviews a vast literature on the subject (pp. 15-133).

14. Katz, Elihu (1957). "The Two-Step Flow of Communication: An Up-to-Date Report on an Hypothesis," *Public Opinion Quarterly*, XXI, 61-78, provides an exhaustive review of the topic.

15. Freidson, Eliot (1953). "The Relation of the Social Situation of Contact to the Media of Mass Communication," *Public Opinion Quarterly*, XVII, 230-38. For an earlier insight, see Cooper, Eunice and Johoda, Marie (1947). "The Evasion of Propaganda," *Journal of Psychology*, XXIII, 15-25.

16. Janis, Irving L. and King, B. T. (1954). "The Influencing of Role-Playing on Opinion Change," *Journal of Abnormal and Social Psychology*, XLIX, 211-18; King, B. T. and Janis, Irving L. (1953). "Comparison of the Effectiveness of Improvised Versus Non-Improvised Role-Playing in Producing Opinion Change." Paper presented before the Eastern Psychological Association; Kelman, Herbert C. (1953). "Attitude Change as a Function of Response Restrictions," *Human Relations*, VI, 185-214, all of which is summarized and evaluated in Hovland, Janis and Kelley (1953), also Michael, Donald N. and Maccoby, Nathan (1953). "Factors Influencing Verbal Learning from Films under Varying Conditions of Audience Participation," *Journal of Experimental Psychology*, XLVI, 411-18.

17. Janis, Irving L. (1954). "Personality Correlates of Susceptibility to Persuasion," *Journal of Personality*, XXII, 504-18; Hovland, Janis and Kelley (1953), chap. vi; Janis, et al. (1959). *Personality and Persuasibility*. New Haven: Yale University Press.

18. Maccoby, Eleanor E. (1954). "Why Do Children Watch TV?" *Public Opinion Quarterly*, XVIII, 239-44.

19. e.g., Klapper (1948); Klapper (1949), pp. IV-20-27; Wiebe, Gerhard D. (1952). "Responses to the Televised Kefauver Hearings," *Public Opinion Quarterly*, XVI, 179-200.

20. Wiebe, Gerhard D. (1951). "Merchandising Commodities and Citizenship on Television," *Public Opinion Quarterly*, XV, 679-91.

21. Berelson, Bernard (1948). "Communication and Public Opinion," in Schramm, Wilbur, *Communications in Modern Society*. Urbana, Ill.: University of Illinois Press, p. 172.

22. Berelson, Bernard; Lazarsfeld, Paul F. and McPhee, William N. (1954). *Voting: A Study of Opinion Formation in a Presidential Campaign*. Chicago: University of Chicago Press, p. 234 for "hypodermic effect."

23. Klapper, Joseph T. (1957-58). "What We Know About the Effects of Mass Communication: The Brink of Hope," *Public Opinion Quarterly*, XXI, 4.

24. Berelson, Lazarsfeld, and McPhee (1954), p. 234.

25. Katz and Lazarsfeld (1955).

26. Riley and Riley (1951) and Maccoby (1954).

27. e.g., The experimental program described in Hovland, Janis and Kelley (1953), Hovland et al. (1957) and Janis et al. (1959).

28. Occasions on which it does so serve are noted in generalizations 3, 4, and 5.

29. Key, V. O. (1955). "A Theory of Critical Elections," *Journal of Politics*, XVII, p. 4.

1.2 ▬▬▬

The Influence and Effects of Mass Media

Denis McQuail

Editor's Note. It is clear from recent research that questions about the effects of the mass media cannot be answered in broad generalities. Scholars have learned to ask about various types of effects, on various types of people and institutions, at various levels of society, under various conditions. Denis McQuail provides an overview of these contingencies in a diverse array of important media situations. In addition to discussing the general nature of mass media effects, McQuail traces the history of research findings produced by several kinds of investigations. His bibliography is an excellent starting point for review of the English language literature on media effects through 1976.

McQuail is a professor of sociology and mass communication at the University of Amsterdam in the Netherlands. He has taught at the University of Southampton, England, and at the University of Leeds. He has written several books on the sociology of mass communication. The following selection is from *Mass Communication and Society*, ed. James Curran, Michael Gurevitch, and Janet Woolacott (Beverly Hills, Calif.: Sage Publications, 1979).

The questions most insistently asked of social research on mass communication, and perhaps least clearly answered, have to do with the effects and social influence of the different mass media. The reasons for asking are understandable enough, given the amount of time spent attending to the mass media in many countries and the amount of resources invested in mass media production and distribution. Although much has been written by way of answer and a good deal of research carried out, it has to be admitted that the issue remains a disputed one—both in general about the significance of mass media and in particular about the likely effect of given instances of mass communications.

From *Mass Communication and Society*, edited by J. Curran, M. Gurevitch, and J. Woolacott, pp. 70-93. Copyright © 1979 by Sage Publications, Inc. Reprinted by permission of Sage Publications, Inc.

Inevitably, this discussion has to begin with some clarifiction of terms, since one of the perennial difficulties in the case has been the lack of communication between those who have investigated the question of media influence on the one hand and, on the other, the public, media producers and those concerned with public policy for the media.

Perhaps it should first be claimed that the question of effects is a somewhat unfair one, one rarely asked of comparable institutions like religion, education or the law which all in their way communicate to the public or to particular publics and where questions about effects as well as aims could well be asked. The mass media are highly diverse in content and in forms of organization and include a very wide range of activities which could have effects on society. To make the question not only more fair, but also more meaningful, we need to introduce a number of qualifications and specifications.

First, we can distinguish between effects and effectiveness, the former referring to any of the consequences of mass media operation, whether intended or not, the latter to the capacity to achieve given objectives, whether this be attracting large audiences or influencing opinions and behaviour. Both matters are important, but a different set of considerations relates to each. A second, though perhaps minor, point on which to be clear concerns the reference in time. Are we concerned with the past, or with predictions about the future? If the former, we need to be precise. If the latter, and often it is a prediction about what is going on now and its results which is a main concern, then some uncertainty is inevitable.

Third, we need to be clear about the level on which effects occur, whether this is at the level of the individual, the group, the institution, the whole society or the culture. Each or all may be affected in some way by mass communication. To specify the level meaningfully also requires us to name the kinds of phenomena on which influence may be exerted. We can investigate some phenomena at several levels—especially opinion and belief which can be a matter of individual opinion as well as the collective expression of institutions and societies. On the other hand to study the effect of the media on the way institutions operate requires us to look at the relationships between people occupying different roles and at the structure and content of these roles. Politics provides a good example, where the mass media have probably affected not only individual political opinions but also the way politics is conducted and its main activities organized. Political roles may have been changed, as well as our expectations of politicians, the relationships of followers to leaders, and even perhaps some of the values of political life. All this is a matter of historical change, much slower and less reversible than any influence on opinion, attitude or voting behaviour. Again it is clear that difference of level of effect is also related to different time spans. Changes in culture and in society are slowest to occur, least easy to know of with certainty, least easy to trace to their origins, most likely to persist. Changes affecting individuals are quick to occur, relatively easy to demonstrate and to attribute to a source, less easy to assess in terms of significance and performance. Hence we tend to find a situation in which the larger and more significant questions of media effect are most subject to conflicting interpretation and the most certain knowledge we have is most open to the charge of triviality and least useful as a basis for generalization. Perhaps one could usefully add a further set of distinctions which have to be made early on, whatever the level of analysis. This relates to the direction of effect. Are the media changing something, preventing something, facilitating something or reinforcing and reaffirming something? The importance of the question is obvious, but it is worth stressing early in the discussion that a 'no change' effect can be as significant as its reverse and there is little doubt that in some respects the media do inhibit as well as promote change.

The History of Research Into the Effects of Mass Communication

. . . [W]e can characterize the 50 years or more of interest in media effects in terms of three main stages. In the first phase, which lasts from the turn of the century to the late nineteen thirties the media, where they were developed in Europe and North America, were attributed considerable power to shape opinion and belief, change habits of life, actively mould behaviour and impose political systems even against resistance. Such views were not based on scientific investigation but were based on empirical observation of the sudden extension of the audience to large majorities and on the great attraction of the popular press, cinema and radio. The assumption of media power was also acted upon, as it were, by advertisers, government propagandists in the First World War, newspaper proprietors, the rulers of totalitarian states, and accepted defensively by nearly all as the best guess in the circumstances. It is not irrelevant that this stage of thinking coincided with a very early stage of social science when the methods and concepts for investigating these phenomena were only developing.

The second stage extends from about 1940 to the early 1960s and it is strongly shaped by growth of mass communications research in the United States and the application of empirical method to specific questions about the effects and effectiveness of mass communication. The influence of this phase of research is surprisingly great, given the rather narrow range of the questions tackled and relatively small quantity of substantial studies. Most influential, perhaps, were the studies of Presidential elections in 1940 and 1948 by Lazarsfeld (1944), Berelson [*et al.*]

(1954) and the programme of research into the use of films for training and indoctrination of American servicemen undertaken by Hovland *et al.* (1950). An earlier and longer tradition of social-psychological inquiry into the effects of film and other media on crime, aggression and racial and other attitudes should also be mentioned (e.g. Blumer, 1933). In practice, a small number of much cited studies provided the substance for the general view of media effects and effectiveness which was generally being disseminated in social and political science by the end of the 1960s. Where there was research outside the United States (e.g. Trenaman and McQuail, 1961), it was in the same mould and tended to confirm rather than challenge the agreed version of media effects. Basically, this version affirmed the ineffectiveness and impotency of mass media and their subservience to other more fundamental components in any potential situation of influence. The mass media—primarily radio, film, or print at the time most research was conducted—emerged as unlikely to be major contributors to direct change of individual opinions, attitudes or behaviour or to be a direct cause of crime, aggression, or other disapproved social phenomena. Too many separate investigations reached similar negative conclusions for this to be doubted. The comment by Klapper (1960) in an influential view of research, that 'mass communication does not ordinarily serve as a necessary and sufficient cause of audience effects, but rather functions through a nexus of mediating factors' well sums up the outcome of the second phase. Of course, research had not shown the different media to be without effects, but it had established the primacy of other social facts and showed the power of the media to be located within the existing structures of social relationships and systems of culture and belief. The reversal of a prior assumption by scientific investigation was striking and seemed the more complete because the myth of media power was so strong and occasionally uncritical and naive. At the same time, it should be admitted that neither public anxiety about the new medium of television nor professional opinion in the field of advertising and mass communication was much changed by the verdict of science. In fact, hardly had the 'no effect' conclusion become generally accepted than it became subject to re-examination by social scientists who doubted that the whole story had yet been written.

The third phase, which still persists, is one where new thinking and new evidence is accumulating on the influence of mass communication, especially television, and the long neglected newspaper press. As early signs of doubts we could cite Lang and Lang (1959) or Key (1961) or Blumler (1964) or Halloran (1964). The case for re-opening the question of mass media effects rests on several bases. First of all, the lesson of 'no-effects' has been learned and accepted and more modest expectations have taken the place of early belief. Where small effects are expected, methods have to be more precise. In addition, the intervening variables of social position and prior audience disposition, once identified as important, could now be more adequately measured. A second basis for revision, however, rested on a critique of the methods and research models which had been used. These were mainly experiments or surveys designed to measure short-term changes occurring in individuals, and concentrating especially on the key concept of attitude. Alternative research approaches might take a longer time span, pay more attention to people in their social context, look at what people know (in the widest sense) rather than at their attitudes and opinions, take account of the uses and motives of the audience member as mediating any effect, look at structures of belief and opinion and social behaviour rather than individual cases, take more notice of the *content* whose effects are being studied. In brief, it can be argued that we are only at the start of the task and have as yet examined very few of the questions about the effects of mass media, especially those which reveal themselves in *collective* phonomena. Some of these matters are returned to later, and at this point it is sufficient to conclude that we are now in a phase where the social power of the media is once more at the centre of attention for some social scientists, a circumstance which is not the result of a mere change of fashion but of a genuine advance of knowledge based on secure foundations. This advance has been uneven and buffeted by external pressure, but it is real enough. . . .

The Evidence of Effects

In order to discuss the results of research into mass media effects in a meaningful way, it may be helpful to divide up the problem under a set of headings which in a composite way reflects the various distinctions which have already been mentioned: of level; of kind of effect and of process; of research strategy and method. Although the headings which follow do not divide up the field in a mutually exclusive way, they do separate out the main topics which have been discussed, and provide a basis for evaluating research evidence. Basically what is being indicated is a set of media situations or processes which have distinctive features and require separate evaluation. The most important media situations are: (1) the campaign; (2) the definition of social reality and social norms; (3) the immediate response or reaction; (4) institutional change; (5) changes in culture and society.

The Campaign

Much of what has been written about the effects or effectiveness of the media either derives from research on campaigns or involves predictions about hypothetical campaign situations. . . The kinds of media provision which might fall under this heading include: political and election campaigns, attempts at public information; commercial and public service advertising, some forms of education; the use of mass media in developing countries or generally for the diffusion of innovations. We recognize the similarity of these different activities. The campaign shares, in varying degrees, the following characteristics: it has specific aims and is planned to achieve these; it has a definite time-span, usually short; it is intensive and aims at wide coverage; its effectiveness is, in principle, open to assessment; it usually has authoritative sponsorship; it is not necessarily popular with its audience and has to be 'sold' to them; it is usually based on a framework of shared values. The campaign generally works to achieve objectives which in themselves are not controversial—voting, giving to charity, buying goods, education, health, safety, and so on....

... Rather than discuss evidence in detail, which space would not allow, a brief assertion of a general condition of effect is made, with some reference to a source or summarizing work which justifies the assertion. One set of relevant factors has to do with the audience, another with the message and a third with the source or the system of distribution. Amongst audience factors, an obvious primary condition is that a large audience should be reached. Second, the appropriate members of the audience should be reached, since size alone does not guarantee the inclusion of those for whom the campaign is relevant.... Third, the dispositions of the audience should at least be not antipathetic or resistant. Political campaigning is most subject to this constraint and there is evidence that the lack of strong disposition either way and a condition of casual attention may be most favourable to the success of mass propaganda. (Blumer and McQuail, 1968). A part of this condition relates to the need for consistency with the norms of locality and sub-culture as well as the presence of broad societal consensus. Fourth, success is likely to be greater when, within the audience, the flow of personal communication and structure of relevant interpersonal status is supportive of the mass media campaign and its aims. (Lazarsfeld, [*et al.*] 1944; Katz and Lazarsfeld, 1956; Rogers and Shoemaker, 1971). Fifth, it is important that the audience understands or perceives the message as intended by its originators (Cooper and Jahoda, 1946; Belson, 1967) and does not selectively distort it.

Factors to do with the message or content are also important. First, the message should be unambiguous and relevant to its audience. The factor of relevance and a parallel self-selection by the audience makes it likely that campaigns are most successful at reinforcing existing tendencies or channelling them into only slightly different pathways. Second, the informative campaign seems more likely to be successful than the campaign to change attitudes or opinions. (Howland *et al.*, 195[0]; Trennan and McQuail, 1969.) Third, in general, subject matter which is more distant and more novel, least subject to prior definitions and outside immediate experience responds best to treatment by the campaign. The essential point is that the receiver has no competing sources of information and no personal stake in resisting an appeal or disbelieving information. It is easier to form opinions and attitudes about events abroad than events at home, about unfamiliar than about familiar matters. Fourth, the campaign which allows some immediate response in action is most likely to be effective, since behaviour generally confirms intention and attitude, whether in voting or buying, or donating to a charity. Fifth, repetition can be mentioned as a probable contributor to effect, although this is a common-sense assumption rather than well demonstrated. As far as the source is concerned, we should mention first the condition of monopoly. The more channels carrying the same campaign messages, the greater the probability of acceptance. This is not easy to demonstrate and there are circumstances where an imposed monopoly invites distrust and disbelief. (e.g. Inkeles and Bauer, 1989.) But, in general, this condition is presupposed in several of the conditions already stated. Second, there is evidence that the status or authority of the source contributes to successful campaigning and the principle is applied in most campaigns whether commercial or not. The source of attributed status can of course vary, including the strongly institutionalized prestige of the political or legal system or the personal attractiveness of a star or other 'hero' of society or the claim to expert knowledge. Endorsement by an individual or institution embodying strong claims to trust and attachment can be crucial in a campaign. Third, there is a variable condition of affective attachment to a media source. There is evidence that loyalty and affective ties exist in relations to some media rather than others which may affect their ability to influence. (Butler and Stokes, 1969; Blumler *et al.*, 1975.)

These factors are all important in the process of intentional influence. . . . If we accept the validity of these points we are already very far from thinking the mass media to be ineffective, [n]or can it be said that we have no certain knowledge of the effects of mass media.

The Definition of Social Reality and the Formation of Social Norms

The topics we should look at under this heading are diverse and the processes involved equally so. Here we mainly consider the process of learning through the media, a process which is often incidental, unplanned and unconscious for the receiver and almost always unintentional on the part of the sender. Hence the concept of 'effectiveness' is usually inappropriate, except in societies where the media take a planned and deliberate role in social development. This may be true of some aspects of socialist media (see Hopkins, 1970) or of some media applications in developing countries. (Pye, 1963; Frey, 1973.) There are two main aspects to what occurs. On the one hand, there is the provision of a consistent picture of the social world which may lead the audience to adopt this version of reality, a reality of 'facts' and of norms, values and expectations. On the other hand, there is a continuing and selective interaction between self and the media which plays a part in shaping the individual's own behavior and self-concept. We learn what our social environment is and respond to the knowledge that we acquire. In more detail, we can expect the mass media to tell us about different kinds of social roles and the accompanying expectations, in the sphere of work, family life, political behaviour and so on. We can expect certain values to be selectively reinforced in these and other areas of social experience. We can expect a form of dialogue between persons and fictional characters or real media personalities and also in some cases an identification with the values and perspectives of these 'significant others.' We can also expect the mass media to give an order of importance and structure to the world they portray, whether fictionally or as actuality. There are several reasons for these expectations. One is the fact that there is a good deal of patterning and consistency in the media version of the world. Another is the wide range of experience which is open to view and to vicarious involvement compared to the narrow range of real experience available to most people at most points in their lives. Third, there is the trust with which media are often held as a source of impressions about the world outside direct experience. Inevitably, the evidence for this process of learning from the media is thin and what there is does little more than reaffirm the plausibility of these theoretical propositions. The shortage of evidence stems in part from a failure to look for it, until quite recently, and in part from the long-term nature of the processes which make them less amenable to investigations by conventional techniques of social research than are the effects of campaigns. . . .

A long list of studies can be cited showing the media to have certain inbuilt tendencies to present a limited and recurring range of images and ideas which form rather special versions of reality. In some areas, as with news reporting, the pattern is fairly inescapable; in others the diversity of media allows some choice and some healthy contradiction. What we lack is much evidence of the impact of these selective versions of the world. In many cases discount by the audience or the availability of alternative information must make acceptance of media portrayals at face value extremely unlikely or unusual. We should certainly not take evidence of content as evidence of effect. There is no close correspondence between the two and some studies show this. For example Roshier (1973) found public views about crime to be closer to the 'true' statistical picture than the somewhat distorted version one might extract from the content of local newspapers. Similarly Halloran's study of audience reaction to television reports of the 1968 demonstration shows this to have been rather little affected by the 'one-sided' version presented on the screen. Even so, there is enough evidence as well as good theory for taking the proposition as a whole quite seriously. The case of the portrayal of an immigrant, especially coloured, minority provides a good test, since we may expect the media to be a prominent source of impressions for those in Britain who have little or very limited personal contact with 'immigrants.'. . . .

[T]he media are associated with a view of immigrants as likely to be a cause of trouble or be associated with conflict. It also seems that impressions attributed to the media as source show a rather higher degree of internal similarity and to be in general less evaluative than those derived from personal contact. The main contribution of the mass media is not, according to this study, to encourage prejudice (often the reverse) but in defining the presence of immigrants as an 'objective' problem for the society.

. . . [T]he terms 'amplification' and 'sensitization' and 'polarization' have been used to describe the tendency of the media to exaggerate the incidence of a phenomenon, to increase the likelihood of it being noticed and to mobilize society against a supposed threat. In recent times, it has been argued that this treatment has been allotted to drug-taking (by Young, 1973), to mugging and to left-wing militants. It is notable that the groups receiving this form of polarizing treatment tend to be small, rather powerless and already subject to broad social disapproval. They are relatively 'safe' targets, but the process of hitting them tends to reaffirm the boundaries around what is acceptable in a free society.

When the question of media effects on violence is discussed, a rather opposite conclusion is often drawn. It seems as if general public opinion still holds the media responsible for a good deal of the increasing lawlessness in society (Halloran, 1970), a view based probably on the frequency with which crime and violence is portrayed, even if it rarely seems to be 'rewarded.' It is relevant to this section of the discussion to explore this view. American evidence obtained for the Kerner Commission on Violence and reported by Baker and Ball (1969) shows there certainly to be much violence portrayed on the most used medium, television. It also shows that most people have rather little contact with real violence in personal experience. The authors chart the public expression of norms in relation to violence and also television norms as they appear in content and find a gap between the two. Thus, while public norms cannot yet have been much affected directly, the gap suggests that the direction of effects is to extend the boundaries of acceptable violence beyond current norms. In brief then, the authors of this study lend support to one of the more plausible hypotheses connecting crime and violence with the media—that the tolerance of aggression is increased by its frequent portrayal and it becomes a more acceptable means of solving problems whether for the 'goodies' or the criminals. It should not be lost sight of, even so, that most dependable research so far available has not supported the thesis of a general association between any form of media use and crime, delinquency or violence. (Halloran, 1970.) The discussion linking social norms with violence takes place on the level of belief systems, opinions, social myths. It would require a long-term historical and cultural analysis to establish the propositions which are involved. Nor should we forget that there are counter-propositions, pointing for instance to the selectivity of public norms about violence and aggression. It is not disapproved of in general in many societies, only in its uncontrolled and non-institutionalized forms. . . .

. . . It has already been suggested that the media help to establish an order of priorities in a society about its problems and objectives. They do this, not by initiating or determining, but by publicizing according to an agreed scale of values what is determined elsewhere, usually in the political system. Political scientists have been most alert to the process and the term 'agenda-setting' has been given to it by McCombs and Shaw (1972). They found the mass media to present a very uniform set of issues before the American public in the 1968 presidential election and found public opinion to accord in content and order rather closely to this pattern. The phenomenon had been noted earlier in election campaign studies, where order of space given to issues in media content was found to be predictive of changes in order of importance attributed to issues over the course of the campaign. (Trenaman and McQuail, 1961; Blumler and McQuail, 1968.) In one sense the media only record the past and reflect a version of the present but, in doing so, they can affect the future, hence the significance of the 'agenda' analogy. . . .

Given the sparseness of evidence, it is not surprising that we cannot so adequately state the conditions for the occurrence or otherwise of effects from the media in the sphere of forming impressions of reality and defining social norms. In particular, we are dealing with society-wide and historically located phenomena which are subject to forces not captured by normal data-collecting techniques in the social sciences. However, if we re-inspect the list of conditions associated with media campaign success or failure, a number will again seem relevant. In particular, we should look first at the monopoly condition. Here what matters is less the monopoly of ownership and control than the monopoly of attention and the homogeneity of content. Uniformity and repetition establish the important result of monopoly without the necessity for the structural causes to be present. The more consistent the picture presented and the more exclusively this picture gains wide attention then the more likely is the predicted effect to occur. (cf. Noelle-Neumann, 1974.) We can suppose, too, that matters outside immediate experience and on which there are not strongly formed, alternative views will also be most susceptible to the level of influence spoken of. Further, we can think that here, as with media campaigns, a trust in the source and an attribution of authority will be an important factor in the greater extension of media-derived opinions and values. Other conditions of social organization must also be taken into account. It is arguable, but untestable, that circumstances of greater individuation and lower ties of attachment to intermediary groups and associations will favour an influence from the media. Finally, we might hypothesize that conditions of social crisis or danger might also be associated with strong short-term effects from the media on the definition of problems and solutions.

Immediate Response and Reaction Effects

To discuss this, we return to questions relating largely to individuals and to direct and immediate effects. We are concerned exclusively with unintended, generally 'undesirable,' effects which fall into two main categories. One relates again to the problem of crime and violence, another to cases of panic response to news or information, where collective responses develop out of individual reception of the media. . . .

. . . One school of thought is now convinced that media portrayals of aggression can provoke aggression in child audiences. (e.g. Berkovitz, 1964.) Another favours the view that the effect of fictional evidence is more likely to be a cathartic or aggression-releasing tendency. (Feshbach [and Singer], 1971) Many experiments have been inconclusive and majority opinion seems inclined to the cautious conclusion that direct effects involving disapproved behaviour are rare or likely to occur only where there is a strong disposition in that direction amongst a small minority of the already disturbed. . . .

The possibility that information received from the mass media will 'trigger' widespread and collective panic responses has often been canvassed, but rarely demonstrated. The 1938 radio broadcast of Wells' *War of the Worlds* which involved simulated news bulletins reporting an invasion from Mars is the case most often cited in this connection mainly because of [research by Cantril *et al.* (1940)] after the event. An event with some similarities in Sweden in 1973 was investigated by Rosengren *et al.* (1976) and the results cast doubt on the thesis as a whole. It seems that in neither case was there much behavioural response, and what there was was later exaggerated by other media. Investigations of news transmission in times of crisis, for instance the studies by Greenberg of the dissemination of news of the assassination of Kennedy (Greenberg [and Parker], 1965) tells us a good deal more of the processes which begin to operate in such circumstances. Essentially, what happens is that people take over as transmitters of information and those who receive news seek independent confirmation from other media or trusted personal sources. The circumstance of solitary, unmediated, reception and response is unusual and short-lived. Shibutani (1966) reminds us that rumour and panic response are the outcome of situations of ambiguity and lack of information and, on the whole the mass media operate to modify rather than magnify these conditions.

In dealing with this aspect of potential media effects, more attention should perhaps be paid to various kinds of 'contagion' or spontaneous diffusion of activities. The situations most often mentioned relate to the spreading of unrest or violence. For instance at times during the late 1960s when urban violence and rioting was not uncommon in American cities it was suggested that television coverage of one event might lead to occurrences elsewhere. Research into the possibility (e.g. Pal[e]tz and Dunn, 1967) does not settle the matter and it remains a reasonable expectation that given the right preconditions, media coverage could spread collective disturbance by publicity alone. Political authorities which have the power to do so certainly act on the supposition that unrest can be transmitted in this way and seek to delay or conceal news which might encourage imitators. The imitation of acts of terrorism or criminality, such as hijacking, seems also likely to have occurred, although the proof is lacking and the phenomenon is different because of its individual rather than collective character. In many areas where there is no institutionalized prohibition there is little doubt that spontaneous imitation and transmission do occur on a large scale by way of the mass media. In the sphere of music, dress, and other stylistic forms, the phenomenon is occurring all the time. It is this which has led to the expectation that the media on their own are a powerful force for change in developing countries (Lerner, 1958), through their stimulation of the desire first to consume and then to change the ways of life which stand in the way of earning and buying. Research evidence (e.g. Rogers and Shoemaker, 1971) and more considered thought (e.g. Golding, 1974) have led to the realization, however, that facts of social structure and of social institutions intervene powerfully in the process of imitation and diffusion. Even so, we should beware of dismissing the process as a misconception or, where it occurs, always as trivial. It is at least plausible that the movement for greater female emancipation owes a good deal to widely disseminated publicity by way of mass media.

Consequences for Other Social Institutions

It was emphasized at the outset that the 'effects' of mass media have to be considered at a level beyond that of the individual audience member and the aggregate of individual behaviours. The path by which collective effects are produced is, in general, simple enough to grasp, but the extent to which effects have occurred resists simple or certain assessment and has rarely been the subject of sustained investigation or thought. As the mass media have developed they have, incontrovertibly, achieved two things. They have, between them, diverted time and attention from other activities and they have become a channel for reaching more people with more information than was available under 'pre-mass media' conditions. These facts have implications for any other institution which requires allocation of time, attention and the communication of information, especially to large numbers and in large quantities. The media compete with other institutions and they offer ways of reaching continuing institutional objectives. It is this which underlies the process of institutional effect. Other social institutions are under pressure to adapt or respond in some way, or to make their own use of the mass media. In doing so, they are likely to alter. Because this is a slow process, occurring along with other kinds of social change, the specific contribution of the media cannot be accounted for with any certainty.

If this argument is accepted, it seems unlikely that any institution will be unaffected, but most open to change will be those concerned with 'knowledge' in the broadest sense and which are most universal and unselective in their reach. In most societies, this will suggest politics and education as the most likely candidates, religion in some cases and to a lesser degree, legal institution[s]. In general we would expect work, social services, science, [and] the military to be only tangentially affected by the availability of mass media. Insofar as we can regard leisure and sport as an institution in modern society this should perhaps be added to politics and education as the most directly interrelated with the mass media. . . .

. . . The challenge to politics from media institutions has taken several forms, but has been particularly strong just because the press was already involved in political processes and because the introduction of broadcasting was a political act. The diversion of time from political activity was less important than the diversion of attention from partisan sources of information and ideology to sources which were more accessible and efficient, often more attractive as well as authoritative, and which embodied the rather novel political values of objectivity and independent 'expert' adjudication. As we have seen, it has increasingly seemed as if it is the mass media which set the 'agenda' and define the problems on a continuous, day to day, basis while political parties and politicians increasingly respond to a consensus view of what should be done. The communication network controlled by the modern mass party cannot easily compete with the mass media network. . . .

Changes of Culture and Society

If we follow a similar line of analysis for other institutions, it is not difficult to appreciate that we can arrive at one or more versions of ways in which culture and social structure can be influenced by the path of development of media institutions. If the content of what we know, our way of doing things and spending time and the organization of central activities for the society are in part dependent on the media, then the fact of interdependence is evident. Again, the problem is to prove connections and quantify the links. The 'facts' are so scarce, open to dispute and often puny in stature that the question is often answered by reference to alternative theories. For some, the answer may still be provided by a theory of mass society of the kind advanced by Mills (1956) or Kornhauser (1959) and criticized by Shil[s] (1975). Such a theory suggests that the mass media encourage and make viable a rootless, alienated, form of social organization in which we are increasingly within the control of powerful and distant institutions. For others, a Marxist account of the mass media as a powerful ideological weapon for holding the mass of people in voluntary submission to capitalism (Marcuse, 1964; Miliband, 1969) provides the answer to the most important effects of the rise of the mass media.

A more complex answer is offered by Carey (1969), in his suggestion that the mass media are both a force for integration and for dispersion and individuation in society. Gerbner [and Gross (1976) see] the key to the effects of mass media in their capacity to take over the 'cultivation' of images, ideas and consciousness in an industrial society. He refers to the main process of mass media as that of 'publication' in the literal sense of making public: 'The truly revolutionary significance of modern mass communication is ... the ability to form historically new bases for collective thought and action quickly, continuously and pervasively across the previous boundaries of time, space and status.' The ideas of McLuhan (1962 and 1964), despite a loss of vogue, remain plausible for some (e.g. Noble, 1975), especially in their particular reference to the establishment of a 'global village' which will be established through direct and common experience from television. The various theories are not all so far apart. A common theme is the observation that experience, or what we take for experience, is increasingly indirect and 'mediated' and that, whether by chance or design, more people receive a similar 'version' of the world. The consequences for culture and society depend, however, on factors about which the theories are not agreed, especially on the character and likely tendency of this version of reality. Similarly, the available theories are not agreed on the basis of the extraordinary appeal of the mass media, taken in general. Do they meet some underlying human needs? If so, what is the nature of these needs? Alternatively, is the apparent 'necessity' of the media merely the result of some imposed and artificial want? Certainly, the question of what most wide-ranging consequences follow from the media must also raise the question of motivation and use.

The Social Power of Mass Media—A Concluding Note

It has been the intention of this whole discussion to make very clear that the mass media do have important consequences for individuals, for institutions and for society and culture. That we cannot trace very precise causal connections or make reliable predictions about the future does not nullify this conclusion. The question of the power of the mass media is a different one. In essence, it involves asking how effectively the mass media can and do achieve objectives over others at the will of those who direct, own or control them or who use them as channels for messages. The history of mass media shows clearly enough that such control is regarded as a valued form of property for those seeking political or economic power. The basis for such a view has already been made clear in the evidence which has been discussed. Control over the mass media offers several important possibilities. First, the media can attract and direct attention to problems, solutions or people in ways which can favour those with power and correlatively divert attention from rival individuals or groups. Second, the mass media can confer status and confirm legitimacy. Third, in some circumstances, the media can be a channel for persuasion and mobilization. Fourth, the mass media can help to bring certain kinds of publics into being and maintain them. Fifth, the media are a vehicle for offering psychic rewards and gratifications. They can divert and amuse and they can flatter. In general, mass media are very cost-effective as a means of communication in society; they are also fast, flexible and relatively easy to plan and control. . . .

The general case which can be made out along these lines for treating the mass media as an instrument of social power is sufficiently strong for many commentators to regard it as settled. In this view, all that remains is to discover not *whether* the media have power and how it works, but *who* has access to the use of this power. Generally this means asking questions about ownership and other forms of control, whether political, legal or economic. It is arguable, however, that we need to take the case somewhat further and to probe rather more carefully the initial general assumption. That is, we cannot assume that ownership and control of the means of mass communication does necessarily confer power over others in any straightforward or predictable way. . . .

. . . [M]ore attention should be given to the various structures of legitimation which attract and retain audiences and which also govern their attitudes to different media sources. There are critical differences between alternative forms of control from above and between alternative types of orientation to the media, both within and between societies. This is, as yet, a relatively unexplored area but meanwhile we should be as wary of trying to answer questions of power solely in terms of ownership as we should be of doing so in terms of 'effects.'

References

Baker, R. K. and Ball, S. J., 1969: *Mass Media and Violence*. Report to the National Commission on the Causes and Prevention of Violence.

Belson, W., 1967: *The Impact of Television*. Crosby Lockwood.

Berelson, B., Lazarsfeld, P. F. and McPhee, W., 1954: *Voting*. University of Chicago Press.

Berelson, B., and Steiner, G., 1963: *Human Behaviour*. Harcourt Brace.

Berkovitz, 1964: 'The effects of observing violence.' *Scientific American*, vol. 210.

Blumler, H., 1933: *Movies and Conduct*. Macmillan.

Blumler, J. G., 1964: 'British Television: the Outlines of a Research Strategy,' *British Journal of Sociology* 15 (3).

Blumler, J. G. and McQuail, D., 1968: *Television in Politics: its uses and influence*. Faber.

Blumler, J. G., Nossiter, T. and McQuail, D., 1975: *Political Communication and Young Voters*. Report to SSRC.

Blumler, J. G. and Katz, E. (eds.), 1975: 'The Uses and Gratifications Approach to Communications Research.' *Sage Annual Review of Communication*, vol. 3.

Butler, D. and Stokes, D., 1969: *Political Change in Britain*. Macmillan.

Cantril, H., Gaudet, H. and Herzog, H., 1940: *The Invasion from Mars*. Princeton University Press.

Carey, J. W., 1969: 'The Communications Revolution and the Professional Communicator.' In Halmos, P., (ed.), *The Sociology of Mass Media Communicators*. Sociological Review Monograph 13. University of Keele.

Cohen, S., 1973: *Folk Devils and Moral Panics*. Paladin.

Cooper, E. and Jahoda, M., 1947: 'The evasion of propaganda.' *Journal of Psychology* 15, pp. 15-25.

De Fleur, M., 1964: 'Occupational roles as portrayed on television.' *Public Opinion Quarterly* 28, pp. 57-74.

Etzioni, A., 1967: *The Active Society*. Free Press.

Feshbach, S. and Singer, R., 1971: *Television Aggression*. Jossey-Bass.

Franzwa, H., 1974: 'Working women in fact and fiction.' *Journal of Communication*, 24 (2), pp. 104-9.

Frey, F. W., 1973: 'Communication and Development.' In de Sola Pool, I. and Schramm, W. (eds.) *Handbook of Communication*, Rand McNally.

Galtung, J., and Ruge, M., 1965: 'The structure of foreign news.' *Journal of Peace Research*, vol. 1.

Gerbner, G. and Gross, L., 1976: 'The scary world of TV's heavy viewer.' *Psychology Today*, April.

Golding, P., 1974: 'Mass communication and theories of development.' *Journal of Communication*, Summer.

Greenberg, B. and Parker, E. B. (eds.), 1965: *The Kennedy Assassination and the American Public*. Stanford University Press.

Halloran, J. D., 1964: *The Effects of Mass Communication*. Leicester University Press.

Halloran, J. D. (ed.), 1970: *The Effects of Television*, Paladin.

Halloran, J. D., Brown, R. and Chaney, D. C., 1970: *Television and Delinquency.* Leicester University Press.

Halloran, J. D., Elliott, P. and Murdock, G., 1970: *Demonstrations and Communication*. Penguin.

Hartmann, P., 1976: 'Industrial relations in the news media.' *Journal of Industrial Relations* 6(4) pp. 4-18.

Hartmann, P. and Husband, C., 1974: *Racism and the Mass Media*. Davis-Poynter.

Hopkins, M. W., 1970: *Mass Media in the Soviet Union*. Pegasus.

Hovland, C. I., Lumsdaine, A. and Sheffield, F., 1950: *Experiments in Mass Communication*. Princeton University Press.

Inkeles, A. and Bauer, R., 1959: *The Soviet Citizen*. Harvard University Press.

Katz, E. and Lazarsfeld, P. F., 1956: *Personal Influence*. Free Press.

Key, V. O., 1961: *Public Opinion and American Democracy*. Knopf.

Klapper, Joseph T., 1960: *The Effects of Mass Communication*. Free Press.

Kornhauser, F. W., 1959: *The Politics of Mass Society*. Routledge.

Lang, K. and Lang, G., 1959: 'The Mass Media and Voting.' In Burdick, E. J. and Brodbeck, A. J. (eds.), *American Voting Behaviour*, Free Press.

Lazarsfeld, P. F., Berelson, B. and Gaudet, H., 1944: *The People's Choice*. Columbia University Press.

Lerner, D., 1958: *The Passing of Traditional Society*. Free Press.

McCombs, M. and Shaw, D. L., 1972: 'The agenda-setting function of mass media.' *Public Opinion Quarterly* 36.

McLuhan, M., 1962: *The Gutenberg Galaxy*. Routledge.
    1964: *Understanding Media*. Routledge.

McQuail, D., 1970: 'Television and Education.' In Halloran, J. D. (ed.), *The Effects of Television*. Panther.

Marcuse, H., 1964: *One-Dimensional Man*. Routledge.

Mills, C. W., 1956: *The Power Elite*. Free Press.

Miliband, R., 1969: *The State in Capitalist Society*. Weidenfeld and Nicolson.

Noble, G., 1975: *Children in Front of the Small Screen*. Constable.

Noelle-Neumann, E., 1974: 'The spiral of silence.' *Journal of Communication*, Spring.

Paletz, D. H. and Dunn, R., 1967: 'Press coverage of civil disorders.' *Public Opinion Quarterly* 33, pp. 328-45.

Pye, Lucian (ed.), 1963. *Communication and Political Development*. Princeton University Press.

Roberts, D. F., 1971: 'The nature of communication effects.' In Schramm, W. and Roberts, D. F., *Process and Effects of Mass Communication*, University of Illinois Press, pp. 347-87.

Rogers, E. and Shoemaker, F., 1971: *Communication and Innovations*. Free Press.

Rosengren, K. E., 1976: *The Bäxby Incident*. Lund University.

Roshier, B., 1973: 'The selection of crime news by the press.' In Cohen, S. and Young, J. (eds.), *The Manufacture of News*, Constable.

Seymour-Urc, C., 1973: *The Political Impact of Mass Media*. Constable.

Shibutani, T., 1966: *Improvised News*. Bobbs-Merrill.

Shils, E., 1975: 'The Theory of Mass Society.' In *Centre and Periphery*, Chicago University Press.

Star, S. A. and Hughes, H. M., 1951: 'Report on an educational campaign.' *American Journal of Sociology* 55 (4), pp. 389-400.

Trenaman, J. and McQuail, D., 1961: *Television and the Political Image*. Methuen.

Weiss, W., 1969: 'Effects of the Mass Media of Communication.' In Lindzey, G. and Aronson, E. (eds.) *Handbook of Social Psychology*, 2d edn., vol. V.

Young, J., 1973: 'The amplification of drug use.' In Cohen, S. and Young, J. (eds.) *The Manufacture of News*, Constable.

1.3 ■■■■■■

Newspapers

Walter Lippmann

Editor's Note. In this classic study, Walter Lippmann shows how journalists point a flashlight rather than a mirror at the world. Accordingly, the audience does not receive a complete image of the political scene; it gets a highly selective series of glimpses instead. Reality is tainted. Lippmann explains why the media cannot possibly perform the functions of public enlightenment that democratic theory requires. They cannot tell the truth objectively because the truth is subjective and entails more probing and explanation than the hectic pace of news production allows.

Lippmann's analysis raises profound questions about the purity and adequacy of mass media sources of information. Can there be democracy when information is invariably tainted? Are there any antidotes? The answers remain elusive.

Walter Lippmann, who died in 1974, was a renowned American journalist and political analyst whose carefully reasoned, lucid writings influenced American politics for more than half a century. He won two Pulitzer Prizes, the Medal of Freedom, and three Overseas Press Club awards. In addition to books, he also wrote articles for *The New Republic*, the New York *World*, and the New York *Herald Tribune*. This selection is from *Public Opinion* (New York: Free Press, 1965). It was published originally in 1922.

The Nature of News

. . . In the first instance . . . the news is not a mirror of social conditions, but the report of an aspect that has obtruded itself. The news does not tell you how the seed is germinating in the ground, but it may tell you when the first sprout breaks through the surface. It may even tell you what somebody says is happening to the seed under ground. It may tell you that the sprout did not come up at the time it was expected. The more points, then, at which any happening can be fixed, objectified, measured, named, the more points there are at which news can occur. . . .

Wherever there is a good machinery of record, the modern news service works with great precision. There is one on the stock exchange, and the news of price movements is flashed over tickers with dependable accuracy. There is a machinery for election returns, and when the counting and tabulating are well done, the result of a national election is usually known on the night of the election. In civilized communities deaths, births, marriages and divorces are recorded, and are known accurately except where there is concealment or neglect. The machinery exists for some, and only some, aspects of industry and government, in varying degrees of precision for securities, money and staples, bank clearances, realty transactions, wage scales. It exists for imports and exports because they pass through a custom house and can be directly recorded. It exists in nothing like the same degree for internal trade, and especially for trade over the counter.

It will be found, I think, that there is a very direct relation between the certainty of news and the system of record. If you call to mind the topics which form the principal indictment by reformers against the press, you find they are subjects in which the newspaper occupies the position of the umpire in the unscored baseball game. All news about states of mind is of this character: so are all descriptions of personalities, of sincerity, aspiration, motive, intention, of mass feeling, of national feeling, of public opinion, the policies of foreign governments. So is much news about what is going to happen. So are questions turning on private profit, private income, wages, working conditions, the efficiency of labor, educational opportunity, unemployment,[1] monotony, health, discrimination, unfairness, restraint of trade, waste, "backward peoples," conservatism, imperialism, radicalism, liberty, honor, righteousness. All involve data that are at best spasmodically recorded. The data may be hidden because of a censorship or a tradition of privacy, they may not exist because nobody thinks record important, because he thinks it red tape, or because nobody has yet invented an objective system of measurement. Then the news on these subjects is bound to be debatable, when it is not wholly neglected. The events which are not scored are reported either as personal and conventional opinions, or they are not news. They do not take shape until somebody protests, or somebody investigates, or somebody publicly, in the etymological meaning of the word, makes an *issue* of them. . . .

Let us suppose the conditions leading up to a strike are bad. What is the measure of evil? A certain conception of a proper standard of living, hygiene, economic security, and human dignity. The industry may be far below the theoretical standard of the community, and the workers may be too wretched to protest. Conditions may be above the standard, and the workers may protest violently. The standard is at best a vague measure.

However, we shall assume that the conditions are below par, as par is understood by the editor. Occasionally without waiting for the workers to threaten, but prompted say by a social worker, he will send reporters to investigate, and will call attention to bad conditions. Necessarily he cannot do that often. For these investigations cost time, money, special talent, and a lot of space. To make plausible a report that conditions are bad, you need a good many columns of print. In order to tell the truth about the steel worker in the Pittsburgh district, there was needed a staff of investigators, a great deal of time, and several fat volumes of print. It is impossible to suppose that any daily newspaper could normally regard the making of Pittsburgh Surveys, or even Interchurch Steel Reports, as one of its tasks. News which requires so much trouble as that to obtain is beyond the resources of a daily press. . . .

If you study the way many a strike is reported in the press, you will find, very often, that the issues are rarely in the headlines, barely in the leading paragraphs, and sometimes not even mentioned anywhere. A labor dispute in another city has to be very important before the news account contains any definite information as to what is in dispute. The routine of the news works that way, with modifications it works that way in regard to political issues and international news as well. The news is an account of the overt phases that are interesting, and the pressure on the newspaper to adhere to this routine comes from many sides. It comes from the economy of noting only the stereotyped phase of a situation. It comes from the difficulty of finding journalists who can see what they have not learned to see. It comes from the almost unavoidable difficulty of finding sufficient space in which even the best journalist can make plausible an unconventional view. It comes from the economic necessity of interesting the reader quickly, and the economic risk involved in not interesting him at all, or of offending him by unexpected news insufficiently or clumsily described. All these difficulties combined make for uncertainty in the editor when there are dangerous issues at stake, and cause him naturally to prefer the indisputable fact and a treatment more readily adapted to the reader's interest. The indisputable fact and the easy interest, are the strike itself and the reader's inconvenience.

All the subtler and deeper truths are in the present organization of industry very unreliable truths. They involve judgments about standards of living, productivity, human rights that are endlessly debatable in the absence of exact record and quantitative analysis. And as long as these do not exist in industry, the run of news about it will tend, as Emerson said, quoting from Isocrates, "to make of moles mountains, and of mountains moles." [2] Where there is no constitutional procedure in industry, and no expert sifting of evidence and the claims, the fact that is sensational to the reader is the fact that almost every journalist will seek. Given the industrial relations that so largely prevail, even where there is conference or arbitration, but no independent filtering of the facts for decision, the issue for the newspaper public will tend not to be the issue for the industry. And so to try disputes by an appeal through the newspapers puts a burden upon newspapers and readers which they cannot and ought not to carry. As long as real law and order do not exist, the bulk of the news will, unless consciously and courageously corrected, work against those who have no lawful and orderly method of asserting themselves. The bulletins from the scene of action will note the trouble that arose from the assertion, rather than the reasons which led to it. The reasons are intangible. . . .

Every newspaper when it reaches the reader is the result of a whole series of selections as to what items shall be printed, in what position they shall be printed, how much space each shall occupy, what emphasis each shall have. There are no objective standards here. There are conventions. Take two newspapers published in the same city on the same morning. The headline of one reads: "Britain pledges aid to Berlin against French aggression; France openly backs Poles." The headline of the second is "Mrs. Stillman's Other Love." Which you prefer is a matter of taste, but not entirely a matter of the editor's taste. It is a matter of his judgement as to what will absorb the half hour's attention a certain set of readers will give to his newspaper. Now the problem of securing attention is by no means equivalent to displaying the news in the perspective laid down by religious teaching or by some form of ethical culture. It is a problem of provoking feeling in the reader, of inducing him to feel a sense of personal identification with the stories he is reading. . . . In order that he shall enter he must find a familiar foothold in the story, and this is supplied to him by the use of stereotypes. They tell him that if an association of plumbers is called a "combine" it is appropriate to develop his hostility; if it is called a "group of leading businessmen" the cue is for a favorable reaction.

It is in a combination of these elements that the power to create opinion resides. . . . This is the plight of the reader of the general news. If he is to read it at all he must be interested, that is to say, he must enter into the situation and care about the outcome. But if he does that he cannot rest in a negative, and unless independent means of checking the lead given him by his newspaper exists, the very fact that he is interested may make it difficult to arrive at that balance of opinions which may most nearly approximate the truth. The more passionately involved he becomes, the more he will tend to resent not only a different view, but a disturbing bit of news. That is why many a newspaper finds that, having honestly evoked the partisanship of its readers, it can not easily, supposing the editor believes the facts warrant it, change position. If a change is necessary, the transition has to be managed with the utmost skill and delicacy. Usually a newspaper will not attempt so hazardous a performance. It is easier and safer to have the news of that subject taper off and disappear, thus putting out the fire by starving it.

News, Truth, and a Conclusion

The hypothesis, which seems to be the most fertile, is that news and truth are not the same thing, and must be clearly distinguished.[3] The function of news is to signalize an event, the function of truth is to bring to light the hidden facts, to set them into relation with each other, and make a picture of reality on which men can act. Only at these points, where social conditions take recognizable and measurable shape, do the body of truth and the body of news coincide. That is a comparatively small part of the whole field of human interest. In this sector, and only in this sector, the tests of the news are sufficiently exact to make the charges of perversion or suppression more than a partisan judgment. There is no defense, no extenuation, no excuse whatever, for stating six times that Lenin is dead, when the only information the paper possesses is a report that he is dead from a source repeatedly shown to be unreliable. The news, in that instance, is not "Lenin Dead" but "Helsingfors Says Lenin is Dead." And a newspaper can be asked to take the responsibility of not making Lenin more dead than the source of the news is reliable; if there is one subject on which editors are most responsible it is in their judgment of the reliability of the source. But when it comes to dealing, for example, with stories of what the Russian people want, no such test exists.

The absence of these exact tests accounts, I think, for the character of the profession, as no other explanation does. There is a very small body of exact knowledge, which it requires no outstanding ability or training to deal with. The rest is in the journalist's own discretion. Once he departs from the region where it is definitely recorded at the County Clerk's office that John Smith has gone into bankruptcy, all fixed standards disappear. The story of why John Smith failed, his human frailties, the analysis of the economic conditions on which he was shipwrecked, all of this can be told in a hundred different ways. There is no discipline in applied psychology, as there is a discipline in medicine, engineering, or even law, which has authority to direct the journalist's mind when he passes from the news to the vague realm of truth. There are no canons to direct his own mind, and no canons that coerce the reader's judgment or the publisher's. His version of the truth is only his version. How can he demonstrate the truth as he sees it? He cannot demonstrate it, any more than Mr. Sinclair Lewis can demonstrate that he has told the whole truth about Main Street. And the more he understands his own weaknesses, the more ready he is to admit that where there is no objective test, his own opinion is in some vital measure constructed out of his own stereotypes, according to his own code, and by the urgency of his own interest. He knows that he is seeing the world through subjective lenses. He cannot deny that he too is, as Shelley remarked, a dome of many-colored glass which stains the white radiance of eternity.

And by this knowledge his assurance is tempered. He may have all kinds of moral courage, and sometimes has, but he lacks that sustaining conviction of a certain technic which finally freed the physical sciences from theological control. It was the gradual development of an irrefragable method that gave the physicist his intellectual freedom as against all the powers of the world. His proofs were so clear, his evidence so sharply superior to tradition, that he broke away finally from all control. But the journalist has no such support in his own conscience or in fact. The control exercised over him by the opinions of his employers and his readers, is not the control of truth by prejudice, but of one opinion by another opinion that is not demonstrably less true. . . .

. . . It is possible and necessary for journalists to bring home to people the uncertain character of the truth on which their opinions are founded, and by criticism and agitation to prod social science into making more usable formulations of social facts, and to prod statesmen into establishing more visible institutions. The press, in other words, can fight for the extension of reportable truth. But as social truth is organized today, the press is not constituted to furnish from one edition to the next the amount of knowledge which the democratic theory of public opinion demands. This is not due to the Brass Check, as the quality of news in radical newspapers shows, but to the fact that the press deals with a society in which the governing forces are so imperfectly recorded. The theory that the press can itself record those forces is false. It can normally record only what has been recorded for it by the working of institutions. Everything else is argument and opinion, and fluctuates with the vicissitudes, the self-consciousness, and the courage of the human mind.

If the press is not so universally wicked, nor so deeply conspiring . . . it is very much more frail than the democratic theory has as yet admitted. It is too frail to carry the whole burden of popular sovereignty, to supply spontaneously the truth which democrats hoped was inborn. And when we expect it to supply such a body of truth we employ a misleading standard of judgment. We misunderstand the limited nature of news, the illimitable complexity of society; we overestimate our own endurance, public spirit, and all-round competence. We suppose an appetite for uninteresting truths which is not discovered by any honest analysis of our own tastes.

If the newspapers, then, are to be charged with the duty of translating the whole public life of mankind, so that every adult can arrive at an opinon on every moot topic, they fail, they are bound to fail, in any future one can conceive they will continue to fail. It is not possible to assume that a world, carried on by division of labor and distribution of authority, can be governed by universal opinions in the whole population. Unconsciously the theory sets up the single reader as theoretically omnicompetent, and puts upon the press the burden of accomplishing whatever representative government, industrial organization, and diplomacy have failed to accomplish. Acting upon everybody for thirty minutes in twenty-four hours, the press is asked to create a mystical force called Public Opinion that will take up the slack in public institutions. The press has often mistakenly pretended that it could do just that. It has at great moral cost to itself, encouraged a democracy, still bound to its original premises, to expect newspapers to supply spontaneously for every organ of government, for every social problem, the machinery of information which these do not normally supply themselves. Institutions, having failed to furnish themselves with instruments of knowledge, have become a bundle of "problems," which the population as a whole, reading the press as a whole, is supposed to solve.

The press, in other words, has come to be regarded as an organ of direct democracy, charged on a much wider scale, and from day to day, with the function often attributed to the initiative, referendum, and recall. The Court of Public Opinion, open day and night, is to lay down the law for everything all the time. It is not workable. And when you consider the nature of news, it is not even thinkable. For the news, as we have seen, is precise in proportion to the precision with which the event is recorded. Unless the event is capable of being named, measured, given shape, made specific, it either fails to take on the character of news, or it is subject to the accidents and prejudices of observation.

Therefore, on the whole, the quality of the news about modern society is an index of its social organization. The better the institutions, the more all interests concerned are formally represented, the more issues are disentangled, the more objective criteria are introduced, the more perfectly an affair can be presented as news. At its best the press is a servant and guardian of institutions; at its worst it is a means by which a few exploit social disorganization to their own ends. In the degree to which institutions fail to function, the unscrupulous journalist can fish in troubled waters, and the conscientious one must gamble with uncertainties.

The press is no substitute for institutions. It is like the beam of a searchlight that moves restlessly about, bringing one episode and then another out of darkness into vision. Men cannot do the work of the world by this light alone. They cannot govern society by episodes, incidents, and eruptions. It is only when they work by a steady light of their own, that the press, when it is turned upon them, reveals a situation intelligible enough for a popular decision. The trouble lies deeper than the press, and so does the remedy. It lies in social organization based on a system of analysis and record, and in all the corollaries of that principle; in the abandonment of the theory of the omnicompetent citizen, in the decentralization of decision, in the coordination of decision by comparable record and analysis. If at the centers of management there is a running audit, which makes work intelligible to those who do it, and those who superintend it, issues when they arise are not the mere collisions of the blind. Then, too, the news is uncovered for the press by a system of intelligence that is also a check upon the press.

That is the radical way. For the troubles of the press, like the troubles of representative government, be it territorial or functional, like the troubles of industry, be it capitalist, cooperative, or communist, go back to a common source: to the failure of self-governing people to transcend their casual experience and their prejudice, by inventing, creating, and organizing a machinery of knowledge. It is because they are compelled to act without a reliable picture of the world, that governments, schools, newspapers and churches make such small headway against the more obvious failings of democracy, against violent prejudice, apathy, preference for the curious trivial as against the dull important, and the hunger for sideshows and three legged calves. This is the primary defect of popular government, a defect inherent in its traditions, and all its other defects can, I believe, be traced to this one.

Notes

1. Think of what guess work went into the Reports of Unemployment in 1921.
2. From his essay entitled *Art and Criticism*. The quotation occurs in a passage cited on page 87 of Professor R. W. Brown's *The Writer's Art*.
3. When I wrote *Liberty and the News*, I did not understand this distinction clearly enough to state it, but *cf.* p. 89 ff.

1.4 ▬▬▬

El Salvador's Civil War as Seen
in North and South American Press

Walter C. Soderlund and Carmen Schmitt

Editor's Note. In the previous selection, Walter Lippmann pointed to the difficulty of capturing reality in news stories. Walter C. Soderlund and Carmen Schmitt demonstrate that the problem is even more complex than Lippmann described. Images of reality not only are inadequate, they also differ among media and vary from country to country. This essay compares and contrasts the diverse images of the civil war in El Salvador presented in 1981 in major newspapers in Argentina, Chile, Canada, and the United States. Judging by their media, audiences in these countries were apt to form quite varied images about this remote war and its international ramifications. Obviously, different media produce different worlds when journalists disagree about which political actors and actions deserve the spotlight and which should be regarded positively, negatively, or neutrally.

Aside from the substantive findings, this study is interesting because it compares major media in several countries that vary from one another in language and in cultural traditions. Despite these differences, and despite the use of disparate news sources, there are substantial similarities in coverage. It is also striking that the South American and Canadian papers depended predominantly on U.S. and European sources rather than on their own. By contrast, U.S. newspapers rarely relied on foreign sources, evidence of what the authors term "extreme parochialism."

At the time of writing, Soderlund was professor of political science at the University of Windsor, Canada. Carmen Schmitt, who holds a master's degree in communication studies from the University of Windsor, was a television journalist in Chile. The selection comes from "El Salvador's Civil War as Seen in North and South American Press," *Journalism Quarterly* 63:2 (Summer 1986): 268-274. One table has been omitted.

The way in which media interpret events involving international conflict is recognized increasingly as important in international relations.[1] El Salvador was, during the final months of 1981 (as of course it has

---

Reprinted by permission from Summer 1986 *Journalism Quarterly.*

continued to be), one of the most dangerous "hot spots" of a rekindled cold war: a Western hemisphere society ripped apart by a civil war that has attracted international participation.

This research reports on the "pictures of reality" regarding events in El Salvador as conveyed to readers by major newspapers in Argentina, Chile, Canada and the United States. What is reported by the press about El Salvador (or any other foreign crisis), is important because most of us are simply unable to evaluate independently such situations. Rather, we of necessity, must depend on the media for most of our information. Thus, in a real sense, a great deal of what we "know" about a given situation is based upon media reporting.

In this particular study we examine press coverage of El Salvador over a 10-week period in the Fall of 1981. The major question which we seek to answer is whether media images of "reality" regarding El Salvador differ for readers of newspapers in four different countries, located on two different continents. The newspapers selected for study are: in Argentina *La Nacion* and *La Prensa*, in Chile *El Mercurio* and *La Tercera*, in Canada the Toronto *Globe and Mail* and the Ottawa *Citizen*, and in the United States the Washington *Post* and the New York *Times*.[2]

The sampling frame began with a date randomly selected in the first week of October and continued using a two-day skip interval, through to the end of the second week of December. Twenty-seven issues per newspaper were included in the sample. Each issue was examined in its entirety for items dealing with El Salvador. Items were coded as to (1) *Type of content:* front page news, inside page news, feature columns, editorials, and cartoons; (2) *source of content:* local staff and special correspondents, columnists, and the various wire services; (3) *thematic coverage:* specific issues and actors discussed; (4) *evaluative direction:* whether a given item reflected positively or negatively on five major domestic and international political actors, the FDR/FMLN, the Salvadorean junta, the United States, Cuba and Nicaragua. Items were coded mixed if both positive and negative material was included, or neutral;[3] and (5) the extent to which a "cold war" mentality based on language was evident in reporting.[4]

Findings

Our content analysis research produced a data set of 160 news items dealing with El Salvador, broken down nearly equally between those appearing in the South American newspapers (78) and those in the North American newspapers (82). In South America, Argentine papers led Chilean in coverage 42 stories to 36, while in North America, the American papers led the Canadian, 55 stories to 27.

With regard to type of content, . . . [w]hat is clear is that there was a lack of in-depth, analytical material on El Salvador, to place day-to-day events in a coherent framework. This deficiency was especially apparent in the South American papers.

... The role of the United States in the crisis was the leading issue reported on overall, surpassing its nearest competitor by well over a 10% margin. Also, in terms of internationalization, we see the roles of Nicaragua and Cuba figuring prominently.... Peace-making efforts on the part of Mexico and refugee problems along the Honduran border accounted for the presence of these countries' activities among the top 10 issues.

The domestic factors which found their way into press reporting were the role of the guerrillas, the role of the Salvadorean military, actual reports of military action, backgrounders on the scheduled March 1982 Constituent Assembly election, and analyses of the politico-military strategies of both the FDR/FMLN [guerrilla forces] and the Salvadorean government. There was scarcely any attention paid to social or economic conditions within El Salvador....

Table 1 shows ... thematic coverage ... broken down by country.... The role of the United States showed up in 73% of the news items appearing in American papers. It was also the leading theme in Canadian news coverage (52%), as well as the number two theme in Argentine reporting (58%). In Chile, the role of the United States was not as prominently featured, (fourth in rank order), appearing in only 28% of news items. Roles played by Nicaragua and Cuba also dominated American newspaper reporting, second and third in rank order. Canadian reporting on Nicaragua earned that nation's activities a fourth place on the rank order list, while Nicaragua occupied the fifth and sixth positions on the Argentine and Chilean agendas. Cuban activities likewise merited less attention in Canada, Argentina, and Chile, occupying the sixth, eighth and ninth positions in these nations' reporting.

The role of guerrilla forces received most coverage in Argentina, with the theme appearing in 64% of news items, and in Chile (47%). Clearly, this theme was less salient in Canada and the United States. Reports of military action were featured prominently in the Chilean press and noticeably absent in Canadian coverage. Canada was also low in reporting on the politico-military strategy of the FDR/FMLN, as was Chile. Chilean newspapers also seemed unconcerned with the role of Mexico. American newspapers featured proportionately less material on Honduras than did the papers of the other three countries.

Table 2 presents data which show the way in which major actors in the Salvadorean crisis were portrayed in South American and North American newspapers. On this dimension, we see evidence of major differences in treatment with respect to almost all the major participants. With regard to the Salvadorean junta, South American papers were mainly

Table 1 News Coverage on Major Issues Dealing with El Salvador, by Country (percent)

	Country				
Issue	Argentina ($N=42$)	Chile ($N=36$)	Canada ($N=27$)	United States ($N=55$)	Cramer's V
Role of the U.S.	57.1	27.8	51.9	72.7	.33[b]
Role of guerrilla forces	64.3	47.2	37.0	25.5	.31[b]
Role of Salvadorean military	42.9	25.0	40.7	20.0	.22[a]
Role of Nicaragua	28.6	22.2	29.6	38.2	.13
Politico-military strategy of the junta	31.0	33.3	14.8	30.9	.14
Report of military action	28.6	41.7	11.1	20.0	.24[a]
Role of Cuba	23.8	11.1	18.5	36.4	.23[a]
Election of March 1982	26.2	13.9	25.9	20.0	.12
Role of Mexico	21.4	2.8	14.8	16.4	.19
Politico-military strategy of FDR/FMLN	16.7	5.6	11.1	18.2	.15
Role of Honduras	19.0	13.9	18.5	7.3	.15

Note: Columns add to more than 100% because of multiple coding.
[a] $p<.05$.
[b] $p<.01$.

neutral, with equal percentages (22%) falling in the positive and mixed categories. Only 15% of material on the junta was negative. North American papers presented quite a different picture of the junta. Here 64% of reporting was negative, 28% neutral, while only 8% was positive. Considering just the balance between positive and negative categories, the junta had a positive balance of +7 in South American papers, but a negative balance in North American papers of −56.[5]

While evaluation of the FDR/FMLN was not exactly the mirror image of that of the junta, the trend was definitely toward the opposite direction. Thus in South American papers, negative reporting on the FDR/FMLN predominated, appearing in 62% of coverage. Positive and mixed categories each accounted for 15%. In the case of North American papers, neutral reporting predominated, but in the balance between positive and negative coverage, the FDR/FMLN had a positive balance of +7. The corresponding negative balance in South American papers was −47.

Table 2   News Coverage Dealing with El Salvador Reflecting on Major Actors in the Crisis, by South American and North American Newspapers (percent)

Issue	N	South America			
		Positive	Mixed	Negative	Neutral
Portrayal of junta	27	22.2	22.2	14.8	40.7
Portrayal of FDR/FMLN	13	15.4	15.4	61.5	0
Portrayal of United States	27	59.3	7.4	18.5	14.8
Portrayal of Cuba	11	0	9.1	90.9	0
Portrayal of Nicaragua	16	0	12.5	75.0	12.5

	N	North America			
		Positive	Mixed	Negative	Neutral
Portrayal of junta	25	8.0	0	64.0	28.0
Portrayal of FDR/FMLN	15	20.0	6.1	13.3	60.0
Portrayal of United States	48	2.1	2.1	16.7	79.2
Portrayal of Cuba	23	0	0	21.7	78.3
Portrayal of Nicaragua	24	0	0	20.8	79.2

Perhaps the most startling finding of all deals with the evaluation of the American role in the conflict. In South American papers, approval of American involvement was apparent in very nearly 60% of reporting while only 19% was categorized as negative. Thus, there was a +41 positive balance of coverage regarding the American role. In the North American papers, by way of contrast, there was a decided lack of support for U.S. policy. While it is true that almost 80% of reporting was neutral, 17% was negative, while only 2% viewed American actions as favorable. This yields a negative balance regarding United States involvement of −15 on the part of North American papers.

Portrayals of Nicaragua and Cuba were consistent on each continent. In South American papers these countries were portrayed negatively, for the most part, with some mixed and neutral reporting. In North American papers, it was the neutral category which predominated, with the balance accounted for by negative reporting.

Country by country analysis on this dimension is difficult due to the very small N's in a number of the categories. However, with respect to the Salvadorean junta, Argentine newspapers were the most opinionated overall, with 25% of items coded in the positive category and 19% in the negative category. By way of contrast, Chilean papers were mostly neutral (64%). In North America, Canadian papers ran no material which reflected positively on the junta, while 13% of American press items did.

Table 3   Source of News Coverage on El Salvador (percent)

Source	Argentina (N=42)	Chile (N=36)	South America (N=78)	Canada (N=27)	United States (N=55)	North America (N=82)
Local staff/special correspondents	19.0	0	10.3	20.8	51.0	41.3
Canadian columnists	0	0	0	8.3	0	2.7
American wire services	54.8	36.1	46.3	33.3	27.5	29.3
American columnists	0	0	0	12.5	15.7	14.7
European wire services	26.2	63.9	43.6	25.0	5.9	12.0

However, both countries' reporting was highly unsympathetic to the junta, more than 60% of items in both Canadian and American newspapers reflected adversely on the junta.

The other actor on which we have a sufficient number of cases to do a country by country analysis is the United States. Here, both the Argentine and Chilean press reporting is overwhelmingly favorable, 67% and 63% respectively. Canadian reporting falls entirely in the neutral category, whereas in the United States, while most items were neutral (74%), the percentage of negative items (22%) far surpassed the positive items (3%). Thus it is clear that press criticism of American policy on El Salvador in North American papers was found in American, not Canadian newspapers.

Data in Table 3 show the source of Salvadorean news coverage. The various wire services provided the majority of news items. The American wire services included AP, UPI, and New York Times, and these accounted for 38% of total coverage. The European wire services included Reuters, EFE (Spain) and ANSA (Italian), and these provided 28% of total coverage. Local staff or special correspondents added another 25% of content, while American and Canadian columnists produced the balance of material.

Interesting variations, both by continent and country, are apparent in this distribution. South American papers were heavily dependent on the wire services for coverage of El Salvador; European services providing only slightly less copy than American. An interesting side point is that none of the Latin American press agencies provided any information to our sampled Argentine or Chilean newspapers. The North American papers were less dependent on wire services overall, with the largest single source of information coming from local staff writers or special correspondents.[6] North American columnists furnished approximately 15% of total material.

The country by country breakdown is perhaps more interesting. It shows a clearly different pattern of Salvadorean information flow into Argentina and Chile. Argentina was linked primarily to the American wire services while Chile was highly dependent on the European services. The Canadian-American comparison is also revealing. The Canadian newspapers were the most balanced of all regarding where information came from, while the American press showed evidence of extreme parochialism. Only 6% of Salvadorean news came from non-American employed sources. However, given that 51% of copy was written by special correspondents and local staff, there appeared to be both greater personal contact with events in El Salvador and greater personal expertise on the part of American writers. Nonetheless, the amount of non-American perspective present in the reporting of both American newspapers was small indeed. Perhaps what is most ironic, (and no doubt due to the two papers chosen in the United States, both of which rely very heavily on local staff and special correspondents), is that American newspapers appeared less dependent on American wire services than did the newspapers in the other three countries.

Our final question is the degree to which reporting on El Salvador was characterized by a "cold war" orientation. This orientation was operationalized by whether the item used language such as Communist, Marxist-Leninist, leftist, Soviet-backed or Cuban-backed. Overall, this Cold War orientation was present in 42.5% of Salvadorean related news items. The cold war orientation was most prominent in material written by American columnists (73%) and least evident in material provided by the European wire services (28%). Canadian columnists and American wire services used cold war frames in 50% of their material while 44% of Local Staff Special Correspondent material contained cold war descriptive terms.

Source of information is crucial in explaining both continent and country variations in the intensity of cold war preoccupation. While cold war orientation was marginally higher in North American papers (45% vs. 40% for South American papers), it is in the country by country analysis that major differences are seen. Specifically, Chilean newspapers presented by far the least amount of cold war-oriented material (25%), while the Argentine newspapers featured the most (52%). American and Canadian figures were 47% and 41% respectively. This pattern is no doubt a reflection of the extent to which Chile received its news from the European wire services, which of course, featured by far the least amount of cold war-oriented material.

Conclusions

First, with regard to volume of coverage, American newspapers featured more material on El Salvador than did the newspapers from the other countries. Even here, however, one story per day (usually on the inside pages) was not a particularly impressive amount of coverage. Salvadorean material had least salience for Canadian newspapers, with Chilean and Argentine newspapers occupying intermediate positions. However, with regard to the specific issues discussed relative to El Salvador, the degree of similarity was quite strong.

The major area where differences became evident was that of evaluation. Here we found, in general, that the South American papers portrayed the Salvadorean junta, and especially the United States, positively, while critical of the FDR/FMLN, Cuba, and Nicaragua. North American papers, on the other hand, were quite negative with regard to the performance of the junta and more positive than negative with respect to the FDR/FMLN. Involvement of all foreign actors was covered mainly in a neutral manner in North American papers, with almost no positive portrayals (even of American involvement), and a good deal of negative evaluation of all outside involvement.

Differences were also very apparent with respect to where Salvadorean news came from. In this case, country was more revealing than continent, as different patterns were seen in Argentina and Chile regarding the use of American or European wire services. Canada and the United States also differed, with Canadian information (which was heavily American in origin), balanced by local staff writers and special correspondents and the Reuters wire. American newspapers, as was pointed out, were singularly dependent upon American news sources.

Finally, with respect to cold war orientation, Argentina topped the list, the United States and Canada followed closely behind, while Chile trailed significantly. Again, the degree to which Chilean information came from European rather than American sources seems to explain this variation.

Overall, then, what we have is a situation where the impact of news flows on the reporting of factual information on El Salvador is somewhat ambiguous. American and Canadian readers were more likely to see the situation in "international" rather than "domestic" terms, but this was only a matter of degree. However, South American readers were given an essentially positive evaluation of the Salvadorean junta and United States efforts to support it against the FDR/FMLN backed by Nicaragua and Cuba, all of which were portrayed negatively. While the North American papers were more "international" in their portrayal of the crisis, they did not present this international involvement in a positive light. This was true whether the involvement was on the part of the United States or Nicaragua and Cuba. Also, little sympathy was shown for the Salvadorean junta.

Notes

1. See for example, Harold and Margaret Sprout, "Environmental Factors in the Study of International Politics," *Journal of Conflict Resolution*, 1:309-328 (1957); and Michael Brecher, Blema Steinberg, and Janice Stein, "A Framework for Research on Foreign Policy Behavior," *Journal of Conflict Resolution*, 13:75-101 (1969); Charles W. Kegley, Jr. and Eugene R. Wittkopf, *American Foreign Policy: Pattern and Process*, 2nd ed. (New York: St. Martin's Press, 1982).

2. *La Prensa, La Nacion* and *El Mercurio* are listed among the 20 most prominent papers in Latin America; see John C. Merrill, ed., *Global Journalism: A Survey of the World's Mass Media* (New York: Longman, 1983), p. 265, 275, 305; while the New York *Times*, the Washington *Post* and the *Globe and Mail* make the list of the world's 50 greatest newspapers; see John C. Merrill and Harold A. Fisher, *The World's Great Dailies: Profile of Fifty Newspapers* (New York: Hastings House Publishers, 1980), pp. 138-143, 220-230, 343-352.

3. These data must be interpreted with care. Positive or negative codes may not necessarily reflect media bias in favor of the actions or goals of a particular actor, but may indicate a factual situation that either favors or detracts from a particular actor.

4. In a post-study intercoder reliability test, an intercoder reliability coefficient of 81.6% was achieved. See Ole R. Holsti, *Content Analysis for the Social Sciences and Humanities* (Reading, Mass.: Addison-Wesley, 1969), p. 140.

5. These findings appear to challenge the charge leveled by Edward Herman in his book, *The Real Terror Network: Terrorism in Fact and Propaganda* (Boston: South End Press, 1982, pp. 139-199), that American media are reluctant to criticize the failings of America's dictatorial cold war allies.

6. Past research has shown, however, that local staff writers occasionally base their stories on wire service copy without indicating the ultimate source. Thus this finding may be less significant than it at first appears. Also, the wire services provided a smaller percentage of material on El Salvador to North American papers than they did on general regional news. See Schmitt and Soderlund, "Television and Newspaper Coverage of Latin American and Caribbean News," *Canadian Journal of Latin American Studies*, p. 61. It is clear that when a situation reaches crisis proportions, newspapers send their own correspondents to the scene, thus lessening the dependence on the wire services.

1.5 ▬▬

Before and After *The Day After:*
The Unexpected Results of a Televised Drama

William C. Adams, Dennis J. Smith, Allison Salzman,
Ralph Crossen, Scott Hieber, Tom Naccarato,
William Vantine, and Nine Weisbroth

Editor's Note. Just as Shakespeare's Hamlet urged his friend Horatio to welcome the unexpected because "there are more things in heaven and earth, Horatio, than are dreamt of in your philosophy" (act 1, scene 5, line 166), so William C. Adams urges researchers to be alert to unanticipated media effects. Failure to find effects may be failure to hypothesize actual effects coupled with an unwillingness to go on intellectual fishing expeditions. Besides discovering some unexpected effects from a broadcast about a fictional nuclear attack, the article demonstrates that political insights may flow as readily from fictional as from factual programs, a fact that political leaders know and attempt to control. Finally, the article suggests why some of the anticipated effects did not materialize.

Adams is a professor in the Department of Public Administration at The George Washington University. He is a well-known, prolific writer about television coverage of domestic and international politics. His co-authors were students at The George Washington University at the time of writing. The selection comes from "Before and After *The Day After*: The Unexpected Results of a Televised Drama," *Political Communication and Persuasion* 3:3 (1986): 191-213.

On Sunday evening, November 20, 1983, over 80 million Americans watched *The Day After,* ABC's drama about the horror and devastation of nuclear war. It was one of the most widely watched and debated dramatic programs in television history.

Nuclear-freeze advocates such as the director of the Campaign Against Nuclear War praised the program as "a 7 million dollar advertising job for our issue." Some conservatives denounced the movie as

From *Political Communication and Persuasion* 3, no. 3 (1986): 191-213. Reprinted by permission of Taylor and Francis.

"blatant political propaganda." Meanwhile, White House strategists worked to minimize any damage the show might do to President Ronald Reagan's defense policies, and the Secretary of State was dispatched to present an immediate televised response.

One television critic predicted that the movie, as a "shared national experience," would "touch our emotions, our attitudes and our hopes for the future." He added:[1]

> No one will be able to forget it. . . . As has rarely happened in television history, a work of fiction has achieved the urgency and magnitude of live coverage of a national crisis. . . . The actual impact will probably be . . . a pervasive shading of popular attitudes toward nuclear weaponry in general and the Reagan administration's New Brinkmanship in particular.

The advance billing was that *The Day After* would be a compelling drama that could create a "pervasive" shift in public attitudes. If this was to be a turning point in the national consciousness, it was important to measure the degree and character of that change.

Our study was designed to assess the effect of *The Day After* on a variety of subjects, including attitudes toward the following: (1) defense spending, (2) a bilateral nuclear freeze, (3) unilateral nuclear disarmament, (4) the likelihood of nuclear war, (5) the severity of nuclear war, (6) personal political efficacy on the issue of war and peace, and (7) the likelihood of nuclear war under the presidency of Ronald Reagan or Walter Mondale. We also appraised behavioral changes by examining public communication to the White House, the Congress, the ABC network counseling services, and antinuclear groups. *The Day After*, we discovered, produced a surprising pattern of reactions.

Methodology

On the evening of the broadcast, we conducted random nationwide telephone surveys both before and after *The Day After*. Working with Smith, Berlin & Associates, a Washington polling firm, and several dozen student volunteers, we surveyed a total of 928 people.

Our short questionnaire consisted of a dozen key attitudinal and demographic questions. Calling began about ninety minutes before the start of *The Day After* in each time zone. We interviewed only those people who said they were about to watch the program, and who were 17-years-old or older. (Most 17-year-olds would be eligible to vote in November 1984.) Thanks to the enormous audience, brief questionnaire, and intense public interest in the subject, we were able to complete 510 pre-test interviews.

A separate post-test sample was surveyed to obtain post-test data that would not be sensitized by the pre-test questions. Telephoning began the minute *The Day After* ended in each time zone and continued for about 45 minutes. People who had not seen the drama were screened out.

The questionnaire was identical to that used for the pre-test, with the addition of an inquiry as to whether respondents had been watching the special "Nightline" discussions about the movie. Viewers were eager to describe their opinions and refusals were unusually infrequent (under 5 percent). We completed 418 post-test interviews.

Random selection of subjects resulted in pre-test and post-test groups that were highly similar in their demographic composition. No statistically significant differences were found between the two groups on any of the available variables (age, sex, education, region, and party identification). Scores of the pre-test group could thus serve as baseline measures against which to contrast the scores of their counterparts in the post-test group.

Attitude Stability:
Defense Policy, Nuclear War, and Efficacy

Those who had predicted that *The Day After* would produce at least a short-term bonanza in additional antinuclear sentiment among the general public were completely wrong. Even with our sizable sample, we were unable to detect even a trivial shift on key questions. There were no statistically significant changes on any of the questions about defense policy or nuclear war.

Defense Policy.   Table 1 presents responses to the initial three questions. Opinions toward current defense spending were unchanged. Both before and after the movie, about 37-39 percent said too much was being spent, while about 16-17 percent said too little.

Three-fourths of those surveyed already favored a mutual freeze on nuclear weapons before they witnessed *The Day After*. There was no significant change afterward. Before the show, only 14 percent were opposed to a mutual freeze—about the same share as previous national surveys had found. After the show, the fraction was almost identical.

Just as Americans overwhelmingly supported a mutual nuclear freeze, they overwhelmingly opposed unilateral nuclear disarmament. In the pre-test, only 12 percent said they would unilaterally scrap all U.S. nuclear weapons; in the post-test, the proportion was 11 percent. Americans were opposed to one-sided nuclear disarmament by a ratio of about 8 to 1 prior to the program. The imagery of a nuclear holocaust did not dislodge that opposition.

Nuclear War.   Many people had speculated that *The Day After* would, at a minimum, convince Americans of the terror and slaughter of a thermonuclear war. Others predicted its graphic depiction would also

Table 1   Defense Armaments Attitudes Before and After *The Day After* (percent)

	Pre-test (N=510)	Post-test (N=418)
Do you think current U.S. government spending on the military and national defense is too much, too little, or about the right amount?		
Too much	38.6	36.7
Too little	16.3	17.2
About right	34.1	31.3
Uncertain	11.0	14.8
Would you support or oppose an agreement for both the U.S. and the Soviet Union to freeze nuclear weapons at current levels?		
Support	75.9	78.7
Oppose	14.3	13.2
Uncertain	9.8	8.1
Would you support or oppose a plan for the United States to scrap all U.S. nuclear weapons, regardless of what the Soviet Union does?		
Support	12.0	10.8
Oppose	81.2	83.5
Uncertain	6.9	5.7

increase fears that the movie was a premonition of a real future. We found no indication, however, of any alteration in attitudes about the severity or likelihood of nuclear war.

As shown in Table 2, those surveyed in the pre-test were just as pessimistic about their chances of surviving a nuclear war as were those who had seen the ABC program. Before the movie, 47 percent said they had absolutely no chance of living through a nuclear war. After the movie, the figure was 45 percent, a statistically insignificant difference.

Watching the atomizing of Lawrence, Kansas, also produced no shift in the proportion of those who thought a "full-scale nuclear war" was likely within the next ten years. Before the show, 45 percent said it was likely. Following the drama, 47 percent thought it was likely, a statistically insignificant difference.

Political Efficacy.   Before *The Day After* was aired, some commentators guessed it might stimulate grass-roots participation in the nuclear freeze movement, while others supposed it would spread feelings of helplessness toward such colossal issues. The latter idea would be consis-

Table 2   Nuclear War Attitudes Before and After *The Day After* (percent)

	Pre-test (N=510)	Post-test (N=418)
In your opinion how likely is a full-scale nuclear war within the next ten years?		
Extremely likely	10.4	12.4
Somewhat likely	34.5	34.9
Somewhat unlikely	32.5	28.9
Extremely unlikely	16.1	15.8
Uncertain	6.5	7.9
If there were a nuclear war, what do you think would be your chance of living through it?		
A good chance	0.8	2.6
About 50-50	11.6	11.5
A poor chance	35.1	36.4
No chance at all	47.1	44.5
Uncertain	5.5	5.0

tent with findings of Michael Robinson[2] and others that television messages often inflate the viewer's sense of frustration, confusion, and powerlessness.[3]

The Day After neither discouraged nor promoted feelings of personal political efficacy. . . .

Nearly two-thirds of those surveyed disagreed with the statement, "There is nothing I can do to influence war or peace," both before and after the drama. (Again, differences were not statistically significant.)

Subgroup Similarity

Having found none of the expected changes in the aggregate, we turned to an examination of major demographic and political subgroups. Perhaps *The Day After* was particularly powerful for younger adults (thought to have been especially vulnerable to its appeals), for women (often more dovish than men), or for Democrats and Independents (because Republicans may have heeded conservative warnings).

When controlling for age, education, sex, and party identification, however, the data still revealed no marked attitudinal shifts. . . . Attitudes toward defense spending, among all of the subgroups, were essentially unchanged. . . .

Attitudes before and after *The Day After* on six issues—defense spending, nuclear weapons freeze, unilateral nuclear disarmament, likelihood of nuclear war, severity of nuclear war, and personal political efficacy on the issue of war—were examined separately for all nine subgroups: men, women, college, noncollege, ages 17-29, ages 30 and over, Democrats, Independents, and Republicans. None of these 54 crosstabulations showed any significant pre-test-post-test differences. . . . Thus, there was no evidence that *The Day After* notably influenced any one subgroup more than it did the general population.

Warmongers and Presidents

Up to this point, we have seen consistency and stability in opinions. There was, however, one area in which we unexpectedly found a statistically significant fluctuation. That area was the image of Ronald Reagan.

Republican strategists had feared that the movie might boost pacifistic feelings and jeopardize President Reagan's military budget, foreign policy tactics, and even damage his reelection chances. . . .

As it turned out, there was a statistically significant shift on the subject of Reagan and nuclear war. In sharp contrast to the worry at the White House and the hopes of Democrats, the change was actually in Ronald Reagan's favor.

We asked the following question: "Do you think a major nuclear war would be more likely if the President were Ronald Reagan or Walter Mondale?" After television's vision of the apocalypse, the share of people pointing to Reagan as the more dangerous President declined significantly from 36 to 27 percent. As shown in Table 3 Mondale's proportion stayed virtually the same (17 to 15 percent). A large plurality of the respondents refused to accept the forced-choice alternatives; nearly 47 percent on the pre-test and 58 percent on the post-test refused to label either Reagan or Mondale as more likely to preside over a nuclear war.

Similar findings appeared in two *Washington Post* polls which asked if "Reagan's handling of foreign affairs is increasing or decreasing the chances for war"? Results from the poll of November 3-5 showed 57 percent saying Reagan was increasing chances of war. The poll taken the day following *The Day After* produced a major drop of 14 percentage points—only 43 percent remained critical of Reagan for increasing the chances of war.

Neither Reagan nor Mondale is mentioned in the script of the show. Why should there be a large drop in the proportion of people believing nuclear war is more likely under Reagan? Although the decreased criticism of Reagan was more pronounced among men, the college-educated, Independents, and those under 30, his ratings improved in every demographic subgroup.

We can suggest two explanations. It may well be that many of those

Table 3　Nuclear War and the President (percent)

	Pre-test (N=510)	Post-test (N=418)
Do you think a major nuclear war would be more likely if the President were Ronald Reagan or Walter Mondale?		
Ronald Reagan	36.1	27.3
Walter Mondale	16.9	15.1
No difference (volunteered)	47.1	57.7

Note: p>.005

who would have—perhaps casually—linked Reagan to nuclear war before *The Day After* might have seen that charge as excessive, overly partisan, and slanderous after being reminded of the slaughter and suffering that would soon follow any launching of ICBMs. Accordingly, they may have tempered their evaluations.

A second possibility is that the program may have artificially produced a version of the "rally-round-the-flag" effect often noted during international crises. In the wake of the movie's ersatz hostilities, some citizens may have been less willing to criticize the Commander-in-Chief.

In the post-test, nearly six out of ten respondents rejected the implicit premise of the question and denied that either Reagan or Mondale as President might be culpable for the onset of the kind of carnage they had just seen dramatized on television. Respondents sometimes volunteered that no American President would initiate such a conflict and that if war broke out, it would be due to the Russians or to circumstances beyond the control of the President.

All of this did not mean that Reagan was invulnerable on the campaign issues of peace. However, chalking up another score for unanticipated consequences of mass media messages, Reagan's problems in that area were not exacerbated by *The Day After* and appear to have been, at least temporarily, partially assuaged. . . .

Behavior

Except for the increased reluctance to link Ronald Reagan to nuclear war, there was no evidence of even minor movement in opinions toward defense policy and nuclear war. However, it is possible that *The Day After* reinforced the intensity of public sentiment and stimulated a zealous minority to action. Thus, rather than confine our analysis entirely to reported attitudes, we examined public behavior as well.

We investigated public responses toward (1) ABC and its affiliate stations, (2) the White House, (3) the Congress, (4) psychological counseling services, and (5) antinuclear groups, such as Ground Zero. If *The Day After*—though not changing opinions—did mobilize viewers into action, we should have ample measures of such behavior.

ABC and Affiliates. . . . Despite the controversy surrounding *The Day After*, there was no outpouring of telephone calls, pro or con, to ABC stations. Those who did call were disproportionately more critical of the program than was, according to our sample, the national viewing audience. At least as far as this small indicator of behavior goes, it suggests that *The Day After* stimulated its critics more than its proponents.

The White House.   A modest response was also tallied at the White House. . . .

Within 24 hours after the broadcast, the White House got only 596 telephone calls. (Of these calls, 77 percent said they believed the President was "doing a good job" in this area.) By comparison, the White House recorded 4,592 calls following the President's October 26 speech on Grenada and Lebanon. . . .

Congress.   . . . Pegging their campaign to the TV drama, a coalition of thirty groups opposed to nuclear arms sponsored television and newspaper ads promoting a toll-free number to call for "Nuclear War Prevention Kits." The kits stressed the importance and techniques of writing members of Congress. With these efforts added to an audience of over 80 million, what happened to Congressional mailboxes following *The Day After?*

We surveyed the correspondence staffs of 21 Senators and 30 Representatives, selecting a wide variety of officeholders from all parts of the country, and from the liberal, moderate, and conservative wings of both the Democratic and Republican parties. Most offices maintain records of mail trends, and we asked for comparisons of the mail received on defense policy, arms control, and nuclear war for the week before and the week after November 20. . . . The nearly unanimous response was that there was no outpouring of mail in the ten-day period following the program. . . .

Antinuclear Groups.   One of the leading groups in the general antinuclear area was Ground Zero. Theo Brown, its director, told us his organization experienced an extremely small increase in mail in the period after November 20, and only a minor increase in donations.

Brown's own conclusion was that *The Day After* was too antiseptic, too apolitical, and, having been oversold in advance, too anticlimactic to be influential. Nevertheless, Brown believed the program helped focus public attention on the subject, and saw that as its "greatest contribution." People in other antinuclear groups who consented to give us information, told a similar story. . . .

Psychological Aid.   Much was made in the press about the potentially disturbing consequences of viewing the drama. Concern was
expressed that vulnerable individuals might be depressed and emotionally
upset by the show. To check this final issue, we surveyed mental health
hotlines.

Did people telephone hotlines to talk about their problems coping
with the trauma of *The Day After?* A survey of long-established hotlines in
the Washington, D.C., area found little or no reaction to the program.
Psychologists and psychiatrists appear to have spent far more time talking
to television station reporters than to disturbed patients.

Intensity, Inoculation, Enervation, and Ennui

Aside from the increased reluctance to link Reagan with nuclear war,
The Day After produced no significant evidence of changed attitudes or
behavior. It was neither the salvation nor subversion the left and the right
had claimed it would be. Why did it have so little influence on its
viewers?

There appear to be four possible explanations: First, the controversy
surrounding the program might have "immunized" many viewers so that
they would be on guard against new ideas. Second, the special *Viewpoint*
discussion immediately following *The Day After* may have mitigated some
of its influence. Third, attitudes may have already been so strongly held
that they were unlikely to be swayed by a two-hour show. Fourth, *The
Day After* may have been more soporific than shattering, and a dull show
would hardly be unsettling, no matter how much Hollywood hype had
preceded it.

Inoculation.   The week leading up to the ABC broadcast had been
filled with news stories about the controversial show. Jerry Falwell and
Phyllis Schlafly led the attack. Mushroom-cloud cover stories were
featured in magazines such as *Newsweek* and *TV Guide.* Television shows
like *Nightline, Sixty Minutes,* and morning news shows featured defenders
and detractors of the forthcoming spectacle. Antinuclear groups mobi-
lized to profit from what they hoped would be a windfall of antinuclear
outrage. In this atmosphere, many viewers might have set up extra
perceptual barriers to resist being influenced.

To measure suspicions about *The Day After,* we asked the following
question: "Do you think that the movie about nuclear war is going to be
politically fair or do you think it will be mainly propaganda?" (Past tense
was used in the post-test version.)

Attitudes toward the movie itself did change before and after its
presentation. Only a modest plurality of 40 percent were willing to say in
advance that they were confident the show would be fair. On the other
hand, one-quarter of the audience said they expected the movie to be

"mainly propaganda." Despite our forced-choice question, over one-third insisted they were reserving judgment—they would wait and see. . . .

After seeing *The Day After*, the proportion who said it was "politically fair" grew from 40 to 63 percent. At the same time, the share saying it was "propaganda" shrunk from 26 to 20 percent. The fraction who were undecided was cut in half, although 17 percent of the respondents still would not characterize the movie even after having seen it. . . .

These figures fall short of being a resounding endorsement, but they do show substantial movement toward considering the program fair. Probably, most or all of those who said they had just watched a propagandistic show had already decided so in advance; there was certainly no increase in their numbers after the show. Nonetheless, one-quarter of the audience was primed to expect a loaded political message, and about one-third was at least prepared to find it slanted ("wait and see").

To examine whether this wary viewership limited the persuasive effects of *The Day After*, we first threw out those who labeled the movie "propaganda" and looked for attitude change among the balance of the audience. Once again, . . . there were no statistically significant differences before and after the movie on any of the five defense and nuclear questions. Even among those presumably most open to the movie there were no signs of change.

We tried another variation on this approach. We separately analyzed the before-and-after responses of those who had called the movie "fair," "propaganda," or were undecided. Again . . . we were unable to find traces of opinion shifts. . . .

. . . [T]he broader finding here was that the movie's failure to induce attitude shifts could not be easily attributed to 100 million people all having their defenses up. The less skeptical portion of the audience gave even less hint of change than did the critics.

Nightline. If the conservative brigade did not torpedo the movie before it was shown, did Ted Koppel's platoon shoot it down immediately after it was shown? Consistent with national TV ratings, nearly three-fourths of those surveyed stayed tuned after the end of *The Day After* to watch a special *Viewpoint* edition of *Nightline*. They first heard Secretary of State George Shultz minimize the prospect of nuclear war. Then they heard an assortment of mostly former government officials debate deterrence theory and defense strategies. (Some wags called the discussion "more frightening" than the movie.)

Previous research has demonstrated that the "coda effects" of subsequent commentaries can blunt the effects of a televised documentary[4] and that "instant analysis" can also dissipate the mood and impact of a presidential address.[5] Might the *Viewpoint* discussion have similarly undercut the power of *The Day After*?

Contrasting the opinions of those who did and those who did not watch *Viewpoint* failed to uncover significant differences. . . .

Intensity.   Neither conservative attacks on *The Day After* nor *Viewpoint* discussions of it explained the absence of opinion change. What then about that usual bulwark against change—intensely-held attitudes? A truism verified by decades of communication research is that strong, long-held opinions do not yield easily to change.

. . . [S]everal decades of public opinion polls suggest that Americans have a long-standing appreciation of the destruction and death that would result from nuclear war. They strongly endorse efforts for mutual U.S.-Soviet limits and reductions of nuclear arms. . . .

Americans have embraced arms control proposals as surely as they have acknowledged the dangers of nuclear warfare. Overwhelming and immediate public support greeted the idea of a nuclear freeze. Almost no matter how the question is phrased, 70 to 85 percent of the public will voice support for a mutual freeze on nuclear weapons.

. . . [T]hese past findings . . . indicate that Americans had not been oblivious to the threat of nuclear war and were historically sympathetic to arms control. In dramatizing the anguish of the aftermath of nuclear war, *The Day After* did not tell its audience anything new.

Ennui.   Along with the factor of prior convictions, one other major explanation can be offered: *The Day After* was not as sensational and heartrending as its promotions had promised.

Given the magnitude of violence in popular entertainment and a decade of disaster movies, *The Day After* had tough acts to follow. Moreover, its depiction of the aftermath of World War III appeared to have been less horrible, less gruesome than many viewers had imagined. Some authorities also argued that the movie's images were optimistic compared to the likely consequences of a worldwide rain of nuclear warheads. ABC conceded as much with a printed coda stating that its scenario was "in all likelihood less severe than what would actually occur."

Communication Theory and Unexpected Effects

Much of the debate in political communication research continues to center on the "minimum effects" (or no effects) view versus the "substantial effects" (or at least "more than minimum effects") view.[6] However, the findings of this study of *The Day After* suggest that too little attention has been paid to oblique or corollary effects. Just because viewers do not accept the exact message or learn the particular lesson predicted by the researcher does not mean that no lessons have been learned.

By focusing on narrowly defined effects, researchers can miss the unexpected oblique influences of mass communication. And, by their nature, unexpected effects are difficult to study. The researcher may not contemplate many possible consequences, and other effects may seem too illogical or farfetched to merit study. The argument here is not just that many viewers may reach conclusions opposite those presented in the mass media. . . .

Beyond the matter of opposite reactions, viewers may frame the story in different terms, may see different issues at stake, and may draw verdicts on different questions than those assumed by the scholar. *The Day After* data showed an audience response that varied markedly from expectations. A "rally" effect had not been imagined; issues and potential main effects had been conceptualized in other ways. . . .

An audience may not share the researchers' agenda or world-view. More expansive methodologies are needed to capture communication reactions that may escape the range of most researchers' few narrow effects variables. And a study that is headlined "no effects" ought to more properly claim that no effects were found in specific areas.

Notes

1. Tom Shales, "Must Viewing for the Nation: Devastating Images of Horror," *Washington Post*, November 18, 1983, p. C1.
2. Michael J. Robinson, "Public Affairs Television and the Growth of Political Malaise," *American Political Science Review* 70 (June 1976): 409-432.
3. William C. Adams, "Why the Right Gets It Wrong in Foreign Policy," *Public Opinion* 6 (August/September 1983): 12-15.
4. Michael J. Robinson, op. cit.
5. David L. Paletz and Richard J. Vinegar, "Presidents on Television: Effects of Instant Analysis," *Public Opinion Quarterly* 41 (Winter 1977-78): 488-497.
6. William C. Adams, Allison Salzman, William Vantine, Leslie Suelter, Anne Baker, Lucille Bonvouloir, Barbara Brenner, Margaret Ely, Jean Feldman, and Ron Ziegel, "The Power of *The Right Stuff:* A Quasi-Experimental Field Test of the Docudrama Hypothesis," *Public Opinion Quarterly* 49 (Autumn 1985): 330-339.

1.6 ■■■■■■

Attitudes About the Media:
A Five Country Comparison

Laurence Parisot

Editor's Note. Media influence depends, in part, on the credibility of the media and on the esteem with which their audiences regard them. Drawing on public opinion polls in four European countries and the United States, Laurence Parisot shows how confidence in the media in these countries compares with confidence in nine other major institutions. The media have negative ratings in all four European countries but a positive score in the United States. Confidence in the media ranks at the bottom in France. Only Spain ranks the media highly in the group of ten, placing them third from the top. These figures do not bode well for media credibility.

It must be remembered, however, that audiences lack sources other than the national media for most current information. They may not believe what they hear and see, but they have no alternative images to which they can turn. Despite credibility problems, most audience members therefore believe that the media are a powerful influence on public opinion. European audiences believe that the media have much less influence on the three branches of government; American respondents, rightly or wrongly, credit the media with a great deal of influence over governmental institutions.

Parisot is general manager of the public opinion polling firm Louis Harris, France. She is a graduate of the Institut d'Etudes Politiques de Paris and also has earned a law degree. The selection is from "Attitudes about the Media: A Five Country Comparison," *Public Opinion* 10:5 (January/February 1988): 18-19, 60. Several tables have been omitted.

> *The press has become the most powerful force in Western countries. It has surpassed in power the executive, legislative, and judiciary.*
>
> —Alexsander Solzhenitsyn
> Harvard University, June 1978

In France, the press is a fourth power of State; it attacks all yet no one attacks it. It reprimands recklessly. It asserts a domination over politicians and men of letters that is not reciprocated, claiming that its protagonists are sacred. They say and do horribly foolish things; that is their right! It is high time we took a look at these unknown, second-rate men who hold such importance in their time and who are the moving force behind a press with a production equal to that of books.
—Honoré de Balzac
1840

Critiques of the press have spanned a century and several continents. Whether or not one would go as far as Solzhenitsyn and Balzac, nearly everyone acknowledges that the media play a powerful role in our public and private lives. Opinions about the media and estimates of their influence on society's other institutions can be important barometers of democracy's functioning. Various organizations have assessed the media's standing in individual countries, but little systematic work has been done to compare those evaluations from nation to nation. In early April 1987, Louis Harris France undertook such a project for *L'Express* and the Institut International de Géopolitique, and surveyed adults in France, West Germany, Great Britain, Spain, and the United States.

The Media: A Controversial Institution

. . . One way to gauge our impressions of the media is to compare our confidence in them to confidence in other institutions. In their 1983 book, *The Confidence Gap*, Seymour Martin Lipset and William Schneider explored the extent to which Americans had confidence in society's institutions. The authors documented a decline in confidence in virtually every major institution, but they also found that faith in the legitimacy of the system was strong and abiding. The 1987 Louis Harris France survey gives us pieces of the same kind of information for Europe and the United States, and enables us to look at confidence in nine key institutions. Although freedom of information is regarded as fundamentally important, the disseminators of information, the media, fare less well.

Perhaps the most striking finding is that Americans have significantly greater confidence in their institutions than Europeans have in theirs. This is as true for the media as for other institutions; majorities in three countries—Germany, Great Britain, and Spain—have only a little or no confidence in the media, while 69 percent of Americans have complete or some confidence. In France opinion is split with 48 percent saying they have at least some confidence in the media, and 49 percent saying they have little or none. With the exception of Spain, the media rank near the bottom of the list of all institutions surveyed. (See Table 1.)

Do the media have too much power? Pluralities in three countries—

Table 1   Confidence in Institutions (percent)

Confidence in:	France	Germany	Britain	Spain	United States
The schools					
Great deal/some	82	82	53	59	82
Hardly any/no	14	17	43	35	17
The church					
Great deal/some	53	66	56	38	85
Hardly any/no	43	34	41	60	14
The military					
Great deal/some	59	69	79	36	86
Hardly any/no	36	31	16	60	13
The police					
Great deal/some	72	80	80	44	88
Hardly any/no	27	20	20	54	12
The Supreme Court					
Great deal/some	58	80	—	38	86
Hardly any/no	21	19	—	43	13
The judicial system					
Great deal/some	62	72	56	35	77
Hardly any/no	35	28	40	61	21
The media/press, radio/television					
Great deal/some	48	41	38	46	69
Hardly any/no	49	59	60	51	30
Labor unions					
Great deal/some	36	43	29	26	52
Hardly any/no	59	56	66	65	45
Business community					
Great deal/some	30	44	55	26	84
Hardly any/no	55	55	34	58	15
Congress					
Great deal/some	55	64	52	30	83
Hardly any/no	32	36	46	61	16

Source: Survey by Louis Harris France, April 9-13, 1987; Emnid Institute GMBH and Co. (Germany), April 11-13, 1987; The Harris Research Centre (Great Britain), April 3-5, 1987; SOFEMASA (Spain), April 4-9, 1987; and Louis Harris and Associates (United States), April 10-15, 1987.

Note: The question was: "How would you rate your confidence in the following (name of country) institutions? Would you say you have a great deal of confidence, only some confidence, hardly any confidence, or no confidence at all in... ?"

Table 2 Media Power (percent)

	France	Germany	Britain	Spain	United States
Media have . . .					
Too much power	29	32	43	46	49
Not enough power	14	6	10	22	10
Just the right amount of power	45	48	41	26	39

Note: The question was: "In general, would you say that, in (name of country) the media have too much power, not enough power, or just the right amount?"

Spain, Britain, and the United States—said they do. In France and Germany strong pluralities felt that the media have "just about the right amount" of power, but in France twice as many respondents said the media have too much, as opposed to too little power (29-14 percent). In Germany one-third believed that the media have too much power, while a slim 6 percent said they have too little. In each of the countries . . . the percentage saying the media have too much power exceeds the percentages saying "not enough power." (See Table 2.)

Do the media influence other key institutions of society? That is, how much power do they really have? Substantial majorities, ranging from 88 percent in the United States to 70 percent in Spain, say that the media have a large influence on public opinion. The media's actual influence cannot be measured by this survey, despite our respondents' strong belief in the power of the press. A number of sociologists who specialize in communications, particularly Paul Lazarsfeld, have demonstrated the partly illusory, partly mythical, character of media influence. But the public believes the influence is there, and that is when myth can become reality. Public opinion, according to this survey, exerts far less influence on the media than the media exert on it.

Separation of Powers: The Fourth Power

The survey also assesses the media's influence on three central institutions of government—the executive, the legislature, and the judiciary. Here, the media are controversial. (See Table 3.) Some accuse the media of undermining the separation of powers that is the foundation of democracy. Our survey cannot say whether the media actually impede the operation of the other three institutions, but it does document the public's evaluation of media influence on government.

Here, Americans diverged from Western Europeans once again. In the United States, 81 percent of the respondents said that the media's

Table 3   Media Influence (percent)

	France	Germany	Britain	Spain	United States
Influence exerted by media on . . . is large[a]					
Judiciary	46	29	40	32	69
Legislature	37	44	48	38	78
Executive branch/ government	48	46	44	41	81
Public opinion	77	71	80	70	88

Note: The question was: "Would you say that the influence exerted by the media on (name institutions) is very large, somewhat large, not very large, or not large at all?"
[a] Large = all "very large" and "somewhat large" responses.

influence on the executive branch is very or quite strong, compared to 48 percent in France, 46 percent in West Germany, 44 percent in Great Britain, and 41 percent in Spain. Americans were also far more likely than Western Europeans to believe that the media have a substantial influence on the legislature. Seventy-eight percent of Americans said that the media's influence on the legislature was strong, compared to 48 percent in Great Britain, 44 percent in West Germany, 38 percent in Spain, and 37 percent in France. The same pattern appeared with the judiciary. Sixty-nine percent of Americans considered the influence of the media on the judiciary to be strong, compared to 46 percent in France, 40 percent in Great Britain, 32 percent in Spain, and 29 percent in West Germany.

There are some important differences in the responses of Europeans to the issue of media influence. The Spanish see the fourth estate's power as more limited than others did. The French believe the media have less influence on the legislature than on the judicial system or the executive. In Germany, Britain, and Spain, respondents felt that the media have more influence on the legislature and the executive than on the judicial system.

The other side of this coin is the influence of each of these institutions on the media. Does the public see the media as tools of these institutions? Those in the United States believe that the media have far more influence on government institutions than the institutions have on the media. The British answers are precisely the opposite: all three government branches exert more influence on the media than the reverse.

The press has become, as Solzhenitsyn said, a powerful force in our societies. As such, it invites much scrutiny. Public perceptions—on both sides of the Atlantic—will be an important part of the critique.

2. SHAPING THE POLITICAL AGENDA

T he American humorist Will Rogers said long ago, "All I know is just what I read in the papers." For many Americans there is a good bit of truth in this aphorism; what they know about ongoing political events comes primarily from the news media. In this section we focus on the media as a supplier of information that the general public and political elites need to form political opinions and make political decisions. If the media guide our attention to certain issues and influence what we think about, it stands to reason that they also influence the choice of issues that will be matters of political concern and action. That, in essence, is the reasoning behind the agenda-setting hypothesis of scholars such as Maxwell E. McCombs and Donald L. Shaw.

In their essay, McCombs and Shaw describe how and to what extent the topics selected by news people for presentation by the mass media become the issues the public regards as important. Their findings have been confirmed by numerous other studies demonstrating that issues featured by the media become correspondingly important to the public. By contrast, issues receiving little media coverage are unlikely to arouse public concern or to engender political action.

Most agenda-setting research begins after media have featured an issue and attempt to fathom the relation between media concerns and the concerns of various audiences. But how are media concerns aroused? What circumstances and efforts are required to attract media attention sufficient to catapult a particular issue into the spotlight of political attention and action? Barbara J. Nelson explores this question as part of her study of the emergence of child abuse as a social issue requiring political action. Whether similar patterns hold true for other social issues remains to be tested.

Phillip J. Tichenor, George A. Donohue, and Clarice N. Olien examine the agenda-setting role of mass media for a group of issues that aroused community conflict. They scrutinize the ways mass media bring conflicts to pubic attention and highlight particular aspects of a conflict so that they become the focus of public discussion and action. The authors' primary conclusion is that the media's agenda-setting power lies in their ability to bestow publicity or to deny it in conflictual situations. Contrary to widespread beliefs, media do not initiate and shape conflicts.

Benjamin I. Page, Robert Y. Shapiro, and Glenn R. Dempsey claim a more important role for the media when it comes to shaping public opinion about a broad array of public policies. They examine changes in policy preferences expressed in successive public opinion polls in light of the intervening television news stories. Their sample of polls, covering eighty issues over fifteen years, demonstrates convincingly that television news stories affect policy preferences. Like other scholars, the authors point out that various contextual factors determine the degree and direction of news impact. The Page-Shapiro-Dempsey study illustrates how a major research venture, simultaneously involving many different issues over an extended time, can bring results when other, less ambitious studies fail to attain conclusive findings.

Most agenda-setting studies have combined content analysis of news media and interviews of media audiences to assess how well media priorities and audience priorities coincide. Shanto Iyengar's approach has been different. To make certain that audiences actually have been exposed to the particular news stories whose influence is under investigation, and to eliminate extraneous influences on their thinking as much as possible, Iyengar designed a series of laboratory tests. Subjects were exposed to stories with carefully controlled content and subsequently were tested in the laboratory for various types of agenda-setting effects. The experiment reported in Iyengar's essay demonstrates that news stories can guide the way audiences think about the causes of various social problems. It remains an intriguing but unanswered question, however, to what extent the artificial laboratory setting influences the results.

The last selection answers some questions—and raises several more—about the ultimate effects of television news and entertainment programs on public thinking and the democratic process. George Gerbner, Larry Gross, Michael Morgan, and Nancy Signorielli discuss how popular entertainment programs affect the political thinking of people who spend four hours or more each day watching television. They also describe how television reality, although grossly distorted compared with the real world, becomes embedded in people's images of society.

2.1

The Agenda-Setting Function of the Press

Maxwell E. McCombs and Donald L. Shaw

Editor's Note. A major factor in reviving the pace of media effects research, after it had been throttled by the minimal effects findings of the 1960s, was a seminal article by Maxwell E. McCombs and Donald L. Shaw. It appeared in 1972 in *Public Opinion Quarterly* and focused on the agenda-setting capacity of the news media in the 1968 presidential election. McCombs and Shaw concentrated on information transmission. This change away from attitudinal effects to an examination of what people actually learn from news stories sparked a spate of empirical research that demonstrated the media's importance as transmitters of political information.

Agenda-setting research continues to be productive in demonstrating and defining the relation between media coverage and the public's thinking. Like much research on political communication, it first was used to study the media's influence on public perceptions of presidential candidates, but it has moved beyond that narrow realm. In recent years, researchers have looked at a wider array of elections as well as at the influence of agenda setting in other political domains, such as public policy formation and perceptions about foreign affairs.

At the time of writing, both authors were associate professors in the School of Journalism at the University of North Carolina at Chapel Hill. McCombs and Shaw are widely viewed as the intellectual godfathers of the agenda-setting research approach. Although there are a few other claimants to that title, none have contributed as much to the continued vigor and development of current agenda-setting research. The selection is from *The Emergence of American Political Issues: The Agenda-Setting Function of the Press* (St. Paul: West Publishing, 1977).

The Popular View

Certainly in the popular view mass communication exerts tremendous influence over human affairs. The ability of television, newspapers,

---

magazines, movies, radio, and a whole host of new communications technologies to mold the public mind and significantly influence the flow of history is a widely ascribed power. In the political arena, candidates spend substantial sums for the services of image-makers—a new kind of mass communication artist and technocrat who presumably works magic on the voters via the mass media.

Early social scientists shared with historians, politicians, and the general public a belief in the ability of mass communication to achieve significant, perhaps staggering, social and political effects. But beginning with the benchmark Erie County survey conducted during the 1940 presidential campaign,[1] precise, quantitative research on the effects of mass communication in election campaigns, public information campaigns, and on numerous public attitudes soon gave the academic world a jaundiced view of the power of mass communication. . . .

We moved from an all-powerful *1984* view to the *law of minimal consequences*, a notion that the media had almost no effect, in two decades! But despite the "law," interest in mass communication has proliferated during the past 15 years. Political practitioners, especially, continue to emphasize the use of mass communication in election campaigns.[2] Surely all this is not due simply to cultural lag in spreading the word about the law of minimal consequences. Rather it is because *mass communication does in fact play a significant political role*. This is not to say that the early research was wrong. It simply was limited. To gain precision, science must probe carefully circumscribed areas. Unfortunately, the early research on mass communication concentrated on attitude change. Given the popular assumption of mass media effects, it was not a surprising choice. But the chain of effects that result from exposure to mass communication has a number of links preceding attitude and opinion change. In sequence, the effects of exposure to communication are generally catalogued as:

Awareness —> Information —> Attitudes —> Behavior

Early research chose as its strategy a broad flanking movement striking far along this chain of events. But as the evidence showed, the direct effects of mass communication on attitudes and behavior are minimal. . . . So in recent years scholars interested in mass communication have concentrated on earlier points in the communication process: awareness and information. Here the research has been most fruitful in documenting significant social effects resulting from exposure to mass communication. People do learn from mass communication.

Not only do they learn factual information about public affairs and what is happening in the world, they also learn how much importance to attach to an issue or topic from the emphasis placed on it by the mass media. Considerable evidence has accumulated that editors and broadcasters play an important part in shaping our social reality as they go about their day-to-day task of choosing and displaying news. In reports both prior to and during political campaigns, the news media to a considerable degree determine the important issues. In other words, the media set the "agenda" for the campaign.

This impact of the mass media—the ability to effect cognitive change among individuals, to structure their thinking—has been labeled the *agenda-setting function of mass communication.* Here may lie the most important effect of mass communication, its ability to mentally order and organize our world for us. In short, the mass media may not be successful in telling us what to think, but they are stunningly successful in telling us what to think *about.*[3]

Assertions of Agenda-Setting

The general notion of agenda-setting—the ability of the media to influence the salience of events in the public mind—has been part of our political culture for at least half a century. Recall that the opening chapter of Walter Lippmann's 1922 book *Public Opinion* is titled: "The World Outside and the Pictures in Our Heads." As Lippmann pointed out, it is, of course, the mass media which dominate in the creation of these pictures of public affairs.[4]

More recently this assumption of media power has been asserted by presidential observer Theodore White in *The Making of the President, 1972.*

> The power of the press in America is a primordial one. It sets the agenda of public discussion; and this sweeping political power is unrestrained by any law. It determines what people will talk and think about—an authority that in other nations is reserved for tyrants, priests, parties and mandarins.[5]

The press does more than bring these issues to a level of political awareness among the public. The idea of agenda-setting asserts that the priorities of the press to some degree become the priorities of the public. What the press emphasizes is in turn emphasized privately and publicly by the audiences of the press. . . .

Cognitive Effects of Mass Communication

This concept of an agenda-setting function of the press redirects our attention to the cognitive aspects of mass communication, to attention, awareness, and information. . . . [T]he history of mass communication research from the 1940 Erie County study to the present decade can be viewed as a movement away from short-range effects on attitudes and toward long-range effects on cognitions.[6]

Attitudes concern our feelings of being for or against a political position or figure. *Cognition* concerns our knowledge and beliefs about political objects. The agenda-setting function of mass communication clearly falls in this new tradition of cognitive outcomes of mass communication. Perhaps more than any other aspect of our environment, the political arena—all those issues and persons about whom we hold opinions and knowledge—is a secondhand reality. Especially in national politics, we have little personal or direct contact. Our knowledge comes primarily from the mass media. For the most part, we know only those aspects of national politics considered newsworthy enough for transmission through the mass media.

Even television's technological ability to make us spectators for significant political events does not eliminate the secondhand nature of our political cognitions. Television news is edited reality just as print news is an edited version of reality. And even on those rare occasions when events are presented in their entirety, the television experience is not the same as the eyewitness experience.[7]

Our knowledge of political affairs is based on a tiny sample of the real political world. That real world shrinks as the news media decide what to cover and which aspects to transmit in their reports, and as audiences decide to which news messages they will attend.

Yet, as Lippmann pointed out, our political responses are made to that tiny replica of the real world, the *pseudoenvironment*, which we have fabricated and assembled almost wholly from mass media materials. The concept of agenda-setting emphasizes one very important aspect of this pseudoenvironment, the *salience* or amount of emphasis accorded to various political elements and issues vying for public attention.

Many commentators have observed that there is an agenda-setting function of the press and Lippmann long ago eloquently described the necessary connection between mass communication and individual political cognitions. But like much of our folk wisdom about politics and human behavior, it was not put to empirical test by researchers for over half a century.

Empirical Evidence of Agenda-Setting

The first empirical attempt at verification of the agenda-setting function of the mass media was carried out by McCombs and Shaw during the 1968 U.S. presidential election.[8] Among undecided voters in Chapel Hill, North Carolina there were substantial correlations between the political issues emphasized in the news media and what the voters regarded as the key issues in that election. The voters' beliefs about what were the major issues facing the country reflected the composite of the press coverage, even though the three presidential contenders in 1968 placed widely divergent emphasis on the issues. This suggests that voters—at least undecided voters—pay some attention to all the political news in the press regardless of whether it is about or originated with a favored candidate. This contradicts the concepts of selective exposure and selective perception, ideas which are central to the law of minimal consequences. Selective exposure and selective perception suggest that persons attend most closely to information which they find congenial and supportive.

In fact, further analysis of the 1968 Chapel Hill survey showed that among those undecided voters with leanings toward one of the three candidates, there was less agreement with the news agenda based on their preferred candidate's statements than with the news agenda based on all three candidates.

While the 1968 Chapel Hill study was the first empirical investigation based specifically on agenda-setting, there is other scholarly evidence in the mass communication/political behavior literature which can be interpreted in agenda-setting terms. Let's briefly consider several examples.

The first example comes from the 1948 Elmira study. . . . For an optimum view of the agenda-setting influence of the press, one should examine those Elmira voters with minimal interpersonal contact. . . . [F]or those voters the political agenda suggested by the media is not mediated, interpreted, or confronted by interpersonal sources of influence. These voters would seem especially open to the agenda-setting influence of the press.

And the influence was there. These Elmira voters moved with the trend of the times more than did the other voters. Like the national Democratic trend that mounted during the 1948 campaign, these Elmira voters moved rapidly into the Democratic column. The cues were there in the media for all. But persons without the conservative brake of interpersonal contacts moved most rapidly with the national trend reported in the media.

The second example of agenda-setting comes from a study of county voting patterns in an Iowa referendum.[9] In this example it is easy to see the agenda-setting effects of both mass media and interpersonal news sources.

The question before the voters was calling a constitutional convention to reapportion legislative districts. Since large counties stood to gain and small counties to lose from reapportionment, the study anticipated a strong correlation between county population and proportion of votes in favor of the convention. In short, it was hypothesized that counties would vote their self-interest. And, overall, this was strikingly the case. Across all counties, the correlation is $+.87$ between county population and vote.

But now let us consider whether this pattern is facilitated by the presence of agenda-setting institutions. Two sources of heightened awareness were considered: a citizens' committee in favor of the convention and a daily newspaper in the county.

In the 41 counties where the citizens' committee was active, the correlation was +.92 between vote and population. In the 58 counties without such a group, the correlation was only +.59. Similar findings are reported for the presence or absence of a local daily newspaper. In the 38 counties with a local daily, the correlation was +.92. In the 61 counties without a daily, the correlation was only +.56.

Each agenda-setting source made a considerable difference in the outcome. What about their combined impact? In 28 countries with both a local daily and a citizens' committee the correlation was +.92. Where only one of these sources was present, the correlation declined to +.40; and when neither agenda-setter was present, the correlation declined to +.21.

Self-interest may have motivated many voters. But unless the issue was high on the agenda—placed there via the newspaper and local citizens' committee—this motivation simply did not come into play.

A similar "necessary condition" role for agenda-setting is found in a study of the distribution of knowledge among populations.[10] Generally, there is a knowledge gap between social classes concerning topics of public affairs, typically documented by a rather substantial correlation between level of education and knowledge of public affairs. That is to say, as level of education increases, so does the amount of knowledge about public affairs. But as communication scientist Phillip Tichenor and his colleagues discovered, the strength of this correlation, at least for some topics, is a direct function of the amount of media coverage. They found a monotonic relationship between media coverage and the strength of the education/knowledge correlation. The more the press covers a topic, the more an audience—especially audience members with more education—learn.

The Concept of Agenda-Setting

Agenda-setting not only asserts a positive relationship between what various communication media emphasize and what voters come to regard as important, it also considers this influence as an inevitable by-product of the normal flow of news.

Each day editors and news directors—the gate-keepers in news media systems—must decide which items to pass and which to reject. Furthermore, the items passed through the gate are not treated equally when presented to the audience. Some are used at length, others severely cut. Some are lead-off items on a newscast. Others follow much later.

Newspapers clearly state the value they place on the salience of an item through headline size and placement within the newspaper—anywhere from the lead item on page one to placement at the bottom of a column on page 66.

Agenda-setting asserts that audiences learn these saliences from the news media, incorporating a similar set of weights into their personal agendas. Even though these saliences are largely a by-product of journalism practice and tradition, they nevertheless are attributes of the messages transmitted to the audience. And as the idea of agenda-setting asserts, they are among the most important message attributes transmitted to the audience.

This notion of the agenda-setting function of the mass media is a relational concept specifying a strong positive relationship between the emphases of mass communication and the salience of these topics to the individuals in the audience. This concept is stated in causal terms: increased salience of a topic or issue in the mass media influences (causes) the salience of that topic or issue among the public.

Agenda-setting as a concept is not limited to the correspondence between salience of topics for the media and the audience. We can also consider the saliency of various attributes of these objects (topics, issues, persons, or whatever) reported in the media. To what extent is our view of an object shaped or influenced by the picture sketched in the media, especially by those attributes which the media deem newsworthy? Some have argued, for example, that our views of city councils as institutions are directly influenced by press reporting with the result that these local governing groups are perceived to have more expertise and authority than they actually possess.[11]

Consideration of agenda-setting in terms of the salience of both topics and their attributes allows the concept of agenda-setting to subsume many similar ideas presented in the past. The concepts of status-conferral, stereotyping, and image-making all deal with the salience of objects or attributes. And research on all three have linked these manipulations of salience to the mass media.

Status-conferral, the basic notion of press agentry in the Hollywood sense, describes the ability of the media to influence the prominence of an individual (object) in the public eye.

On the other hand, the concept of stereotyping concerns the prominence of attributes: All Scots are thrifty! All Frenchmen are romantic! Stereotyping has been criticized as invalid characterization of objects because of its overemphasis on a few selected traits. And the media repeatedly have been criticized for their perpetuation of stereotypes, most recently of female roles in our society.

The concept of image-making, now part of our political campaign jargon, covers the manipulation of the salience of both objects and attributes. A political image-maker is concerned with increasing public familiarity with his candidate (status-conferral) and/or increasing the perceived prominence of certain candidate attributes.

In all cases, we are dealing with the basic question of agenda-setting research: How does press coverage influence our perception of objects and their attributes?

Issue Salience and Voting

Political issues have become salient as a factor in voter behavior in recent years. The importance of party identification, long the dominant variable in analysis of voter decisions, has been reduced. This stems both from a conceptual rethinking of voter behavior and from an empirical trend. . . .

. . . In 1960 the Michigan Survey Research Center, whose earlier work has provided much of the evidence for the key role of party identification, added a new set of open-ended questions to its interview schedule seeking information about the voter's own issue concerns—that is, those issues which were salient to the individual voter—and the perceived link between those issues and the parties.

Analysis of these questions reveals a major role for issue salience in the presidential vote decision. For example, in predicting voting choice in 1964 the weights were .39 for candidate image, .27 for party identification, and .23 for issues. (Each weight controls for the influence of the two other factors.) . . .

In 1972 issues took center stage. Summing up its analysis of that election, the Survey Research Center concluded: "Ideology and issue voting in that election provide a means for better explaining the unique elements of the contest than do social characteristics, the candidates, the events of the campaign, political alienation, cultural orientations, or partisan identification." [12]

Voters do respond to the issues. The new evidence on the impact of issues appearing in the late 1960s and early 1970s provided empirical vindication for V. O. Key, Jr.'s view that "voters are not fools." Key had long contended that voters in fact responded to the issues and to the events creating and surrounding those issues.[13] Again, anticipating the concept of an agenda-setting function of the press operating across time to define political reality, Key argued that the "impact of events from the inauguration of an administration to the onset of the next presidential campaign may affect far more voters than the fireworks of the campaign itself." [14] Even the benchmark Erie County survey found that events between 1936 and 1940 changed more than twice as many votes as did the 1940 presidential campaign itself.

It is, of course, the press that largely structures voters' perceptions of political reality. As we shall see, the press can exert considerable influence on which issues make up the agenda for any particular election. Not only can the press influence the nature of the political arena in which a campaign is conducted but, on occasion, it can define (albeit inadvertently) an agenda which accrues to the benefit of one party. To a considerable degree the art of politics in a democracy is the art of determining which issue dimensions are of major interest to the public or can be made salient in order to win public support.

In 1952 the Republicans, led by Dwight Eisenhower, successfully exploited the three "K's"—Korea, Corruption, and Communism—in order to regain the White House after a hiatus of twenty years. The prominence of those three issues, cultivated by press reports extending over many months and accented by partisan campaign advertising, worked against the incumbent Democratic party. Nor is 1952 an isolated example. One of the major campaign techniques discussed by political analyst Stanley Kelley in *Professional Public Relations and Political Power* is nothing more than increasing the salience of an issue that works to an incumbent's disadvantage.[15]

These are what social scientist Angus Campbell and his colleagues[16] call *valence issues* in contrast to our usual consideration of *position issues* on which voters take various pro or con stances. A valence issue is simply a proposition, condition, or belief that is positively or negatively valued by all the voters. At least two, if not all three, of the 1952 K's were valence issues. . . . To the extent that the press (via its agenda-setting function) has a direct impact on the outcome of a particular election, it is likely to be through the medium of valence issues which directly accrue to the advantage or disadvantage of one political party. . . .

Notes

1. Paul Lazarsfeld, Bernard Berelson, and Hazel Gaudet, *The People's Choice* (New York: Columbia University Press, 1948).
2. Ray Hiebert, Robert Jones, John Lorenz, and Ernest Lotito (eds.), *The Political Image Merchants: Strategies in the New Politics* (Washington: Acropolis Books, 1971).
3. See Bernard C. Cohen, *The Press and Foreign Policy* (Princeton: Princeton University Press, 1963), p. 13; also Lee Becker, Maxwell McCombs, and Jack McLeod, "The Development of Political Cognitions," in Steven H. Chaffee (ed.), *Political Communication*, Vol. 4, Sage Annual Reviews of Communication Research (Beverly Hills: Sage Publications, 1975), pp. 21-63.
4. Walter Lippmann, *Public Opinion* (New York: Macmillan, 1922).
5. Theodore White, *The Making of the President, 1972* (New York: Bantam, 1973), p. 327.
6. Maxwell McCombs, "Mass Communication in Political Campaigns: Informa-

tion, Gratification, and Persuasion," in F. Gerald Kline and Phillip J. Tichenor (eds.), *Current Perspectives in Mass Communication Research*, Vol. 1, Sage Annual Reviews of Communication Research (Beverly Hills: Sage Publications, 1972).

7. Kurt Lang and Gladys Engel Lang, *Politics and Television* (Chicago: Quadrangle, 1968).

8. Maxwell E. McCombs and Donald L. Shaw, "The Agenda-Setting Function of Mass Media," *Public Opinion Quarterly*, 36:176-87 (Summer 1972).

9. David Arnold and David Gold, "The Facilitation Effect of Social Environment," *Public Opinion Quarterly*, 28:513-16 (Fall 1964).

10. G. A. Donohue, Phillip J. Tichenor and C. N. Olien, "Mass Media and the Knowledge Gap: A Hypothesis Reconsidered," *Communication Research*, 2:3-23 (January 1975).

11. David L. Paletz, Peggy Reichert, and Barbara McIntyre, "How the Media Support Local Governmental Authority," *Public Opinion Quarterly*, 35:80-92 (Spring 1971).

12. A. H. Miller, W. E. Miller, A. S. Raine, and T. A. Brown, "A Majority Party in Disarray: Policy Polarization in the 1972 Election," Mimeographed report, University of Michigan.

13. V. O. Key, Jr., *The Responsible Electorate* (New York: Vintage Books, 1966).

14. Ibid., p. 9.

15. Stanley Kelley, *Professional Public Relations and Political Power* (Baltimore: Johns Hopkins Press, 1956).

16. Angus Campbell, Philip E. Converse, Warren E. Miller, and Donald E. Stokes, *Elections and the Political Order* (New York: John Wiley and Sons, 1966), p. 170.

2.2   ■

The Agenda-Setting Function
of the Media: Child Abuse

Barbara J. Nelson

Editor's Note. Among the perennial puzzles of human history, few are
as intriguing as why ideas emerge and disappear. How do some issues
capture public and legislative attention and become public policy while
others perish without action? Research often points toward the mass media as
the catalyst. Barbara J. Nelson's essay provides an interesting case study. She
probes several major questions: how media decide that a state of affairs
should be "news"; how they pursue a topic and frame it until large numbers
of people are aroused and action is taken; and how and why media drop
many topics after relatively brief spans of attention so that the pressure for
action dissipates.

    Besides its exposition of the role that media played in bringing the issue
of child abuse to the fore, the essay is also theoretically significant. It tests
political economist Anthony Downs's theory of the "issue-attention cycle,"
which postulates that issues arise when intolerable conditions have come to
public attention and fade when media coverage begins to bore the public or
when solutions require economic redistribution. Nelson demonstrates that
the predictions derived from the theory coincide only partly with what
happened in the case of child abuse. Contrary to the theory, child abuse has
remained a long-term interest of the media, and pressure for public action
remains strong.

    Nelson is a professor at the Hubert Humphrey Institute of Public Affairs
at the University of Minnesota. Her scholarship in the public policy field has
been recognized in many ways, including a Kellogg Foundation National
Fellowship, a visiting fellowship at the Russell Sage Foundation, and major
grants from Guggenheim and the National Academy of Sciences. The
selection comes from "The Agenda-Setting Function of the Media: Child
Abuse," in *Making an Issue of Child Abuse: Political Agenda Setting for
Social Problems* (Chicago: University of Chicago Press, 1984), 51-75. Several
tables and footnotes have been omitted.

What part did the media play in transforming the once-minor charity concern called "cruelty to children" into an important social welfare issue? We would expect the media's role to be very important, because the media exist at the boundary between the private and the public. Their task is to discover, unveil, and create what is "public." To do so they often wrench "private deviance" from the confines of the home. In the case of child abuse the media also helped to establish a new area of public policy. . . .

The "Issue-Attention Cycle"

In order to gain a full understanding of the media's role, we must examine how political issues are usually covered by the media, particularly how and when coverage of an issue is sustained. Anthony Downs has presented the most compelling description of the "issue-attention cycle" to date.[1] Downs predicts that problems begin to fade from the media's and the public's attention when their solutions imply the necessity of economic redistribution, or when media coverage begins to bore an ever-restless public.

. . . [N]ineteenth-century coverage of the problem conforms to Downs's formulation, but, perhaps surprisingly, twentieth-century coverage does not. Rather than fading from prominence, child abuse has received constant, even growing, attention from the media. Careful investigation into *how* and *why* the media covered child abuse at various times leads us to revise Downs's issue-attention cycle. As we shall see, it appears that issues can have a much longer attention cycle than previously supposed, a finding which has important consequences, one of which is that political agendas become increasingly crowded, a fact significant for the real and perceived efficiency of government.

Just as there are many more issues, concerns, and conflicts than government can address, there are many more potential stories than the media can report. The problem of deciding "what's news" is severe. Tom Wilkinson, Metro Editor for the *Washington Post*, has written that "the *Washington Post*, like other large media outlets receives approximately one million words every day . . . [and] has the capacity to publish about 100,000 words—or 10 percent of the information received. Competition for this space is fierce."[2]

. . . Downs suggests, there is the pre-problem stage, where the objective conditions of the problem are often more severe and pervasive than in the second stage, called "alarmed discovery and euphoric enthusiasm." With deadly accuracy, Downs notes that Americans have a touching blend of horrified concern and wide-eyed, cotton-candy confidence which leads them to assert "that every problem can be solved . . . *without any fundamental reordering of society itself.*"[3] Government begins to try to solve the problem at this point. Soon, however, the initial enthusiasm for solving the problem gives way to the third stage, a more sober realization that significant progress will be costly not only in terms of money but also in terms of social stability. When the need for redistribution or social reordering seems to be part of the solution to a particular problem, Downs suggests that the cycle enters its fourth stage, where both the media and their audiences begin to lose interest. In step five an issue enters the "post-problem stage." Whatever response has been initiated by government becomes institutionalized. Once innovative and exciting programs become part of the business-as-usual processes of government. The issue retains routine coverage, but the public, hungry for novel news, implicitly demands a new set of issues.

Intuitively, Downs's description of the issue-attention cycle seems to be accurate. Certainly the cognoscenti of the media, the regular readers, listeners, and viewers, sense the pattern of the media's (and government's) attention to particular issues. Downs's formulation has not been put to the test, however. Indeed, it is difficult to do so because his objective was to sketch the overall pattern of the issue-attention cycle, not to specify its processes. By attempting to understand child abuse coverage in terms of Downs's formulation, we learn a great deal about what sustains media interest and coverage.

The Mary Ellen Case

Downs's issue-attention cycle aptly describes media, public, and governmental interest in child maltreatment at the point when the problem was "discovered" in 1874, and when the now-familiar Mary Ellen case tugged at the hearts of fashionable New York. It is fair to say that without media coverage of the Mary Ellen case, child protection might never have become institutionalized as a social problem distinct from the Scientific Charity movement's more general interest in reducing sloth, pauperism, and dependence on the public purse. Without a doubt the living and working conditions of many children during the Gilded Era conform to Downs's pre-problem stage. The misery of poverty and a tradition of legal and religious precepts supporting a father's right to raise a child as he saw fit probably made violence toward children fairly prevalent. The ideal of a protected childhood, which encouraged the recognition of child abuse as a social problem, was just beginning to develop.

It was the Mary Ellen case, however, which ushered in the second stage of "alarmed discovery and euphoric enthusiasm." [4] In the spring of 1874 the *New York Times*[5] and the other New York papers reported that Mary Ellen Wilson had been chained to her bed and whipped daily with a rawhide cord by her stepmother. The *Times* was not yet governed by the motto "All the News That's Fit to Print," which was adopted in 1897.[6] Nonetheless, the *Times* only rarely carried stories about cases of even such blatant abuse as that suffered by Mary Ellen, and even when the *Times* did cover such stories, it was in a tone much more moderate than that used by papers with larger circulations such as the *New York Herald* and the *World*. In fact, the *Times* covered only one other instance of a child similarly abused in the two years prior to Mary Ellen's case.

Even Mary Ellen's story might never have become part of the public record had not Henry Bergh [the founder of the American Society for the Prevention of Cruelty to Animals] been informed of the abuse by "a lady who had been on an errand of mercy to a dying woman in the house adjoining [Mary Ellen's]." [7] The ensuing trial of Mary Ellen's stepmother, who received a one-year penitentiary term, and the decision about what to do with Mary Ellen, who was eventually sent to the Sheltering Arms children's home, remained in the news through June of that year. As 1874 drew to a close, Mary Ellen's plight reemerged in the *Times*, this time as the reason for the formation of the New York Society for the Prevention of Cruelty to Children (New York SPCC), the nation's first charitable organization dedicated to identifying ill-treated children.

Of course, the Mary Ellen case was not the first instance of cruelty to children to receive newspaper coverage. The bizarre brutalization of children and public horror over it always received a modicum of attention in the press. The significance of the Mary Ellen case rests with its label— cruelty to children—which like the later labels unified seemingly unrelated cases, and in the fact that it precipitated the formation of an organization whose purpose was to keep this issue alive.

The label "cruelty to children" and the Mary Ellen case did not, however, ensure sustained media attention. Two measures of the issue's rapid decline from prominence can be garnered from the *New York Times Index*. In the 1874 volume of the *Index* the entry "Children, Cruelty to" appears for the first time. However, this subject entry disappears from the *Index* beginning in July, 1877, and does not reappear until 1885, after which time it occurs only infrequently until World War I. During the first three years of recognition, the *Times* published fifty-two news articles it specifically categorized as dealing with "cruelty to children." But the deletion of the cruelty to children subject heading did not signal the end of coverage of the topic. By searching all the subject entries about children, articles on child abuse cases and the activities of prevention societies can be found. Most frequently, instances of abuse and neglect are classified under the ignominious heading "Children, miscellaneous facts about." In the judgment of librarians of that period, cruelty to children ceased to be a problem important enough to warrant special reference.

A century later, it is difficult to determine whether the issue's short tenure in the spotlight was indeed caused by the reason Downs suggests, i.e., that a meaningful response to the problem includes a major revamping of society. Certainly, a concerted response to child abuse must include an examination and reordering of economic and social arrangements—a protected childhood is not possible without it. . . .

. . . [A]fter the novelty of the Mary Ellen case wore off, newspapers and professional journals gave the problem only sporadic coverage. Indeed, almost ninety years elapsed before the issue again took center stage in the media, in the form of the now-famous article "The Battered-Child Syndrome" by [pediatrician] Dr. C. Henry Kempe and his associates, published in the July 7, 1962 issue of the *Journal of the American Medical Association*.[8] With the publication of this article, a tiny trickle of information grew into a swollen river, flooding mass-circulation newspapers and magazines and professional journals alike. In the decade prior to the article's appearance doctors, lawyers, social workers, educators and other researchers and practitioners combined published only nine articles specifically focusing on cruelty to children. In the decade after its publication, the professions produced 260 articles. Similarly, mass-circulation magazines carried twenty-eight articles in the decade after Kempe's article, compared to only three in the decade before, two of which recounted instances of bizarre brutalization.[9]

Even television displayed an interest in the problem. Although it is harder to document this medium fully, it seems that child abuse was virtually absent from early television scripts, whereas after "The Battered-Child Syndrome" appeared, soap operas and prime-time series alike created dramas based on the problem. The plight of Mary Ellen's fictional brothers and sisters was first beamed into millions of households in episodes of *Dr. Kildare, Ben Casey, M.D.,* and *Dragnet*.[10]

These figures on the emergence of child abuse in the media suggest that Downs's formulation of the issue-attention cycle needs to be amended. Contrary to Downs's hypothesis, media attention to child abuse grew steadily rather than declined, and the public has sustained a loyal interest in what might on the surface be thought of as a small, even unimportant, issue. Admittedly, Downs does not speculate on how long the issue-attention cycle takes to run its course. Nonetheless, findings so strikingly at variance with the tenor of Downs's formulation deserve closer attention.

Four factors contribute to the continuing coverage of child abuse and suggest that media attention to a host of issues can be more long-lived than previously assumed. These factors include topic differentiation, issue aggregation, the link between the professional and the mass media, and the growing appeal of human interest stories (especially ones with a medical deviance twist).

First and foremost, coverage of abuse increased because stories about *specific types* of abuse were added to the earlier, more general reports. In other words, coverage increased because the general problem of abuse was differentiated into more narrowly defined topics such as the relationship between illegitimacy and abuse, or abuse within military families. Second, child abuse coverage increased because the issue was also linked with larger, more over-arching concerns, such as intrafamilial violence, which now includes abuse of a spouse, parent, or even grandparent. The scope of the problem is thus simultaneously decreasing and increasing.

Topic differentiation and issue aggregation are themselves explained by a third factor which encourages sustained media attention to child abuse. To a large extent the mass media carefully and consistently monitor professional and scientific journals in search of new stories. This symbiotic relationship is perhaps the most neglected factor contributing to ongoing media coverage of issues. Despite the lack of attention paid to it, the relationship between the mass media and professional outlets is well institutionalized, and serves both parties admirably, providing fresh stories for journalists and (for the most part) welcome publicity for scholars. Moreover, this relationship provides a regular source of "soft (i.e., interesting) news" about child abuse. Indeed, the fourth factor contributing to the durability of child abuse coverage is the fact that "soft news"—human interest stories—has been added to "hard news" stories, which have traditionally focused on child abuse cases as crime news. This last factor should not be confused with the first two. Soft news stories extend the range of story *types*, whereas differentiation and aggregation extend the range of story *topics*.

By investigating each of these factors we can show how media coverage both created the demand for, and was a product of, governmental action. The first three factors—differentiation, aggregation, and the relationship between the professional and mass media—can be considered together. These three factors are linked through the recognition that child abuse was initially a research issue, and that research on a problem has a life cycle of its own. This life cycle can greatly affect the prominence of an issue in the media.

. . . [P]hysical abuse was a research problem long before it was a public policy issue in the conventional sense. During the decade between 1946 and 1957 radiologists reluctantly pieced together evidence revealing that a fair number of children had bruises and broken bones, the cause of which could only be parental violence. This research, however, never crossed the bridge from scientific publications to the mass media. Indeed, not until 1960 did the Children's Bureau even mention these medical studies in its *Annual Report. . . .*

In 1962 the situation changed, however. Dr. C. Henry Kempe and his colleagues published "The Battered-Child Syndrome" in the AMA *Journal.* The article and its companion editorial caused a storm in medical circles and in the mass media as well. Indeed, the article and editorial are routinely used to date the rediscovery of abuse. In this instance, medical research and opinion did cross the bridge to the mass media, primarily through the vehicle of the AMA press release "Parental Abuse Looms in Childhood Deaths." [11] The message of the article and editorial was clear: Kempe and his co-workers had "discovered" an alarming and deadly "disease" which menaced the nation's children. The article was measured in tone and eminently professional, although its findings were later sensationalized through less careful retelling. But the editorial presented problems from the beginning.

The most important characteristic of the article is that it provided a powerful, unifying label in the phrase "the battered-child syndrome." Kempe purposefully chose the term to emphasize the medical, and downplay the criminal, aspects of the problem. . . .

. . . Like many professional associations, the AMA routinely issues press releases about important findings reported in its journal. This practice constitutes the first link in a chain which keeps mass media personnel abreast of medical, scientific, and technical developments. At the other end of the chain are the beat reporters who cultivate the sources behind the news releases. The chain, little studied in the policy-making literature but well institutionalized, transmitted Kempe's findings to journalists responsible for medical news.

Within a week of the news release, *Time* magazine summarized the article as the second feature in its "Medicine" section. . . . *Newsweek*, however, beat *Time* to the punch. In the April 16, 1962 edition of *Newsweek*, the findings of "The Battered-Child Syndrome" were reported.
. . . Together, *Time* and *Newsweek* informed millions of readers that a new "disease" imperiled the nation's children.[12]

If these two magazines informed a somewhat selective and small audience, the *Saturday Evening Post* and *Life* had more popular appeal. The *Post* published an article entitled "Parents Who Beat Children: A Tragic Increase in Cases of Child Abuse Is Prompting a Hunt for Ways to Select Sick Adults Who Commit Such Crimes" on October 6, 1962.[13]

Like the news magazine articles, the author of the *Post*'s article interviewed the medical experts. . . . But in the *Post* article, these interviews were juxtaposed with a recitation of the gory details of child abuse. . . .

In a double-barreled shot, photojournals and news magazines introduced child abuse to the American public. The articles can be considered the point at which an invisible problem became a public concern, and soon a major public policy issue. . . .

For the next twenty years, popular magazines began what seemed to be a campaign to publicize the problem. The *Readers' Guide to Periodical Literature* cites 124 articles published from 1960 through 1980. . . . [T]he articles cluster around significant research breakthroughs and political events. But the tempo of coverage was constant. Abuse has remained a staple in popular magazines as different as *Woman's Day* and *Scientific American.*

The durability of coverage was in part caused by new "events" (research or action) which continually revitalized interest. Thus Downs underestimated the extent to which his formulation assumed that individual or closely clustered events trigger the issue-attention cycle. Though every professional article did not get the recognition of "The Battered-Child Syndrome," over *1,700* articles on child abuse or related subjects have been published in professional journals over the last thirty years. Together they kept a steady stream of information flowing to beat reporters and issue partisans.

Once child abuse and neglect were adopted as policy issues, public funds supported much of the research reported in professional journals. The Children's Bureau spent over a million dollars between 1962 and 1967, and $160 million was authorized (though not all was appropriated) under [the Child Abuse Prevention and Treatment Act] and its reenactments through 1983. But public interest in child abuse was not limited to scientists and practitioners. The attention of the mass public was also engaged, quite deliberately in fact, by professionals who felt that government should take a greater responsibility for child protection. . . .

Newspaper Coverage

Newspaper accounts of abuse were extremely important in setting the government's and the citizenry's agendas. In the same year that "The Battered-Child Syndrome" was published, the Children's Division of the American Humane Association reviewed the major newspapers in forty-eight states to determine how many child abuse cases were reported by papers. They learned of 662 incidents, of which 178, or almost one-fourth, led to the death of the child.

. . . [W]hat had formerly appeared as isolated incidents of psychopathic behavior could now be understood as a patterned problem when over 600 cases were identified nationwide.

The 662 abuse cases found by the AHA typified newspaper coverage early in the issue's life. During the early 1960s, child abuse was covered as crime news and the press found stories of bizarre brutalization especially newsworthy. But as time went on, newspaper coverage began to include—even be dominated by—stories reporting research findings. Of course, there could not be any reporting on research when there was no research to cover. But it is the *addition* of research-related stories which accounts for the durability of child abuse articles in the *New York Times.* Space for research-based stories on abuse became increasingly available as the *Times* editorial staff decided to give more space to human interest stories, especially those with a medical or scientific slant.[14]

The crime-and-victims approach to covering child abuse cases always assured a minimum of coverage for the issue. Reviewing research on newspaper coverage of crime, Joseph R. Dominick found that "a typical metropolitan paper probably devotes around 5-10% of its available space to crime news. Further, the type of crime most likely reported is individual crime accompanied by violence."[15] Thus, even if the media should tire of reporting other aspects of child abuse, child-abuse-as-crime coverage will remain. Indeed, it was always present at some level; it merely lacked a label to unify seemingly unrelated events.[16]

But child abuse reporting is not merely crime reporting: it is crime reporting with an important twist. There is a certain unfreshness about the act of abusing a child which adds a sense of personal and social deviance to the existing criminality. If a person robs a bank, it's a crime; but if a child is beaten, it's something more. One obvious motivation for emphasizing the most unusual and extreme forms of abuse is that newspapers can then titillate their readers with stories that are unwholesome as well as violent. The penny press of the nineteenth century and its twentieth-century descendents made no bones about seeking out just this type of story. "Respectable" newspapers, on the other hand, feel the need to cloak the decision to run such articles behind a cloud of scientific justifications. Adolph Ochs, who bought the *New York Times* in 1896, perfectly captured the nuances of this perspective: "When a tabloid prints it, that's smut. When the *Times* prints it, that's sociology."

. . . [T]he reporting of child abuse follows a fairly consistent pattern in which unwholesomely criminal cases where the child survives are preferred to what might be considered the more serious, but somehow more routine, cases where the child dies. The titillation of bizarre brutality accounts in part for this pattern, but other factors also contribute to newspapers' apparent preference for this type of story. Part of this preference can be traced to the organizational needs of newspapers. From the perspective of news managers, more information unfolds in a case of brutality than in one where the victim dies. This fact in itself sustains coverage.

But factors more subtle than an editor's bent for sensationalism are involved in sustaining newspaper coverage of child abuse stories. Most importantly, the press enjoys playing an advocative role in maintaining cultural norms that protect children and defend the integrity of the home. These expressions are part of the Progressive Era values sustained by the media in general.[17] Additionally, abuse which results in death is murder, or at least manslaughter. Society has clearly defined sanctions which are invoked in cases of murder. No similarly straightforward response existed for child abuse in 1964. Under the doctrine of "the best interest of the child," there was a presumption that a child ought to remain at home unless the situation was hopeless. With only limited temporary shelter facilities available and permanent placement options restricted to foster care or—what was even less likely—adoption, an abused child was frequently returned to his or her parents. The implicit difficulty in determining what was a safe environment for a child and the common-law precedent supporting strong parental rights together created a tension in bizarre brutalization cases which led to sustained coverage of these cases. The bizarre brutalization of young girls may also account for the newspapers' continuing interest.

In a 1965 nationwide public opinion survey conducted by David G. Gil, newspapers were cited more frequently than other media as a source of information on physical abuse: 72.0% of Gil's respondents mentioned newspapers as an information source, 56.2% specified television, and 22.7% cited magazines.[18] The newspapers' tradition of reporting child abuse as crimes of bizarre brutalization helps to explain why approximately 30% of Gil's sample felt that parents or other abusers should be "jailed or punished in some other way." [19] Indeed, with the extremely brutal images provided by reporting abuse as a crime, we may do well to wonder why over two-thirds of those queried preferred a more therapeutic approach to dealing with abusers, believing close supervision or even leaving the abuser alone if the injury was not too serious (or not intervening at all) to be a sufficient response. The message of "The Battered-Child Syndrome," which portrayed abuse as medical deviance, was clearly in accord with more general attitudes defining social problems involving violence as psychological in origin.

Once child abuse was rediscovered as a social problem, newspapers began to cover cases more frequently and intensively. But not all the growth in the coverage of child abuse was a result of papers' interest in bizarre brutalization. As legislative response to child abuse grew, so did that type of newspaper coverage. Every state passed a child abuse reporting law between 1963 and 1967, and all amended and reamended their law several times, with each legislative action renewing newspaper interest in the problem. In addition, newspapers also began to run human interest stories on child abuse, in part aided by the now defunct Women's News Service, which provided feature stories on child abuse for the home, style, and fashion pages of subscribing newspapers. Local human interest stories focused on nearby programs to prevent or treat abuse, and special training sessions for county and state workers.

In deciding to investigate or publish a particular story, journalists quickly learn that "hard" and "soft" news are not accorded the same value. "Hard news," according to Gaye Tuchman, "concerns important matters and soft news, interesting matters." [20] Soft news does not have the "quickening urgency" which Helen MacGill Hughes asserts is the life-blood of newspapers.[21] In other words, soft news is timeless and durable—

although many would say insignificant—which means it appears at the back of a newspaper.

The special titillation of violent deviance accounts for the durability of child abuse as soft news. Newspapers usually feature such news in the portions of the papers devoted to women's interests. . . .

The role of human interest stories in sustaining newspaper coverage of child abuse can be seen by examining the *New York Times* stories in 1964 and again in 1979. The sixteen stories on child abuse published in 1964 split evenly between cases and legislative reports. Fifty child abuse stories made the *Times* in 1979. In that year the activities of various charitable groups and the results of numerous scientific research projects constituted *one-half* of the coverage. Cases, legislation, even criminal proceedings took a back seat to soft-news articles.

The pattern of newspaper coverage of abuse and neglect over the last thirty years is quite illuminating. Once again relying on the *New York Times Index*, we find that during the early 1950s child abuse stories were quite common, thinning to just a few stories a year until the late 1960s when coverage took a dramatic jump. . . . The sheer volume of coverage is remarkable. Between 1950 and 1980 the *Times* published 652 articles pertaining to abuse, certainly enough to keep the issue in the public's eye.

Of course, the media can lead the public to water, so to speak, but cannot always make it drink. The information was available to anyone who wanted it, but how many people read which articles (or watched which television programs) cannot be ascertained. And the information grew year by year, to an unprecedented volume, providing a climate of public awareness which initially encouraged elected officials to recognize the problem and ultimately caused them to maintain an interest in it.

In sum, we can say that child abuse achieved the public's agenda because the interest of a few pioneering researchers crossed the bridge to mass-circulation news outlets. Public interest was sustained and grew, however, because the media have both many *sources* of news and many *types* of audiences to whom they present the news. Through topic differentiation, issue aggregation, professional and mass-circulation linkages, and the growth in human interest newspaper reporting, child abuse remains a lively topic of media coverage. The public's interest in this newly recognized social problem prompted state legislatures into action. And act they did, out of humanitarian interest to be sure, but also from the recognition that child abuse was the premier example of no-cost rectitude. . . .

Would media attention decline if research funds continued to decline? I imagine so, but not quite for the reasons Downs proposed. Coverage may decline because there is less to report. There may be less to report because there is less research money spent. And there is less research money because of the conflicting values over the size of the budget and the role of the federal government in social programs. Conflicting values over the propriety of intervening in the family are not directly driving the budgetary decision making about federal child abuse legislation, although the social conservatives like the Moral Majority have raised these questions. In ways not evident during an era of plenty and growth, the issue-attention cycle may be significantly affected by larger macroeconomic and political concerns.

The downward spiral of decreasing research and media coverage may induce further programmatic and policy changes as well. The consequences of reduced research and coverage could include less public awareness and declining "demand" for public programs. In the long run, reporting of suspected cases to welfare offices might decline as well, the product of citizen apathy and fiscal difficulties in staffing reporting and service systems. A public convinced of bureaucratic unresponsiveness would be further discouraged to report. The great fear of advocates of public policy against abuse is that declining media coverage and declining reporting will be used to assert that the actual incidence of abuse is declining. . . .

Notes

1. Anthony Downs, "Up and Down with Ecology—'The Issue Attention Cycle,'" *Public Interest* 32 (Summer 1972): 38-50. See also Mark V. Nade, "Consumer Protection Becomes a Public Issue (Again)," in James E. Anderson, ed., *Cases in Public Policy Making* (New York: Praeger, 1976), pp. 22-34; and P. F. Lazarsfeld and Robert K. Merton, "Mass Communication, Popular Taste, and Organized Social Action," in W. Schramm and D. F. Roberts, eds., *The Process and Effects of Mass Communication* (Urbana, Ill.: University of Illinois Press, 1971), pp. 554-578.
2. Tom Wilkinson, "Covering Abuse: Context and Policy—Gaining Access," in George Gerbner, Catherine J. Ross, and Edward Zigler, eds., *Child Abuse: An Agenda for Action* (New York: Oxford University Press, 1980), p. 250.
3. Downs, "Up and Down," p. 39.
4. Ibid., p. 39.
5. In recounting the public's introduction to the problem we depend heavily on the accounts of the Mary Ellen case carried in the *New York Times*. This is a decision based on the exigencies of research, not on the *Times*'s stature during that period. . . .
6. Michael Schudson, *Discovering the News: A Social History of American Newspapers* (New York: Basic Books, 1978), p. 112.
7. The *New York Times*, April 10, 1874, p. 8.
8. C. Henry Kempe et al., "The Battered-Child Syndrome," pp. 17-24.
9. The figures reported here were derived by summing the articles listed under the appropriate headings in the following indexes. For the professional media: *Index Medicus*, the *Index of Legal Periodicals*, the *Social Science*

Index, the *Humanities Index,* and the *Education Index.* Figures for mass-circulation magazines derived from the *Readers' Guide to Periodical Literature.* No reductions were made for the possibility of double counting.

10. For two perspectives on television's response to child abuse and other social problems, see Donn H. O'Brien, Alfred R. Schneider, and Herminio Tratiesas, "Portraying Abuse: Network Censors' Round Table"; and George Gerbner, "Children and Power on Television: The Other Side of the Picture," in Gerbner et al., *Child Abuse,* pp. 231-238, 239-248.

11. American Medical Association, "Parental Abuse Looms in Childhood Deaths," news release, July 13, 1962.

12. "When They're Angry . . . ," *Newsweek,* April 16, 1962, p. 74; and "Battered Child Syndrome," *Time,* July 20, 1962, p. 60.

13. Charles Flato, "Parents Who Beat Children: A Tragic Increase in Cases of Child Abuse is Prompting a Hunt for Ways to Select Sick Adults Who Commit Such Crimes," *The Saturday Evening Post,* October 6, 1962, pp. 32-35.

14. Harrison Salisbury, *Without Fear or Favor: The New York Times and Our Times* (New York: Time Books, 1980), pp. 558-560.

15. Joseph R. Dominick, "Crime and Law Enforcement in the Mass Media," in Charles Winick, ed., *Deviance and Mass Media* (Beverly Hills, Cal.: Sage, 1978), p. 108.

16. Gans's research on the content of the the CBS and NBC nightly news and the news magazines *Time* and *Newsweek* shows that crime-and-victim news also forms a steady part of news offerings in these outlets. . . . Herbert Gans, *Deciding What's News* (New York: Pantheon, 1979), p. 13 from table 3.

17. Gans, *Deciding What's News,* pp. 203-206; and Schudson, *Discovering,* pp. 77-87.

18. David G. Gil, *Violence against Children* (Cambridge, Mass.: The Harvard University Press, 1973), p. 61, table 5: "Sources of Respondent's Knowledge of the General Problem of Child Abuse during the Year Preceding the Survey." Respondents could mention more than one source.

19. Ibid., p. 66, table 10: "What Respondents Thought Should be Done About Perpetrators of Child Abuse."

20. Gaye Tuchman, "Making News by Doing Work: Routinizing the Unexpected," *American Journal of Sociology* 79, no. 1 (July 1973): 114.

21. Helen MacGill Hughes, *News and the Human Interest Story* (Chicago: University of Chicago Press, 1940), p. 58.

2.3 ■■■■■

Communication and Community Conflict

Phillip J. Tichenor, George A. Donohue, and Clarice N. Olien

Editor's Note. The authors explain the roles played by the media when conflicts erupt in various types of communities. Phillip J. Tichenor, George A. Donohue, and Clarice N. Olien approach the media from a neglected perspective showing them embedded in their social setting and interacting with their environment. Viewed in this way, the media are an integral part of the political power structure; they serve some contenders in the power struggle and injure others.

The findings reported here are based on surveys of general populations, on interviews with political elites, and on newspaper content analysis data drawn from nineteen Minnesota communities. These ranged from hamlets of less than 2,000 people to urban and suburban communities of 100,000 people. The conflict situations for which the role of the media was examined include safety concerns about the location of a nuclear power plant and a high voltage power line, environmental issues raised by sewage and industrial waste disposal, protection of wilderness areas from mining and logging, and massive job losses through closure of an obsolete steel plant.

The authors have worked as an interdisciplinary team at the University of Minnesota to study links between community structures and roles of the press. Tichenor is professor of journalism and mass communication; Donohue is professor of sociology; and Olien is professor of rural sociology. The selection is from *Community Conflict and the Press* (Beverly Hills, Calif.: Sage Publications, 1980).

Where Does Information Come From?

While the need for greater citizen understanding of issues may be generally agreed upon, ways of creating that understanding are not. There is, on the one hand, the traditional belief that responsible concerned citizens will inform themselves (Hennessy, 1975). Parallel with that view is the belief that information media such as newspapers, broadcast stations, and educational institutions have a responsibility and should provide the needed knowledge. The view that individual citizens should bear the *sole* responsibility for finding out about issues is not viable, especially when the information and the system for dissemination within the community may be inadequate or nonexistent. As society becomes more diverse and complex, there is a growing expectation that the information agencies, particularly the mass media, will deliver information and interpretations through the use of experts and news analysis.

Growing diversity in society has been mirrored in the information delivery system, with increased use of such techniques as specialized sections of modern newspapers which appeal singly and in combination to different groups. Rapid growth of specialized magazines and publications targeted to limited and specific audiences also reflects this diversity. . . . The increasing number of purposive communicators (such as educators, public information and public relations specialists, and advertisers) illustrates not only the increased number of special interest groups but also the interdependence of groups attempting to control both generation and dissemination of knowledge.

A large portion of the information available, then, depends on an information delivery system which reflects the pluralistic organization and vested interests of the society in which it exists. Information appears to be generated and disseminated as a result of joint activity of professionals within the mass media channels and professionals who have advocacy functions for interdependent special interest groups. . . .

Newspapers and Community Controversy

The role of newspapers and other mass media in community conflict is often recognized, and frequently the media are charged with creating the conflicts. They may be accused of "sensationalizing" and "blowing things out of proportion" or of "covering up" and "not paying attention to all sides" of a controversy (Gerald, 1963; Rivers and Schramm, 1969). Members of the media profession often answer the first accusation by saying that bringing things into the open is a necessary contribution to democratic processes (Small, 1970); the second criticism may be answered by the argument that newspapers are not simply conduits but must themselves make judgments about selection and presentation of news if they are to meet their professional obligations to the community in a responsible manner (Hulteng, 1976). In doing so, media professionals may argue, they must decide how much and what kind of play to give each side, risking the possibility that both sides may believe that their views have been underrepresented in the press. . . .

. . . Neither the newspaper nor the broadcast station is organized to create new ideas or proposals for community consideration. They are only rarely equipped or motivated to examine proposals from different sectors of the community in an evaluative or critical way, let alone create new proposals of their own. Fundamentally, the newspaper and community broadcast station deal with the ideas and initiatives of their sources.

A fundamental hypothesis, then, is that newspapers tend to serve ancillary rather than initiating roles in the development of community conflicts. Concerted social action requires a degree of planning, coordination, and organized activity beyond the staff and capabilities of the newspaper. The organizational processes of governmental agencies, city councils, and legislatures may be neither understood nor appreciated by the individual journalists who report them. It is not unusual to find editors and reporters highly critical, if not hostile, toward committee activity and organizational procedure which are at the core of social action in both public and private sectors.

But if newspapers and other media do not initiate action, from whence comes the belief that community projects may be impossible without the media? The answer in theory is that newspapers like most mass media draw attention to organized activity that is already under way. The power or lack of power of the press stems in large measure from its ability and need to be selective (within limits) in choosing what to accelerate and what to leave languishing. For every urban renewal or environmental project given newspaper publicity in a community, informed citizens can usually name scores of other projects that never gained attention in print or were ignored in broadcast reports. A big question is, "who had the power to be selected for attention by the mass media?"

It may seem contradictory to argue that newspapers deal regularly in conflict while hardly ever initiating it. But the contradiction fades when one realizes that newspapers are regular recipients of ideas and information from a myriad of organized sources. There is very real competition from parties in a conflict for media space and time; even so-called investigative reporting is often a matter of deciding which overtures from news sources to accept (Bethell, 1977). The ordinary front page of a newspaper contains few items that resulted from journalistic initiative alone. A large portion of material is published because someone with a vested interest in the subject brought it to the newspaper's attention. Sigal (1973) found, for example, that nearly 74% of the information channels for foreign and national news in a sample of New York *Times* and Washington *Post* editors were *other* than reporter "enterprise." Press conferences and press releases alone accounted for 42% of the news channels.

If it is true that newspapers choose and select under varying degrees of pressure from items brought in by others, it is equally true that newspapers live with the most intense conflicts of their communities. But by living with these conflicts, newspapers do not necessarily turn the conflicts into public issues. They may play these conflicts down or avoid them entirely as often occurs in small communities or they may give the conflicts sustained front page play as often happens in the metropolitan press. Part of the nature of the newspaper's decision or judgment is a result of the social structure in which the newspaper operates. The characteristic differences between the rural and urban press result from the differences in the newspaper's environment; the environment does not differ because of the newspaper. The content decisions, dependent as they are on community structure, constitute a pattern of information control that has far-reaching implications for what the community will hear about, think about, and talk about.

To say that media are engaged in information control is not to say that diabolical forces are necessarily at work. The potential for such forces is there, however, and may be exploited in certain instances. Information control is one aspect of all information activities, including the conduct of social conflict. Decisions about information are made daily, and growing social and political complexity of the milieu in which communities thrive or falter creates a potential for a wealth of information on diverse topics. It is never possible to transmit or reproduce all of the information available; some decision about what to publish will be made. What is called "news judgment," "censorship," or "publicity" is, in each case, a decision about information and therefore an act of control. There may well be thousands of journalists, officials, functionaries, and citizens who make information judgments without thinking about the consequences, but those decisions are control acts despite this lack of deliberate consciousness.

Newspapers, Conflict, and Knowledge Gaps

There is the traditional viewpoint that resolution of social problems is related to inputs of information. Accordingly, if a system is sufficiently saturated with information, a general understanding of the topic will develop within the system. Once understanding is at hand, resolution is assumed to be at hand.

Behind that viewpoint are at least three assumptions. One is that information itself contributes to resolution of social problems. That assumption is not challenged here. Open for study and examination, however, are two additional assumptions. The first, based on the educational principle of repetition, is that a medium of communication, such as a newspaper, can through sheer redundancy raise the overall level of understanding in the community. The second is that higher levels of information input will lead to a general equalization of knowledge throughout the system. Hence, more effective decision making is assumed to occur.

Both of these assumptions have been brought into question by systematic studies. The first, that redundancy of newspaper reporting can increase levels of understanding, has been difficult to demonstrate in some studies of publicity campaigns (Hyman and Sheatsley, 1947; Star and Hughes, 1950), in which levels of understanding of issues changed little or not at all following media campaigns. The second assumption, that more information inputs lead to equalization of knowledge, is even more strongly questioned. Selective self-exposure to information has frequently been found to be related to level of education. Furthermore, data in recent years indicate that the problem is not so much one of increasing knowledge but, frequently, one of relative deprivation of knowledge. A gap in knowledge between segments within a total system is entirely possible, and since social power is in part based on knowledge, relative deprivation of knowledge may lead to relative deprivation of power (Tichenor, Donohue, and Olien, 1970; Rogers, 1974; Katzman, 1973).

Specifically, several studies have supported the hypothesis that as the flow of information into a social system increases, groups with higher levels of education often tend to acquire this information at a faster rate than those with lower levels of education. This higher rate of acquisition results from the different roles and positions of more highly educated segments in the social system. Groups with higher education have higher verbal skills and more media resources available to them. Educational training creates habits that include a higher rate of attention to certain kinds of media content, including public affairs, and a trained capacity for understanding and retaining that information. Similarly, more highly educated groups are trained to recognize the relevance of information for their particular position in the social structure and for maintenance of that position.

As a result of the differential rates of acquisition, gaps in knowledge between segments with different levels of education tend to increase rather than decrease. Knowledge of space research is an example; after several years of heavy media attention to space rocketry and satellites, the gap in knowledge about that research across educational levels was greater than it had been before the space research program began. Similarly, knowledge gaps widened over time for the smoking and cancer issue.

Many of the findings on knowledge of national issues support the knowledge gap hypothesis. But these findings raise a question of major theoretical and social significance: Under what conditions does it increase and under what conditions, if any, might this knowledge gap be reduced or eliminated? If such gaps widen as the flow of information to specialized groups is increased, then that tendency should be reduced as a public issue is made relevant to the plurality of the groups involved. There may be basic concerns in communities, but the key question may be the extent to which groups singly or in interaction succeed in *defining* the issue as one of basic concern.

Newspaper coverage may be more likely to equalize levels of understanding to the extent that it contributes to the intensity of conflict in a neighborhood. This stimulation may overcome—at least partially— some of the selective dissemination and selective self-exposure patterns that contribute to the widening of the knowledge gap on topics of specialized interest.

If indeed research data indicate that newspaper coverage may lead to increased controversy, which in turn increases equalization of knowl- edge, the implications may be disturbing. Among dominant community values, frequently, is a belief that calls for quick resolution of conflict, if not elimination of it in the first place. There is also the popular belief that "nobody learns anything in a controversy." The general proposition for study here holds quite the opposite, that controversy draws attention to information which (1) has a bearing on competition between interest groups and (2) potentially puts one group in a better power position as a result of having the information. Underlying this reasoning is the assumption that redistribution of social power among constituent groups is one of the most basic concerns in society generally. . . . A group seeking to maintain the status quo will be as concerned about redistribution as a group that considers itself deprived and therefore seeks a power realign- ment. As a result of these concerns, there is an increased likelihood in a conflict that citizens of all status levels will acquire information relevant to that conflict. While there may be limits, the implication would be that intense controversies may lead to greater realization of a general demo- cratic ideal: the sharing of an equalized quantity of information about a situation by nearly everyone. . . .

[Role of the Press in Conflict]

The analysis of conflict situations provides abundant evidence that newspapers and other media of communication are not the independent, self-styled social agents that either they or members of the public may imagine them to be. The efficacy of viewing the press, or any other mass medium, as constituting a separate "fourth estate" is doubtful at best. The press is an integral subsystem within the total system, and its strong linkages with other system components impinge upon it as much as it impinges upon them, if not more. . . .

As an integral part of the community, the newspaper reflects the concerns of the dominant power groupings. The term *reflects* is appropriate in the sense that it is neither a total nor an undistorted reproduction of current events and institutions. Newspapers reflect selectively, in ways determined not by editorial idiosyncrasy but by the structure and distribution of social power in the community. A newspaper in a one-industry town is unlikely to report that industry in a critical way. It will reflect community consensus about that industry through reporting socially noncontroversial aspects of that industry and generally avoid reports that would question it. . . .

While the press does serve as a mirror, however contorted its reflective curvature, it is part of a reciprocal process, being affected *by* that system and affecting it in turn. Rather than being an initiator of basic positions, the press is normally pushed into reporting events by organized forces in the system and its reports become an integral part of the social process which bears on the nature of future events. Community groups may use the press and journalists as sources of intelligence, as indications of reaction of the public to events, and as a device for creating awareness and defining problems. The performance of the press or other medium typically becomes part of the controversy.

. . . Just as "no man is an island," subsystems are integrated into larger systems. The press is no exception, and the generalizations presented below are illustrative of this perspective.

Newspapers and Information Control

One generalization is that information is part of a general process of social control which includes media participation within different social structures. Information is a prime resource in the creation and maintenance of social power, a point which may become increasingly visible as social conflicts progress. Importance of information control is illustrated by the increasing development of specialized communication centers in business, government, education, and other agencies and interest groups. It is a rare collective action group that does not develop an organizational role or set of roles in communications, carrying titles such as public relations, publicity, outreach, or even "communication specialist.". . .

Community Structure, Media and Media Use

A second generalization is that since communication subsystems are themselves creations of the larger structures in which they operate, both media personnel performance and media use patterns of citizens will differ according to structural characteristics.

In a more highly specialized and diverse urban structure, the reporter is more likely to have a relationship with sources that are limited to the news gathering function, compared with a reporter in the more homogeneous small-town structure. As a consequence, the urban reporter is more autonomous within the system as a whole, vis-à-vis the sources, since the more pluralistic structure tends to reinforce separation of roles according to professional specialization and relationships. . . .

Similarly, media use patterns differ according to community structure. In a small, more tradition-oriented rural community, the local weekly newspaper tends to be dominated by local news, and citizens are less likely to read daily newspapers than are citizens of larger urban centers served by dailies. . . .

These differential media uses lead to different combinations of use patterns that organized groups must take into account if they are to reach the larger public through the various channels that exist. The question of how interest groups develop strategies for different community and media structures is a fruitful area for further study. These strategies require far more than analyzing the audience, finding the media that achieve high audience attention, and placing messages in those media. The "media event" techniques, such as demonstrations or whatever form they take, often involve the media personnel in such a way that they lead to quite different content than might occur if a press release were simply "placed" through routine editorial handling of purposive communications. Reporter involvement in reporting a media event does not necessarily mean the reporter thereby will be sympathetic to the organization staging the event, even though the possibility exists for such sympathy to develop. What is crucial for the strategy of countervailing groups, typically, is that the event be covered and given prominent display by the media. Reports of demonstrations, confrontations, and other media events in a newspaper may gain a level of public awareness and salience which a press release from one side alone is unlikely to have. . . .

System Reinforcement of the Media Role

A third generalization is that since they are dependent upon other parts of the system, newspapers and other media participate in social conflict in circumscribed ways which are reinforced within the system. Media will tend to reflect the perspectives of organizational power centers, which is apparent not only in small, homogeneous communities but is also illuminated in communities or regions where values and outlooks on major issues are highly diverse. Where there is diversity in social power, media tend to reflect the orientations of those segments that are higher on the power scale. In the American experience, this means having the general outlook of the business community, as a number of observers have pointed out (Hennessy, 1976; Davis, Bredemeier, and Levy, 1949; Breed, 1958). This tendency to reflect the outlook of . . . dominant power groups can have consequences in conflict situations. . . .

Structurally, it is predictable that media reports will tend to "back the winner," that is, to reflect the locus of social power and to be reinforced within the system for doing so.... It would be structurally unreasonable to expect any mass medium serving a community as a whole to continue backing, through editorials or portrayals, what has come to be known as a lost cause.... Within the local community, it is the power elite that ultimately shapes the media outlook and which therefore receives reciprocal reinforcement *from* those media.

Information and Conflict

A fourth generalization considers knowledge as a power resource and conflict as an aspect of the process that coalesces the generation, distribution, and acquisition of knowledge. This generalization runs counter to the view that conflict produces mostly confusion, rumor, and social disorder, a view based on the belief that "emotional" issues lead to "irrationality" with "nobody listening to reason." While it is true that a wide range of intense emotions on the individual level may be aroused and expressed in a conflict, and while break-offs in communication may occur among individuals and groups, the conflict process generally creates greater need for communication at various levels and tends to increase the distribution and acquisition of knowledge among different interest groups....The type of information generated and distributed tends to vary according to the needs of different groups within the structure at different stages of the conflict....

A perspective in general education holds that in reporting ... confrontations, reporters and editors "aren't doing their job" unless they devote large amounts of space to "background" reports based on evidence from scientists and technologists. Such a perspective, however, fails to take into account the nature of the conflict process and the structural principle that editors and reporters at all stages are dependent upon the acts and statements of the various interest groups. From a structural standpoint, it is very understandable why reporters *do* become immersed in the day-to-day chronology of conflict events rather than in background analyses when the conflict reaches a phase of organized confrontations and demonstrations....

Conflict and the Knowledge Gap

A fifth generalization ... is that through being an integral part of a conflict process within a social structure, mass media in performing their particular roles may contribute to either the widening or narrowing of disparities in knowledge within the system. Whether the consequence is to widen knowledge gaps or not depends at least partially upon the nature of conflict itself. Conflict is rooted in social differentiation, and newspapers and other media may contribute to increasing intensity and broadening of the scope of these conflicts while performing according to their traditional roles. This participation may serve to reinforce the differences in orientations and outlooks between different interest groups and sectors of society. . . .

The finding of increasing knowledge gaps in a variety of situations does not mean, however, that the gaps will *always* increase. There are conditions that may lead to a decrease in gaps and to greater equalization of knowledge within a social system. One of these conditions is the existence of increasingly intense levels of social conflict, particularly that associated with community issues that touch basic concerns of different groups among the population. Conflict not only results in generation and dissemination of new knowledge but it is also an intervening variable in coalescing the concern of participating groups to acquire that knowledge. Conflict increases the amount of interaction at various points within the system and leads to a sharpening of the definition of group interests and to greater clarification in the definition of social problems. In this process, conflict leads to clarification of values of groups vis-à-vis other groups in the system and to a sharpening of each group's position. Effective group positions in social controversies include articulation of the relevance of the issue to the interests of other groups. A basic conflict strategy is to engage groups in the larger public which may have previously seen the issue as a distant fray over "somebody else's problem." A small group of employees in a container factory may conduct a strike which is not recognized by any union and may receive the "wildcat" label in newspaper headlines and broadcast news reports. The strikers' organization might then set up a media event, such as a demonstration or press conference, in which they argue that if the companies and "big unions" can join forces to squelch the protest of one small group of workers, they can also do so for other groups in the community. The strikers may also argue that the issue shows how local people are being overrun by external interests, through suggesting that the companies, unions, and perhaps the National Labor Relations Board are creatures of Washington or New York which are not responsive to local concerns. . . .

Knowledge Gaps and Organizational Strategy

. . . Existence of knowledge gaps is not necessarily dysfunctional for attainment of such social goals as community development. . . . During times of conflict, elite groups may serve as vital community resources. . . . In fact, existence of knowledge elites may serve to alert the rest of the community to the relevance of the legislation to local interests and thereby create initial awareness. . . .

Another question about the knowledge gap phenomenon is whether new and more specialized forms of information technology will also tend to widen gaps. A hypothesis which may be offered for future study is that technologies which are organized so as to increase the degree of differential selection of information among groups will increase the disparity in information between the have and have not groups in society. One would also expect such employment of technologies to lead to knowledge gaps on more topics, since these technologies typically are structured to provide information to specialized groups. . . . Cable television has been promoted in some communities as a means for informing a wide range of citizens about community topics, in others as a means of providing highly specialized information to special interest groups. The latter outcome is more likely to occur, however, considering the nature of broadcast systems. In radio broadcasting, for example, the increased number of stations with specialized programming would be expected to contribute to increasing differentials in knowledge particularly in the entertainment area, among different groups, to which the stations direct their differential appeals.

Information, Education, and Attitudes

A final generalization is that opinions and knowledge may be related, but not in the simple and direct way that many observers suggest. Again, the existence of conflict appears to be a central variable. There is little evidence to support the contention that the more people know about a particular course of action being advocated by some group, the more they will support it. Any time there is a dispute within the system, the dispute is a result of vested interests, and the groups use information and knowledge as a source of support for their interests. . . . The intensity of a community conflict appears to reduce the likelihood that individual points of view can be predicted from their educational status or from their levels of knowledge. As a conflict develops, the highly educated individuals become more likely to turn to their vested interests and to the question of whose ox is being gored as a basis for action. . . .

References

Bethell, T. (1977) "The myth of an adversary press." Harpers Magazine (January): 33-40.

Breed, W. (1958) "Mass communication and social integration." Social Forces 37:109-116.

Davis, K., H. C. Bredemeier, and M. J. Levy, Jr. (1949) Modern American Society: Readings in the Problems of Order and Change. New York: Holt, Rinehart & Winston.

Gerald, E. J. (1963) The Social Responsibility of the Press. Minneapolis: University of Minnesota Press.

Hennessy, B. (1975) Public Opinion. Belmont, Calif.: Wadsworth.

Hulteng, J. (1976) The Messenger's Motives: Ethical Problems of the News Media. Englewood Cliffs, N.J.: Prentice-Hall.

Hyman, H. and P. Sheatsley (1947) "Some reasons why information campaigns fail." Public Opinion Quarterly 11:413-423.

Katzman, N. (1973) "The impact of communication technology: some theoretical premises and their implications." NIH Information Science Training Program Colloquium. Palo Alto, Calif.: Stanford University Press.

Rivers, W. and W. Schramm (1969) Responsibility in Mass Communication. New York: Harper & Row.

Rogers, E. M. (1974) "Social structure and communication strategies in rural development: the communications effect gap and the second dimension of development." Presented at Cornell-CIAT International Symposium on Communication Strategies for Rural Development, Cali, Colombia.

Sigal, L. V. (1973) Reporters and Officials: The Organization and Politics of Newsmaking. Lexington, Mass.: D. C. Heath.

Small, W. (1970) To Kill a Messenger: Television News and the Real World. New York: Hastings House.

Star, S. and H. Hughes (1950) "Report of an educational campaign: the Cincinnati Plan for the United Nations." American Journal of Sociology 55: 389-400.

Tichenor, P. J., G. A. Donohue, and C. N. Olien (1970) "Mass media and differential growth in knowledge." Public Opinion Quarterly 34: 158-170.

2.4 ▰▰▰▰▰▰

What Moves Public Opinion?

Benjamin I. Page, Robert Y. Shapiro, and Glenn R. Dempsey

Editor's Note. Benjamin I. Page, Robert Y. Shapiro, and Glenn R. Dempsey believe that shortcomings in research design explain why many studies of media impact on public opinion do not detect substantial media effects. The authors point out that most research designs focus on instant changes in opinions about single events or classes of events, rather than changes produced over longer periods of time by a multiplicity of media stimuli. Investigators seldom develop baselines that would allow them to assess opinions before news exposure. In cross-sectional studies, control groups are rarely as free from media exposure as the research demands. When the potency of media stimuli is measured, researchers usually fail to analyze the appeal of stories, their manner of presentation, and the sources who transmit the news.

Choosing a more realistic design, the authors examine media impact on a variety of issues by comparing opinions about public policy issues before and after audiences have been exposed to a wide range of news stories. The initial opinion and the pre-poll news stories furnish the baseline by which changes in opinion can be accurately assessed. To judge which factors make stories influential, stories were classified according to different content and format features that have a bearing on salience, credibility, and appeal. The findings reported in the essay demonstrate clearly that television news affects citizens' policy preferences. The influence varies, depending on the sources who advocate particular policies. News commentators' views were most influential, ranking ahead of the views of experts and high officials, such as popular presidents. Television news commentators have become powerful agenda setters for national public opinion.

At the time of writing, Page was the Frank C. Erwin, Jr., Centennial Professor of Political Science at the University of Texas at Austin; Shapiro was assistant professor of political science at Columbia University; Dempsey was a graduate student in political science at the University of Chicago. The selection comes from "What Moves Public Opinion?" *American Political Science Review* 81:1 (March 1987): 23-43. Several tables and notes have been omitted.

Rational Citizens and the Mass Media

. . . [N]ew information that modifies relevant beliefs can change the expected utility of policies for citizens. This should occur if five conditions are met: if the information is (1) actually received, (2) understood, (3) clearly relevant to evaluating policies, (4) discrepant with past beliefs, and (5) credible. (For related views of attitude change, see Jaccard 1981; Zaller 1985.)

When these conditions are met to a sufficient extent, new information should alter an individual's preferences and choices among policies. Further, if the conditions are met in the same way for many individuals, there may be a change in collective public opinion that shows up in opinion polls. For example, if many citizens' policy preferences depend critically on the same belief (e.g., "We must spend more on national defense because the Russians are overtaking us") and if highly credible, well publicized new information challenges that belief (e.g., U.S. military spending is reported to rise sharply and a CIA study concludes that Soviet spending has changed little since 1976), then enthusiasm for increased military spending may drop.

Since most people have little reason to invest time or effort learning the ins and outs of alternative policies (Downs 1957), we would not expect new information ordinarily to produce large or quick changes in public opinion. Indeed the evidence indicates that aggregate public opinion about policy is usually quite stable (Page and Shapiro 1982).

By the same token, however, for whatever they do learn about politics, most people must rely heavily upon the cheapest and most accessible sources: newspapers, radio, and television, especially network TV news. When news in the media reaches large audiences and meets our five conditions for many individuals, we would expect public opinion to change.

Television news often meets the exposure condition. Most U.S. families own television sets, and most tune in to network news broadcasts from time to time. Viewers may wander in and out; they may eat or talk or be distracted by children; but every day millions of U.S. citizens catch at least a glimpse of the major stories on TV news. Others see the same stories in newspaper headlines or get the gist of the news from family and friends. Over a period of weeks and months many bits and pieces of information accumulate.

The conditions of comprehension and relevance, too, are often met. The media work hard to ensure that their audiences can understand. They shorten, sharpen, and simplify stories, and present pictures with strong visual impact so that a reasonably alert grade-schooler can get the point. Often stories bear directly upon beliefs central to the evaluation of public policies.

Credibility is a more complicated matter. Rational citizens must sometimes delegate the analysis or evaluation of information to like-minded, trusted agents (Downs 1957, 203-34). The media report the policy-relevant statements and actions of a wide variety of actors, from popular presidents and respected commentators, to discredited politicians or self-serving interest groups. News from such different *sources* is likely to have quite a range of salience and credibility, and therefore quite a range of impact on the public (see Hovland and Weiss 1951-52). The analysis of effects on opinion should allow for such variation.

News may also vary greatly in the extent to which it is or is not discrepant with past beliefs. If it closely resembles what has been communicated for many months or years, if it simply reinforces prevalent beliefs and opinions, we would not expect it to produce change. If, on the other hand, credible new information calls into question key beliefs and opinions held by many people, we would expect changes in public opinion. The extent of discrepancy with past news and past opinions must be taken into account.

We are, of course, aware of the curious notion that the contents of the mass media have only minimal effects (Chaffee 1975; Klapper 1960; Kraus and Davis 1976; McGuire 1985; but cf. Graber 1984; Noelle-Neumann 1973, 1980, 1984; Wagner 1983). This notion seems to have persisted despite findings of agenda-setting effects upon perceptions of what are important problems (Cook, Tyler, Goetz, Gordon, Protess, Leff, and Molotch 1983; Erbring, Goldenberg, and Miller 1980; Funkhauser 1973; Iyengar, Peters, and Kinder 1982; McCombs and Shaw 1972; MacKuen 1981, 1984).

We believe that the minimal effects idea is not correct with respect to policy preferences, either. It has probably escaped refutation because of the failure of researchers to examine collective opinion over substantial periods of time in natural settings and to distinguish among news sources. One-shot quasi-experimental studies (e.g., of presidential debates) understandably fail to find large, quick effects. Cross-sectional studies seek contrasts between media attenders and media "nonattenders" that hardly exist: nearly everyone is exposed either directly or indirectly to what the media broadcast (see Page, Shapiro, and Dempsey 1985a, 2-4). A more appropriate research design yields different results.

Data and Methods

Taking advantage of a unique data set in our possession, we have carried out a quasi-experimental study that overcomes several of the limitations of previous research. The design involved collecting data from many pairs of identically repeated policy preference questions that were asked of national survey samples of U.S. citizens; coding TV news content from broadcasts aired in between (and just before) each pair of surveys; and predicting or explaining variations in the extent and direction of opinion change by variations in media content.

Our design facilitated causal inferences and permitted comparison across types of issues and historical periods. The use of natural settings meant that all real world processes could come into play, including major events and actions, the interpretation of news by commentators and others, and the dissemination of information through two-step or multiple-step flows and social networks (cf. Katz and Lazarsfeld 1965). The examination of moderately long time periods (several weeks or months) allowed enough time for these natural processes to work and for us to observe even slow cumulative opinion changes. In addition, our measurement scheme permitted us to distinguish among different sources of news and to take into account the extent of news story relevance to policy questions, the degree of discrepancy between current and previous media content, and the credibility of news sources.

As part of our ongoing research project on public opinion and democracy, we have assembled a comprehensive collection of survey data on U.S. citizens' policy preferences. It includes the marginal frequencies of responses to thousands of different policy questions asked by various survey organizations since 1935. Among these data we have identified several hundred questions that were asked two or more times with identical (verbatim) wordings, by the same survey organization. (For a partial description, see Page and Shapiro 1982, 1983a.)

For the present research we selected 80 pairs of policy questions from the last 15 years (for which TV news data are readily available) that were repeated within moderate time intervals averaging about three months.

These 80 cases are not, strictly speaking, a sample from the universe of policy issues or poll questions but (with a small number of exceptions) constitute either a random sample of the available eligible survey questions and time points for a given survey organization or *all* the available cases from an organization. They are very diverse, covering many different kinds of foreign and defense ($n=32$) and domestic ($n=48$) policies. In nearly half the cases public opinion changed significantly ($p<.05$; 6 percentage points or more), and in a little more than half, it did not—nearly the same proportion as in our full data set of several hundred repeated items. A list of cases and a more detailed methodological discussion is available in Page, Shapiro, and Dempsey (1985a, b).

The dependent variable for each case is simply the level of public opinion at the time of the second survey (T2), that is, the percentage of the survey sample, excluding "don't know" and "no opinion" responses, that endorsed the most prominent (generally the first) policy alternative mentioned in the survey question. As will be seen, our method of using T2 level of opinion as the dependent variable and including first survey (T1) opinion as a predictor yields nearly identical estimates of media effects as does using a difference score—the magnitude and direction of opinion *change*—as the dependent variable.

For each of the 80 cases, we and our research assistants coded the daily television network news from one randomly selected network (in a few low-salience cases, *all* networks) each day, using the summaries found in the *Television News Index and Abstracts* of the Vanderbilt Television News Archive. These summaries, while rather brief and not intended for such purposes, were generally satisfactory in providing the fairly straight-forward information we sought, especially since they were aggregated over several weeks or months. We coded all news stories that were at least minimally relevant to the wording of each opinion item, beginning two months before the T1 survey—in order to allow for lagged effects and for discrepancies or changes in media content—and continuing with every day up to T1 and through to the date of the T2 survey.

Being interested in the effects of particular actors or *sources*— particular providers of information, or Downsian "agents" of analysis and evaluation—whose rhetoric and actions are reported in the media, we distinguished among the original sources found in each news story. We used 10 exhaustive and mutually exclusive categories: the president; fellow partisans and members of his administration; members of the opposing party; interest groups and individuals not fitting clearly into any of the other categories; experts; network commentators or reporters themselves; friendly (or neutral) foreign nations or individuals; unfriendly foreign states or individuals; courts and judges; and objective conditions or events without clearly identifiable human actors (e.g., unemployment statistics, natural disasters, unattributed terrorist acts).

Our independent variables characterize *reported statements or actions by a specified source.* Each such *source story,* or "message," constitutes a unit of analysis in measuring aggregate media content over the time interval of a particular case. For each reported statement or action by a particular source—each source story—we coded the following: 1) its degree of *relevance* to the policy question (indirectly relevant, relevant, or highly relevant); 2) its *salience* in the broadcast (its inclusion in the first story or not, its proximity to the beginning of the broadcast, its duration in seconds; 3) the pro-con *direction* of intended impact of the reported statement or action in relation to the most prominent policy alternative mentioned in the opinion item; 4) the president's popularity (measured by the standard Gallup question) as an indication of his *credibility* as news source at the time of his statement or action; and 5) some judgments—not used in this paper—concerning the quality of the information conveyed, including its logic, factuality, and degree of truth or falsehood.

The most important part of the coding effort concerned the directional thrust of reported statements and actions in relation to each opinion question. Proceeding a little differently from the method of our earlier work on newspapers (Page and Shapiro 1983b, 1984), we measured directional thrust in terms of the intentions or advocated positions of the speakers or actors themselves. We took considerable care in training and supervising coders and in checking the reliability of their work. We prepared detailed written instructions and held frequent group discussions of coding rules and the treatment of problematic cases. All pro-con coding decisions, and those on other variables central to our analysis, were validated by a second coder and also by one of the present authors, who made the final coding decisions.[1] We masked the public opinion data so that coders would not be affected in any way by knowledge of whether or how policy preferences changed; we gave them only the exact wording of each opinion item and the time periods to be examined, not the responses to the questions.

As a result of these efforts we are confident that very high quality data were produced. It proved rather easy to code reported statements and actions on a five-point directional scale with categories "clearly pro," "probably pro," "uncertain or neutral," "probably con," and "clearly con" in relation to the main policy alternative outlined in each opinion question.

For each type of news source in each opinion case, we summed and averaged all the numerical values of pro-con codes (ranging from $+2$ to -2, with 0 for neutral) in order to compute measures of total and average directional thrust of the news from each source. The sums and averages of directional codes for television news content prior to T1 and between T1 and T2—for all messages coming from all sources combined and for messages coming separately from each distinct source—constitute our main independent variables. Most of our analysis is based on measures restricted to "relevant" or "highly relevant" source stories because we found that inclusion of less relevant source stories weakened the observed relationships.

Our principal mode of analysis was ordinary least squares regression analysis, in which we estimated the impact of each news source (or all sources taken together) along with opinion levels at T1, upon the level of public opinion at T2. We analyzed all cases together and also each of our two independently selected subsets of 40 cases, as well as subsets of cases involving different kinds of issues (e.g., foreign versus domestic policies), different time periods, and different levels of source credibility (popular versus unpopular presidents).

After testing hypotheses and exploring the aggregate data, we closely examined individual cases of public opinion change, scrutinizing media-reported statements and actions and the precise sequence of events. This served two purposes. First, it helped us with causal inference, shedding light on possibilities of spuriousness or reciprocal influence. Second, it enabled us to generate some new hypotheses about effects on opinion by certain sets of actors not clearly differentiated in our aggregate data.

Findings

. . . News commentary (from the anchorperson, reporters in the field, or special commentators) between the T1 and T2 surveys is estimated to have the most dramatic impact. A single "probably pro" commentary is associated with more than four percentage points of opinion change! This is a startling finding, one that we would hesitate to believe except that something similar has now appeared in three separate sets of cases we have analyzed. It was true of editorial columns in our earlier analysis of 56 two-point opinion series using the *New York Times* as our media source (Page and Shapiro 1983b), in the first 40 TV news cases we collected (Page, Shapiro, and Dempsey 1984), and in the 40 new TV cases, which we analyzed separately before doing all 80 cases together.

We are not convinced that commentators' remarks in and of themselves have such great potency, however. They may serve as indicators of elite or public consensus (Hallin 1984; McClosky and Zaller 1984; Noelle-Neumann 1973, 1980). Or the commentaries may—if in basic agreement with official network sentiment or the attitudes of reporters (perhaps providing cues for reporters . . .) —indicate slants or biases in media coverage that are transmitted to citizens in ways that supplement the statements of the commentators. These could include the selection of news sources and quotes, the choice of visual footage, the questions asked in interviews, camera angles, and so forth.

Certain other estimated effects on opinion are probably important even though some do not reach the .05 level of statistical significance according to a conservative two-tailed test. . . . Most notably—and clearly significantly—a single "probably pro" story about experts or research studies is estimated to produce about three percentage points of opinion change, a very substantial amount. Presidents are estimated to have a more modest impact of about three-tenths of a percentage point per "probably pro" story, and stories about opposition party statements and actions may also have a positive effect.

There are indications, on the other hand, that interest groups and perhaps the courts (in recent years) actually have negative effects. That is, when their statements and actions push in one direction (e.g., when corporations demand subsidies or a federal court orders school integration through busing) public opinion tends to move in the opposite direction. We are not certain about the negative effect of courts, however, because of the instability of coefficients across data sets.

Certain kinds of news appear on the average to have no direct effect at all upon opinion, or less impact than might be expected. The president's fellow partisans, when acting independently of the president himself, do not appreciably affect opinion. Events may move public opinion indirectly, but they do not speak strongly for themselves. They presumably have their effects mainly through the interpretations and reactions of other news sources. The same applies to statements and actions from foreign countries or individuals, whether friends or foes. U.S. citizens apparently do not listen to foreigners directly but only through interpretations by U.S. opinion leaders.

The marked distinctions among types of news fits well with our idea that information from different sources has different degrees of credibility. It is quite plausible, for example, that the public tends to place considerable trust in the positions taken by network commentators and (ostensibly) nonpartisan experts. Some other sources may be considered irrelevant. Still others, like certain interest groups that presumably pursue narrowly selfish aims, may serve as negative reference points on public issues (see Schattschneider 1960, 52-53). Similarly, the federal courts may have served as negative referents in the 1970s and the early 1980s because of their unpopular actions on such issues as busing and capital punishment. In any case, it is clearly important to distinguish among sources of news. . . .

When presidents are popular, they tend (though the estimate falls short of statistical significance) to have a small positive effect on public opinion. Each "probably pro" statement or action is estimated to produce more than half a percentage point of opinion change. Part of the effect is undoubtedly temporary and part reciprocal. The impact presumably could not be multiplied indefinitely by talkative presidents because of potential saturation and overexposure of the reporters' and editors' desires for fresh topics to cover. Still, this constitutes some evidence that a popular president does indeed stand at a "bully pulpit." On an issue of great importance to him he can hammer away with repeated speeches and statements and can reasonably expect to achieve a 5 or 10 percentage point change in public opinion over the course of several months (see Page and Shapiro 1984).

Unpopular presidents, in contrast, apparently have no positive effect on opinion at all. They may try—like Glendower in *Henry IV*—to call spirits from the vasty deep, but none will come.

There are some indications that the effects of other news sources interact with presidential popularity. . . . [C]ommentaries may have their strongest effects when presidents are unpopular. Perhaps news commentators substitute for a respected leader, challenging the one that is out of favor. In addition, administration officials and the president's fellow partisans in Congress and elsewhere, when acting independently of a popular president, appear to have a slightly negative impact on opinion, whereas they may have positive effects when presidents are unpopular. The opposition party, rather strangely, seems especially potent when presidents are popular. In short, there may be some substantial differences in the dynamics of opinion change depending upon whether the president in office at a particular time is popular or not.

Discussion

Our examination of a number of specific cases of opinion change has bolstered our general confidence in the aggregate findings. . . .

News Commentary

The most dramatic finding . . . is the strong estimated impact of news commentary. Our examination of specific cases provides a number of instances in which the statements of news commentators and reporters clearly parallel opinion change. Examples include Howard K. Smith's praise for Nixon's policies and his criticism of calls for unilateral withdrawal from Vietnam in 1969; various newsmen's support for continued slow withdrawal from Vietnam during 1969-70; commentary favoring conservation and increased production rather than stopping military aid to Israel in order to get cheap oil during 1974-75; Smith's and others' support for more attention to the Arabs during 1974-75 and during 1977-78; Eric Severeid's, David Brinkley's, and Smith's advocacy of campaign contribution limits in 1973; Brinkley's and Smith's backing of stricter wage and price controls during 1972-73; John Chancellor's editorializing on the importance of fighting unemployment (versus inflation) in 1976; Smith's support for federal work projects in 1976; and commentaries in the spring of 1981 that Reagan's proposed tax cuts would benefit the wealthy.

. . . We would not claim that individual news commentators like Howard K. Smith—for all the esteem in which they are held—are, in themselves, the biggest sources of opinion change (but cf. Freeman, Weeks, and Wertheimer 1955). We do not believe that Walter Cronkite single-handedly ended the Vietnam War with his famous soul-searching broadcast in 1968.

Instead, the commentary we have examined may reflect the positions of many journalists or other elites who communicate through additional channels besides TV news or even a widespread elite consensus in the country (see McClosky and Zaller 1984). Or commentators' positions may be indicators of network biases, including subtle influences of reporters and editors upon the selection of news sources and upon the ways in which stories are filmed and reported. Or, again, commentators and other sources with whom they agree may (correctly or not) be perceived by the public as reflecting a climate of opinion or an emerging national consensus on an issue, which may weigh heavily with citizens as they form their own opinions (see Lippmann 1922; Noelle-Neumann 1973). With our present data, we cannot distinguish among these possibilities. But news commentators either constitute or stand for major influences on public opinion.

Experts

. . . [T]hose we have categorized as "experts" have quite a substantial impact on public opinion. Their credibility may be high because of their actual or portrayed experience and expertise and nonpartisan status. It is not unreasonable for members of the public to give great weight to experts' statements and positions, particularly when complex technical questions affect the merits of policy alternatives.

The existence of a reciprocal process, influence by public opinion upon experts, cannot be ruled out (particularly to the extent that the audience-seeking media decide who is an expert based on the popularity of his or her policy views), but it is probably limited in the short run because experts do not face immediate electoral pressures—that is, public attitudes may ultimately influence who are considered experts and what their basic values are, but once established, experts are less likely than presidents or other elected officials to bend quickly with the winds of opinion.

One striking example of the influence of expert opinion as reported in the media concerns the Senate vote on the SALT II arms limitation treaty. Public support for the treaty dropped 5.5% from February to March 1979 and 19% from June to November. During both periods many retired generals and arms experts spoke out or testified against the treaty, citing difficulties of verification and an allegedly unequal balance of forces favoring the Soviets.

Presidents

. . . [N]umerous cases support the inference that popular presidents' actions and statements reported in the media do affect public opinion. These include President Nixon's persistent opposition to accelerating U.S. troop withdrawals from Vietnam during 1969, 1970, and 1971; Reagan's 1981 argument for AWACS airplane sales to Saudi Arabia; Carter's 1977-78 increased attention to Arab countries; Carter's early 1980 movement (during a temporary peak in popularity) toward toughness in the Iranian hostage crisis; Reagan's 1982 bellicose posturing toward the Soviet Union; Ford's 1974-75 defense of military spending; Ford's 1976 and Carter's

1980 advocacies of cuts in domestic spending; and, perhaps, Nixon's 1972-73 support for wage and price controls.

On the other hand, as our regression results showed, unpopular presidents do not have much success at opinion leadership. In a number of cases unpopular presidents made serious efforts to advocate policies but failed to persuade the public. This was true of Ford's attempts to increase military spending in 1976 and his resistance to jobs programs and health and education spending in the same year. Jimmy Carter in early 1979, with his popularity at 43% approval and falling, failed to rally support for SALT II. Carter was also unsuccessful at gaining significant ground on gasoline rationing, the military draft, or the Equal Rights Amendment in 1979 and 1980. Even Ronald Reagan, when near a low point of popularity (44%) in mid-1982, failed to move opinion toward more approval of a school prayer amendment to the Constitution. Because this distinction between popular and unpopular presidents emerged clearly in our previous analysis of newspaper data (Page and Shapiro 1984), we are inclined to believe that it is real (though modest in magnitude) even though the popular president effect does not quite reach statistical significance. . . .

Interest Groups

Our regression analysis indicated that groups and individuals representing various special interests, taken together, tend to have a negative effect on public opinion. Our examination of the cases supports this point but also suggests that certain kinds of groups may have positive effects while others have negative impact.

We found many cases (more than 20) in which public opinion unequivocally moved *away* from positions advocated by groups and individuals representing special interests. In some cases the groups may have belatedly spoken up after public opinion had already started moving against their positions, producing a spurious negative relationship. But in many instances they seem actually to have antagonized the public and created a genuine adverse effect.

Such cases include Vietnam War protestors from 1969 to 1970, protestors against draft registration in 1980, and perhaps the nuclear freeze movement in 1982. U.S. citizens have a long history of opposition to demonstrators and protestors, even peaceful ones, and apparently tend not to accept them as credible or legitimate sources of opinion leadership. . . .

In general, the public apparently tends to be uninfluenced (or negatively influenced) by the positions of groups whose interests are perceived to be selfish or narrow, while it responds more favorably to groups and individuals thought to be concerned with broadly defined public interests. The best examples of the latter in our data are environmental groups and perhaps also general "public interest" groups like Common Cause.

From 1973 to 1974, for example, support for leasing federal land to oil companies declined as TV news reported conservationists challenging the positions of the profit-seeking and presumably less credible oil companies. During the same period, support for a freeze on gasoline, heating, and power prices increased a bit despite opposition by gas station owners and oil companies.

Not only business corporations, but also some mass membership groups representing blacks, women, the poor, Jews, and organized labor seem to have been held in disrepute and to have had null or negative effects on opinion about issues of direct concern to them, including social welfare policies and some Middle East issues. . . .

Conclusion

We believe we have identified the main influences on short-term and medium-term opinion change.

Our analysis does not offer a full account of certain glacial, long-term shifts in public opinion that reflect major social, technological, and demographic changes such as rising educational levels, cohort replacement, racial migration, or alterations in the family or the workplace. The decades-long transformations in public attitudes about civil liberties, civil rights, abortion, and other matters surely rest (at least in an ultimate causal sense) upon such social changes. . . . If news reports play a part in such major opinion shifts, they may do so mainly as transmitters of more fundamental forces.

Within the realm of short- and medium-term effects, however, we have had striking success at finding out what moves public opinion. Our TV news variables, together with opinion at the time of an initial survey, account for well over 90% of the variance in public opinion at the time of a second survey. The news variables alone account for nearly half the variance in opinion change. . . .

The processes of opinion change are not simple. In order to account for changes between two opinion surveys, for example, it is essential to examine media content before the first survey. *Discrepancies* between current news and prior news (or prior opinion) are important. Part of the media impact is temporary so that there is a tendency for opinion in the T1-T2 period to drift back, to move in a direction opposite to the thrust of the media content prior to T1.

Moreover, it is important to distinguish among news *sources* rather than aggregating all media content together. The effects of news from different sources vary widely.

Among the sources we examined, the estimated impact of news commentary is strongest of all, on a per-story basis, though such messages are aired less frequently than those from other sources. The causal status of this finding, however, is uncertain. Commentary may be an indicator of broader influences, such as media bias in the selection and presentation of other news, of consensus among the U.S. media or elites generally, or of a perceived public consensus.

Experts, those perceived as having experience and technical knowledge and nonpartisan credibility, also have very sizable effects. A policy alternative that experts testify is ineffective or unworkable tends to lose public favor; an alternative hailed as efficient or necessary tends to gain favor.

We found that messages communicated through the media from or about popular presidents tend to have positive effects on opinion. Presidents respond to public desires, but they can also lead public opinion (see Page and Shapiro 1984). Active presidential effort can be expected to yield a 5- or 10-percentage point change in opinion over the course of a few months.

News commentators, experts, and popular presidents have in common a high level of credibility, which we believe is crucial to their influence on the public. Rational citizens accept information and analysis only from those they trust. In contrast, news sources with low credibility, such as unpopular presidents or groups perceived to represent narrow interests, generally have no effect, or even a negative impact, on public opinion.

Some of these findings might be thought to be limited to the recent period we studied, in which the public has relied heavily on TV and is better educated and more attentive to politics than U.S. citizens in the past. Our confidence in the generality of the findings, however, is bolstered by their consistency with our previous analysis (using newspaper stories) of opinion change from 1935 onward (see Page and Shapiro 1983b, 1984). This similarity also reinforces the observation that the national news media in the U.S. are very much of a piece. They all tend to report the same kinds of messages concerning public policy, from the same sources. This can be attributed to the norms and incentives—and the organizational and market structure—of the news industry and especially to the pervasiveness of the wire services (see Epstein 1973; Gans 1980; Roshco 1975). In this respect the contents of one medium is a good indicator of the content of many media.

In terms of our concerns about democratic theory, it is interesting to observe that relatively neutral information providers like experts and news commentators apparently have more positive effects (at least direct effects) than do self-serving interest groups. It is also interesting that popular presidents, who presumably tend to embody the values and goals of the public, are more able than unpopular ones to influence opinions about policy. These findings suggest that objective information may play a significant part in opinion formation and change and that certain of the more blatant efforts to manipulate opinion are not successful.

On the other hand, unobtrusive indirect effects by special interests—through influences on experts and commentators, for example—may be more dangerous than would be a direct clash of interests in full public view. Clearly there is much more to be learned before we can be confident about the fundamental sources of influence on public opinion. The same is true of judging the quality of information received by the public.

In order to judge to what extent the public benefits from constructive political leadership and education and to what extent it suffers from deception and manipulation, we need to examine the truth or falsehood, the logic or illogic, of the statements and actions of those who succeed at gaining the public's trust (see Bennett 1983; Edelman 1964; Miliband 1969; Wise 1973; contrast Braestrup 1983; Robinson 1976; Rothman 1979). This applies to the sources whose messages are conveyed through the media and to the media themselves. There is much to learn about whether various sources lie or mislead or tell the truth; about how accurately or inaccurately the media report what the sources say and do; and about the causes of any systematic distortions or biases in the selection and reporting of policy-related news.

Note

1. . . . Any disagreements about coding were resolved through meetings and discussion. Some reliability analysis was done, with Dempsey and Shapiro coding cases independently. Their intercoder reliability coefficients for the variables coded were in the .7 and .8 range. For the all-important pro-con codes, the two authors never disagreed by more than one unit on the 5-point scale.

References

Bennett, W. Lance. 1983. *News: The Politics of Illusion.* New York: Longman.
Braestrup, Peter. 1983. *Big Story.* New Haven, Conn.: Yale University Press.
Chaffee, Steven H. 1975. *Political Communication: Enduring Issues for Research.* Beverly Hills: Sage.
Cook, Fay Lomax, Tom R. Tyler, Edward G. Goetz, Margaret T. Gordon, David Protess, Donna R. Leff, and Harvey L. Molotch. 1983. Media and Agenda Setting: Effects on the Public, Interest Group Leaders, Policy Makers, and Policy. *Public Opinion Quarterly* 47:16-35.

Davis, James A. 1975. Communism, Conformity, Cohorts, and Categories: American Tolerance in 1954 and 1972-73. *American Journal of Sociology* 81:491-513.

Downs, Anthony. 1957. *An Economic Theory of Democracy.* New York: Harper.

Edelman, Murray. 1964. *The Symbolic Uses of Politics.* Urbana: University of Illinois Press.

Epstein, Edward J. 1973. *News from Nowhere.* New York: Random House.

Erbring, Lutz, Edie N. Goldenberg, and Arthur H. Miller. 1980. Front Page News and Real World Cues: A New Look at Agenda-Setting by the Media. *American Journal of Political Science* 24:16-49.

Freeman, Howard E., H. Ashley Weeks, and Walter J. Wertheimer. 1955. News Commentator Effect: A Study in Knowledge and Opinion Change. *Public Opinion Quarterly* 19:209-15.

Funkhauser, G. Ray. 1973. The Issues of the Sixties: An Exploratory Study in the Dynamics of Public Opinion. *Public Opinion Quarterly* 37:63-75.

Gans, Herbert J. 1980. *Deciding What's News.* New York: Vintage.

Graber, Doris A. 1984. *Mass Media and American Politics.* 2d ed. Washington, D.C.: Congressional Quarterly.

Hallin, Daniel C. 1984. The Media, the War in Vietnam, and Political Support: A Critique of the Thesis of an Oppositional Media. *Journal of Politics* 46:2-24.

Hovland, Carl I., and Walter Weiss. 1951-52. The Influence of Source Credibility on Communication Effectiveness. *Public Opinion Quarterly* 16:635-50.

Iyengar, Shanto, Mark D. Peters, and Donald R. Kinder. 1982. Experimental Demonstrations of the "Not-So-Minimal" Consequences of Television News Programs. *American Political Science Review* 76:848-58.

Jaccard, James. 1981. Toward Theories of Persuasion and Belief Change. *Journal of Personality and Social Psychology* 40:260-69.

Katz, Elihu, and Paul F. Lazarsfeld. 1965. *Personal Influence: The Part Played by People in the Flow of Communications.* Glencoe, Ill.: Free Press.

Klapper, Joseph T. 1960. *The Effects of Mass Communication.* Glencoe, Ill.: Free Press.

Kraus, Sidney, and Dennis Davis. 1976. *The Effects of Mass Communication on Political Behavior.* University Park: Pennsylvania State University Press.

Lippmann, Walter. 1922. *Public Opinion.* New York: Macmillan.

McClosky, Herbert, and John Zaller. 1984. *The American Ethos: Public Attitudes toward Capitalism and Democracy.* Cambridge, Mass.: Harvard University Press.

McCombs, Maxwell E., and Donald L. Shaw. 1972. The Agenda-Setting Function of the Mass Media. *Public Opinion Quarterly* 36:176-87.

McGuire, William J. 1985. The Myth of Mass Media Effectiveness: Savagings and Salvagings. In *Public Communication and Behavior,* ed. George Comstock.

MacKuen, Michael B. 1981. Social Communications and Mass Policy Agenda. In *More than News: Media Power in Public Affairs,* by Michael B. MacKuen and Steven L. Coombs. Beverly Hills: Sage.

MacKuen, Michael B. 1984. Exposure to Information, Belief Integration, and Individual Responsiveness to Agenda Change. *American Political Science Review* 78:372-91.

Miliband, Ralph. 1969. *The State in Capitalist Society.* London: Quartet.

Noelle-Neumann, Elisabeth. 1973. Return to the Concept of Powerful Mass Media. In *Studies in Broadcasting,* ed. H. Eguchi and K. Sata, 67-112. Tokyo: The Nippon Hoso Kyokai.

Noelle-Neumann, Elisabeth. 1980. Mass Media and Social Change in Developed Societies. In *Mass Communication Review Yearbook.* Vol. 1, ed. G. Cleveland Wilhoit and Harold de Bock. Beverly Hills: Sage.

Noelle-Neumann, Elisabeth. 1984. *The Spiral of Silence.* Chicago: University of Chicago Press.

Page, Benjamin I., and Robert Y. Shapiro. 1982. Changes in Americans' Policy Preferences, 1935-1979. *Public Opinion Quarterly* 46:24-42.

Page, Benjamin I., and Robert Y. Shapiro. 1983a. Effects of Public Opinion on Policy. *American Political Science Review* 77:175-90.

Page, Benjamin I., and Robert Y. Shapiro. 1983b. The Mass Media and Changes in Americans' Policy Preferences: A Preliminary Analysis. Paper presented at the annual meeting of the Midwest Political Science Association, Chicago.

Page, Benjamin I., and Robert Y. Shapiro. 1984. Presidents as Opinion Leaders: Some New Evidence. *Policy Studies Journal* 12:649-61.

Page, Benjamin I., Robert Y. Shapiro, and Glenn R. Dempsey. 1984. Television News and Changes in Americans' Policy Preferences. Paper presented at the annual meeting of the Midwest Political Science Association, Chicago.

Page, Benjamin I., Robert Y. Shapiro, and Glenn R. Dempsey. 1985a. The Mass Media Do Affect Policy Preferences. Paper presented at the annual meeting of the American Association for Public Opinion Research, McAfee, N.J.

Page, Benjamin I., Robert Y. Shapiro, and Glenn R. Dempsey. 1985b. What Moves Public Opinion. Paper presented at the annual meeting of the American Political Science Association, New Orleans.

Robinson, Michael J. 1976. Public Affairs Television and the Growth of Political Malaise: The Case of "The Selling of the Pentagon." *American Political Science Review* 70:409-32.

Roshco, Bernard. 1975. *Newsmaking.* Chicago: University of Chicago Press.

Rothman, Stanley. 1979. The Mass Media in Post-Industrial Society. In *The Third Century: America as a Post-Industrial Society,* ed. Seymour Martin Lipset, 346-88. Stanford: Hoover Institution.

Schattschneider, E. E. 1960. *The Semisovereign People.* New York: Holt.

Wagner, Joseph. 1983. Media Do Make a Difference: The Differential Impact of the Mass Media in the 1976 Presidential Race. *American Journal of Political Science* 27:407-30.

Wise, David. 1973. *The Politics of Lying.* New York: Vintage.

Zaller, John. 1985. The Diffusion of Political Attitudes. Princeton University. Photocopy.

2.5 ▰▰

Television News and Citizens'
Explanations of National Affairs

Shanto Iyengar

Editor's Note. Most studies of agenda setting involve a combination of
content analysis of news media and interviews with media audiences to assess
the extent to which priorities reflected in news content are shared by media
audiences. By contrast, Shanto Iyengar bases his findings on laboratory
experiments in which he controls the news to which various respondents are
exposed so that effects can be measured more accurately. The drawback in
laboratory studies is making laboratory situations totally realistic.

Iyengar's study sheds light on an important aspect of agenda setting—
the power of newspeople to present news in various contexts and, in the
process, to suggest various types of causes for the happenings. In turn, the
causes of a situation suggest what the appropriate remedies might be. Like
other agenda-setting studies, the findings reported here demonstrate that
media influence varies depending on the subject matter and on extraneous
political conditions.

At the time of publication, Iyengar was associate professor of political
science at the State University of New York, Stony Brook. The article is part
of a large research project reported in Shanto Iyengar and Donald R. Kinder,
News That Matters: Television and American Opinion (Chicago: University
of Chicago Press, 1987). The selection comes from "Television News and
Citizens' Explanations of National Affairs," *American Political Science
Review* 81:3 (September 1987): 815-831. Several tables have been omitted.

Explanations as Knowledge

Explanation is an essential ingredient of human knowledge. To
explain events or outcomes is to understand them: to transform the
"blooming, buzzing confusion" of today's world into orderly and meaningful patterns. Psychological research has demonstrated that causal
relationships feature prominently in individuals' perceptions of social

---

Reprinted by permission of the author and the American Political Science Association.

phenomena (Nisbett and Ross 1980; Weiner 1985). In fact, causal thinking is so ingrained in the human psyche that we even invent causation where none exists, as in purely random or chance events (see Langer 1975; Wortman 1976).

Explanatory knowledge is important to political thinking for two reasons. First, answers to causal questions abound in popular culture, making the task of explanation relatively inexpensive. One need not devour the pages of the *Wall Street Journal* or study macroeconomics to "know" why there is chronic unemployment. Second and more important, explanatory knowledge is connotative knowledge. To "know" that unemployment occurs because of motivational deficiencies on the part of the unemployed is relevant to our attitudes toward the unemployed and our policy preferences regarding unemployment. In other words, explanatory knowledge is usable knowledge. Simple factual knowledge, on the other hand (e.g., the current rate of unemployment), does not so readily imply political attitudes and preferences. It is not surprising, then, that opinions, attitudes, feelings, and behaviors in a multitude of domains are organized around beliefs about causation (for illustrative research, see Schneider, Hastorf, and Ellsworth 1979, chap. 2). . . .

Framing Effects in Political Explanation

When individuals engage in causal reasoning, their thinking processes are rarely systematic or exhaustive (see, for example, Kelley 1973). Virtually all forms of human judgment are infinitely labile, with outcomes hinging on a variety of circumstantial and contextual cues (for illustrative evidence, see Kahneman, Slovic, and Tversky 1982). The term *framing effects* refers to changes in judgment engendered by subtle alterations in the definition of judgment or choice problems. Tversky and Kahneman (among others), in a number of ingenious studies, have shown that choices between risky prospects can be profoundly altered merely by altering the description of the alternatives. Framing the prospects in terms of possible losses, for example, induces risk-seeking behavior while describing the identical prospects in terms of potential gains makes people risk averse (Kahneman and Tversky 1982, 1984; for illustrations of framing effects in consumer behavior, see Thaler 1980). In short, the invoking of different reference points triggers completely different strategies of choice or judgment.

Political explanation would seem a particularly promising real-world domain for the occurrence of framing effects. Political stimuli are generally remote from everyday life, and ordinary citizens are unlikely to have developed strong commitments to particular explanations; accordingly, one would expect citizens to be highly susceptible to political framing effects.

Because citizens must depend primarily upon the media for information about the political world, there can be no better vehicle for examining political framing effects than media news presentations in general and television news presentations in particular.[1] The evidence reported here indicates that, according to the manner in which television news frames national issues, individuals' explanations of these issues are altered. Moreover, by altering explanations of national issues, the media alter attitudes toward the incumbent president.

Method

Residents of the Three Village area of Brookhaven Township, Suffolk County, New York, participated in a series of studies described to them as investigations of "selective perception" of television newscasts. Individuals responded to newspaper advertisements offering $10 as payment. This procedure yielded samples that were approximately representative of the local area. . . .

Procedure

When participants arrived at the Media Research Laboratory, they completed an informed consent form and a short pretest questionnaire probing personal and political background variables. They then watched a 20-minute videotape containing seven news stories described as a representative selection of network news stories broadcast during the past six months. On average, each viewing session had two participants. The fourth story on the tape represented the experimental manipulation and, depending on the condition to which participants were assigned (randomly), they saw different coverage of poverty, unemployment, or terrorism. With the exception of the treatment story, the videotapes were identical.

Following viewing of the videotape, participants completed a lengthy posttest (individually, in separate rooms) that included the key questions probing their explanations for the target problem as well as other questions on their issue opinions, their perceptions of President Reagan's issue positions, their assessments of the president's overall performance, his competence and integrity, and his performance in specific domains. On completing the posttest, participants were paid and debriefed.[2]

Measures

I relied entirely on unstructured questions to get at participants' causal accounts. These questions, though unwieldy and coding intensive, are relatively nonreactive. Given the paucity of research into citizens' explanations of political issues, it would have been presumptuous for the researcher to define the appropriate causal categories. The approach was to let each individual choose his or her own categories, with no prompts whatsoever.

The posttest began by asking participants "When you hear or read about ____, what kinds of things do you think about? Please list as many thoughts as you have." Responses to this "thought-listing" question ranged widely. Nevertheless, it was possible to separate explanatory statements from other categories with a high degree of reliability.[3] Statements were coded as explanatory if they made reference to antecedent causes of the target issue either specifically ("If people would try harder to find work, we would all be better off") or vaguely ("Society screws the poor; the rich get richer, the poor poorer"). Later in the questionnaire, participants were asked to identify what they considered to be "the major causes of ____." The thought-listing method was designed to provide evidence on the spontaneity of causal reasoning; the "most-important-causes" question identifies the specific content of causal beliefs.

Study 1: Poverty

We established five experimental conditions. In the first condition *(national poverty)*, participants watched a news story that documented the increase in poverty nationwide and the significant reductions in the scope of federal social-welfare programs under the Reagan administration. In the second condition *(high unemployment)*, participants watched a story that juxtaposed the national unemployment rate with the size of the federal budget deficit. The three remaining conditions all framed poverty in terms of particular instances or victims of economic hardship. The first *(the high cost of heat)* portrayed two families unable to pay their heating bills. The second *(the homeless)* focused on homeless individuals—two black teenagers living on the streets of New York City, and a white couple forced to live in their car in San Diego.[4] Finally, the third case-study condition *(unemployed worker)* described the financial difficulties facing the family of an unemployed auto worker in Ohio. These case-study stories were edited so as to be entirely descriptive; the news stories simply presented the predicament of each victim.

Results

The results of the "thought-listing" procedure revealed quite clearly that causal attributions of poverty figure prominently in participants' store of information. Participants listed a total of 322 thoughts, of which 124 (39%) represented explanatory statements. The causes people cited most often fell into five categories—inadequate motivation, poor education and inadequate skills, welfare dependence, the economy in general, and governmental actions/inactions. Even allowing for the possibility that respondents may have thought of these antecedent factors only in a loose causal sense, it is still impressive that explanatory thoughts take precedence over evaluations or feelings. Respondents were much more likely to offer reasons for poverty than affective reactions.

Turning to the "most-important-causes" question, the categories of causes parallel perfectly those that emerged from the thought-listing question. . . . Participants were far from mystified by the question—a total of 189 causes were cited, for an average of 2.2 per person. Virtually every respondent mentioned at least one cause (98%), and their responses were remarkably homogeneous in that five categories accounted for almost all the responses (183 out of 189). . . .

. . . Causal beliefs were significantly molded by the manner in which the news framed poverty. After watching accounts of specific homeless people, participants were especially drawn to poor motivation or inadequate skills as causal factors. After watching the news story that documented trends in the national poverty rate and federal spending on social programs, participants were especially drawn to economic and governmental/societal factors. If we combine the two systemic response categories (*economy* and *government*), the proportion of systemic attributions ranges from .33 in the *homeless* condition to .81 in the *high unemployment* condition. Conversely, the proportion of dispositional attributions (*motivation, skills,* and *culture*) ranges from a low of .17 in the *high unemployment* condition to a high of .69 in the *homeless* condition.

Framing poverty in terms of individual victims did not always draw individuals to dispositional accounts of poverty. The homeless, the unemployed, and those unable to afford heat all represent people facing economic difficulties, yet they elicit very different explanations of poverty. The type of victim makes a difference. While the homeless trigger personal or dispositional attributions, people unable to pay their utility bills elicit a preponderance of economic and societal attributions, with the unemployed worker falling in between, eliciting a relatively even mix of societal and dispositional attributions.

. . . [T]hese results drive home the point that explanations of poverty depend considerably upon the particular informational context in which poverty is encountered. When poverty is framed as a societal outcome, people point to societal or governmental explanations; when poverty is framed in terms of particular victims of poverty, particularly the homeless, people point instead to dispositional explanations.

To assess whether these framing effects withstand controls for built-in or chronic differences in causal beliefs, the analysis incorporated individuals' socioeconomic status, partisanship and approval of presidential performance, issue opinions, and degree of political involvement. It computed two indexes corresponding to the number of systemic *(governmental* and *economy)* and dispositional *(motivation, skills,* and *culture)* causes mentioned and subjected them to a multiple-regression analysis. . . .

The effects of the framing manipulations emerged relatively unscathed after taking into account longstanding individual differences in causal beliefs.[5] . . .

In sum, though causal knowledge is embedded in individuals' socioeconomic circumstances and partisan attitudes, media frames affect this knowledge independently of these antecedents. When the media direct individuals' attention to national outcomes, explanations for poverty become predominantly systemic; when the media point to particular instances of poor people, explanations for poverty become predominantly dispositional.

The final analysis assesses whether explanations for poverty spill over to evaluations of the president. Specifically, the question was whether individuals who understand poverty as a societal or governmental outcome are less apt to praise President Reagan's performance. In this analysis the reverse possibility must also be considered, since supporters of President Reagan systematically discount systemic causes when asked to account for poverty. . . .

Systemic explanations of poverty exerted powerful effects on participants' ratings of Reagan's overall performance even after controlling for the effects of partisanship, ratings of his performance in the specific issue areas of arms control, the budget deficit, and unemployment, assessments of his competence and integrity, and the reverse effects of his overall performance. . . .

Study 2: Unemployment

Three conditions were established, each providing a different perspective on unemployment. Two of the conditions were taken from the first study—*high unemployment* and *unemployed worker.* The former represents a systemic frame with the focus on the national unemployment rate, while the latter is a case study of a particular victim of unemployment. In between these two extremes was a third level of coverage describing the serious economic difficulties facing the U.S. steel industry. The expectation was that this presentation would trigger *the economy* as the dominant reference point. (Note that all three conditions featured the identical "lead-in" by the newscaster, who noted the persistence of high unemployment.) In all other respects, the procedures and method were identical to those of Study 1.

Results

As was the case with poverty, causal attributions were offered spontaneously. The 40 subjects listed a total of 110 thoughts on unemployment, of which 40 took the form of causal attributions. . . . [T]he framing manipulations had no impact on the relative prominence of economic (or any other) causes. In fact, explanations of unemployment stand in marked contrast to explanations of poverty. While the former is understood uniformly as a systemic problem regardless of the news frame, the latter is seen as having a mix of both systemic and dispositional causes, the precise composition of the mix being significantly influenced by media presentations.

Even though participants' causal beliefs were unaffected by the framing manipulation, these beliefs did carry over to evaluations of President Reagan. . . .

The more dispositional the attribution, the more positive the rating of President Reagan's overall performance. This effect was uncontaminated by any feedback from the Reagan performance ratings because ratings of Reagan's overall performance had no effect on the number of either dispositional or systemic causes for unemployment. Respondents who cited more systemic attributions did tend to be less supportive of the president, but this relationship did not quite attain conventional levels of statistical significance.

Study 3: Terrorism

The target issue in this study was terrorism. The stimulus event was the June 1985 hijacking of TWA Flight 847 and the subsequent hostage drama in Beirut. Following the release of the hostages, all three networks aired detailed recapitulations of the crisis. One such story (ABC's) was edited into three very different versions. The first condition *(U.S. role)* viewed the hijacking incident as a protest against the United States. The U.S. role in the region as the principal ally of Israel was noted as was the hijackers' demands that Israel release the Shiites being held prisoners. President Reagan was shown declaring that the U.S. would never concede to terrorists. The second condition *(local politics)* shifted the focus to the internal politics of Lebanon. The report traced the history of Amal, the Shiite organization holding the hostages, and described its political ideology and its efforts to gain a power base in Beirut. The third condition *(hostages released)* showed the hostages saying goodby to each other prior to their release. Red Cross officials were interviewed regarding the state of the hostages' health and their treatment during captivity. The hostages were then shown arriving in Damascus. Finally, unlike the earlier studies, a control condition was added in which subjects saw no story on the target issue, that is, subjects watched the identical videotape without the story on the hijacking.

Results

As usual, participants were asked to list the things they thought about when they heard or read about terrorism. The 92 participants mentioned a total of 201 thoughts. Cause and effect were prominent in the thoughts listed. Many participants explicitly raised causal *inquiries* (e.g., "Why do people do things like this?"). Causal attributions were also frequent, the most common being dispositional—terrorists as fanatics, deranged extremists, and so on. Terrorism was also traced to situational causes including local political disputes, U.S. policy toward the Middle East, and the support provided terrorist groups by radical leaders such as Colonel Qaddaffi. Causal inquiries and attributions together accounted for 31% of all thoughts. All told, the distribution of responses to the thought-listing question maintained the pattern established in the first two studies, namely, that causal attributions (and questions) are offered spontaneously when individuals think about political issues.

What did participants consider to be the prime causes of terrorism, and to what degree were their causal attributions susceptible to framing effects? Three classes of attributions dominated responses to the "most-important-causes" question. *Dispositional* attributions trace terrorism to personal traits, particularly extremism, fanaticism, and a craving for recognition. *Situational* attributions cover characteristics of the immediate situation and range from general political instability, to governmental oppression, to poverty and injustice. *Policy* attributions encompass actions of the U.S. government, including support for Israel and opposition to the Arab or Palestinian cause, Israeli dominance, and concerted efforts (primarily by "communists") to weaken the U.S. These three broad categories accounted for 175 of the 198 causes mentioned.

. . . Dispositional attributions tended to be greatest in the *U.S. role* condition, followed closely by the condition in which there was no media frame *(hostages released)*. More in keeping with expectations, situational attributions were most frequent in the *local politics* condition (which differed significantly from the *U.S. role* and *hostages released* conditions). Contrary to expectations, individuals given no news of terrorism tended to attribute terrorism to situational rather than dispositional factors. Finally, framing the hijacking as an act of protest against the U.S. did raise the proportion of policy attributions.

. . . [P]articipants were asked to indicate (on a five-point scale) the degree to which they approved or disapproved of the president's performance in dealing with terrorism (this study did not include the question on the president's overall performance).

Both policy and dispositional attributions affected ratings of the president's performance, but in opposite directions. The greater the number of policy attributions, the more critical the terrorism performance rating. This effect was substantial, despite having been purged of the reciprocal influence of participants' evaluations of the president's performance. It was also independent of partisanship, issue opinions, race, gender, and a measure of political interest. The number of dispositional attributions also affected participants' ratings of the president's performance: the more dispositional one's understanding of terrorism, the more positive the rating. This effect, however, was noticeably weaker than that exerted by policy attributions.

To sum up, attributions for terrorism are influenced by the perspectives television news presentations impose on terrorist acts. When these acts are placed in the context of a local political situation, situational attributions predominate; when terrorism is framed as a protest against the U.S., policy and dispositional attributions come to the forefront of individuals' explanations. Finally, as was true for poverty and unemployment, explanations for terrorism are relevant to evaluations of the president, in this case to ratings of the president's performance in regard to terrorism.

Conclusion

People can and do explain the issues and events they encounter in the world of public affairs. These explanations are politically consequential, for they can be and are integrated with evaluations of the incumbent president. The more individuals attribute problems to structural or systemic causes, the more critical they are of President Reagan's performance.

Individuals are quite sensitive to contextual cues when they reason about national affairs. Their explanations of issues like terrorism or poverty are critically dependent upon the particular reference points furnished in media presentations. Whether terrorists are seen as protesting U.S. actions or as attempting to strengthen their political influence has the effect of invoking very different attributions of terrorism. Similarly, whether news about poverty takes the form of particular victims or of nationwide outcomes makes a difference to viewers' attributions of poverty.

The exception to this pattern is unemployment, where attributions are heavily systemic regardless of the media frame used. It may be that the term *unemployment* is itself a sort of semantic frame or wording effect that directs individuals to think of the concept as a collective rather than individual outcome. Asking people to explain "why John Smith was laid off" or "why so many Americans are out of work" may elicit a different set of attributions. Alternatively, the sustained prominence of economic problems in the nation's political rhetoric and policy agenda during the past decade may have served to alert individuals to *the economy* as a catchall cause for unemployment.

It is important to qualify these results by noting the short time interval between the experimental manipulation and the elicitation of participants' causal beliefs. The framing effects may wear off rapidly. As yet I have no evidence bearing on the question of persistence. However, the identical experimental design yielded significant delayed effects (up to a week following exposure to the treatment) on participants' responses to an open-ended question concerning "the most important problems facing the nation" (see Iyengar and Kinder 1987, chap. 3).

All told, these results suggest that it is important to document the degree to which particular media frames are more or less dominant in news coverage of current issues. To take the case of poverty, the tendency of the U.S. public to see the causes of poverty as lying within the poor themselves may be due not only to dominant cultural values like individualism and self-reliance (as argued by Feldman 1983; Kluegel and Smith 1986), but also to news coverage of poverty in which images of poor people predominate. This is in fact the case with television news coverage of poverty, where close-up depictions of personal experience far outnumber depictions of poverty that are societal or nationwide in emphasis. I have examined every story in the *CBS Evening News* from January 1981 through December 1985 that made reference to "welfare," "social programs," "poor people," "hunger," and other such referents of poverty. Ninety-eight stories contained material relevant to poverty, of which 56 (57%) presented a particular victim. The figure is actually higher if 1981 is excluded, since that was the year of the pitched battles between the Reagan administration and the Democratic Congress on appropriations for social programs, thus resulting in an abnormally high number of government-oriented poverty stories. For the 1982-85 period, the percentage of case study stories is 68. U.S. citizens who watched *CBS Evening News* during the period would, understandably, have been drawn to dispositional accounts of poverty, whatever social and economic values they subscribed to. At this point, I can only offer the pervasiveness of case-study coverage as a plausible cause of public beliefs. I do have evidence, however, that the degree to which particular issues are seen as *national* problems is significantly lowered when issue coverage takes the form of the "particular-victim" scenario. Specifically, Kinder and I found that when network news coverage of both pollution and unemployment focused on individuals or families adversely affected by either issue, viewers were less likely to come away believing that either pollution or unemployment were important national problems (Iyengar and Kinder 1987, chap. 4).

The political implications of the "particular-victim" media frame are unmistakable. Citizens' causal attributions will fix upon dispositional rather than structural factors. This is naturally beneficial to the incumbent president—people are less likely to treat the administration and its actions as causal agents. President Reagan's concern in 1982, at the height of the recession, that the networks were providing too much coverage of people who had lost their jobs ("Is it news that some fellow out in South Succotash has just been laid off and that he should be interviewed nationwide?") seems misplaced. In light of the results reported here, the White House should encourage such coverage, for it has the effect of shielding the president from any culpability, deserved or otherwise. . . .

Notes

1. The focus on television news is justified, for it is the most preferred source of public-affairs information for the great majority of the U.S. public (see Bower 1985).

2. In any experimental procedure it is imperative that the researcher guard against the effects of demand characteristics—cues in the experimental situation that suggest to participants what is expected of them. Several such precautions were undertaken including a plausible cover story that disguised the true purpose of the study. In addition, the treatment stories were compiled using studio-quality editing equipment so that participants could not know that the stories had been altered. Finally, the aura of the research laboratory was minimized by inviting participants to bring a spouse, friend, or colleague with them. Most did so and the average session size of two means that a participant typically watched the videotape with someone he or she knew. The concern over experimental demand also dictated the choice of a posttest-only design. Had I asked participants for their explanations of the target issue both before and after exposure to the videotape, this would have provided them with a powerful cue as to the researcher's intent, thereby affecting the posttest responses.

3. Responses fell into four general categories: explanations, prescriptions/remedies, descriptions, and expressions of affect. Using this four-fold classification, two independent coders agreed more than 90% of the time.

4. These were initially separate conditions, as we wished to investigate the effects, if any, of the victim's race. In this particular study, the two conditions elicited responses not significantly different. For purposes of this analysis, therefore, they were merged.

5. In this analysis and those that follow, the remaining attributional categories are included in the equation as control variables. This is because the number of causes falling into a particular category inevitably reduces the number falling into other categories.

References

Bower, Robert. 1985. *The Changing Television Audience in America*. New York: Columbia University Press.

Feldman, Stanley. 1983. Economic Individualism and American Public Opinion. *American Politics Quarterly* 11:3-29.

Iyengar, Shanto, and Donald Kinder. 1987. *News That Matters: Television and American Opinion*. Chicago: University of Chicago Press.

Kahneman, Daniel, Paul Slovic, and Amos Tversky. 1982. *Judgment under Uncertainty: Heuristics and Biases*. London: Cambridge University Press.

Kahneman, Daniel, and Amos Tversky. 1982. The Psychology of Preferences. *Scientific American* 246:136-42.

Kelley, Harold. 1973. The Processes of Causal Attribution. *American Psychologist* 28:107-28.

Kluegel, James, and Eliot Smith. 1986. *Beliefs about Inequality*. New York: Aldine.

Langer, Ellen. 1975. The Illusion of Control. *Journal of Personality and Social Psychology* 32:311-28.

Nisbett, Richard, and Lee Ross. 1980. *Human Inference: Strategies and Shortcomings of Social Judgment*. Englewood Cliffs, N.J.: Prentice-Hall.

Schneider, David, Albert Hastorf, and Phoebe Ellsworth. 1979. *Person Perception*. Reading: Addison-Wesley.

Thaler, Richard. 1980. Toward a Positive Theory of Consumer Choice. *Journal of Economic Behavior and Organization* 1:39-60.

Weiner, Bernard. 1985. "Spontaneous" Causal Search. *Psychological Bulletin* 97:74-94.

Wortman, Camille. 1976. Causal Attributions and Personal Control, in *New Directions in Attribution Research*, vol. 1, eds. John Harvey, William Ickes, and Robert Kidd. Hillsdale, N.J.: Lawrence Erlbaum.

2.6 ■■■■■

Charting the Mainstream: Television's Contributions to Political Orientations

George Gerbner, Larry Gross, Michael Morgan, and Nancy Signorielli

Editor's Note. The authors contend that television entertainment programs mold the perceptions of reality held by "heavy viewers" (those who watch television four or more hours a day) in socially undesirable ways. Television buffs become hard-line conservatives on civil rights issues and put their personal economic well-being ahead of the public's economic welfare.

The selection reports findings from the Cultural Indicators project conducted since 1967 at the Annenberg School of Communications at the University of Pennsylvania. Investigators associated with the project have recorded and analyzed week-long samples of network television dramas each year to establish the kind of world pictured there. They call this approach "message system analysis." Then, in their "cultivation analysis," they have questioned viewers to assess to what degree their perceptions mirror either the television world or the real world, as measured by official records.

The authors compare three demographically matched categories of viewers: light viewers (25 percent), who watch less than two hours of television daily; heavy viewers (30 percent), who watch four or more hours daily; and an intermediate group of viewers (45 percent). The differences in views among these groups constitute the "cultivation differential."

Cultivation analysis findings have been challenged on methodological and philosophical grounds. Specifically, critics have alleged that viewers have been grouped improperly and that the research team has misjudged the ways in which media audiences relate the media world to the real world. Still, the major point made by cultivation analysis remains intact: media images are noticeably reflected in public thinking.

At the time of writing, the authors were members of the Cultural Indicators research team at the Annenberg School of Communications at the University of Pennsylvania. Senior author George Gerbner was dean of the Annenberg School. The selection is from *Journal of Communication* 32 (1982): 100-127. Several tables have been omitted.

Reprinted and abridged from *Journal of Communication* 32, no. 2 (1982): 100-127. Reprinted by permission of Oxford University Press.

. . . Television is a centralized system of storytelling. Its drama, commercials, news, and other programs bring a relatively coherent world of common images and messages into every viewing home. People are now born into the symbolic environment of television and live with its repetitive lessons throughout life. Television cultivates from the outset the very predispositions that affect future cultural selections and uses. Transcending historic barriers of literacy and mobility, television has become the primary common source of everyday culture of an otherwise heterogeneous population.

Many of those now dependent upon television have never before been part of a shared national political culture. Television provides, perhaps for the first time since preindustrial religion, a strong cultural link, a shared daily ritual of highly compelling and informative content, between the elites and all other publics. What is the role of this common experience in the general socialization and political orientation of Americans? . . .

. . . Despite the fact that nearly half of the national income goes to the top fifth of the real population, the myth of [the] middle class as the all-American norm dominates the world of television. Nearly 7 out of 10 television characters appear in the "middle-middle" of a five-way classification system. Most of them are professionals and managers. Blue-collar and service work occupies 67 percent of all Americans but only 10 percent of television characters. These features of the world of prime-time television should cultivate a middle-class or "average" income self-designation among viewers.

Men outnumber women at least three to one. Most women attend to men or home (and appliances) and are younger (but age faster) than the men they meet. Underrepresentation in the world of television suggests the cultivation of viewers' acceptance of more limited life chances, a more limited range of activities, and more rigidly stereotyped images than for the dominant and more fully represented social and dramatic types.

Young people (under 18) comprise one-third and older people (over 65) one-fifth of their true proportion in the population. Blacks on television represent three-fourths and Hispanics one-third of their share of the U.S. population, and a disproportionate number are minor rather than major characters. A single program like "Hawaii Five-O" can result in the overrepresentation of Orientals, but again mostly as minor characters. A study by Wiegel and others (11) shows that while blacks appear in many programs and commercials, they seldom appear with whites, and actually interact with whites in only about two percent of total human appearance time. The prominent and stable overrepresentation of well-to-do white males in the prime of life dominates prime time. Television's general demography bears greater resemblance to the facts of consumer spending than to the U.S. Census (5, 6). These facts and dynamics of life suggest the cultivation of a relatively restrictive view of women's and minority rights among viewers.

The state in the world of prime time acts mostly to fend off threats to law and order in a mean and dangerous world. Enforcing the law of that world takes nearly three times as many characters as the number of all blue-collar and service worker characters. The typical viewer of an average week's prime-time programs sees realistic and often intimate (but usually not true-to-life) representations of the life and work of 30 police officers, 7 lawyers, and 3 judges, but only one engineer or scientist and very few blue-collar workers. Nearly everybody appears to be comfortably managing on an "average" income or as a member of a "middle class."

But threats abound. Crime in prime time is at least 10 times as rampant as in the real world. An average of five to six acts of overt physical violence per hour involves over half of all major characters. Yet, pain, suffering, and medical help rarely follow this mayhem. Symbolic violence demonstrates power; it shows victimization, not just aggression, hurt but not therapy; it shows who can get away with what against whom. The dominant white males in the prime of life score highest on the "safety scale": they are the most likely to be the victimizers rather than the victims. Conversely, old, young, and minority women, and young boys, are the most likely to be the victims rather than the victimizers in violent conflicts. . . .

The warped demography of the television world cultivates some iniquitous concepts of the norms of social life. Except among the most traditional or biased, television viewing tends to go with stronger prejudices about women and old people (5, 6, 7, 9). Children know more about uncommon occupations frequently portrayed on television than about common jobs rarely seen on the screen (1). Viewing boosts the confidence rating given to doctors (10) but depresses that given to scientists, especially in groups that otherwise support them most (4).

Cultivation studies continue to confirm the findings that viewing tends to heighten perceptions of danger and risk and maintain an exaggerated sense of mistrust, vulnerability, and insecurity. We have also found that the prime-time power hierarchy of relative levels of victimization cultivates similar hierarchies of fears of real-world victimization among viewers. Those minority group viewers who see themselves more often on the losing end of violent encounters on television are more apprehensive of their own victimization than are the light viewers in the same groups (8). Television's mean and dangerous world can thus be expected to contribute to receptivity to repressive measures and to apparently simple, tough, hard-line posturing and "solutions." At the same time, however, the overall context of conventional values and consumer gratifications, with their requirements of happy endings and material satisfaction, may suggest a sense of entitlement to goods and services, setting up a conflict of perspectives.

Thus we can expect the cultivation of preference for "middle-of-the-road" political orientations alongside different and at times contradictory, assumptions. These assumptions are likely to include demographically skewed, socially rigid and mistrustful, and often excessively anxious or repressive notions, but expansive expectations for economic services and material progress even among those who traditionally do not share such views. . . .

. . . [T]elevision alters the social significance and political meaning of . . . conventional labels. An example of this transformation is the blurring of class lines and the self-styled "averaging" of income differences. . . . [This] shows that low socioeconomic status (SES) respondents are most likely to call themselves "working class"—but only when they are light viewers. Heavy-viewing respondents of the same low-status group are significantly less likely than their light-viewing counterparts to think of themselves as "working class" and more likely to say they are "middle class." The television experience seems to counter other circumstances in thinking of one's class. It is an especially powerful deterrent to working-class consciousness.

Middle SES viewers show the least sense of class distinction at different viewing levels. They are already "in" the mainstream. The high SES group, however, like the low SES group, exhibits a response pattern that is strongly associated with amount of television viewing. . . . Television viewing tends to blur class distinctions and make more affluent heavy viewers think of themselves as just working people of average income.

These processes show up clearly when we relate television viewing to labels of direct political relevance. We used a relatively general and presumably stable designation of political tendency, most likely to structure a range of political attitudes and positions: the self-designations "liberal," "moderate," and "conservative." We are assuming that . . . most of us locate political positions on a continuum ranging from liberal to conservative (if not farther in either direction), owing in part to the generally accepted and commonplace use of these terms in interpersonal and mass media discourse. Consequently, unlike many things respondents might be asked about, we believe that these self-designations have a prior existence and are not created in response to the interview situation.

. . . The most general relationship between television viewing and political tendency is that significantly more heavy than light viewers in all subgroups call themselves moderates and significantly fewer call themselves conservatives. The number of liberals also declines slightly among heavy viewers, except where there are fewest liberals (e.g., among Republicans). [This] illustrates the absorption of divergent tendencies and the blending of political distinctions into the "television mainstream." [1]

On the surface, mainstreaming appears to be a "centering"—even a "liberalizing"—of political and other tendencies. After all, as viewing increases, the percent of conservatives drops significantly within every group (except Democrats), and the relationships of amount of television viewing with the percent of liberals are generally weaker. However, a closer look at the actual positions taken in response to questions about political issues such as minorities, civil and personal rights, free speech, the economy, etc., shows that the mainstream does not always mean "middle of the road." . . .

. . . [A]ssociations between amount of viewing and these attitudes are sharply different for liberals, moderates, and conservatives. Liberals, who are least likely to hold segregationist views, show some dramatic (and always significant) associations between amount of viewing and the desire to keep blacks and whites separate. Among moderates and conservatives, in contrast, the relationships between viewing and these attitudes are smaller and inconsistent. . . . On busing, moderates and conservatives even show a significant negative association, indicating *less* segregationist attitudes among these heavy viewers; this is an instance of viewing bringing divergent groups closer together from both directions.

In general, these patterns vividly illustrate mainstreaming. There are, to be sure, some across-the-board relationships, but even these are markedly weaker for moderates and conservatives. Overall, these data show a convergence and homogenization of heavy viewers across political groups.

The differences between liberals and conservatives—i.e., the effects of political tendency on attitudes toward blacks—decrease among heavy viewers. Among light viewers, liberals and conservatives show an average difference of 15.4 percentage points; yet, among heavy viewers, liberals and conservatives differ by an average of only 4.6 percentage points ($t = 4.54$, $p < .01$).

Figure 1 shows the mainstreaming pattern for three of these items. In the first, opposition to busing, we can see that heavy-viewing conservatives are more "liberal" and heavy-viewing liberals more "conservative" than their respective light-viewing counterparts. In the second instance, opposition to open housing laws, viewing is not associated with any differences in the attitudes expressed by conservatives, but among liberals we see that heavy viewing goes with a greater likelihood of such opposition. Finally, in response to a question about laws against marriages between blacks and whites, we find that heavy viewers in all groups are more likely to favor these laws than are light viewers in the same categories, but this is significantly more pronounced for liberals.

In sum, the responses of heavy-viewing liberals are quite comparable to those of all moderates and conservatives, and there is not much

Figure 1   Television Viewing and Attitudes about Blacks, by Political
Self-Designation

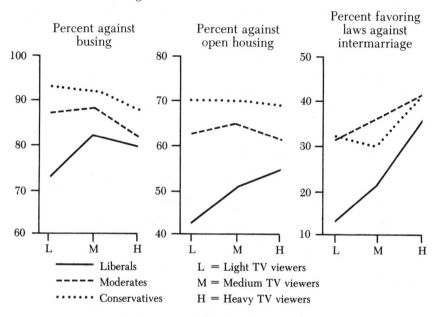

difference between moderates and conservatives. The television mainstream, in terms of attitudes toward blacks, clearly runs to the right.

Many of the fiercest political battles of the past decade have been
fought on the nation's "home front"—around a group of so-called moral
issues which have sharply divided liberal and conservative forces. We find
liberals confronting conservatives over the propriety, morality, and even
legality of personal behavior. The fights involving reproductive freedom,
the rights of sexual minorities, and the Equal Rights Amendment have
become a focus of that confrontation.

. . . In the case of attitudes on homosexuality, abortion, and mari-
juana, there is considerable spread between light-viewing liberals and
light-viewing conservatives (an average of 28 percentage points); the
latter are always much more likely to be opposed. And, once again, the
attitudes of heavy-viewing liberals and conservatives are far closer
together (an average of 13 percentage points; t=16.6, p<.01), due
primarily to the difference between light- and heavy-viewing liberals. . . .
In all instances, the self-designated moderates are much closer to the
conservatives than they are to the liberals. . . .

. . . [T]elevision's relationship to anti-Communist sentiments and to
the tendency to restrict free speech . . . shows the familiar pattern. . . .
Five out of ten light-viewing moderates and six out of ten light-viewing

conservatives consider communism "the worst form [of government] of all." Heavy-viewing moderates and conservatives nearly unite in condemning communism as "worst" by even larger margins (64 and 67 percent, respectively). But viewing makes the biggest difference among liberals: only one-third of light-viewing but half of heavy-viewing liberals agree that communism is "the worst form" of government. . . .

Responses on restricting free speech show similar patterns. Heavy viewers of all three political persuasions are more likely to agree to restrict, in various ways, the speech of "left" and "right" nonconformists than are their light-viewing counterparts. There is little difference between conservatives and moderates. But, again, the most striking difference is between light- and heavy-viewing liberals.

In general, with respect to anti-communism and restrictions on political speech of the left and right, those who call themselves conservatives are in the "television mainstream." Those who consider themselves moderates join the conservatives—or exceed them—as heavy viewers. Liberals perform their traditional role of defending political plurality and freedom of speech only when they are light viewers. Mainstreaming means not only a narrowing of political differences but also a significant tilt in the political balance.

But political drift to the right is not the full story. As we noted before, television has a business clientele which, while it may be politically conservative, also has a mission to perform that requires the cultivation of consumer values and gratifications pulling in a different direction.

A number of surveys have documented the tendency of respondents to support government services that benefit them while taking increasingly hard-line positions on taxes, equality, crime, and other issues that touch deeply felt anxieties and insecurities. The media interpreted (and election results seemed to confirm, at least in the early 1980s) these inherently contradictory positions as a "conservative trend" (2). Television may have contributed to that trend in two ways. First . . . , heavy viewers have a keener sense of living in a "mean world" with greater hazards and insecurities than do comparable groups of light viewers (3, 8). Second, while television does not directly sway viewers to be conservative (in fact, heavy viewers tend to shun that label), its mainstream of apparent moderation shifts political attitudes toward conservative positions.

When positions on economic issues are examined, however, a different if perhaps complementary pattern emerges. . . . We examined patterns of responses to questions about government spending on 11 programs. . . . Seven are traditional "liberal" issues: health, environment, cities, education, foreign aid, welfare, and blacks. . . .

Here, instead of heavy-viewing liberals taking positions closer to conservatives, the opposite happens: heavy-viewing conservatives, as well as moderates, converge toward the liberal position on six of the seven issues. The more they watch, the less they say the U.S. spends "too much." On these six issues, the average distance of 16 percentage points between liberal and conservative light viewers is only 9 percentage points for heavy viewers, with conservatives accounting for most of the convergence ($t=8.2$, $p<.001$). The exception is the relatively distant issue of foreign aid.

The remaining four issues are crime, drugs, defense, and space exploration. . . . Here again, with the exception of space, heavy viewers generally want to spend more. As these are somewhat more "conservative" issues, it is the moderates and conservatives who are in the "television mainstream," taking a position toward greater spending, and heavy-viewing liberals stand close to them. On these four issues an average liberal-conservative spread of nearly 10 percentage points for light viewers compares with a gap of 4 percentage points among heavy viewers ($t=2.2$, $p<.12$).

To investigate further the populist streak in the otherwise restrictive political mix of the typology of the heavy viewer, we looked for . . . respondents who oppose reductions in government spending and yet feel their taxes are too high. . . . [H]eavy viewers are more likely to express this contradictory position in every subgroup (although the relationship remains significant at $p<.05$ only overall and within six of these groups). . . .

As on the other economic issues, liberals and moderates are close together while heavy-viewing conservatives join the liberal-moderate mainstream; the tilt is in the liberal (if conflicted) direction. Heavy-viewing Republicans and Independents also express attitudes closer to the Democratic position than do their light-viewing political counterparts. But all heavy viewers are more likely to want a combination of more social spending *and* lower taxes. . . .

Our analysis shows that although television viewing brings conservatives, moderates, and liberals closer together, it is the liberal position that is weakest among heavy viewers. Viewing blurs traditional differences, blends them into a more homogeneous mainstream, and bends the mainstream toward a "hard line" position on issues dealing with minorities and personal rights. Hard-nosed commercial populism, with its mix of restrictive conservatism and pork-chop liberalism, is the paradoxical—and potentially volatile—contribution of television to political orientations.

The "television mainstream" may be the true twentieth-century melting pot of the American people. The mix it creates is of central significance for the theory as well as the practice of popular self-government. If our charting of the mainstream is generally valid, basic assumptions about political orientations, the media, and the democratic process need to be reviewed and revised to fit the age of television.

Note

1. . . . [T]his moderating effect seems to be a specific correlate of television viewing, and not a general media exposure phenomenon: neither radio listening nor newspaper reading are associated with similar results. . . .

References

1. DeFleur, Melvin L. and Lois B. DeFleur. "The Relative Contribution of Television as a Learning Source for Children's Occupational Knowledge." *American Sociological Review* 32, 1967, pp. 777-789.
2. Entman, Robert M. and David L. Paletz. "Media and the Conservative Myth." *Journal of Communication* 30(4), Autumn 1980, pp. 154-165.
3. Gerbner, George, Larry Gross, Michael Morgan, and Nancy Signorielli. "The 'Mainstreaming' of America: Violence Profile No. 11." *Journal of Communication* 30(3), Summer 1980, pp. 10-29.
4. Gerbner, George, Larry Gross, Michael Morgan, and Nancy Signorielli. "Scientists on the TV Screen." *Society* 18(4), May/June 1981, pp. 41-44.
5. Gerbner, George, Larry Gross, Nancy Signorielli, and Michael Morgan. "Aging with Television: Images on Television Drama and Conceptions of Social Reality." *Journal of Communication* 30(1), Winter 1980, pp. 37-47.
6. Gerbner, George and Nancy Signorielli. "Women and Minorities in Television Drama 1969-1978." The Annenberg School of Communications, University of Pennsylvania, 1979.
7. Morgan, Michael. "Longitudinal Patterns of Television Viewing and Adolescent Role Socialization." Unpublished Ph.D dissertation, University of Pennsylvania, 1980.
8. Morgan, Michael. "Symbolic Victimization and Real-World Fear." Paper presented at the Symposium on Cultural Indicators for the Comparative Study of Culture, Vienna, Austria, February 1982.
9. Signorielli, Nancy. "Television's Contribution to Sex Role Socialization." Paper presented at the Seventh Annual Telecommunications Policy Research Conference, Skytop, Pennsylvania, April 1979.
10. Volgy, Thomas J. and John E. Schwarz. "TV Entertainment Programming and Sociopolitical Attitudes." *Journalism Quarterly* 57(1), 1980, pp. 150-155.
11. Weigel, Russel H., James W. Loomis, and Matthew J. Soja. "Race Relations on Prime Time Television." *Journal of Personality and Social Psychology* 39(5), 1980, pp. 884-893.

3. INFLUENCING ELECTION OUTCOMES

In no area of public life have practicing politicians taken media effects more seriously than in the area of elections. Political campaign organizations spend much time, effort, and money to attract favorable media attention to candidates for major electoral offices. When their candidates lose, they frequently blame the tone of media coverage or the lack of adequate media coverage. Because vigorous, information-rich electoral contests are essential to the democratic process, scholars regularly have put the activities of involved parties, including the media, under the microscope.

The readings in this section deal with the images that media create for political candidates. Selections depict the difficulties campaign staffs and newspeople encounter in covering elections. They also record what types of coverage spell victory or defeat for political contenders. Dean E. Alger's essay sets the stage. It summarizes and critiques the findings of major recent research and presents an overview of the many types of questions that scholars of media influence on campaigns have pursued.

There is an old saying that "there is many a slip 'twixt the cup and the lip." It is one thing for politicians to try to create a particular image and another for that image to be conveyed to newspeople and, through them, to the voting public. Can candidates control the media coverage they receive? Two essays representing the views of practitioners in the field shed light on this issue. F. Christopher Arterton interviewed campaign managers and press secretaries during the 1976 presidential contest. He chronicles how campaign staffs work to gain attention and publicity from the media so that candidates will attract financial support, sustain the morale of their campaign volunteers, and, ultimately, win elections. David Nyhan explains how campaign journalism looks from the perspective of a reporter on a major urban newspaper. Many conflicting pressures must be faced, but the ultimate control is reporters' desire for peer approval. In a rare display of professional self-criticism, Nyhan lays bare some of the faults in news coverage, tempering his negative remarks with a good deal of solid praise.

Thomas E. Patterson dissects the major role that media play in presenting every phase of the campaign as a horse-race scenario. In primary contests, in daily routines, in debates, and in public opinion polls, newspeople always designate winners and losers. Although the supporting evidence for these judgments may be flimsy, the designation nonetheless provides winners with tremendous momentum and drags losers to defeat. Martin Schram focuses on the crucial role that television has come to play in presidential campaigns. He considers it the candidates' most powerful campaign tool. If candidates excel in front of the cameras, good visuals become a teflon coat that wards off the effects of harsh verbal commentary.

The final selection focuses on media coverage of congressional races. Although presidential elections remain by far the chief event in election coverage, interest in congressional election coverage has been growing. Timothy E. Cook explains the significance of media publicity in the representative's district, contrasting it with the role of the national media. The effect of election coverage, Cook notes, may last far beyond election day. A legislator whose pet projects have received favorable commentary during the campaign may find it easier to win legislative battles in the postelection years.

3.1 ▰▰▰▰▰

The Media in Elections:
Evidence on the Role and the Impact

Dean E. Alger

Editor's Note. The impact of mass media coverage on elections has received more attention from political scientists than any other media topic. In this essay, Dean E. Alger reviews and critiques the major studies of election news. He reports findings about the subject matter of news stories, the manner of framing to stress conflict, and the delight with which reporters pounce on candidates' errors and slips of the tongue.

Alger also comments on the significant influence of election coverage on the parties' choice of nominees and the equally significant influence of omissions of important stories. He analyzes the distorting effects of heaping coverage on the winners of the early primaries and caucuses, and he questions the wisdom of gauging winning and losing by scales based on comparisons of expectations with actual outcomes, rather than on the outcomes alone. On the whole, Alger finds the quality of coverage predictably wanting, leaving the public's information supply inadequate when judged by the canons of democratic government.

Alger is associate professor of political science at Moorhead State University in Minnesota. He has written numerous articles analyzing the media's role in politics and has served regularly as news analyst for a network-affiliated television news station. The selection is taken from "The Media in Elections: Evidence on the Role and the Impact," in *The Media and Politics* (Englewood Cliffs, N.J.: Prentice-Hall, 1989), 201-230.

Media Coverage of Presidential Elections and Campaign Response

Nature of Coverage: The Patterson Evidence

Striking patterns of media coverage of the nomination process have been found. The most comprehensive and systematic study is that

From Dean E. Alger, *The Media in Politics,* © 1989, pp. 201-230. Reprinted by permission of Prentice-Hall, Inc.

reported in Thomas Patterson's *The Mass Media Election*. . . .

This study of the media in the 1976 presidential election process found two patterns of fundamental importance in media coverage: (1) the game and strategy in the process, along with candidate style and image, were heavily covered, but issues and candidate qualifications and leadership abilities received comparatively little coverage; and (2) the basic design and intent of the process (delegate selection through 50 states and a gradual weighing of comparative appeal of candidates to voters and party activists) tended to get lost in the coverage of the game. In fact, the very nature of the process has been altered and the outcomes profoundly affected by the nature of the news coverage. . . .

The Game: Issues and "Campaign Issues."   Over all the media he studied (. . . the three networks, *Time* and *Newsweek*, and two newspapers each in two areas), Patterson found that between 51 and 58% of all news on elections was about the *game* (i.e., about who was winning or losing, strategy and logistics, appearances and hoopla). Only 28 to 32% of election news involved the substance of the election (i.e., issues and policies, candidates' leadership traits and records, and endorsements). . . .

It should be noted that the measure of news coverage of "substance" in this study, like most others, does not appear to be terribly demanding. That is (although Patterson is not as specific about this as one would like), news content that included anything more than the briefest mention of the name of an issue or policy was included in the substance column. This does not tell us how many stories involved material that was sufficiently meaningful and substantial that there was a real chance to learn something from it. Patterson did point out, however, that the figures just cited on coverage of the game compared with substance actually understate the media's emphasis on the game. Thus when we look at stories placed in the more frequently read or watched front pages of newspapers or beginning of newscasts, there is an even greater emphasis on the game, style, and image and even less attention to substance.[1]

Patterson also found interesting patterns in the news media's interest in "issues" coverage (broadly conceived of) compared with candidates' interests and efforts. He found that the media preferred to cover "clear-cut" issues, that is, issues that neatly divide the candidates (thus fulfilling the "conflict" news criterion). The candidates generally preferred that more "diffuse" issues be the center of news attention, diffuse issues being those with broad appeal to a general public, which allows a candidate to build a larger set of supporters and offend fewer segments of voters.

To the extent that the media seek candidate discussion of serious policy issues, this tension between a media preference for clear-cut issues versus candidates' preferences for diffuse issues is as it should be; it is a welcome thing for the media to try to "smoke out" the candidates on policy issues. But is that the main emphasis of the media's interest?

Apparently not. The media preference is that these issues "produce disagreement and argument among the candidates; rest on principle rather than complex details or relationships; and can be stated in simple terms, usually by reference to a shorthand label such as busing or detente." [2]

Further, one main media focus in "clear-cut issue" coverage is better referred to as *"campaign* issues" than as substantive issues. Campaign issues are those that arise as a result of incidents in the campaign, typically a mistake in judgment by the candidate or his or her campaign principles. The classic example of this was Gerald Ford's misstatement in one of the 1976 debates with Jimmy Carter that Poland was not under the domination of the Soviet Union. This received a great deal of coverage (egged on, of course, by the Carter campaign); but no serious observer of politics thought this represented Ford's view of the Eastern European situation. [3] The misstatement of his law school record by Senator Joe Biden in September 1987 was an excellent example of this phenomenon early in the campaign 1988 process.

Why the absence of coverage of policy issues—and such emphasis on nonsubstantive campaign issues? Newspeople are aware of the idea of democracy. The factors in and orientations of news production, however, push journalists to see policy statements as quickly losing their "newsworthiness," whereas campaign missteps and the tangible events of the election process are "fresh occurrences." As Patterson said, "once a candidate makes known his position on an issue, further statements concerning that issue decline in news value." [4] The journalists who are principally reporting on each campaign also sit through innumerable repetitions (and some variations) of The Speech, the standard campaign speech used at most stops around the country, which normally contains various general statements about the "issues facing our nation today." Reporters, not surprisingly, begin to question the news value of a statement on issues. Does that mean that questions on the policy issues should not be pursued, however? There is a difference between the numbing drone of a standard campaign speech (after the umpteenth hearing) and a serious effort to cross-examine prospective presidents on the significant policy issues and to find out (1) whether they have adequate knowledge about such matters, and (2) whether their general proposals on such things as budget making really add up.

Coverage of Candidates and the Nomination Process. Those are important findings. But even more striking and important is what Patterson found regarding coverage of the candidates and the nomination process itself. The principal Patterson findings have now been echoed in many other sources, even in the media themselves, in their occasional self-analyses. The findings regarding patterns of coverage of the process and the consequences of that coverage remain of central importance for understanding the media's role in elections.

The news media's criteria for news and other news production factors lead them to focus on tangible, official events, especially the earliest such events, in the election process. And following the conflict and drama criteria, it inclines the media to highlight who has "won" and who has "lost." A candidate who did not "come in first" in the voting but who did much better than the media expected can also receive prominent, positive media coverage (under the right circumstances).

In the 1976 Democratic nomination process, for example, Jimmy Carter received about 30% of the votes cast in the Iowa caucuses, the first delegate-selection event (then held in January). (Carter had spent large amounts of time in the state over the previous two years.) Various other candidates received various lower percentages, but also, reflecting the indecision among the citizenry at that early point in time, nearly 40% of the caucus participants cast votes for uncommitted delegates. The media's response to this very mixed result was to pronounce Carter the unequivocal winner and the rest losers: "He was the clear winner in this psychologically crucial test," said network correspondent Roger Mudd, for example.[5] In New Hampshire, Carter received 28% of the primary vote, while Congressman Udall received 23%, with others dividing up the balance of the vote. Of the slightly more than 80,000 people who voted in the Democratic primary, Carter received 4500 more votes than Udall. This meant that Carter received one or two more delegates than Udall in the proportional allocation.

After Iowa and New Hampshire, Carter had a projected total of about 20 delegates out of more than 3000 to be chosen. The media verdict, however, was that Carter was the clear "front runner." He received massive media coverage, while the other candidates received little or virtually none. Thus *Time* and *Newsweek* put Carter on their cover and gave him 2600 lines of coverage, whereas Udall received only 96 lines, and all the other Democratic candidates combined got only 300 lines. In short, the media treated it as if a new President of the United States of New Hampshire had been elected.[6]

. . . [T]he results are meaningful for the nation as a whole. But neither Iowa nor New Hampshire were or are now representative of the national Democratic populace or the population in general, since neither state had or has any large cities, much in the way of minorities, and so on. . . .

[M]edia coverage usually makes it a winner-take-all system in public perceptions. Indeed, even beyond the first caucus and primary, Patterson found that throughout the entire 13 weeks of the primaries and caucuses, in the "typical week following each primary, the first-place finisher received nearly 60% of the news coverage. . . ."

[T]he problem is best illustrated by the New York and Wisconsin primaries:

In Wisconsin Udall finished second to Carter by less than 1% of the popular vote, gaining 25 delegates to Carter's 29. On the same day, Udall easily bested Carter in New York's primary, receiving 70 delegates to Carter's 35. Thus, Udall collected 95 delegates while Carter received 61, yet Carter got more news coverage and bigger headlines. Why was this? It was because Udall did not "win" either primary.[7]

. . . Other studies of other presidential elections have generally confirmed Patterson's findings. Michael J. Robinson and Margaret Sheehan studied news coverage of the 1980 election on CBS and the UPI wire service.

. . . [T]heir conclusion and key data on issues coverage were:

For both CBS and UPI, the totals for policy issue coverage were not impressive. [W]e found that 59% of the full-fledged presidential campaign news on CBS failed to contain even one issue sentence. On UPI, 55% of the news items made not a single meaningful reference to any one of the ninety-odd policy issues we identified during the course of Campaign '80. Using our less precise measure of general issue coverage, story by story, on CBS, 20% of the news items emphasized issues. On UPI, the figure was 18%.[8]

It is interesting to note that the UPI wire carried even less issues news than CBS. What that also suggests is that readers of local (nonmajor) newspapers receive very little issue news, since those papers rely on the wire services for national news. . . . [I]n another analysis, Michael Robinson found the game dominant in 1980 election news, while candidate qualifications and leadership characteristics were given short shrift: "There were four times as many explicit references to success and failure [in primaries, caucuses, debates . . .] as there were to all other candidate characteristics combined."[9] These are striking omissions in coverage. . . .

One other pattern reported by Robinson and Sheehan is very interesting and important to note; it can be called: "Whatever happened to the Vice-Presidency?" In the general election of 1980, Carter's vice-presidential running mate, Walter Mondale, "was the featured candidate in a grand total of one story" on the UPI wire; and Reagan's running mate, George Bush, was the subject of only two stories. On CBS Bush and independent John Anderson's running mate Patrick Lucey were the subject of one story each; "Mondale got shut out"—no stories at all. They report that other work found the same pattern in the 1968 and 1972 campaigns.

. . . As Robinson and Sheehan importantly point out, "although four of the last six vice-presidents have become president . . . , the national press consistently ignores the vice-presidential ticket-holders, once they have been selected"; in effect, we "lose" the vice-presidency in national election news.[10]

Issues and the Game in the Election of 1984.   Thomas Patterson returned to the fray in 1984, with Richard Davis, and found that it continued to be the case that "election news conveys scenes of political actions, not the values represented by those scenes. . . .Election news concentrates on competition and controversy, not basic questions of policy and leadership." [11]

. . .[T]he presidential candidates, especially in the nominating stage, were not able to get through to the public with their leadership and policy themes and ideas because of the news media's fixation on the game.

. . . Patterson and Davis found that "neither candidate's themes even appeared in more than a tenth of the articles" on the nomination process in the . . . *New York Times* and the *Syracuse Post-Standard*. (The exception was Hart's "new generation of leadership" line.) "Nor were the specific issues that contributed to Hart's and Mondale's themes singled out for heavy coverage. In 114 articles about the Democratic campaign, Mondale's charge that Reagan's tax cuts benefited the rich was mentioned only four times; his 'progressive tax plan' was not mentioned once." [12] . . .

To be as complete as possible, though, we should mention some efforts made by the networks in 1984 to add a bit to the usual level of issues coverage. A few specific examples from the general election period: CBS News ran a standard-length piece in August on winners and losers resulting from Reagan administration policy; NBC, in the "Summer Sunday USA" program in early September ran a (half-hour) review of the candidates, including a fair amount of material on qualifications and issues; CBS aired a fairly long segment (by network news standards) distinguishing the "two [different] visions" of governmental policy and society held by Reagan and Mondale in late October. CBS even made three brief tries at coverage of the Reagan campaign's comprehensive, concerted staging of events and manipulation of the media. . . .

A Note on Coverage of Minor Parties.   . . . In the current media age, third parties are nearly invisible, however, especially on network TV. Robinson and Sheehan found in 1980, for example, that

> minor parties had no significant access to the news. . . . Rounding to the nearest whole number, minor party candidates received 0% of the newstime . . . on CBS and UPI.
>
> In all of 1980, there was only one complete story on CBS weekday news about a minor party presidential candidate [excepting John Anderson's "independent, non-partisan movement"]—a less-than-3-minute piece about Libertarian candidate Ed Clark. On UPI there were two stories featuring Clark, and two featuring Citizen's party candidate Barry Commoner [distinguished biochemist and author of several highly praised books on energy and environmental issues.][13]

These were parties with coherent, intelligent general political philosophies and specific policy proposals (pointed in very different directions), which amounted to intelligent challenges to the status quo of the major parties. But they were virtually invisible to the general public. In 1984, Robinson found the same pattern: "The networks gave practically no time to the minor parties." [14] . . .

The Preprimary Period. . . . [B]efore the first caucuses, candidates build organizations, seek political support and money around the nation, and seek media attention (which confers a sort of legitimacy on the candidacy and helps bring in money). And how is that media attention gained? As Richard Joslyn points out, a principal way "the press decides who should receive media coverage during the invisible primary is by relying on the support for a candidate in Gallup's or Harris' [polls] of presidential contenders"—those registering higher in the polls receive more media attention.[15] Despite the surface logic, however, there are serious problems with this approach; in fact, such preprimary polls are largely a waste of money and news space. These polls, in most cases, do not measure real support levels for candidates; it is simply too early for the vast majority of the public to be interested in these contests. The polls in this stage measure only name recognition.

Senators John Glenn and Gary Hart in the 1984 election cycle were good illustrations of the mistaken nature of these polls and of the consequences.

. . . Glenn was portrayed as the "leader" because he registered high in the polls, well above any of the other candidates other than Mondale in the preprimary stage. But after a few caucuses and primaries were held, where was Glenn? Gone! The "support" he registered in polls was simply a projected name recognition and a vaguely positive image (principally from his astronaut days). Gary Hart, on the other hand, with all his well-articulated issue papers and policy proposals, was generally ignored in the media until his modest, relative success in Iowa and then his "win" in New Hampshire, after which he suddenly received vast coverage and dramatic increases in expressed support, without much public knowledge of who and what he was. This is not a very sensible way to cover potential nominees. . . .

Candidates and the Nomination Process: In 1980 and 1984. The pattern of primary and caucus coverage Patterson found in 1976 has been amply confirmed in succeeding elections.

. . . In 1984, the pattern was again repeated—and strikingly so, with a strong impact. Mondale won 45% of the Iowa caucus vote, while Hart received 15% (second best), and Glenn received 5%. This was 15% of Iowa Democrats who turned out. The result has been documented by scholar William C. Adams:

Despite the tiny size of the electorate, the media verdict was unequivocal, and the self-fulfilling power attributed to the caucuses was monumental: "Senators Hart and Glenn traded places in Iowa. Hart moved up to number two. Glenn became an also-ran. The effect of this surprising reversal already is being felt in their campaigns."—Tom Brokaw, NBC News Feb. 21

Further, Adams found that in the week following the Iowa caucuses Mondale "actually suffered a decline in his relative share of attention on CBS and NBC newscasts"; Hart was awarded new status as prime challenger, and he received ten times the coverage on NBC and five times the coverage on CBS that he had had the week before. Further, "Hart's coverage was virtually free of any harsh criticism, unflattering issues, or cynical commentary." [16]

And then came New Hampshire. Hart "won" New Hampshire, again upsetting media expectations. The coverage was massive. It was a replay of Carter's coverage at the same stage in 1976. Hart's picture was on the cover of *Newsweek* and *U.S. News* and it shared the cover of *Time* with Mondale (each in chariots—the chariot race, rather than the horse race!). And the prose was purple indeed regarding the epic nature of Hart's victory:

"In a single dazzling day, he had won the most electrifying upset primary victory in years—and set off a political chain reaction that transformed campaign '84."

"Suddenly, [Mondale's] entire campaign seemed to be on the fritz."

"Like the once formidable John Glenn, who stumbled home third in the primary, Mondale was suddenly racing for his life."

"Reaction to televised accounts of Hart's victory was strong and immediate." [And *Newsweek*] "detected an electorate awash in a tidal wave of support for the youthful candidate. . . ."

"No poll taken amid the white-hot heat of the Hart explosion should be viewed as conclusive. But the dramatic implosion of Mondale's support. . . ."

All this occurred after Hart received 15% of the 15% Democratic turnout in Iowa, while Mondale received 45%, and after Hart won a sum total of under 12,000 more votes than Mondale in the unrepresentative state of New Hampshire (a number of which voters were not Democrats).[17] This was out of the tens of millions of Democrats nationwide.

In general, as Brady and Hagen document, there was some attention to policy issues in the January "flurry of attention to the impending campaign." But "by February, policy issues and all other subjects were buried under a blizzard of speculation about who was winning and who was losing the nomination campaign." [18]

This, frankly, is just senseless; and it seriously altered the nomination process. As journalist Tom Wicker remarked and lamented, the "unexpected" Iowa showing for Hart produced a wave of publicity that Hart astutely rode to an upset primary victory . . . among New Hampshire's iconoclastic voters. That generated an avalanche of publicity, under which Mondale was buried in Maine . . . and Vermont. . . .

What's wrong with publicity for the candidate with momentum? The problem is that the publicity *is* the momentum. . . ." [19]

What also resulted from such coverage is that many candidates were effectively eliminated after the few earliest primaries and caucuses and people in other states, including such states as New York, Ohio, and California, never got to indicate their preference for a full range of candidates. Effectively, we have a media-elimination tournament, with most candidates being forced to leave the "game" before the sizable majority of the party populace can vote on them. . . .

And how were the candidates themselves treated in the news? Interestingly, Robinson and Sheehan, in their effort to assess how "fairly" the candidates were treated in 1980, came to a generalization which appears to apply to other years as well (although not without some exception): incumbents and distinct "front runners" receive decidedly tougher (at times, hostile) media coverage than other candidates. Robinson concluded that the same was the case in the 1984 general election. . . . In terms of sheer amount of time in the general election, Robinson and colleagues found nearly perfect equality of network and UPI news coverage for the two major party candidates.[20]

. . . And in 1988.   In the 1988 nomination process, with no incumbent involved and with "hot races" in both major parties, the temptations of horse-race journalism were at their height. . . .

. . . [M]edia organs were very interested in the Bush-Dole conflict (and any conflict they could find on the Democratic side). But in their focus on the game and conflict in the Bush-Dole contest, the media largely lost sight of what should have been a truly central policy issue in campaign '88. In the New Hampshire case, the media focused especially on the conflict over Bush's ads saying that Dole would raise taxes and Dole's angry reaction of denial. But the prime, in fact overwhelming, issue facing American government which caused the tax question to be raised in the first place got lost in the conflict obsession: the monumental budget deficits and what action each candidate would take to (realistically) solve that problem.

. . . Clearly, this issue should have been at the center of campaign coverage in 1988, with constant efforts to get answers on solutions from candidates in *both* parties. Instead, with the huge "Super Tuesday" set of primaries and caucuses throughout the South and elsewhere, and with the Democratic Party having an active contest through much of the nomination stage, most of what the public got was the game.

On the plus side, major newspapers did continue the trend in recent elections of running special series of articles on the major party candidates, including often good synopses of background, education, career, qualities as public figure and officer, and a fair amount of material on policy positions. The networks did make a more distinct effort *before* the Iowa and New Hampshire events to point out the unrepresentative nature of those states. The networks also made more effort to give the public more information on the politics and demographics of states holding primaries prior to the events—with help from their whiz-bang, computer-generated graphics capacities....

Systematically establishing the impact of election communications on the public's opinions and behavior is a real challenge. That, in fact, is an understatement. As Richard Joslyn has precisely pointed out ... "Empirical demonstration that campaign communication has a particular effect on public opinion would ideally include prior specification of the hypothesized effect, measurement of the relevant opinions both before and after the campaign communication has occurred, a comparison of the opinions of those exposed to the communication with those who were not exposed, and the elimination of all other possible reasons that those exposed to the communication might differ from those unexposed." [21]

This is indeed a challenge—and those requirements of empirical demonstration should certainly be kept in mind whenever statements are made about such effects....

Thinking and Talking about the Campaign: Media Agenda/Voters' Agenda.   And with all the coverage of the sort we have noted, what did the public think was important, and what did they talk about? By this point it should come as no news flash that what the news media emphasized—the game and the horse race—was just what the public thought was important.

... This public preoccupation with the game as opposed to the substance of electoral choices appears to be a product of the post-1968 resort to primaries and open caucuses and of the mass media treatment of the campaign. Thus Patterson notes that the premier study of the 1948 election found that "67% of voters' conversations were concerned with the candidates' positions and qualifications," while only one-fourth of them discussed which candidate was likely to win. But in 1976, "only 34% of people's conversations were concerned with substance" (with a high of only 43% even in October).[22] Is the contemporary democratic electoral choice process being largely lost in a fog of electoral trivial pursuit?

But Patterson also found a significant variation in that pattern of seeing the game as the election's most important feature—a variation of striking importance. He found that the game "was at the top of the voters' lists at every stage of the campaign but one: It fell behind the debates during the general election," and viewing of both the televised conventions and the debates also increased people's sense of the importance of substance in the election: "Indeed, debate and convention viewing was more closely related than either newspaper or evening newscast exposure to a heightened belief in the significance of policy and leadership matters." [23]

. . . This suggests that when serious communications about the substance of electoral choice are presented to the public (in an interesting fashion) they respond—and begin to act more like democratic citizenship requires. Networks (and even newspapers) are you listening?!

Jimmy Who? Awareness of Candidates.   The nature of the impact of media coverage of the nomination process is perhaps most dramatically evident in people's awareness of the candidates and the consequences for how they vote (our ultimate concern). In the 1976 election Patterson found that most of the public knew little about the candidates for the Democratic nomination at the beginning of the year. . . . Even in February, after the Iowa caucuses, only 20% said they knew anything more about Carter than his name. Media coverage following the New Hampshire primary dramatically changed that for Carter. Patterson found that Carter was the only candidate whose public recognition rose dramatically: 20% said they knew something about him in February, 81% said so by June. But the public's recognition of his Democratic opponents increased only modestly. "Recognition levels rose by 14% for [Congressman Morris] Udall, [Governor Jerry] Brown, and Jackson, and by only 9% for [Senator Frank] Church . . . and even declined for [Senator] Bayh and [Sargeant] Shriver."[24]

And most striking of all was the impact of that awareness, from the nature of media coverage, on the vote.

. . . "Nearly all [voters] picked a candidate they knew something about. . . ." Most specifically, about a quarter of the voters knew only one of the three candidates, usually Carter; he received 90% of those votes. And about 30% knew two candidates, typically Carter and either Jackson or Udall; Carter got 60% of those votes. The nature of campaign coverage, it appears, has a profound impact on the way people vote. This is further confirmed by how people tended to view the candidates—according to who was portrayed as the "winner" and who the "losers."

"Winning Isn't Everything, It's the Only Thing."   That old line of legendary coach Vince Lombardi seems to have been taken to heart by the media, and the public response followed suit in 1976. Who had "won" a primary or caucus event and who was likely to in the future were so prominently and constantly run as news stories that the great majority of the public was certain to have gotten the message. Patterson explained the developments and the impact:

> The first impression that most Democrats had of Carter was that he was doing extremely well in places like Iowa and New Hampshire, an

accomplishment that evoked some surprise and a certain amount of admiration. As they heard more about him, most of them also regarded him as an acceptable nominee. This reaction was not based on the feeling that in Carter they had discovered their ideal candidate, for they *knew very little about his politics or abilities.* But he seemed like a sensible and personable individual and, since he had won the acceptance of voters elsewhere, he must have his good points. These were persuasive perceptions [emphasis added].[25]

This impression and the public perception of winners and losers was an especially potent factor in a nomination process where there were no clearly and strongly dominant figures before the process began, as was the case in 1976 on the Democratic side (and again in 1988). In such coverage, Patterson pointed out, was the making of a bandwagon. . . .

Images (—and Print Media versus TV). . . . Patterson . . . found that newspapers were "more instrumental in the formation of images" and that newspaper reading "particularly contributes to the fullness of people's images." [26] This, he concluded, was because voters' impressions of a candidate's primary victories, political record, and the like are principally dependent on verbal communication, which is the strong suit of newspapers. Patterson . . . acknowledges that "when only the voters' impressions about the candidates' personalities and leadership capacities are considered, television's impact is more apparent"—indeed, in the first half of the nomination period especially, "regular viewing of the evening newscasts was strongly associated with the formation of impressions of Carter's personality." He also noted the predominance of stylistic impressions of Carter, along with the fact that "once a candidate's image has been developed, it's unlikely to be altered significantly" by subsequent news—and that the "large majority" of voters had developed an image of Carter by April.[27] Putting those elements together suggests a larger role played by TV in image building. . . .

Information. On the other hand, Patterson reports convincingly, as have others, that newspaper reading is far more responsible for people's learning of substantive information than is watching newscasts. . . . Two specific forms of TV viewing of election coverage did contribute to people's awareness of the candidates' policy positions. . . . "Heavier convention viewers became significantly better informed about 63% of Carter's positions and 25% of Ford's [the incumbent and hence already better known]," and "exposure to the televised . . . debates . . . was significantly related to higher awareness of 50% of Carter's and Ford's policies." [28] . . .

Finally, Election Night ("Tuned-In TV, Turned-Off Voters"?)

There is one final way that the TV age has notably affected elections—final in a literal sense. Election night is the final act of the election process (the final scene of the election drama). The combination of the competition between the networks and the development of survey sampling techniques (and computers to process the data) has resulted in network projections of a presidential victor well before the polls have closed in some parts of the nation. The election of 1980 was the most notorious case: One network announced its projection of the winner nearly three hours before the polls had closed in most West Coast areas— thereby telling citizens who were preparing to vote during that time, in effect, "your vote is meaningless" (at least for the premier office in the nation). Further, in 1980 a good number of West Coast elections for the House of Representatives were decided by close votes, as will always occur in some number. Correspondingly, if even 5 or 10% of the public which would have voted is discouraged from voting by such projections, the actual outcome of elections can be affected (usually, about 15 to 20% of West Coast voters cast their votes between 6:00 and 8:00 p.m.). There were indeed accounts of voters leaving the voting places after the projections were broadcast in 1980.[29]

The debate over whether this practice has a serious impact and whether such early projections should be allowed has been fairly intense. Unfortunately, systematic evidence (data as well as accompanying logic) has been mixed (what there is of it). . . .

In late 1987, the House of Representatives passed a bill to establish a uniform poll-closing time throughout the nation (7:00 p.m. Western time), and the networks would not be allowed to broadcast projections of winners until then. It is not clear why the election day schedule and the opportunity for citizens to vote must be altered simply because of network competition and lack of responsibility. I cannot resist quoting part of journalist David Sarasohn's response to this action: "Look, if this is too inconvenient for the networks, maybe the West Coast could just give up voting for president entirely."[30] . . .

References

1. Thomas Patterson, *The mass media election* (New York: Praeger, 1980), p. 25.
2. Ibid., Chapter 4; quote from pp. 31-32.
3. Ibid., pp. 34-37.
4. Ibid., p. 30.
5. Ibid., p. 44.
6. Ibid., pp. 44-45.
7. Ibid., pp. 45-47, quotes from pp. 45 and 46 (footnote), respectively.
8. Michael J. Robinson and Margaret Sheehan, *Over the wire and on TV: CBS and UPI in campaign '80* (New York: Russell Sage, 1983), pp. 145-146.
9. Michael J. Robinson, A statesman is a dead politician: Candidate images on

network news, in Elie Abel (Ed.), *What's news* (San Francisco: Institute for Contemporary Studies, 1981), p. 161.

10. Robinson and Sheehan, *Over the wire and on TV*, p. 168.
11. Thomas Patterson and Richard Davis, The media campaign: Struggle for the agenda, in Michael Nelson (Ed.), *The elections of 1984* (Washington, D.C.: Congressional Quarterly Press, 1985), p. 113.
12. Ibid., p. 116.
13. Robinson and Sheehan, *Over the wire and on TV*, p. 73.
14. Michael Robinson, The media in campaign '84, Part II, Wingless, toothless, and hopeless, in Michael J. Robinson and Austin Ranney (Eds.), *The mass media in campaign '84* (Washington, D.C.: American Enterprise Institute, 1985), p. 35.
15. Richard Joslyn, *Mass media and elections* (Reading, Mass.: Addison-Wesley, 1984), p. 121.
16. William C. Adams, Media coverage of campaign '84: A preliminary report, *Public Opinion* (April/May 1984), pp. 10-11.
17. *Newsweek*, March 12, 1984, pp. 20-21; see also Otis Pike column (Newhouse News Service) as run in *The Forum* (Fargo, N. Dak.), March 4, 1984.
18. Henry E. Brady and Michael G. Hagen, The horse-race or the issue?: What do voters learn from presidential primaries, Center for American Political Studies, Harvard University, Occasional Paper (1986 APSA Annual Meeting Paper), p. 8.
19. Tom Wicker, Hart's well-managed windfall, as run in *Minneapolis Star and Tribune*, March 11, 1984, p. 17A.
20. On candidate treatment in 1980, see Robinson and Sheehan, *Over the wire and on TV*, pp. 115-134. On toughness on the incumbent in 1984, see Maura Clancy and Michael Robinson, The media in campaign '84: General election coverage, part 1, in Robinson and Ranney, *The mass media in campaign '84*; on equality of news time, see Robinson and Sheehan, *Over the wire and on TV*, Chapter 5, and Robinson, The media in campaign '84, p. 35.
21. Joslyn, *Mass media and elections*, p. 159.
22. Patterson, *Mass media election*, p. 105.
23. Ibid., pp. 98 and 103.
24. Ibid., pp. 109-110.
25. Ibid, p. 126.
26. Ibid., p. 142.
27. Ibid., pp. 143 and 134-135, respectively.
28. Ibid., p. 157.
29. See the summary in Joslyn, *Mass media and elections*, pp. 150-152.
30. David Sarasohn, A poll-closing scheme designed to keep Westerners from voting, Newhouse News Service, as run in *Minneapolis Star and Tribune*, November 18, 1987, p. 17A.

3.2 ■■■■■

Campaign Organizations Confront
the Media-Political Environment

F. Christopher Arterton

Editor's Note. F. Christopher Arterton describes how the desire to attract appropriate media coverage shapes campaign plans during a presidential contest. Campaign managers deem it essential to dominate the perceptual environment that leads to news production. Therefore, they exercise a tight rein over their candidate's activities and schedules. Four case studies provide illustrations. Arterton's analysis is based on interviews with the campaign managers and press secretaries of all the major contenders in the 1976 presidential race.

The author raises important questions about the merits of a media-dominated primary election system. As currently structured, it allows the victor in the battle for media coverage to stake out a strong claim for the spoils of election victory. The media become the unanointed handicappers of the presidential race. Arterton questions whether it is sound to entrust such a serious responsibility to an institution that is not designed to make well-considered political decisions.

Arterton received his Ph.D. from the Massachusetts Institute of Technology. At the time of writing, he was teaching political science at Yale University. Arterton is no stranger to the world of political maneuvering, having served as policy maker for various Democratic action groups. The selection is from *Race for the Presidency,* ed. James David Barber (Englewood Cliffs, N.J.: Prentice-Hall, 1978).

Campaigning in the Media

. . . Those who manage presidential campaigns uniformly believe that interpretations placed upon campaign events are frequently more important than the events themselves. In other words, the political contest is shaped primarily by the perceptual environment within which cam-

From *Race for the Presidency: The Media and the Nominating Process,* ed. James David Barber, pp. 8-19. New York, The American Assembly.

paigns compete. Particularly in the early nomination stages, perceptions outweigh reality in terms of their political impact. Since journalists communicate these perceptions to voters and party activists and since part of the reporter's job is creating these interpretations, campaigners believe that journalists can and do affect whether their campaign is viewed as succeeding or failing, and that this perception in turn will determine their ability to mobilize political resources in the future: endorsements, volunteers, money, and hence, votes.

Both journalists and campaigners speak of the importance of "momentum," a vague conception that the campaign is expanding, gaining new supporters, and meeting (or, if possible, overachieving) its goals. In other words, in presidential nominations, because of the sequential nature of the process, the perceptual environment established by campaign reporting is seen as the meaningful substitute for political reality.

Reporters and political strategists, not surprisingly, often differ as to the nature of the race and the importance of a particular event to the general process. A passage from Jules Witcover's book *Marathon: The Pursuit of the Presidency, 1972-1976* in which he reacts to a frequently heard complaint illustrates the point:

> One unhappy Udall worker later stated in the *Washington Post* that the candidates themselves and the issues were lost in the efforts to draw press attention, and in the reporters' determination to draw significance from an insignificant exercise. "The reality of a presidential campaign," he wrote in a woeful misunderstanding of the dynamics of the system, "is the delegate count, but no significant number of delegates will be selected until March. . . ." The fact is that the reality in the early going of a presidential campaign is *not* the delegate count at all. The reality at the beginning stage is the psychological impact of the results—the perception by press, public, and contending politicians of what has happened.

Establishing "the psychological impact of the results—the perception by press, public, and contending politicians," however, is an exceedingly difficult judgment.

Consider, for example, a front page article in the *New York Times*, dated January 12, 1976, written by chief political correspondent R. W. Apple:

> A kind of rough standing among the candidates has suddenly started to emerge in the minds of political professionals around the country. . . . In the group from which the nominee is believed most likely to be selected are Senator Henry M. Jackson of Washington, Senator Birch Bayh of Indiana, former Gov. Jimmy Carter of Georgia and Senator Hubert Humphrey of Minnesota.
>
> In the second, candidates given a conceivable chance of being nominated, are former Ambassador Sargent Shriver, former Senator Fred R.

Harris of Oklahoma and Morris K. Udall of Arizona. Some professionals think Mr. Udall belongs in the first category, but not many.

In the third group, those most unlikely to be the nominee, are Senator Lloyd Bentsen of Texas, Gov. Milton Shapp of Pennsylvania, former Gov. Terry Sanford of North Carolina, Senator Frank Church of Idaho, Gov. George C. Wallace of Alabama and Senator Robert C. Byrd of West Virginia.

Such early calculations are highly speculative. . . .

The illustration is not offered in order to criticize Apple's judgment—in fact as subsequent events revealed, his only error was in overrating Bayh's chances—but rather to point out that the criteria for asserting an emerging consensus among political professionals are not readily apparent. Apple refers to visits to twelve states and conversations with hundreds of politicians and activists as the basis for his article.

From the point of view of campaign operatives, this kind of rating has monumental consequences for their nomination prospects in two spheres: first, by facilitating or hampering their efforts to attract political support, and, second, by dictating the amount of news coverage they will subsequently receive. A subtle, reciprocal influence results from the pivotal role ascribed to campaign reporting by those who manage candidate organizations. On the one hand, beyond simply viewing the media as a convenient conduit to the electorate, campaign strategists are [led] to attempting to influence the political judgments of the journalists themselves. Accordingly, the attitudes, beliefs, and behavior of the journalist corps become a milieu for political competition between presidential campaigns. On the other hand, campaigners accommodate their political strategies to the expected nature of campaign reporting. . . .

Media Impact on Presidential Campaign Politics

The assertion that journalists exert an influence over the conduct of presidential campaigning does not imply that they intend such an impact or even that they could prevent the effects if they so desired. Whereas campaigns are quite open in their attempt to persuade journalists, the reverse influence relationship can be quite elusive. Anticipating the reactions of journalists, campaign decision-makers set their strategic plans and their daily behavior with a view toward how the press will report campaign events. The most direct influence of the media upon the campaign process derives primarily from the fact that campaign reporting is fairly predictable, and campaigners are able to design their activities taking these continuities into account.

On a superficial level, the building of campaign behavior around media considerations involves actions such as scheduling the campaign day so that events to be covered take place before deadlines; allowing a break in the schedule for filing stories; providing typewriters and telephones to facilitate the reporters' work; building into one's campaign organization a capacity to handle reporters' baggage and make their hotel and airline reservations; passing out schedules, advance texts of the candidate's major speeches, and other news releases containing reportable information; arranging private interviews with the candidate, family members, and staff personnel; and so on. In terms of organizational resources and candidate time, interactions with journalists comprise a substantial commitment of campaign effort. . . .

Beyond the mechanics of obtaining coverage, which, as noted above, may be taken as a rather trivial impact of news reporting on campaign behavior, campaigners frequently respond directly to criticism emanating from the corps of journalists. To present but a single prominent example, after Jimmy Carter was questioned by a reporter about his lack of a self-deprecating humor, for several days he worked humorous remarks about himself into his public appearances.

The influence of campaign journalism is felt on its most profound level, however, in the formulation of political strategies around media considerations. To the extent that they have control over the activities of their organizations, campaign managers plan with a view toward media interpretations as one facet of practically everything undertaken by the campaign. Major campaign decisions are rarely, however, based *solely* upon expected news reporting; media strategy and political strategy are intertwined as part of the same process. . . . [T]he following case studies are instances in which the participants reported to us the supremacy of predicted news reporting in determining the campaign decisions. These examples extend to every arena in which campaigns must make strategic decisions: campaign organization, fund raising, the timing of decisions, scheduling, and the selection of key primary states.

Case 1: Sanford's "License to Practice"

. . . Like a number of others, Terry Sanford, the former Governor of North Carolina, decided to concentrate his efforts on a few early primaries (New Hampshire, Massachusetts, and North Carolina) and to rely upon his contacts in North Carolina to provide his financial base. Other funds were to be collected by building a financial arm into the primary organizations in states where he would make an effort. Thus, initial money would be raised only in three or four states and later the effort could be extended to the twenty states needed to qualify for federal matching funds.

By the summer of 1975, however, Sanford found his strategy running headlong into a perception among journalists that "qualification" constituted an important test of which candidates should be taken seriously.

Since during the preprimary period, the amount of news space devoted to the coming presidential race is quite limited, judgments as to the newsworthiness of events of candidates can be quite consequential. . . .

The Sanford staff and those of several other candidates had difficulty in obtaining coverage in the absence of meeting the qualifications for federal matching money. They reported being told specifically they would not be covered until they had qualified. As discussed by his press secretary, Paul Clancey, on July 7, 1975:

> That's definitely where the press corps has been known to influence the actions of the campaign, because we [or rather] Sanford maintained for a long time that he was not going to waste his energies on getting up political matching funds, and yet, it has become about the only game in town. . . . He had a major statement on defense spending last week and Udall got all the play because he could qualify in twenty states.

Jim Hightower, Harris' campaign manager, noted similar pressure upon his campaign, July 8, 1975:

> The press had decided that's the way they're going to certify who a candidate is, if you raise a hundred thousand dollars, which is ludicrous, number one, but it is a game they're playing. And not only are they trying to do it, but I think they've succeeded; I think we've got to go raise our $100,000 now. . . .

The attention by news organizations to whether candidates had qualified or not took place despite the widespread recognition among campaigners that the test was meaningless as a real indicator of political strength. The sarcasm of Hightower's comment above was echoed by Sanford's campaign manager, Jean Westwood:

> Everyone thinks that once you've got $100,000, you're viable. Well how far does $100,000 go in a national campaign? And you receive no matching money until the 1st of January no matter how much you raise.

Despite this interpretation of the political realities confronting the campaign, Governor Sanford decided he had to conform to those standards which would facilitate access to news coverage. At his press conference on July 2, 1975, describing qualifications as a "license to practice," he committed his organization to raising the necessary funds within one month, much to the surprise of his finance people. Raising money in twenty states instead of three or four necessitated an entirely different organizational structure, diverting resources away from the states in which he planned to make his early efforts. Staff members would have to be sent into nonessential states to set up "fund raisers" and Sanford's schedule would require him to spend less time in New Hampshire, Massachusetts, and North Carolina. . . .

Case 2: Udall and the Iowa Caucuses

From their initial decision-making in early 1975 to November of that year, the Udall campaign planned to make their first solid effort in the New Hampshire primary under the assumption that, as in years past, the print and broadcast media would devote a great deal of attention to the build-up and results of that first primary. Campaigning in New Hampshire, Udall would attract considerable press coverage; winning New Hampshire (followed, hopefully, by a win in Massachusetts) would catapult him into the front runner status. It was a familiar route: "Our strategy," explained Stewart Udall, the candidate's brother, in a July 8 interview, "has to be a McGovern/Jack Kennedy strategy in the key states, which are New Hampshire, Massachusetts, and Wisconsin." Other interviews confirmed the same strategy; while Udall did have the beginning of an organization in Iowa, which was to hold precinct caucuses on January 19, the first major test was planned for New Hampshire.

Beginning on October 27, however, the national political reporters began to devote so much attention to the upcoming Iowa caucuses that it soon became apparent that the first big splash of the 1976 race would occur there, rather than in New Hampshire. R. W. Apple's piece in the October 27th *New York Times* not only put the spotlight for the first time on Carter's growing strength, but it also signaled the fact that the Iowa caucuses would be an important event from the perspective of news reporting organizations.

The significance of Apple's piece was enhanced by the clairvoyance of his reporting in 1972, interpreting the caucus results in Iowa as demonstrating unexpected McGovern strength. As in 1972, Iowa could be the first opportunity to observe which candidates were "emerging from the pack." According to Witcover in *Marathon:*

> The media's seizing upon Iowa, though it chose only 47 of 3,008 delegates to the Democratic National Convention, was both understandable and defensible . . . in 1976, if there were going to be early signals, the fourth estate was going to be on the scene *en masse* to catch them.

All the attention caused the Udall campaign to reconsider its decision to stay out of Iowa. As frequently happens, the decision caused a split within the campaign. The efforts of key participants to explain their positions after the fact provide a unique opportunity to observe the importance of predicted media coverage in major political decisions. The campaign political director argued for making a major, albeit eleventh hour, effort in Iowa. His position was reinforced by a memo (quoted in *Marathon*) prepared by a key advisor after an exploratory trip into the state. The important passage of that memo read:

> Iowa justifies the expense. It will be covered like the first primary

always has been in the national press. If we can emerge as the clear
liberal choice in Iowa, the payoffs in New Hampshire will be enormous.

Despite the argument by others in the campaign that it was by then too
late to make a successful effort in Iowa, the political director's side finally
won with the additional argument that even if they did not win Iowa, at
least their presence there would keep the (liberal) front runner from
emerging in the headlines until New Hampshire. The Udall campaign
committed about $80,000 and, an even more precious resource, ten days
of the candidate's time to the Iowa effort.

While it can never be ascertained whether this decision to switch
resources away from the New Hampshire effort resulted in a poorer
showing there, it certainly did not improve their New Hampshire
campaign. With hindsight, Udall staffers admitted the preeminence of
the media considerations in their mistaken venture:

> Iowa was regrettable in that we had not inclination or desire to devote
> resources and time and money to Iowa. But it became such a media
> event that I think some of our staff people—national staff and Iowa
> staff—panicked in the face of it, and we rushed in headlong. (Press
> secretary Robert Neumann). . . .

Their discovery that the media planned to cover the Iowa caucuses as
extensively as they would the early primaries led Udall's advisors to
conclude that they could not let the other candidates (principally Bayh
and Carter) get the jump on them either in sheer amount of coverage or
in favorable perceptions of political progress communicated by the media
to New Hampshire voters. Needless to say, by any standard this was a
major campaign decision.

Case 3: Reagan and Schweiker

. . . In the 1976 Republican race . . . the estimates made by the
networks and the *New York Times* . . . were widely accepted as valid
statements of the progress of the race. In the middle of July, for example,
the PFC [President Ford Committee] claimed to have the needed number
of delegates, while the media counts showed Ford not yet there, but
closing in on the nomination.

Obviously the Reagan campaign was in a difficult position. To
counter their deteriorating situation, John Sears arranged for Reagan to
announce that Senator Richard Schweiker would be his choice for the vice
presidential nomination. That announcement raised the possibility of
broadened Reagan coalition, and meant, at a minimum, that delegates
would have to be repolled to record any switches. As it turned out, the day
of the Schweiker announcement, CBS News had been preparing a story
for broadcast *that night*, projecting Ford the nominee on the basis of their

delegate polls. Clearly the proposal of Schweiker as a running mate was a response to the political situation; but the timing of the announcement was related to necessity to forestall exactly such an occurrence in which one of the news reporting organizations would declare Ford the nominee. If that happened, the race would be over:

> We realized that something like that was going to happen fairly soon. There you have a clear situation where we had to try a defense; because if that had ever been broadcast over CBS one night, we would have had much less support than we ultimately had. (John Sears)

Case 4: The Rose Garden Strategy

An incumbent President has a built-in advantage of being newsworthy in everything he does. The Presidency provides a forum from which the occupant can attempt to proselytize voters without giving the appearance of campaigning. The incumbent does not have to struggle to make the news; on the contrary, he has the luxury of deciding what kind of news he wants to make.

During the nomination campaign, Ford's advisors noticed a relationship between his national poll and ratings and the degree to which he was making news *as a candidate:*

> When he went out on the stump, his inexperience as a campaigner showed up. Throughout a day of five or six speeches, he would tend to get more strident and more partisan and harder on the attack, and when people began to see him this way on the evening news every night, his national approval ratings tapered off. Then, when he'd stay in the White House for three or four months, he'd come back a little bit in the national polling. (Robert Teeter, pollster for Ford)

A strategy book prepared for the general election campaign by Stuart Spencer and Robert Teeter recommended that Ford remain in the White House and make the news through presidential business. . . . According to Teeter:

> . . . [T]his was the basis for the campaign strategy in the general election, the Rose Garden strategy. The President simply did better in communicating with the voters when he was perceived as President, not as a candidate for President. (*Campaign for President: The Managers Look at 76*, by Jonathan Moore and Janet Fraser)

While the briefing book emphasized the special role of television, roughly the same argument can be made for print reporting. Given a choice between making the front page of most newspapers by kissing a cowgirl, as happened during the Texas primary, versus greeting a foreign head of state at the White House, it is natural to see why Ford's advisors would lean toward the latter.

Normally, the candidate's time is one of the most precious resources available to a campaign. While Ford's advisors were persuading him not to campaign, their counterparts in the Carter organization were meticulously allocating his campaign days to key states according to an elaborate point system. Yet the Ford campaign decided to dispense with half the available days, because of the impact of campaign reporting.

An important difference exists between the first two case studies examined above and the latter two. The Reagan decision to select a running mate before the convention and the Ford plan to avoid campaign reporting were dictated simply by the fact that presidential campaigns are covered so extensively and intensively by the news media. On the other hand, the earlier campaign decisions are grounded in journalists' assumptions about the presidential race which determine campaign coverage both in substance and in allocation patterns. In the Sanford case, the assumption that qualification for federal matching funds was a reasonable criterion for separating serious from nonserious candidates imposed that standard upon the campaign. For Udall, the decision by many news reporting organizations to cover the Iowa caucuses in depth provided the stimulus for reevaluating the political strategy. The decision to allocate coverage to Iowa, of course, assumes that the Iowa results would be a valid indicator of progress in the national nomination race. The fact that it was the only barometer, or the first, does not, however, make it valid. . . .

3.3 ■

Newspapers in Campaigns

David Nyhan

Editor's Note. David Nyhan reports on the campaign from the perspective of a reporter on a major newspaper. He thinks that major papers are at their best when they police the candidates' activities to make sure that the rules are obeyed and when they scrutinize how candidates treat issues and watch for gaffes. He also discusses the alleged shortcomings of elite papers, although he disagrees with a number of the complaints. He notes, for example, that the press is wrongly criticized for featuring public opinion polls, making them too important. He believes that the effect of polls on the newspaper audience has been exaggerated. He also refutes the charge that the press is overly liberal. In his view, conservatives dominate the news media, especially when one considers that most smaller papers throughout the country are conservative and too timid to battle the established power structure.

He concurs with the charge that the press is too respectful to incumbents and that it focuses too much on the horse-race aspects of the campaign. He chides the press for paying excessive attention to front-runners and grants that the press is often unfair when it covers aspects of the campaign unevenly. Although he believes that reporters on major papers enjoy a great deal of freedom to select what they wish to cover and to inject their opinions into their stories, he acknowledges that they labor under constraints. Chief among them is the desire for peer approval.

At the time of writing, David Nyhan was a political reporter for the *Boston Globe.* He has been a White House reporter and has covered presidential campaigns since 1968. The selection comes from "Newspapers in Campaigns," in *Political Persuasion in Presidential Campaigns*, ed. L. Patrick Devlin (New Brunswick, N.J.: Transaction Books, 1987), 105-117.

. . . Readers are well served by newspapers that make a major commitment to covering the campaign. Some newspapers give readers more information than they can handle. Nobody can keep up with these papers. The Sunday *New York Times* or *Boston Globe* weigh four or five pounds—a couple of million words. Nobody can digest it. Nobody can devote forty-five minutes or an hour a day to reading a series of newspapers. ... There is an information glut, and the average voter cannot absorb what is printed and written about the candidates and delivered on his doorstep if he gets one of these good papers. So they pick and choose. A newspaper is really a supermarket. The papers give you rows and rows of shelves with hundreds of different stories to sample from. We cannot make you read them. But we try to make it entertaining and accurate.

... Most people in this country do not get to read that kind of material, because it takes a tremendous commitment by publishers to make the space available and to pay people to go out, report it, prepare it, and put it in the paper. More papers should do what leading papers do in terms of political coverage. The fact that they do not has a lot to do with ideology. Most papers are extremely conservative and do not like to rouse the rabble by giving readers a wide variety of viewpoints and stands on issues from which to pick and choose. There is not a great spread in political coverage in papers across the country. ...

The political newspapers set the agenda for the political campaign. We cannot herd the candidates in a particular direction. We follow the bell cow. This year it has been Walter Mondale. He is the incumbent in this group. The papers that cover the campaign police the action. We make sure that the rules are applied, more or less fairly and equitably. We tell you where their money is coming from and what they are spending it on. We tell you if their TV advertising is misleading. We are like the referee in a heavyweight title fight. We tell you what is fair and what is foul. And what we say about those details is generally picked up and magnified and its impact increased manifold by national television.

This is an expensive proposition for newspapers and only the prosperous ones can afford to do it. ... The *Boston Globe* has seven reporters on the road more or less full-time covering different candidates in different primary states because this is such a front-loaded year. We will have been in Iowa, New Hampshire, Maine, Vermont, Massachusetts, Rhode Island, and seven other states all before St. Patrick's Day. ... We make a tremendous monetary investment in this. Yet the candidates are limited to spending not more than $400,000 legally in New Hampshire. There are many ways they get around that. They bill a lot of their services and advertising through Massachusetts. And I would be very surprised if you could total up the accurate figure. I would bet that more than $1 million will have been spent on Mondale's behalf in New Hampshire, not just by his campaign, but by the labor unions and independent expenditure groups doing other things before this is over. And the policing, reporting, and sorting out of the details is done by this political press, this relative handful of reporters who discover and publish items and then have an added impact when television picks them up.

We also develop the issues. We do not tell the candidates what they have to say, but we point out to readers when candidates are ducking issues. Much has been made in the last couple of days of the fact that Gary Hart shrewdly asked Mondale in the Iowa debate last Saturday night, "Can you name me one issue that you have taken a stand on that was opposed by the leaders of labor unions?" Mondale ducked it that night. His nonanswer was reminiscent of the time Dwight Eisenhower was president and was asked to name one thing that Richard Nixon had achieved as vice-president, and he said, "Well, give me a week and I'll think of something." It took "Fritz" about three days, and he came up with some examples of some things that he had stood for that labor had opposed. But it is the press that picks up a charge by one candidate or another, and we give it the megaphone. We magnify it, and then when Mondale responds, we report that as well. In politics you always get this two-cushioned shot: charge and countercharge, accusation and response. It is not just one-way. It goes out there. It bounces. And it echoes back.

What we have not had a chance to do this year, that we did in years past, is one of the things we do best. And I say this with a certain amount of relish. We pounce on mistakes. . . . There have not been many mistakes this year. . . . They have not messed up, so we have not had a chance to pounce. But when they do, the press will pounce with a vengeance. These people have been fortunate so far, and they have been restrained and disciplined among themselves. But, there is no pressure on a public figure like that which builds during a presidential campaign. And it gets even tougher in the fall than it is during the primary season. When one of them does make a mistake, or is perceived as having done so, the political press will be there and you will be the first to know. You can read it in your newspaper.

What do we in the media do that is wrong, or that is not so good, or that we could be doing better? You hear that the press makes too much of the polls. And there are responsible newspaper editors who say that we should not use polls, that it is the devil's tool, that you cannot trust them, and that it is only a snapshot in time. All that is true. My own feelings on polls are: Politicians use them; why should we not use them? Even if we do not pay thousands for our own polls, we wind up reporting the polls of others. The networks can afford to do it. The national polls sometimes do not zero in on a state, like Massachusetts, New Hampshire, or Rhode Island, the way a regional newspaper might, but my own feeling is that polls are a legitimate journalistic tool because they are a method of analysis. It does give you a snapshot. I am a defender of the use of polls, even though some people criticize them saying they influence too many people and dry up campaign money for candidates perceived as trailing. . . .

We hear that the press is biased. We hear that, at least, the writers and reporters are flaming, liberal, commies and that the publishers are good old, reliable, stouthearted, free-enterprise conservatives, who do not know that the inmates are running their asylum. And while they are totting up the profits, their hare-brained liberal dreamers who do the reporting are taking the country down the road to ruin.

In 1972 something like 90 percent or more of the newspapers in this country of 1,700 dailies endorsed Richard Nixon, not George McGovern. Few newspapers had the courage to stand up against what was going on in those days. I am very proud to say that my paper was one of them. We endorsed McGovern and I am proud of it to this day. By and large, the press is biased and distorted. But it is distorted in favor of the conservatives, of the right wing, of the business and managerial class—and it is against liberals. It is against those who would share the wealth, those who favor a bigger role for government, and those who favor government regulation.

The vast majority of editorial and op-ed pages in this country is dominated by conservative-to-far-right forces, not by liberals. There are a few liberal columnists in this country, very few. There are far more conservatives, because by far the bulk of newspaper proprietors in this country favor the conservative political viewpoint. So if there is bias in the press in general, I would submit that it is a bias on behalf of the Right against the Left in the majority of American newspapers. I would have to concede that papers like the *Washington Post*, the *New York Times*, and the *Boston Globe* are liberal by most newspaper standards. The vast majority of reporters who work in this business are liberal. Most of them would be considered liberal because it is hard not to be a liberal when you see how society works up close and how power can influence.

Another thing the press does wrong is the tendency to be too respectful of incumbents. It is not just true of President Reagan. It was true of Carter. I was a White House correspondent in 1975 and 1976 right after Jerry Ford had taken over for Nixon. At that time, the press was too hard on Jerry Ford. We were slow to get Nixon, so we said, "Let's take it out on Ford. He's a meathead." . . .

Ford never got a break from the press because there was this delayed reaction: Nixon had picked him so he must be something evil; there must be something wrong with him. Jimmy Carter played this very skillfully. Carter unfairly charged and the press reported, unfair accusations against Ford and some ties with funny money right at the end of the 1976 campaign that hurt Ford. That was an example of less than scrupulous fairness by the media toward the end of that campaign.

With the exception of Ford, the press is not tough enough on incumbents. . . . There is a lot to be said for Reagan's self-confidence, optimism, and his ability to inspire people with his speeches, which has rendered him untouchable by current standards of political criticism. But the press lets him get away with murder: 270 marines dead in Lebanon. Forget it. Grenada, here we come. He neutralized it. By invading Grenada he neutralized the political fallout from Beirut. . . . The press, after Watergate, decided that it had to pull in its horns, because people began to feel that the press had become too powerful and influential, and we were maybe bullying people. We had to chasten ourselves a little. . . . We have some dirty laundry in our own profession, and one of the results of that has been that incumbents get generally better treatment than they deserve from the press. . . . After Nixon, the press decided to think long and hard before taking out after a guy. This is true for Reagan. It did not happen to be true for Carter, who seemed to lose his self-confidence and then became fair game for the press. Carter invited a lot of attack upon himself in a way that Reagan has not.

Another thing the political press may be faulted on is making too much of a horse race of primary campaigns. We did it with the Republicans in 1980, and we can be faulted for doing the same thing now. We concentrate too much on who is ahead now, or who has the best machine. . . . The press has become enamored of political machines, more so than issues, records, or the character and personality of the individual. I do not think that is true of readers. . . . Voters are a lot less impressed by the reputation or efficiency of a political machine than they are with their subjective, personal, and emotional estimates of character and personality. Once we sense an upset, once we sense a guy has made a mistake, once a front-runner has been humbled, get out of the way, because the press is going to stampede. In 1976 it was Jimmy Carter in Iowa, Jimmy Carter in New Hampshire, *Time* cover, *Newsweek* cover, network specials. We are easily spooked. And if it happens this way, for a John Glenn, Gary Hart, or Jesse Jackson, get out of the way, because there is going to be an avalanche of news coverage. It is not really pack journalism, it is a reaction to a stimulus. All the press will rush from one side of the boat, from covering Mondale, to covering whoever the new star is, and the whole media ship is going to tip. . . .

In the case of a political correspondent, a presidential campaign means a year out of your life, you are traveling a great deal. You are in a different hotel all the time, eating out all the time. Most political writers do it because they love the action. They love the game. They love the chase. . . .

I like to highlight issues. The ability to highlight an issue, to focus it, and force politicians to respond to it, is a big power. . . . [W]e can sit them down for an hour and a half and drill them on foreign policy in an intellectual, demanding, rigorous format and make them address things in a way they might not in a stump speech. When you can do that you do not feel helpless. So it is rewarding to be a political journalist.

You just do not work for your editors. You work for the approval of your peers, who are often your competition. And if you are "snookered," to use a John Glenn phrase, or if you are seduced into writing something that proves to be ill-conceived, you lose esteem within the political writing fraternity. This is a powerful force for correcting abuses before they happen, but it also has a tendency to make reporters think twice about whether they should go with their instinct. . . .

The press is unfair. Much of the press is biased in one way or another, and also hostile. Many reporters abuse their powers and a lot of unfair things are written. Politics is not pristine. It takes place in the hurly-burly of the marketplace. It is Darwinian, survival of the fittest, and you have to have a certain resilience, strength, instinct, courage, character, luck, charm, and appeal. There are a lot of things that go into it. All I can say is, by the time the candidate gets to the voters, he has been through the wringer a few times with the press, and you see him, more or less, warts and all. It may not be fair. It may look like we are picking on him, but nobody ever stuck a gun to his head and said, "Gary Hart, your sentence for your crime is that you have to run for president." They want to be there. They welcome it. They come to the media and say, "Put my name in the paper."

3.4 ■■■■

Views of Winners and Losers

Thomas E. Patterson

Editor's Note. In a book that became an instant classic, Thomas E. Patterson talks about creating winner and loser images, particularly during the primaries when they are most important. Early in the campaign the winner image can create a bandwagon effect. Money, volunteers, and votes are attracted to candidates who bear the winner label. In this way media prophecies about who will win and who will lose become self-fulfilling.

Patterson's study was based on a massive collection of two types of data: media content and voters' beliefs and attitudes. Media data came from content analysis of election news in television, newspaper, and news magazine sources that voters used in Erie, Pennsylvania, and Los Angeles, California, during the 1976 presidential campaign. Audience data were obtained through multiple, lengthy interviews with panels of up to 1,236 voters conducted in Erie and Los Angeles. The voters were interviewed five times during 1976 so that evolving attitudes could be chronicled.

Patterson is professor of political science at Syracuse University. His extensive research concerning mass media effects during the 1972 and 1976 presidential elections was made possible by major grants from private and public foundations. The selection is from *The Mass Media Election* (New York: Praeger, 1980). Several tables have been omitted.

The dominant theme of presidential election news coverage is one of winning and losing. The returns, projections, and delegate counts of the primaries and the frequent polling and game context of the general election make the candidates' prospects for victory a persistent subject of news coverage throughout the campaign. The outcomes of the races are of considerable interest to the voters as well; in 1976 this was the most frequently discussed political subject during the primaries and continued to be a large part of political conversation during the general election.

The voters' opinions about the candidates' chances are heavily dependent on information received from the news media. To decide where a candidate stands on the issues, voters might rely on what they know of the candidate's partisanship, but for knowledge of the candidates' competitive positions, they must depend for the most part on news about primary outcomes, poll results, and so on. Indeed, in 1976 people's perceptions of the candidates' chances for nomination and election followed closely what the news coverage indicated those chances to be. When press accounts indicated uncertainty about likely winners and losers, the judgments of the electorate mirrored that uncertainty. When the news spoke of an almost certain winner, the voters expressed the same optimism for that candidate. . . .

Winning and Losing: Two Examples

. . . When the Ford-Reagan race changed direction midway through the primaries, voters revised their perceptions greatly. On April 27 Ford wrapped up his eighth first-place finish in Pennsylvania, the state of the ninth primary. Only Reagan's win in North Carolina on March 23 prevented Ford's sweep of the early primaries. But Reagan then retaliated with a winning streak of his own, winning in Texas on May 1 and in both Indiana and Georgia on May 4, then winning in Nebraska but losing in West Virginia on May 11.

The interviews conducted between April 28 and May 18 indicate that people's estimates of the two candidates' chances were highly sensitive to these developments. . . . People interviewed in the three days immediately following Pennsylvania's primary regarded Ford as an almost certain nominee and saw Reagan's chances as slim. As the days passed and Reagan's victories accumulated, however, there was a significant change in these estimates. Reagan's prospects were thought to have improved somewhat following his win in Texas, to have improved dramatically after his double victory in Indiana and Georgia, and then to have leveled off after he split Nebraska and West Virginia with Ford. Meanwhile people's estimates of Ford's chances slipped gradually before stabilizing near the end. Over the intervening period, voters felt that Ford's advantage over Reagan had declined by about 60 percent. In their minds Reagan still trailed Ford, but by a much narrower margin than before.

Close attention to the news during this period sharpened people's reactions and judgments. First, those with heavier news exposure reacted more quickly to the changing situation. In early May, for example, nearly every voter thought that Reagan was gaining ground on Ford, but those who followed television or the newspaper regularly came to this conclusion two to three days sooner than most nonregulars. Also, the reactions of

Table 1 The Effect of News Exposure on the Evaluation of Debate Winner or Loser (percent)

Which candidate they felt won the debate	Time elapsed between interview and second debate	
	12 hours or less	12 to 48 hours
Ford	53	29
Undecided	12	13
Carter	35	58
Total	100	100

close followers of the news were stronger. Collectively, those having attended carefully believed that Reagan had closed Ford's lead by 65 percent, nonregulars felt the gap between the candidates had shrunk by 55 percent.

The impact of new information on public judgment is even more evident in a competitive situation of another kind—the presidential debates. After each debate, the news focused on analysis of its outcome. The journalistic consensus after the second debate was that Ford had lost because he had mishandled the question on Eastern Europe. Although a number of hours passed before this message reached the voters, its effect was dramatic, for while respondents who were interviewed within 12 hours of the second debate felt that Ford had won, most of those interviewed later felt Carter had won. The passing of time required for the news to reach the public brought with it a virtual reversal of opinion (see Table 1). The change was clearly due to news exposure, for in their evaluation of the debate only 10 percent of the people interviewed early mentioned Ford's statement on Eastern Europe. On their own, voters failed to see in his remark the significance that the press would later attach to it. Yet over 60 percent of those interviewed late discussed his Eastern Europe statement, most indicating that they, like the press, saw it as a major error causing him to lose the second debate.

In this situation close attention to the news again intensified people's reactions. About 50 percent of nonregular news users interviewed late believed that Carter had won the debate, but nearly 65 percent of news regulars interviewed felt he had won. News regulars also were a third more likely to cite Ford's statement on Eastern Europe as the reason for his defeat.

The Making of a Bandwagon

Information about the candidates' chances can result in a bandwagon—the situation where large numbers of voters choose to back the candidate who is ahead. For a bandwagon to occur, however, two conditions must be met: first, voters must be largely unfettered by other influences; second, they must be convinced that the leading candidate is almost certain to win.

A case in point is the 1976 Democratic nominating contest. When the Democratic primaries began, most rank-and-file Democrats had few constraints on their thinking. They were concerned about the nation's unemployment level and still troubled by Watergate, but this discontent was directed at the Republican party. Unlike Vietnam in 1968 and 1972, no issue dominated their thoughts about the party's primaries. Excepting Wallace, most Democrats had no strong feelings one way or the other about their party's active candidates. . . .

Lacking any firm notion of what or whom they wanted, many Democrats were influenced by the news coverage and outcomes of the early primaries. When a voter is firmly committed to a particular candidate or viewpoint, this attitude provides a defense against change. The commitment leads voters to see events and personalities selectively, in the way they want to see them, thus resulting in the reinforcement of existing attitudes. When voters' attitudes are weak, their perceptual defenses also are weak. When this occurs, as Herbert Krugman, Muzafer Sherif, and others have noted, voters are likely to accept incoming information in a rather direct way, thus developing a conception of the situation consistent with this information. Their perspective becomes that of the communicator, a change that directs their attention toward certain ways of acting and away from other modes of behavior. Their perception of the situation may even point toward a single option, one that they find entirely satisfactory because they had no strong initial preference. They then act upon this choice and, in doing so, form attitudes consistent with their choice. Voters, in short, have been persuaded through perceptual change rather than attitude change. Their perceptions were altered first, and then appropriate attitudes were developed.[1]

This was the process of decision for many Democratic voters during the 1976 primaries. They had no strong commitments before the campaign began, but developed perceptions of the race that led them to accept Carter and reject his opponents. In their minds the central concern became the candidates' electoral success and, once the race was seen in this way, they embraced the winner and rejected the losers. Except for Udall, the candidates who were labeled as losers by the press lost favor with the voters. . . . Jackson, Bayh, Wallace, Shriver, and Harris were regarded much less favorably after they failed to run strongly in the early primaries. This cannot be explained by the fact that Democrats had come to know and dislike these candidates' politics, for they acquired very little information of this kind during the primaries. . . . The only impression that most voters gained of any of these candidates was that they were not doing well in the primaries.

. . . The first impression that most Democrats had of Carter was that he was doing extremely well in places like Iowa and New Hampshire, an accomplishment that evoked some surprise and a certain amount of admiration. As they heard more about him, most of them also regarded him as an acceptable nominee. This reaction was not based on the feeling that in Carter they had discovered their ideal candidate, for they knew very little about his politics or abilities. But he seemed like a sensible and personable individual and, since he had won the acceptance of voters elsewhere, he must have his good points. These were persuasive perceptions. The rush to Carter's side was not because large numbers of Democratic voters wanted to be in the winner's camp; that type of bandwagon effect was not operating during the early Democratic primaries. Rather, Carter's approval by other voters, his apparent command of the nominating race, and his lack of liabilities made him the natural choice of an electorate attuned to the race and devoid of strong preferences. . . .

. . . Democrats' opinions about a candidate tended to align with their perceptions of his chances. If they regarded a candidate as having a good chance, they usually had acquired more favorable feelings toward him by the time of the next interview. On the other hand, less favorable thoughts usually followed the perception that a candidate did not have much of a chance. . . .

. . . [F]rom the evidence available it is certain that most Democrats reached a conclusion about a candidate's prospects before developing a firm opinion about him. Considering the uncertainty that the Democratic respondents expressed in the interviews completed just before the first primary, and the fact that the large majority did not even know Carter at the time, it is inconceivable that great numbers of them selected Carter before hearing about his success in the opening primaries. Thus this dual change reflects mostly the pull of their judgments about the candidates' chances on their feelings toward the candidates.

Interestingly, frequent followers of the news were slightly more likely than infrequent users to judge the candidates on the basis of performance. . . . The opposite might have been predicted, since more attentive citizens generally have stronger political convictions, ones that might retard band-wagon effects. Nevertheless, heavier exposure to the newspaper and television was related to the tendency to respond favorably to winners and unfavorably to losers. Perhaps frequent users' heavier exposure to the news media's conception of the Democratic race impressed it more thoroughly on them.

An alternative explanation for why heavy media users were more responsive to winners and losers relates to the uncertainties surrounding the Democratic race—uncertainties about the identity of the candidates, about their prospects, and about their politics. Jacques Ellul posits that conditions of uncertainty make attentive citizens particularly vulnerable to mass persuasion. According to Ellul, attentive citizens feel a greater need to understand situations, and thus feel a greater compulsion to resolve uncertainty when it exists. Because the events they wish to understand are beyond their direct observation, however, they are susceptible to the media's interpretations of reality.

. . . [O]nly a very small percentage of citizens can receive information about an event and then draw unique and perceptive inferences about it. The ordinary response of the attentive citizen is to accept the communicator's definition of the situation. The inattentive citizen, in contrast, may not care or know enough to try to understand the situation, thus being somewhat less likely to adopt the media's interpretation.[2]

Obstacles to Bandwagons

Unlike Democrats, Republicans were largely unaffected by the outcomes of their party's primaries. About 75 percent of the Republican respondents had chosen between Ford and Reagan before the campaign began, some selecting their candidate because they liked or disliked Ford's handling of the presidency, others choosing one of the two men because of a conservative or moderate preference. Moreover, the large majority of these Republicans stayed with their candidate; in June 80 percent preferred the same candidate they had preferred in February. Reasonably sure about which candidate they wanted and why, their commitments shielded them from bandwagon effects. . . . Among rank-and-file Republicans, then, the candidates' successes were generally unimportant to public response. Indeed, another pattern was evident—Republicans tended to think highly of their preferred candidate's chances. There is in fact a general tendency for voters to be optimistic about the prospects for the candidate they favor. People like to think that others will develop equally high opinions of their favorite contender; consequently, they overrate his prospects. Throughout the 1976 race, each candidate's supporters rated his chances more highly than did other voters, but the degree of exaggeration varied. People were especially positive when the indicators were soft or conflicting, as they were before the first primaries, when without a solid basis for assessing how the contests would go, voters were reasonably hopeful about their candidates' chances. It is true that Ford's backers were more confident than Reagan's and Democrats backing Jackson, Carter, and Humphrey were more optimistic than those behind other candidates, but each side held on to the possibility of victory.

Carter's success in the primaries, however, quickly dampened the hopes of opposing Democrats. Halfway through the primaries, regardless of whom they favored, Democratic voters saw Carter as the likely winner. Only Brown's supporters felt their candidate still had a reasonable chance.... Carter's showing had simply overwhelmed the ability of opposing voters to rationalize.

Republicans were less strongly affected by developments. After Ford's victory in Pennsylvania extended his domination of the early primaries, most of Reagan's supporters believed that Ford had the advantage. They were not convinced, however, that the race was virtually over, but felt that Reagan still had time to turn things around, an optimism apparently justified by the winning streak Reagan began in early May. His wins did more than simply persuade his supporters that his chances had improved; many felt that he had edged ahead of Ford. They were less optimistic than Ford's supporters that their candidate would prevail, but they felt he could prevail. Each side continued to feel confident through the remaining primaries—an outlook made possible by the reality of a close race. Almost certainly this impeded any bandwagon effect—most Republicans already believed their side had a good chance.

All of this helps to explain why the Republican and Democratic races, despite similar appearances at the outset, took such different routes. Ford and Carter each began the primaries with a series of victories, but only Carter's success produced a bandwagon. Once he had control of the headlines, there was little to stem the flow of Democrats to his side. To be sure, some people voted against Carter because he was winning. Jackson in Pennsylvania and Brown in California gained some votes because people saw them not as their first choice, but as capable of stopping Carter, thus enabling another candidate, such as Humphrey, to gain nomination. Voters of this type, however, were easily outnumbered by those attracted to Carter because of his success.

The Republican vote was decidedly more stable. Despite the appearance from early losses that his voters were deserting him, Reagan actually retained the large majority of his supporters throughout the early primaries, and won handily when the campaign finally reached the states dominated by conservative Republicans. Had Ford maintained his streak through the early weeks of May, Reagan supporters might have given up hope and reconciled themselves to accepting Ford as their candidate (as they did after the Republican convention). Or had a national crisis occurred, Ford might have been able to rally enough of Reagan's weaker supporters to generate a bandwagon. Or had Reagan committed a major blunder, his support might have evaporated. As things were, however, the strength of his candidacy and the commitment of his followers provided them with an effective shield from persuasion by the outcome of the early primaries.

By the same process, bandwagon effects are limited in nature during a general election. Although a third of the respondents delayed or changed their preferences during the general election, they did not gravitate toward the candidate they felt was leading. Indeed, Carter, who after the summer conventions was thought by most respondents to be ahead, lost votes during the general election. If anything, the fact that Carter appeared likely to win the presidency led voters to examine his candidacy more critically than they previously had. For the most part, changes during the general election reflected people's party, issue, and leadership preferences, influences that rather easily overrode their perceptions of the candidates' chances. Regardless of what they thought about the candidates' prospects, for example, Democrats developed increasingly negative opinions of Ford, and Republicans grew increasingly critical of Carter.

In the general election, people apparently find it easier to believe that their side can win—poll results seem to have less impact on their thinking than primary outcomes and delegate counts. When Carter led by two to one in postconvention polls, Ford's supporters felt Carter was more likely to win, but they hardly conceded him the advantage that opposing Democrats had granted him halfway through the primaries. Shortly before the general election day, when the polls had Carter narrowly in the lead, Ford backers rated Ford's chances as slightly better than Carter's, while Carter backers felt the victory would be a Democratic one. Not surprisingly, then, when a voter was faced with the possibility that his preferred candidate would lose the general election, he was more likely to change his belief about the likely winner than he was to switch candidates.

Notes

1. Herbert Krugman, "The Impact of Televised Advertising," *Public Opinion Quarterly*, Fall 1965, pp. 349-65; Carolyn W. Sherif, Muzafer Sherif, and Roger E. Nebergall, *Attitude and Attitude Change* (Philadelphia: W. C. Saunders, 1965), chap. 1; Muzafer Sherif and Carl Hovland, *Social Judgment* (New Haven, Conn.: Yale University Press, 1961).
2. Jacques Ellul, *Propaganda.* New York: Vintage Books, 1965, pp. 112-16.

3.5 ▬▬▬

The Great American Video Game

Martin Schram

Editor's Note. Martin Schram, a print journalist who has watched video-age presidential campaigns closely, has concluded that seeing is believing, no matter what the words may say. A candidate like Ronald Reagan who built his campaign around visual images, was playing the great American video game, knowing that viewers rely more on their eyes than on contrary messages delivered through their ears or derived from logical thinking. The selection presented here tells how this lesson was driven home to veteran television reporter Lesley Stahl during the 1984 presidential campaign.

Schram also describes how politicians devise elaborate television news strategies and carry them out and how journalists try, and often fail, to avoid manipulation by the political image makers. In the game of video politics, the politicians thus far seem to be ahead of the journalists, and the politician with the best video strategies and skills seem to prevail at the voting booth.

Is the public well-served by video politics? Schram thinks it is, calling television news "the nation's greatest hope" because it permits the public to assess candidates "in those intangible, up-close-and-personal ways that the newspaper can never fulfill."

Schram, at the time of writing, was associate editor of the *Chicago Sun-Times*. He has covered every presidential campaign since 1968, writing for the *Washington Post* and other papers. Besides the book from which these excerpts were taken, Schram has written books about the 1976 and 1980 presidential campaigns. The selection comes from "The Great American Video Game," in *The Great American Video Game: Presidential Politics in the Television Age* (New York: Morrow, 1987), 23-29, 224-226, 305-310. Several footnotes have been omitted.

Lesley Stahl, one of television's greatest stars of network news, sat in silence, listening to an ominous sound she feared could seal her fate at the White House. From the speaker of a small Sony television set wedged between plastic coffee cups and old press releases in the cramped CBS cubicle at the White House press room, about three hundred feet from the Oval Office, she sat listening to the sound of her own voice. She heard herself saying things she had long thought about Ronald Reagan and his aides, but had never dared say publicly before.

For almost four years, Reagan and his advisers had been using television newscasts to create an image of the Reagan presidency that just did not square with the policies of the Reagan presidency. Now Stahl was telling America precisely that—in the most toughly worded piece she had done in her six years of covering the White House for *The CBS Evening News*.

Night after night, Reagan had had his way with the television news. He had succeeded in setting their agenda and framing their stories by posing for the cameras in one beautiful and compelling setting after another. (Reagan officiating at the handicapped Olympics; Reagan dedicating a senior-citizens housing project.) And the networks had duly transmitted those scenes to a grateful nation on the nightly news, even though the pictures of the president conveyed impressions that were quite the opposite of the policies of the president. (Reagan actually had proposed cutting the budget for the disabled; Reagan actually had proposed cutting federal housing subsidies for the elderly.)

The president couldn't control what the correspondents would be saying; but, due to the unintended compliance of the networks, he could certainly control what America would be seeing while they said it.

Now, for five minutes and forty seconds—about three times longer than most stories she got on the air—Stahl told America all about it. Her piece had been the subject of much internal concern and even tension within CBS. "I went over that script as intensely as any script I've ever gone over," recalled Lane Vernardos, who was executive producer of the CBS *Evening News with Dan Rather* in that era. "This was a very sensitive piece. It certainly was a sensitive issue. . . . I thought, 'This is a tough piece. I know I'm going to take a lot of flak for this—not CBS flak, but the phones ring off the hook and Larry Speakes [the White House deputy press secretary] will call.' Larry calls every three or four weeks to complain about something. Larry will be on the phone with this one."

In her script, Stahl told it like it really had been:

How does Ronald Reagan use television? Brilliantly. He's been criticized as the rich man's president, but the TV pictures say it isn't so. At seventy-three, Mr. Reagan could have an age problem. But the TV pictures say it isn't so. Americans want to feel proud of their country again, and of their president. And the TV pictures say you can. The orchestration of television coverage absorbs the White House. Their goal? To emphasize the president's greatest asset, which, his aides say, is his personality. They provide pictures of him looking like a leader.

Confident, with his Marlboro Man walk. A good family man. They also
aim to erase the negatives. Mr. Reagan tries to counter the memory of
an unpopular issue with a carefully chosen backdrop that actually
contradicts the president's policy. Look at the handicapped Olympics,
or the opening ceremony of an old-age home. No hint that he tried to
cut the budgets for the disabled and for federally subsidized housing for
the elderly. . . .

Another technique for distancing the president from bad news—
have him disappear, as he did the day he pulled the marines out of
Lebanon. He flew off to his California ranch, leaving others to hand out
the announcement. There are few visual reminders linking the president
to the tragic bombing of the marine headquarters in Beirut. But two
days later, the invasion of Grenada succeeded, and the White House
offered television a variety of scenes associating the president with the
joy and the triumph. . . . President Reagan is accused of running a
campaign in which he highlights the images and hides from the issues.
But there's no evidence that the charge will hurt him because when
people see the President on television, he makes them feel good, about
America, about themselves, and about him.

And as she spoke, to illustrate her sharply worded points, viewers
were treated to four years of Reagan videos:

The president basking in a sea of flag-waving supporters, beaming
beneath red-white-and-blue balloons floating skyward, sharing concerns
with farmers in a field out of Grant Woods, picnicking with Mid-
Americans, pumping iron, wearing a bathing suit and tossing a football
. . . more flags . . . wearing faded dungarees at the ranch, then a suit with
Margaret Thatcher, getting a kiss and a cake from Nancy, getting the
Olympic torch from a runner, greeting wheelchair athletes at the
handicapped Olympics, greeting senior citizens at their housing project,
honoring veterans who landed on Normandy, honoring youths just back
from Grenada, countering a heckler, joshing with the press corps,
impressing suburban schoolchildren, wooing black inner-city kids, hug-
ging Mary Lou Retton . . . more flags . . . red, white, and blue smoke
emissions from parachutists descending, red-white-and-blue balloons as-
cending.

Stahl turned off the Sony, and as she sat alone in the silence of that
cubicle in the nearly deserted press room on the night of October 4, 1984,
a certain occupational tenseness—a mix of nervousness and apprehension—began to build within her. Reporters are an internally contradictory
lot; on the one hand we want to be tough, ever-vigilant as we pursue our
subjects, yet we know that the reward for tough reporting is often a deep
freeze. Phone calls go unreturned, scoops suddenly drop into the laps of
competitors.

And so it is understandable that this concern, which can be defined
as journalistic fear of freeze-out, began to well within Stahl as she thought

about what she had just told the nation in this extraordinarily long piece. ("I was worried," she recalled later. "It was a tough piece—it insinuated that the campaign wasn't being totally honest about the president's record, and I did have to go back there the next day. And, you know, it's never pleasant if they're angry at you.")

The ringing of the telephone startled her. As she reached to pick it up, she knew what to expect. It was, just as she feared, one of the president's assistants. The Reagan man had wasted no time in punching up the number of the CBS phone at the White House; he couldn't wait to give Stahl a piece of his mind after having monitored with the rest of America her evening's journalism.

"Great piece," the Reagan man said.

Stahl thought she was not hearing right.

"We loved it," he continued.

"You what?" Stahl said.

"We loved it!" he said.

"What do you mean you loved it?" Stahl asked. (It should be pointed out that, for a journalist, there is perhaps one weapon a subject-victim can use to retaliate that is worse than a deep freeze—it is high praise.) "How can you say you loved it—it was tough! Don't you think it was tough?"

"We're in the middle of a campaign and you gave us four and a half minutes of great pictures of Ronald Reagan," said the Reagan assistant. "And that's all the American people see."

Stahl, a veteran on the White House beat and star moderator of CBS's Sunday news showcase *Face the Nation*, was suddenly in no mood to take yes for an answer—she went on to repeat all the tough things she had said in her piece.

The president's man listened to this off-the-cuff replay, and then replied. "They don't listen to you if you're contradicting great pictures," he said, patiently explaining a truth his White House had long held to be self-evident. "They don't hear what you are saying if the pictures are saying something different."

So it is that Ronald Reagan has been able to maintain his public support and dominate America's politics in the 1980s, even when all the public-opinion polls were showing that Americans had seemingly fundamental differences with many of their president's policies. . . . He succeeded because he was able to employ an appeal more fundamental than government policies. He skillfully mastered the ability to step through the television tubes and join Americans in their living rooms; and together they would watch these policies of Washington's and shake their heads—and occasionally their fists—at Washington's policymakers. Americans came to understand that if they were happy with Reagan's policies, the president deserved the credit; and if they were unhappy with them, the president was right there with them, plainly disgusted too.

Reagan accomplished all that because he was able to have his way with a television medium that is represented on the air by journalists who, in many cases, are considered to be decidedly more liberal than he. He did it not by catering to them or debating with them—he did it by making America's most famous television stars irrelevant. He stepped right past these stars and took his place alongside the Americans in their living rooms, and together they paid no great mind to what these media elites were saying. . . . Television watching has become America's true national pastime, and Ronald Reagan has shown the nation's political strategists how it is possible to reduce the pronouncements of the medium's news stars to mere dugout chatter.

Reagan accomplished this in part—but only in part—because he was a former actor who has essentially played the same aw-shucks-cum-John-Wayne part throughout his careers in Hollywood, Sacramento, and Washington. He mainly accomplished it because of the careful strategy-making by top advisers who made the making of the President's image their prime political task and highest presidential calling.

A whole new generation of political advisers has now gone to school on the teachings of Reagan and his videologists, most notably Michael K. Deaver, who functioned for more than four years in the White House as the creator and protector of the president's image. . . .

Ever since the television age of politics was born in the 1952 campaign of Dwight Eisenhower versus Adlai Stevenson, the ability to use the medium has been increasingly essential to electoral success. In 1960, John F. Kennedy's video persona in his televised debate with Richard Nixon proved his margin of victory. In 1968, Joe McGinniss captured America's political imagination with his book *The Selling of the President,* which unfolded from the inside the machinations of Richard Nixon's television advertising campaign. In 1976, Jimmy Carter co-opted television in the Democratic primaries to help him create a candidacy that was larger than life, and then failed to master that medium and went on to appear as president smaller than the office he held.

And in 1984, the Democrats in their primaries and Ronald Reagan throughout his presidency proved that the visual medium had become the political message. Success on the TV news has come to overshadow success with TV ads; and in the primaries, success on the local newscasts in the primary states has come to overshadow the much shorter network evening news shows as shapers of electorate opinion.

In all the presidential primaries of that year, it was the candidate's ability to get his daily message out on the nightly television news that unquestionably was the single greatest factor in determining the winner. This was even true in the caucus states, where traditional political punditry maintained that machine organization was key and television impact was minimal.

When people vote for president, they are most interested not in policy specifics but in taking the measure of the candidate—what kind of leader will he or she be? How will the candidate react in the crisis to come, which involves issues unknown? That is the greatest service television performs in this democracy's rites of succession. Television's greatest disservice is its difficulty in dealing with governmental policies and their consequences and showing that they are in fact very much a part of the candidate's real leadership skills.

In the years of the Reagan presidency, the White House advisers have succeeded in getting the television news shows to do their bidding whether the electronic journalists realized it or not. They were able to do this in part because of the nature of the medium. And they were able to do it because there are some pols who understand TV better than the TV people themselves.

They understood early that in areas of government policy and global complexity the nature of the medium is tedium. And so by controlling the pictures, they could control the pacing—and the entertainment quality—of the news shows. . . .

. . . [T]he Reagan campaign of 1984 showed that a shrewd and politically sophisticated group of strategists and a willing and communicatively sensitive candidate can manipulate the messages of the spring and summer so they work *for* their campaign. They showed that it is possible to use the mix of television news and ads to in effect achieve victory—or at least lay the groundwork for victory—before the traditional Labor Day kickoff.

This crucial public mood of patriotism and optimism was designed and nurtured by Reagan's top strategists—James Baker, Michael Deaver, and their associates on the White House staff—plus the group of some forty Madison Avenue advertising-agency brainstormers who called themselves the Tuesday Team (named for Election Day) and worked to produce commercials to sell Ronald Reagan as skillfully as they had sold Campbell's soup, Prego spaghetti sauce, Pepsi-Cola, Gallo wine, and Yamaha motorcycles. . . .

Michael Deaver said that watching the way the Democrats conducted their televised primary-election debates convinced him of the direction the Reagan news and ad-message campaigns should take. "I thought the way the Democrats handled the primary situation was abominable," said Deaver. "It was far too scrappy and disagreeable. No one emerged as acting presidential". . . . If that is what the public was getting from the Democrats—political harangues and lectures about what was wrong with America—then the Reagan campaign would give the public just the opposite. Deaver recalled one meeting of the Reagan strategy-makers in Baker's White House office. "We decided early on that the best thing we had going were all these guys [the Democrats] screaming and scratching. . . . While all these people are fighting, we've got to go with nice old couples walking down the street eating ice cream cones, and kids waving the American flag, and people buying houses, and more people getting married, and more people believing in America again. . . .

"We felt not only because of the Olympics, but a feeling we got through [polling] research . . . that this idea of making people feel good was the way to go. As long as it worked, we ought to use it forever. . . . That's the Reagan constituency; all we were trying to do was show that visually."

The orchestral theme music, soothing and uplifting at the same time, plays in the background, and the scenes that drift through the Reagan ad are done in soft-focus photography, which complements the soft-sell messagery. First there is an ideal factory, then people working, a cowboy dusting himself off, people getting married, people building a house.

ANNOUNCER: It's morning again, in America. Today more men and women will go to work than ever before in our country's history. With interest rates at about half the record highs of 1980, nearly 2,000 families today will buy new homes, more than at any time in the past four years. This afternoon, 6,500 young men and women will be married, and with inflation at less than half what it was just four years ago they can look forward with confidence to the future. It's morning again, in America. And under the leadership of President Reagan, our country is prouder and stronger and better. Why would we ever want to return to where we were less than four short years ago? . . .

The instrument of television has taken control of the presidential-election process. It is the single greatest factor in determining who gets nominated every fourth summer and who gets elected that fall. Some politicians and strategists have shown remarkable skill at regulating and even manipulating the television news coverage. The most successful of them have also enjoyed a good bit of luck.

Television news has become the greatest force in the nation's presidential process; it also stands as the nation's greatest hope. It remains the only medium that can give the public what it wants most: the ability to take the measure of the candidates for president in those intangible, up-close-and-personal ways that the newspaper page can never fulfill.

This is of great and perhaps even overriding importance, because a vote for president is a special and rather personal thing for many people, a bit like casting a vote for father, or grandfather (or maybe, in the case of John F. Kennedy, a vote for husband). People often find it difficult to sort through the complexities of even the best-explained national issue, to decide which position they believe is right and which they believe is wrong. But they often find it easy to look at the candidates and decide which they would most like to lead the nation through the next crisis, whatever that crisis may be. The task of television-news journalists is to do their journalistic best to tell people what is really going on, to make the issues and controversies as understandable as possible, even as the camera provides the crucial, close, personal insights into the candidates. . . .

In The Great American Video Game, the goal of the politicians and image-makers is relatively simple: to design visual settings that will put the candidate and his or her policies in the best possible light, images that encourage television journalists to focus their stories around the photo opportunities provided.

The goal of the television journalists (reporters, editors and producers, and executives) is much more difficult—tougher than that of the politicians or the image-makers, and certainly tougher than that of the print journalists. It is to withstand the designs and schemes of the image-makers and to maintain journalistic control of their news product. It requires an unceasing effort to withstand the temptation to build a story around an event—such as Ronald Reagan's Fourth of July, 1984—simply because it was a day of fascinating pictures. It means they must build the story around his statements that day, relegating the pictures of stockcar racing and holiday spirit to their proper and secondary perspective.

The Great American Video Game will always produce competition verging on warfare between the pols and the television journalists. The task of the journalists is to see that their relationship with the candidates and image-makers remains healthily adversarial rather than symbiotic.

America's television news and its voters do not have to lose every time the Great American Video Game is played. . . .

Behind the examples of television news's failures to resist the enticements of campaign image-makers in 1984, there is also this central reality: There is nothing that television news correspondents or anchors or producers could have done that would likely have altered the outcome of the 1984 campaign. Reagan would likely have won reelection no matter what—even if the television networks had not catered to his made-for-television pageants and his visually compelling ways.

Reagan's campaign hummed in perfect political harmony with its blend of feel-good imagery and economic fact. Beating a president in a time of relative peace and prosperity is as unlikely as it sounds. The unenviable job of having to show the nation that the "peace" was problematic, what with those 261 marine deaths in Lebanon and the efforts to overthrow the Sandinistas in Nicaragua, was left to Mondale and his strategists. And it was left to Mondale and his strategists to convince their countrymen that the prosperity they felt and saw every time they went to the store was not real, and that a deficit they could not see, feel, or understand loomed as the economic undoing of their children or themselves.

But it is also true that Mondale and his strategists were singularly not up to the challenge of this tough assignment in message politics in 1984. Reagan and his advisers were masterful. And the television networks were often unable to cope with and unable to gain control of their own medium.

3.6 ▬▬▬

Show Horses in House Elections:
The Advantages and Disadvantages
of National Media Visibility

Timothy E. Cook

Editor's Note. Timothy E. Cook discusses the increasing importance of mass media publicity for members of Congress. Work horses, who concentrate on legislative duties, are turning into show horses, who prance around seeking publicity. Media coverage is particularly crucial during elections, when name recognition boosts a member's chances of being elected. Local coverage is generally more helpful than national coverage, however. Local newspeople usually feature the representative's achievements in matters of high concern to constituents. Reporters for the national media are apt to be more negative and to write stories that may be of limited local interest.

The study combines two research approaches: content analysis of national nightly television news and the *New York Times*, and interviews with press secretaries whose views about the value of media coverage were elicited in two surveys. Contrary to political folklore, frequency of coverage by the national news media did not influence vote totals, but it did have other effects. Negatively, national coverage tended to attract stronger, better-financed rivals, thereby reducing the chances of reelection. Positively, it helped representatives become national spokespersons for issues of special interest to them and created national constituencies for these issues. Being a show horse thus ultimately aids the work horse role. It may also indirectly help reelection by strengthening the representative's legislative record.

Cook is associate professor of political science at Williams College, specializing in legislative and electoral politics. In 1984-1985, he served as a congressional fellow in the office of Ohio representative Don Pease. The selection comes from "Show Horses in House Elections: The Advantages and Disadvantages of National Media Visibility," in *Campaigns in the News: Mass Media and Congressional Elections,* ed. Jan Pons Vermeer (New York: Greenwood Press, 1987), 161-181. Several tables and footnotes have been omitted.

The unabridged version of this essay appears in *Campaigns in the News: Mass Media and Congressional Elections,* Jan Pons Vermeer, ed. (Greenwood Press, Inc., Westport, Ct., 1987), pp. 161-182. Copyright © 1987 by Jans Pons Vermeer. Abridged and reprinted with permission.

A familiar complaint in current assessments of Congress has been to decry the preoccupation in both the House and the Senate with publicity. According to numerous scholars, beginning with Mayhew's (1974a) influential essay, Congress is nowadays organized less to address constructively public problems than to provide maximum opportunities for self-promotion. The "work horse," some say, has been succeeded by the "show horse," to the point that the mass media's effects on Congress include exacerbating the dispersion of power, increasing the dilemmas of coalition building in the institution, and contributing to the decline of Congress as a national policy-making body (see especially Robinson, 1981, Ornstein, 1983, and Ranney, 1983; a journalistic account that stresses this shift is Broder, 1986).

Evidence abounds that members of both the House and the Senate devote increasing resources to the search for publicity, not only through self-promotional efforts like trips home and mass mailings but also through the mass media. For example, the recent institutionalization of a designated press secretary position in House offices attests to the importance of the media as one focus for congressional activity. As of the Ninety-eighth Congress, in 1984, only 28 percent of House offices listed no staffers with press responsibilities—a striking shift from the Ninety-first Congress, in 1970, in which 84 percent of House offices had no designated press aide (Cook, 1985). Likewise, the national publicity accorded to House members has expanded during the same time period; whereas only 24 percent of House members were covered *at all* by the network news in 1970, more recent figures are as high as 55 percent in 1981 (Cook, 1986). Members may then be spending more time publicizing themselves and their activities, and they may be receiving more coverage, but it is less clear why they are doing so, how they are doing so, and with what effect.

The most common presumption has been that members of Congress pursue publicity to ensure reelection. There can be little doubt that the mass media play an important and growing role in congressional elections and reelections. Recognition of the competing candidates is a central determinant of voting decisions, and is highly affected by media coverage. As media advertising takes ever larger chunks of campaign finances, receiving free media exposure becomes crucial (see especially Goldenberg and Traugott, 1984). However, our knowledge approaches completeness only on the impact of local media coverage of the incumbent on congressional elections, where the symbiotic relationship of members and local media appears to work to the decisive benefit of the incumbent.[1] By providing newsworthy items to report, the members help the local media fill their newsholes; by reporting about the incumbents uncritically, the local media not only assure their own continued access to the newsmaking members, but also help to boost the incumbents' name recognition and favorable popular assessments of their activities.

The local media, however, make up only one part of what Robinson (1981) nicely terms the members' "media mix." We understand far less about the importance and impact of another component—national media visibility—on congressional elections, even though it is there that "show horses" often direct their attention. National media visibility has traditionally been assumed to be an advantage to members seeking reelection. For instance, Mayhew's (1974a) concept of advertising and Payne's (1980) consideration of "show horses" both suggest the national media as a key conduit of publicity with presumably beneficial effects on getting returned to Congress. Likewise, some members of Congress were initially prone to anticipate the incursion of national media into the House—especially the broadcasting of floor proceedings—as helping in reelection. In 1979 then-Representative John Anderson, a Republican from Illinois, called the nascent House television system "one more incumbent protection device at taxpayers' expense [that will] distort and prolong our proceedings by encouraging more and longer speeches for home consumption" (in Cooper, 1979, p. 252). On the other hand, there is reason to doubt that national media attention is seen to be as much of a plus for members in reelection as has been commonly assumed. Robinson (1981), for one, contends that most members of Congress see the national media as being tougher and less fair to them than the pliant local media. And insofar as news coverage of Congress does tend to be more negative than positive (see Miller et al., 1979; Robinson and Appel, 1979; Tidmarch and Pitney, 1985), members may wish to avoid any guilt by association with the disdained institution far from the home district where the incumbent's support is best nurtured and reinforced.

It is then unclear whether the national media help or hurt the incumbents' pursuit of reelection. . . . [National] media coverage could empirically influence congressional election outcomes in interrelated ways. First, there could be a direct relationship between media visibility and the percentage of votes received by the incumbent; voters could respond directly, whether favorably or unfavorably, to noticing their representative in the national news. . . .

Second, and probably more likely, given the even chances that a representative will not be mentioned in the network news in a given year (Cook, 1986) and the general inattentiveness of the mass public to nightly network news (Comstock et al., 1977), there could be an indirect relationship mediated through the strength of the challenger as measured by the funds he or she is able to raise and spend (Jacobson, 1980). . . .

To test these suggestions, data were collected for a variety of activities engaged in by members at least in part for electoral benefit (e.g., trips home, bills co-sponsored, district staff allocations), the member's position within the House (e.g., leadership status, seniority), and electoral liabilities (e.g., estimates of policy discrepancy from the district, ethical accusations), as well as indicators of partisan strength and the incumbent's past electoral performance in previous years, in order to assess the impact of media coverage over and above those variables more commonly thought to affect congressional elections. . . .

The media visibility variables are straightforward. For visibility in the network news, a count was made of the number of times each member was mentioned on any nightly network news broadcast according to the Vanderbilt Television News Abstracts and Indices. . . . For visibility in the national print media, a similar count was taken using the *New York Times Index.* . . .

. . . [I]n neither 1978 nor 1980 did network news visibility have a significant direct effect on the vote totals; instead, the election returns were best explained by long-term and short-term partisan conditions, the challengers' expenditures and political experience, and accusations of ethical improprieties. Appearing on the network news had no independent impact on the vote totals. Similar results obtain if visibility in the *Times* is included in the equation in lieu of the media visibility variable. . . .

Interestingly, media coverage in the network news did have an effect on challengers' strength as measured either by their expenditures or their political action committee (PAC) contributions. The effect is negative in 1978 but is not significant at a .05 level. In 1980, however, network news visibility *positively* predicted challenger moneys, and similar effects were in evidence on challengers' PAC contributions (see Ragsdale and Cook, 1987). Whether or not one was covered by the nightly news apparently increased one's chances of facing a strong opponent, even over and above the effects of variables that would best predict media visibility such as leadership status and ethical accusations.[2] Moreover, at the same time that incumbents' media visibility apparently assisted challengers in their abilities to raise and spend funds, it had no similar effects for incumbents attempting to match challengers' efforts. . . . In sum, national media coverage either in print or over the air seems not to be, at best, a credible strategy for incumbents in seeking reelection, and, at worst, it may be a way to enhance the strength of one's opponent.

Members and National Media: The Press Secretaries' Perspective

The results from the 1980 election show the perils of national media visibility. Members more visible in the national news were more likely to face credible opponents than those not covered. Receiving what "show horses" seek—coverage by the national media—not only seems not to pay dividends at the polls; it may actually hurt, indirectly but effectively, the member's chances for reelection.

Yet, despite ... empirical indicators and Robinson's (1981) contention that members and their staffs see the national media as tough and
unfair, we know that members of Congress seldom hide from national
attention. Of course, it may be that the national media may be worth the
reelection risks in order to attain other goals—public policy accomplishments, influence in Washington, progressive ambition, or just plain ego
gratification—but could there be subtle benefits from national news
attention about which members and staffers are aware?

To estimate whether and why House press operations would pay
attention to the national media, I proceeded in two complementary ways.
First, I conducted forty semistructured interviews with a representative
sample of press secretaries in the fall directly preceding the 1984 election.
All interviews were held under "not-for-attribution" conditions in which
strict anonymity for member and staffer alike was guaranteed. A
semistructured format was chosen in order to ask particular questions
while permitting the interviewee to digress into potentially important
areas. Although this format does not permit easy quantification, it
provides a rich basis for conclusions. Second, through the Association of
House Democratic Press Assistants, a three-page questionnaire composed
by myself and Lynn Drake, then-president of the association, was sent out
in November 1984, after the election, to all Ninety-eighth Congress
Democratic House offices, asking the press secretary to respond to
questions pertaining to their media operations and their perceptions of a
number of strategies and news outlets. The response rate was a reasonably
strong 46 percent (N=123), an acceptable percentage considering that
numerous House offices do not have any one designated press aide. Only
Democrats were studied because of the importance of being able to
determine the member for which particular press secretaries worked, and
because of the sensitivity of press strategies. Although each of these
approaches is imperfect, our ability to triangulate between the two studies
enhances the confidence with which one can make conclusions. Moreover,
although these surveys cannot give the perceptions of members themselves (or, for that matter, fellow staffers) on the presumed importance of
the national media to congressional operations, they do provide solid
indications of the strategies preferred by those most closely working with
the press and the approaches that they bring to the relationship of
Congress and the media.[3]

During the semistructured interviews I asked what the major focus of
the press secretaries' jobs were, what they spent the most time doing, who
they dealt with, and the strategies they used to get their members' names
in the news. Questions about the national media were expressly reserved
until later in the interview. Frequently, at this point, the respondents had
mentioned nothing about the national media—either electronic or print.
Moreover, to the pursuant question, "Do the national media help in

Table 1   Democratic Press Secretaries' Evaluation of Media Outlets and Strategies

	Mean	Standard deviation
Local dailies	9.0	1.5
Local weeklies	8.2	2.0
Press releases	8.1	1.8
Newsletters	7.8	2.0
Local television news	7.4	2.6
Targeted mail	6.7	2.7
Radio actualities	5.6	3.3
Recording studio	4.9	2.9
Weekly columns	4.8	3.2
Washington Post	4.7	3.1
Network television news	4.4	3.2
New York Times	4.3	3.1
Televised floor proceedings	3.8	2.7

Source: Calculated by the author from Democratic press secretary questionnaire, November-December 1984.

Note: The question was: "Please rate how valuable each is in getting your job done (on a scale of 1 to 10 with 1 being very low and 10 being very high)." $N \geq 120$.

getting the job done?" press secretaries were often incredulous, some indicating that nobody in the district read the *Washington Post* or the *New York Times*. National media do not seem to help most press secretaries in their daily work, as can be seen by the results from the questionnaires of Democratic press secretaries. Table 1 reports the mean ratings (on a scale running from a low of 1 to a high of 10) for various outlets and strategies that help to get the press secretaries' jobs done. There was strong consensus on the positive value of local newspapers—either dailies or, to a lesser extent, weeklies—and a slightly weaker agreement on the worth of local television news. However, the national media, whether electronic or print, are rated considerably lower in their value to press secretaries. . . .

. . . [T]here were strong indications that the local media came first. One press secretary said early on, "We'd rather get in the [hometown paper] than the front page of the *New York Times* any day," and only one press secretary among the forty semistructured interviews disagreed with that statement. Getting mentioned on the front page of the *Times* is unlikely, and similar results obtain with a more realistic choice, as found in the questionnaire: only 15 percent disagreed with the statement "I'd rather get on the front page of my hometown daily than in the *New York Times* or the *Washington Post* any day," as reported in Table 2.

The national media are then not central to the aims of the vast

Table 2 Democratic Press Secretaries' Attitudes on Local Versus National Media

	"I would rather get in the front page of my hometown daily any day than the *New York Times* or the *Washington Post.*"	"The local media are fairer to my boss than the national media."
Agree strongly	45% (56)	7% (9)
Agree somewhat	26% (32)	19% (23)
Neither agree nor disagree	10% (13)	59% (73)
Disagree somewhat	12% (15)	9% (11)
Disagree strongly	3% (4)	6% (7)
No answer	3% (4)	1% (1)
Total	99% (124)	101% (124)

Source: Calculated by the author from Democratic press secretary questionnaire, November-December 1984.

Note: Columns do not add to 100% due to rounding.

majority of press secretaries, who generally see their task as getting the member's name and accomplishments publicized back home. The national media are not viewed as less fair to their bosses. Few emphasized that their member discouraged, explicitly or implicitly, national media attention in general. In the survey of Democratic press secretaries, asked to agree or disagree with the statement "The local media are fairer to my boss than the national media," the bulk (59 percent) neither agreed nor disagreed; only 26 percent agreed. Likewise, in Dewhirst's (1983) survey of sixty-two press secretaries in 1981-1982, thirteen rated the national media as fairer, fifteen rated the district media as fairer, and the remainder reported no difference (p. 142). The national media are thus less important to House press operations than local media, but they are not shunned as being unfair or negative. . . .

. . . [D]espite . . . potential advantages of using the national media for reelection, not to mention other goals like internal influence and policy accomplishments, virtually all press operations in the House primarily focus on the local media.[4] However, the possible liabilities of national visibility that were apparent in 1980 do not seem to weigh heavily on press secretaries' minds. Instead, several other factors propel press operations to favor local over national media in the pursuit of reelection.

First, the local media are the main customers for their product. Not only do press secretaries find local outlets more valuable, but local reporters are generally in much closer contact, sometimes on a daily basis, than national reporters. Local media, after all, come to depend on individual members to regularly make news for them. In the words of the press secretary to a four-term midwestern Republican from a rural district, "journalists are glad to talk to a member of Congress. It's an easy story, it's good copy cause anything he says is news. It makes the day easier to fill twenty column-inches or thirty seconds that way instead of a leaves-turning-color story." Not only may representatives provide stories of grants being awarded or local heroes being recognized, their reactions can provide a local angle to a national story, making the event more saleable to editors and (presumably) audiences. Most interactions are then with local newspersons; Dewhirst found his sample of sixty-two press secretaries estimating on the average that 76 percent of their time was spent dealing with district media, as compared with 18 percent with national media and 11 percent with statewide media, even though the press releases sent out were approximated to be just about evenly divided between national and local issues (1983, p. 142). It is then difficult to establish rapport with national media, who have numerous reporters covering Congress, sometimes by issues rather than by beat, and with whom contact is sporadic. Keeping regular customers happy and willing to come back to buy a product again is something every enterprise aims for; congressional enterprises are no exception.

Second, even if the member is newsworthy to both local and national media, the latter has different needs, which places an angle on the story that deemphasizes the member's personal role in favor of the issue or controversy concerned. The national media cannot be expected to find 1 out of 435 newsworthy in the same way that the local outlets find the lone representative important. Unlike in the local media, obtaining almost any member's reactions to some national event would not be considered nationally newsworthy unless that member had a base of legitimation as an "authoritative source." The distinction is then not only between local media attending to members versus national media ignoring, but also in what each level considers important, especially since what is newsworthy to the national media can often get covered without covering the member pushing it. . . .

. . . [A]s a result of these two factors, any national coverage on one's own terms requires much more expenditure of resources than it would cost to obtain an equivalent or greater amount of local coverage. This is especially true of network television news, the national medium most

Table 3   Correlates of Democratic Press Secretaries' Perceived Value of National Media

Importance of long-term goals	Pearson's r with index of value of national media
Building name recognition of member in district	.06
Creating national constituency for issue	.51[a]
Enabling member to run for higher office	.19[b]
Serving as liaison to different constituent groups	.05
Making member national spokesperson on an issue	.52[a]

Source: Calculated by the author from Democratic press secretary questionnaire, November-December 1984.

[a] $p < .001$.

[b] $p < .05$; all other coefficients not statistically significant at $p < .05$.

likely to directly reach the voters but where the vagaries of the twenty-two minute constraints are unpredictable and where the preparation involved is daunting. As the press secretary to a southern Democratic committee chair concluded, "to do an interview here, it takes up thirty or forty minutes just to get set up and then some more to do it. And then he gets seven seconds of time. Sure seems like a lot of trouble for not very much meat.". . . Given that serving the needs of the local media could easily become a full-time job in any media market, devoting resources to enticing the national media with only uncertain prospects for beneficial results is not an efficient way to ensure that the member almost continually makes news.

Thus dealing with the national media is seldom pursued for reelection purposes. Why, then, do members have any interest in national media visibility? . . . In the questionnaire of the Democratic press secretaries, the respondents were asked to rate the importance of five long-term goals in their work; these variables were then correlated with an index of the value of national media in general. . . .

As reported in Table 3, the index of the value of national media was highly correlated with two goals: national spokespersonship and creating national constituencies for an issue. By contrast, the correlations were insignificant with the two constituent-oriented goals and only marginally significant with the goal of progressive ambition.

. . . The national media, it seems, are largely important for national goals. Even considering a run for a more salient office only somewhat impels House press operations to find national media more useful, and they are seldom perceived as an effective way to gain the local benefits, which, more often, are, at best, a useful by-product.

Conclusion

Members of Congress have sought publicity throughout history. The show horse—work horse 'distinction is far from new to students or members of the national legislature. What is new are the allegations that the incentives and rewards for being a show horse now outstrip those for being a work horse. Yet the results here suggest that if being a show horse is primarily oriented toward national media visibility, the main incentives do not include winning reelection, the usual "proximate goal" (Mayhew, 1974a) of members of Congress. Aggregate analyses of election outcomes in 1978 and 1980 show that the aim of show horses, national media visibility, does not seem to help in reelection; the only significant effect was to bolster the campaign moneys and PAC contributions of challengers in 1980. Nor do the interviews with and questionnaires from House press secretaries in 1984 display any dependence on national media attention for getting reelected. Local media are seen as more reliable and predictable outlets, more eager not only to cover the member's activities, but also to stress the member's role itself as the most newsworthy aspect of a story. The national media, it appears, are seldom spurned, but they are not openly pursued in most House offices for reelection. Despite the frequently perceived advantages of the publicity that "trickles down" from national to local coverage, it is simply too costly to spend limited resources getting in the national news when other, less expensive means of publicity exist for the folks back home.

It may well be that more and more members of the House are courting national publicity in a manner once reserved for senators (see, e.g., Ornstein, 1981). However, it seems that national media visibility is sought for national goals that cannot be achieved through the local press—especially influence in Washington and attainment of public policy goals. In that sense, members' attentiveness to national media is much more an element exclusively of their Washington styles, not their home styles, to recall Fenno's (1978) crucial distinction. Particularly with the ascendancy of a president, much of whose power rests on the ability to control the agenda through the media (see, e.g., Sinclair, 1985), and with an exceedingly complex Congress in which consensus is difficult to achieve by the old rules of bargaining, members can find that strategies to work with and through the national media are central ways to attain goals inside the institution through such an outside strategy. If there are some slight advantages for reelection as a by-product, so much the better; if there are risks involved, as the aggregate findings from 1980 suggest there may be, most members do not apparently conclude that such risks rule out the importance and value of dealing with the national media.

"Show horses" in Congress are not, then, primarily receiving a boost for reelection, nor are they primarily getting ego gratification from their names in the national headlines and their faces on the nightly news. Even if they do not exploit such strategies much for reelection, being a show horse is rationally goal-oriented more than it is an effect of personality dynamics alone—oriented toward goals that make being a show horse and being a work horse more compatible than mutually exclusive. If members were interested only in reelection, we might not see them paying any attention to the national media. That the national media are not ignored is then testimony to two crucial arguments: members of Congress have important multiple goals beyond reelection and, just as important, media effects must be presumed to go beyond electoral politics in a way whereby the audience usually studied, the mass public, is not directly involved. Whether legislative styles geared toward and dependent on national media are effective ways to get things done in Congress cannot be answered here; all we can conclude is that such styles are not efficient tools for reelection. National media visibility is indeed a resource much more accessible to incumbents than to challengers. But, unlike its local counterpart, its effects as a key perquisite of office are mixed.

Notes

1. . . . Book-length treatments that underscore this point include Clarke and Evans (1983) and Goldenberg and Traugott (1984).
2. It has been suggested that 1979 might have been a year of unusually bad news. Yet, despite the well-known tribulations of the Carter administration, 1979 was, in most ways, a typical news year for Congress. . . .
3. The two samples are fairly representative of the larger populations. In the sample of House press secretaries who were selected from semistructured interviews, Southerners are slightly underrepresented, whereas Northeastern-ers are slightly overrepresented; fortunately the biases were reversed in the questionnaire of Democratic press secretaries. The questionnaire also over-represents press secretaries to freshmen representatives, although this bias will help us to distinguish more clearly the differences between those engaging in the "new apprenticeship" of the first term and those who have gotten past their first reelection.
4. Even in the Senate, long known for being a publicity chamber and president incubator, a recent study concludes that most senators' press operations are largely focused on the home state media (Hess, 1986).

Bibliography

Broder, David. (1986). "Who Took the Fun Out of Congress?" *Washington Post Weekly Edition* (February 17): 9-10.
Clarke, Peter and Susan H. Evans. (1983). *Covering Campaigns: Journalism in*

Congressional Elections. Stanford, California: Stanford University Press.

Comstock, George et. al. (1977). *Television and Human Behavior.* New York: Columbia University Press.

Cook, Timothy E. (1985). "Marketing the Members: The Ascent of the Congressional Press Secretary." Paper presented at the annual meeting of the Midwest Political Science Association, Chicago, Illinois.

————. (1986). "House Members as Newsmakers: The Effects of Televising Congress." *Legislative Studies Quarterly.* 11:203-26.

Cooper, Ann. (1979). "Curtain Rising on House TV Amid Aid-to-Incumbent Fears." *Congressional Quarterly Weekly Report.* (February 10): 252-54.

Dewhirst, Robert E. (1983). "Patterns of Interaction Between Members of the U.S. House of Representatives and Their Home District News Media." Ph.D. dissertation, University of Nebraska-Lincoln.

Fenno, Richard F., Jr. (1978). *Home Style: House Members in Their Districts.* Boston: Little, Brown.

Goldenberg, Edie N. and Michael W. Traugott. (1984). *Campaigning for Congress.* Washington, D.C.: CQ Press.

Hess, Stephen. (1986). *The Ultimate Insiders: The Senate and the National Press.* Washington, D.C.: The Brookings Institution.

Jacobson, Gary C. (1980). *Money in Congressional Elections.* New Haven, Connecticut: Yale University Press.

Mayhew, David R. (1974a). *Congress: The Electoral Connection.* New Haven, Connecticut: Yale University Press.

Miller, Arthur H., Edie N. Goldenberg, and Lutz Erbring. (1979). "Type-set Politics: The Impact of Newspapers on Public Confidence." *American Political Science Review.* 73:67-84.

Ornstein, Norman J. (1981). "The House and the Senate in the New Congress." In Thomas Mann and Norman Ornstein, eds., *The New Congress.* Washington, D.C.: American Enterprise Institute, pp. 363-83.

————. (1983). "The Open Congress Meets the President." In Anthony King, ed., *Both Ends of the Avenue.* Washington, D.C.: American Enterprise Institute, pp. 185-211.

Payne, James L. (1980). "Show Horses and Work Horses in the United States House of Representatives." *Polity.* 12:428-56.

Ragsdale, Lyn and Timothy E. Cook. (1987). "Representatives' Actions and Challengers' Reactions: Limits to Candidate Connections in the House." *American Journal of Political Science.* 31:45-81.

Ranney, Austin. (1983). *Channels of Power: The Impact of Television on American Politics.* New York: Basic Books.

Robinson, Michael J. (1981). "Three Faces of Congressional Media." In Thomas E. Mann and Norman J. Ornstein, eds., *The New Congress.* Washington, D.C.: American Enterprise Institute, pp. 55-96.

Robinson, Michael J. and Kevin R. Appel. (1979). "Network News coverage of Congress." *Political Science Quarterly.* 94:407-13.

Sinclair, Barbara. (1985). "Agenda Control and Policy Success: Ronald Reagan and the 97th House." *Legislative Studies Quarterly.* 10:407-13.

Tidmarch, Charles and John Pitney. (1985). "Covering Congress." *Polity.* 17:446-83.

4. AFFECTING POLITICAL ACTORS AND THE BALANCE OF POWER

A ll politics involve actors. This part differs from earlier ones only in its more concentrated focus on the effect of the mass media on the political fates of various participants. The section begins with a look at normal coverage patterns for the presidency, the office most in the media limelight. It then turns to routine coverage of Congress and its members. The contrast between media impact on senators and representatives and media impact on the president puts the distinctions between these political actors into sharper focus. An example of presidential news coverage when the presidency is in crisis follows. It points out how all parties to a major conflict use the media to compete for favorable public opinion. The section concludes with two selections that show how media coverage affects two types of interest groups: ordinary people at the fringes of the power structure and ordinary people who defy the mores of the established culture.

The first selection presents what happens at a typical news conference where newspeople confront the president with pointed, often hostile questions. The president tries to control the situation, but often fails. The news conference is followed by a report based on a systematic analysis of media coverage of presidents over a sixteen-year period. Fred T. Smoller delineates how impressions about presidents are created by the media. He explains why these impressions are so politically potent and contends that, on balance, they have diminished the stature and power of the presidency.

David L. Paletz and K. Kendall Guthrie remind us that one cannot talk generically about media coverage as if it were all alike. Individual media vary considerably in thrust and tone of particular stories, which may create images ranging from positive to negative. Michael J. Robinson delineates variations in media treatment of Congress. Stories differ in nature and impact depending on whether they appear in the national or local press or in publications issued by the legislator's office or campaign. Robinson also points out that publicity that may hurt a political institution may, at the same time, help its office holders, and vice versa.

What happens when a president is under serious attack? Do newspeople close in for the kill like a wolf pack stalking wounded prey? Gladys Engel Lang and Kurt Lang reach surprising conclusions after examining the role played by the mass media in the resolution of the

Watergate scandal. Their study also sheds light on the media's function in defining public opinion for policy makers.

From people in formal positions of power, the discussion turns to citizens who band together to seek governmental remedies for shared problems or who strive to gain favorable public attention for their chosen causes. Gadi Wolfsfeld describes how three types of groups tried different techniques, matched to their resources, to attract the media attention they needed. Their efforts met with mixed success. In the final selection, Todd Gitlin explores the services and disservices performed by the media for social protest movements that advocate radical political change. He uses Students for a Democratic Society, a New Left student movement of the 1960s, as an example.

4.1 ▬▬▬

President Bush's News Conference
March 7, 1989

Editor's Note. We begin our look at coverage of the presidency with the transcript of portions of a typical presidential news conference, an event that has occurred regularly since Grover Cleveland's presidency in 1885. In earlier days, presidents protected themselves against unwanted questions by responding only to written queries submitted in advance or by prohibiting all direct quotations unless specifically authorized. Dwight D. Eisenhower was the first president to allow full quotations, including radio and television broadcasts of his conferences. These broadcasts usually were delayed to permit editing. Live-broadcast news conferences started with President John F. Kennedy in 1961.

Presidents always have enjoyed as well as dreaded these public confrontations with reporters. If presidents perform well, and if they are masters of repartee, news conferences can enhance their image and their effectiveness. If they perform poorly, or if they misstate an important fact or make an unfortunate slip of the tongue, the results can be disastrous, especially when errors are made in front of a television audience of millions of people.

To prepare for news conferences, modern presidents are briefed about all current problems that are likely to surface. After digesting this information, some have held dress rehearsals in which aides quiz the president, mimicking the inquisitorial style of news reporters. Presidents also may receive a seating chart of reporters, complete with pictures, so that they can call on reporters whom they deem friendly. But all these preparations are never enough. With reporters ready with hundreds of questions, and the time for framing answers measured in seconds, misstatements are almost unavoidable.

The news conference reported here from the *New York Times* transcript illustrates several common practices: the president's use of an opening statement in the vain hope of guiding the discussion, the reporters' sharp and at times antagonistic questioning, the broad sweep of issues that the president must be prepared to discuss, and the groping for appropriate formulations of questions and answers. The headings have been added to the original text.

[Opening Statement]

. . . I want to take this brief opening statement opportunity to restate my belief that free collective bargaining is the best means of resolving the dispute between Eastern Airlines and its unions. I continue to feel that it would be inappropriate for the Government to intervene and to impose a solution. This dispute has gone on for more than 17 months and it's time for the parties involved to get down to serious business and reach an agreement. The action forcing event in this case is the strike and that is the tool at the disposal of labor and they're properly going forward with that. Management and labor now have to find a settlement.

But let me just say that I hope my position on secondary boycotts is well known. Thankfully these boycotts have not yet materialized and I hope they don't. Temporary restraining orders have been in effect yesterday and today in the New York and Philadelphia areas, but even when those restraining orders lapse, I remind all parties that secondary boycotts are not in the public interest. And I will send legislation to Congress to forbid them if that is necessary. It is not fair to say to a commuter on a train coming in from Long Island that you're going to be caught up and victimized by a strike affecting an airline. It simply isn't fair in my view.

... The Department of Transportation and the F.A.A. have taken every precaution to insure airline safety during this period. And I understand that the pilots are talking about a work slowdown beginning today. Certainly, I must recognize their special concerns for safety during this period, but I also would urge them not to make the traveling public— the innocent traveling public, a pawn in this dispute. So that's my view on the airline strike and I hope that it is settled in the traditional way: management, labor sitting down and working out an agreement. . . .

[Questions and Answers]

[Signs of Policy Drift]

Q. Mr. President, your struggle to win the confirmation of Senator Tower and the seeming lack of direction has caused a lot of criticism that your Administration is in drift, there is malaise. What is your response and what are you going to do about it?

A. My response is that it's not adrift and there isn't malaise. And I talked to a fellow from Lubbock, Tex., the other day, which is the best phone call I've made. And he says all the people in Lubbock think things are going just great. . . .

Q. Do you really think you're doing fine, when nobody—

A. I think we're on track.

Q. —knows where your Administration is going?

A. Well, let me help you with where I think it's going. First place, in a very brief period of time, we addressed ourselves to a serious national problem, the problem of the S & L bailout. That is still moving forward. It takes a little time. I've challenged the Congress to act.

Secondly, we came up in a very short period of time with great amount of detail, far more than the two previous Administrations, regarding the budget, sound proposals. The No. 1 problem facing this country, in my view, is getting this Federal budget deficit down. Not only did we address it, but we addressed it in considerable detail and talks are going on right now to try to solve that problem.

There, we've—I've taken a substantive foreign policy trip that took me not only to three countries, but where I met with, I think, some 19 representatives of 19 countries and talked about their objectives and mine for foreign policy. Our Secretary of State has not only touched base with all the NATO leaders, but has had a productive meeting with Mr. Shevardnadze. The defense reviews and the other foreign policy reviews are under way and I will not be stampeded by some talk that we have not come up with bold new foreign policy proposals in 45 days. . . .

We're confident of the confirmation of Bill Bennett and he is charged with a six-months mandate to do something, map out the drug program, and he will be very serious about going forward on that. I appointed early on an ethics commission, which will be—has been meeting and will be coming out with, I think sound proposals and so we'll start moving forward legislatively there.

I spelled out in my speech, an education agenda, and that will be followed, the speech, very shortly with legislative initiatives. . . .

So I would have to urge, and we—everyone here is familiar with my position on child care. That's going to take legislation, but I think the Congress clearly knows where we want to go there. So I would simply resist the clamor that nothing seems to be bubbling around, that nothing is happening. A lot is happening. Not all of it good, but a lot is happening.

[Intervention in Airline Strike]

Q. Mr. President, on the air strike, your opposition on Capitol Hill—many of the Democrats up there—wanted you to intervene in this strike. Should you have to go to Congress for emergency legislation to deal with secondary boycotts, it is likely they are going to say, "No, no, we want you to intervene first." If the Eastern pilots succeed, and the machinists succeed in imposing secondary boycotts, you seem to be on a collision course there. Will your policy hold firm?

A. It will hold firm. The Secretary is testifying, I think at this very moment, about the kind of legislation you're talking about; and some wanting to compel the President to convene this board. So there are two schools of thought. I still feel that the best answer is a head-on-head, man-to-man negotiation between the union and the airline. And I think that is better, and more lasting incidentally—the agreement that would stem from that—more lasting than an imposed Government settlement which could cause the airline to totally shut down. So I think there could be some, you know, confrontation. But I will stick with my view and I will— and if, indeed, innocent parties are threatened through the secondary boycott mechanism, I will move promptly with the Congress. And what will happen—what would happen, and I don't want to buy into a lot of hypothesis here—but you would have an outcry from the American people on the basis that I mentioned about that commuter. It is not fair, you know, to have innocent people victimized by a struggle between Eastern Airlines and the machinists union. . . .

Q.   If that should happen, sir, you must recognize that there would be great pressure on you to at least stop it for 60 days. Are you intent on not doing that?

A.   I'm intent on staying with what I've outlined is our Administration's policy, and it is the correct policy and I think it's the best way to have a solution to this question. We'll go right across here and then start down there.

[Tower Confirmation Debate]

Q.   Mr. President, back to Helen's question, the sort of sense that's developing that, let's say, the John Tower fight is sapping you of your ability to get on with other issues. How long are you willing to fight this fight, let the debate go on? Are you ready to now call for them to have a vote, say today or tomorrow, just to get this behind you one way or the other?

A.   No. No. Because, Lesley, in the first place there are two major principles: fair play and, secondly, the right of the President to have— historical right—to have who he wants in his Administration. And I've heard a lot of judgments on Tower based on reports; varying people reading the same report and coming out with different judgments. I want him. I believe he is the best man for the job. There are a lot of historical precedents behind my desire to have him, and you might say "right" to have him, barring any very clear reason not to. And therefore, I will stay with it.

And secondly, it's the Senate that controls when they vote or not, and I will—I will leave that to Bob Dole and to George Mitchell, both of whom I think are conducting themselves very well.

Q.   May I ask you—

A.   Here's a follow-up, yes.

Q.   May I ask you a question about the chain-of-command question, because the Senator admits to excessive drinking which would disqualify him for a job in the so-called chain of command. Does this not disturb you at all, that that's the qualification for a job?

A.   No, I think he'll measure up to that qualification. Indeed he has said he'd never touch another drop of liquor, and you'll have 25,000 people in the Pentagon making sure that's true. So what—I mean, here's, I'd say, a fail-safe guarantee. It doesn't bother me.

Q.   The past—

A.   No, I think he—I think when you look at the record and look at the testimony as I have—and I haven't had one single senator, not one, who served with him over the years say: "I have seen him. My first-hand evidence is this man is ineligible because of his consumption of spirits." Not one. Now isn't that a little bit unusual? So I go right back to the President's right to have his choice. . . .

And, Lesley, it isn't iron-willed stubbornness, there's a question of fundamental principle here. And I've spelled out my call for fair play and I'm going to keep reiterating it. So let the Senate work its will; it's not going to hurt. And this concept that you can never work in the future because people disagree with you in the Senate, I simply don't accept that.

[Release of Confidential Data]

Q.   Mr. President, you have said that the F.B.I. report guns down the accusations against Senator Tower and yet you have also said that there can be no release in practical terms because of the confidentiality of people interviewed. Have you given consideration, given the problem with the nomination, to asking those interviewed to waive the right of confidentiality so that the public doesn't have to take your word for it as to the degree to which this report exonerates the Senator.

A.   Or the word of the opponents, yes. We have thought about that, and I'm not sure where our counsel's office stands on it. But I'll tell you, the precedent is troubling. When you take testimony and then—and then certainly you can't go ahead and release. I mean, I just could not do that. And I think it's very damaging in the future. So I am saying, I have read it, this is my view, and it is—it's inhibiting because it does confine the debate on the floor. But I really worry about the precedent, so I have not been pushing for sanitization and then release, or for selective release, or for—I hadn't thought about this concept of going to somebody and saying, "Would you release us from confidentiality." I think that would chill future proceedings.

[Gun Control]

Q.   Mr. President, this is supposed to be, the theme of the week is drugs this week. And you mentioned again this morning your commitment to ridding the country of drugs. But your designate for drug czar, William Bennett, has said that as part of that, the way that he would like to help end drug violence would be to consider a ban on semiautomatic weapons, which is opposed to your own viewpoint. And we're getting more and more evidence from doctors and police that there's gunfire in the streets and wounds that they haven't seen since the Vietnam War because of these weapons. What do you say to people whose families have—family members have been maimed by these kinds of weapons?

A.   I say the same thing I say to a person whose family had been maimed by a pistol or an explosive charge or whatever else it might be, fire. This is bad and we have got to stop the scourge of drugs. And I talked to Bill Bennett about that because I—I said, Bill, what can be worked out with finality on AK-47s. What can be done and still, you know, do what's right by the legitimate sportsman? I'd love to find an answer to that, Rita, because I do think that there has to be some assurance that these—that these automated attack weapons are not used in the manner they're being used.

So I'd like to—and I told Bill, I said look I don't worry about what you said up there. I said I can identify with what was behind your thinking on that, very, very easily. I'd like to find some accommodation. The problem as you know is, that automated AK-47s are banned, and semiautomated are not, so in they come and then they get turned over to automated weapons by—through some filing down. It isn't as easy as it seems to those who are understandably crying out, do something, do something. But I've . . . said Bill, work the problem, find out. And I'm not so rigid that I can't—if you come to me with a sensible answer that takes care of the concerns I've felt over the years, I'll take a hard look at it and I'll work with you to that end.

[Central American Policy]

Q.   Mr. President, on foreign policy, there's some confusion over how you feel about linkage, about linking Soviet good behavior, particularly in Central America, to granting them technological transfers and economic credits. If Gorbachev helps you in Central America, specifically Nicaragua, are you willing to help him economically?

A.   Look, the more cooperation we can get on regional objectives, our regional objectives in this instance, the democratization in Central America, the more help we can get towards that end by the Soviets with pulling back their large amount of military support, the better it would be between relations. So there is linkage, but when it gets to the specifics of what I'll be willing to do, that'll—that'll come out under this whole policy review. . . .

Q.   Mr. President, nonmilitary aid to the contras will run out at the end of the month. Do you plan to propose new aid to the contras and some package of carrots and sticks for the Sandinistas?

A. Well, I hope there are some—I hope there is some understanding on the Hill that these people must not be left without humanitarian aid. . . .

[Middle Eastern Policy]

Q. Mr. President, on another regional question. Yasir Arafat has refused to criticize any of the raids within Israel that have been carried out. Is he backing down on his promise against terrorism?

A. I hope not. And I'd like to see him forthrightly condemn any— any terror that might be perpetrated by the Palestinians. I stop short of saying he's condoning it or that he is—that he is furthering it. Not saying that. But I'd like to see him speak out. It would do wonders. It would be very good for future dialogue.

Q. Well, is he jeopardizing the dialogue as it sits now?

A. To the degree terroristic acts are condoned, it doesn't help the dialogue.

4.2 ■■■■■

The Six O'Clock Presidency: Patterns of
Network News Coverage of the President

Fred T. Smoller

Editor's Note. Analysis of CBS news coverage over a sixteen-year period
provides support for Fred T. Smoller's theory that the emergence of
television as a primary news source about presidents has contributed to the
decline of the presidency. This finding runs counter to assertions by other
scholars that television has enhanced the power of the presidency, particularly in relation to Congress, and that it has vastly increased presidents'
ability to mobilize public opinion to support their programs.

Smoller contends that news practices designed to keep tales about the
presidency exciting on a daily basis undermine the dignity and efficiency of
the office. Exceptional rather than normal occurrences are featured and
conflicts are exaggerated. The need for pictures makes reporters focus on the
superficial. Good news becomes better and bad news becomes worse than the
situation warrants. When Washington insiders are asked to comment about
the president, reporters usually call on the president's antagonists because
their comments make a racier story. To twist a familiar saying, when it
comes to covering the presidency, "good news is no news." In the presidencies from Nixon to Reagan, negativism tended to increase as time progressed.
Smoller credits Reagan with partially surmounting this trend through his
skilled use of the media opportunities under his control, such as presidential
speeches, radio commentary, and chances to be photographed.

Smoller is assistant professor of political science at Chapman College in
California. His research has focused on the impact of electronic media on the
presidency. The selection comes from "The Six O'Clock Presidency: Patterns
of Network News Coverage of the President," *Presidential Studies Quarterly* 16:1 (Winter 1986): 31-49. Several tables, figures, and footnotes have
been omitted.

Introduction

The Constitution makes no provision for television networks, nor
does any act of Congress mandate their existence. Nevertheless, the three

networks (ABC, CBS, and NBC) and their nightly news programs are major actors in American politics. They are the primary source from which the public gains its information both about the state of the nation and the conduct of the nation's public officials in promoting its general welfare. This pivotal role gives them immense power to shape the direction of American politics. This power is particularly evident in the area of presidential politics, since the president is the nation's single most important political official and therefore the special object of attention by the nightly news programs.

The great power of the network news programs, and their special attention to the presidency, enable them to play a major role in determining the fate of modern presidents, as well as the fate of the institution itself. This essay will argue, in fact, that the networks, seeking to realize their own goals, set in motion a dynamic pattern that can unravel the career of individual presidents and the public's support for the Office of the Presidency. Thus, the era of televised news coverage has produced a tendency for the modern presidency to be defined by, and systematically destroyed by, the image of presidential performance presented on the evening news. I call this phenomenon the Six O'Clock Presidency because its origins are the needs of the commercial networks rather than the values implicit in the Constitution.

The purpose of this essay is to explore the existence of the Six O'Clock Presidency through two strategies. First, it will present the argument that suggests how and why networks may systematically, if inadvertently, pursue organizational interests that can undermine the presidency. This argument is bolstered by interviews with television news executives, correspondents and technicians, primarily from CBS News, and observations made as a participant-observer in the White House press room during the spring of 1982. Second, it will then look at the actual pattern of news coverage of one network, CBS, from January, 1969 to January, 1985, seeking to document the nature of the negative coverage. . . .

Decisions concerning news coverage and the implementation of network policies are made in the Washington bureau. This is where presidential news stories are "built," and where the limitations imposed by the nature of the medium are accommodated. Three factors in particular—format constraints, the need for pictures, and assumptions about the nature of the viewing audience—systematically influence television news coverage of the president.

Format of the Evening News

The fixed time limit of the evening news program (22 minutes, without commercials) coupled with the belief that the audience will be bored with pieces that run for more than a few minutes, mean that news reports must be short (usually no more than two minutes in duration, frequently less), and therefore uncomplicated, producing, in Walter Cronkite's words, "inadvertent and perhaps inevitable distortion." [1] This means that complexity of the presidency is rarely captured in news reports. Dan Rather put it this way:

> [T]here is no way that I, or any other White House correspondent . . . can come out there in a minute and 15 seconds and give the viewer even the essence, never mind the details or the substance [of a president's policies] . . . One of the great difficulties of television is that it has a great deal of trouble dealing with any subject in depth. [2]

The Need for Pictures

Television news uses its technology ("pictures") to compete with other news media. The need for pictures affects news coverage of the president in three ways. First, it makes the reporting of complicated stories that focus on complex issues more difficult. Second, it highlights those aspects of the Office that are amenable to pictures and ignores those that are not. Finally, the need for "interesting" pictures reinforces journalism's penchant for the novel and the unusual (e.g., presidential faux pas).

The need for pictures contributes to the distortion of the presidency because pictures capture, condense, simplify and exaggerate complex political phenomena. Pictures often portray politics in "black" and "white," "good" or "evil" terms. The "grays," the qualifications, the nuances, are often lost. News pictures, like political cartoons, are effective devices for symbolic communication (which is why television is ideally suited to political campaigning). Thus, when presidents or candidates control media access, they have a formidable political tool at their disposal. But because pictures present complex political phenomena in symbolic terms reality is often exaggerated. This is how a producer for ABC's "World News Tonight," who was formerly a deputy White House press secretary during the Carter Administration, explained to me:

> Basically, when things aren't going well at the White House, the evening news' portrayal is worse than in fact the reality is. And then when things are going well for an Administration the stories suggest that things are far better than they are. There is a tendency to extremes because television is so dependent on pictures.
>
> The Camp David peace agreement between Israel and Egypt is a good example. Those pictures of Carter and Begin and Sadat embracing are just wonderful visuals. The impression they leave is that what occurred was 100 percent positive. A newspaper reporter, however, might go on for two-thirds of his story about what a great achievement

it was. But might for the last third talk about the history of the problem and certainly how insurmountable it has been up to this point. He might also add that this achievement hasn't been as great as it may appear.

A negative example would be hecklers at an event who threw tomatoes at the president. This is so visually compelling that the resulting story will be a one minute spot that says, yes, the president spoke, but he was heckled throughout, and following his speech the crowd threw three tomatoes. The visuals of the tomatoes splattering on the secret service agent would be the lasting impression that you would come away with. It would have to be arguably ten times more dramatic to come across in print. So in print you would talk about what was said in the speech and so forth, that he was heckled throughout, and then three tomatoes were thrown.[3]

The need for pictures also biases news coverage toward those aspects of the presidency that are amenable to visual portrayal. Many times this is due to White House restrictions. There are aspects of the Office, however, that simply cannot be photographed. For example, President Carter's efforts to get the hostages released could not be shown in pictures. Instead descriptions of the president's actions had to compete with visually and emotionally engrossing pictures of angry Iranian students burning the American flag. Presidential actions such as the ordering of troops on a mission to free the hostages will receive more coverage than stories concerning the evolution of that policy decision, or, more important, the constraints which inhibit the exercise of presidential power. Because actions (e.g., ceremonies, bill signing, a presidential tour of a disabled nuclear power plant) receive more attention and have greater impact than "processes" (such as the development of policy options, negotiations, the evolution of ideas, the structure and functioning of the office, or the constraints on presidential power) the power, purpose, and functioning of the Office is systematically exaggerated and distorted. This is a direct consequence of the environmental constraints affecting television coverage of the president.

Finally, the need for interesting pictures reinforces journalism's penchant for the unusual, the departure from the norm. Thus, network news coverage of presidential faux pas and clumsiness (e.g., presidents falling down stairs, dropping their election ballot, being attacked by a "killer rabbit," bumping their head on a helicopter door) and visually compelling but often gratuitous, trivial, and unrepresentative stories containing compelling visuals receive more coverage than they might otherwise merit solely because of their value in pictures. In addition, the need for pictures encourages coverage of conflict and controversy and other melodramatic events rather than the plain, routine functioning of government, which is not amenable to interesting pictures. As one producer for the CBS Evening News explained to me:

There is a real big mandate for pieces to not be boring; no standup, no bland looking stuff. [CBS News] wants it to be more visually enticing. So you try to be more creative. People are not going to watch if it is just a standup. And Que polls show that they like what we are doing, which is pepping up the news. I covered President Reagan when he went to Pittsburgh. There were the angriest demonstrators in the two years that I have been travelling with him. However, if I just had the two crews that was the normal standard on the road I couldn't have gotten good pictures of those demonstrators. I had another crew sent in from New York just to cover them, and that became the main focus of the story.[4]

Audience Assumptions

News coverage of the president is also greatly influenced by network policies which stem from their understanding of the nature of the viewing audience. Specifically, that viewers have a very limited attention span. The first assumption is that "reports are more likely to hold a viewer's attention if cast in the form of the fictive story, with narrative closure."[5] Producers attempt to keep their reports light and entertaining by accentuating conflict and drama and by telling their stories based on a "narrative form."

The narrative form reinforces television's simplistic, abbreviated, and truncated portrayal of the president. In particular, it accentuates reporting of conflict within the administration, and between the administration and other political actors, notably the congress. I am not suggesting that this conflict does not exist; only that the format of the television news story leads itself to its being highlighted. Of course when a president is successful (when his programs are being passed by the congress, and critics have not yet emerged) during the initial months of a new Administration this works in the president's favor. Later, however, when the president is more moderately successful, or simply less successful, the tendency to report the extreme increases the negative portrayal of the president.

The White House and Media Coverage

The White House has a virtual monopoly over information about the president through its control over news gathering. Nevertheless, reporters do not rely solely on the White House for news stories because over-reliance on the White House is frowned on by the producers of the Evening News and because a unitary executive cannot generate enough news to meet the network's demand.[6] To get "airtime," which is necessary for professional advancement, White House reporters must produce stories that meet the needs of the bureau: the stories must be short, uncomplicated, visually interesting when possible, and contain, when possible, elements of conflict, drama, and balance, stressing analysis and criticism over description.[7] Given the factors which constrain and influence correspondent's news judgment (e.g., deadline pressure, rapid turnover, competition, journalistic norms) White House reporters frequently turn to interviews with Washington-based elites for stories about the president. Interviews provide original ideas for new stories and new angles on old ideas. Interviews generally require a minimum of effort on the reporter's part: they can be obtained quickly (often over the phone), are beyond the White House's control, do not require in-depth, time consuming research or specific expertise in a policy area, and can provide the elements of conflict and drama favored by the narrative form.

News stories based on interviews with Washington based elites, however, often contribute to a negative portrayal of the president. If a source is from an interest group, he or she is prone to evaluate the president along narrow or self-interested lines. If the source is a Member of Congress, he or she has partisan and institutional interests to protect. And if the source is a permanent member of the Washington Community, he or she may have reasons for disliking the president which have little or no bearing on the performance of the president's official duties—such as the president's and his staff's ability to conform to the norms and mores of Washington Society (e.g., Carter's "Georgia" mafia, Nancy Reagan's redecorating the White House). Most important, because "president judging" is such a major topic of conversation, it is arguably the case that Washingtonians tend to judge the president sooner and more harshly, and perhaps with a different set of standards, than those who live outside the nation's capital.

The Growth of Negative News Coverage
of Presidents and the Presidency

I have argued so far that the networks have reason to give the president extensive coverage and for the bulk of this coverage to be negative in character. But the Six O'Clock Presidency involves more than extensive-negative coverage. It involves: 1) a tendency toward a growth in negative coverage during a president's term of Office, 2) a growth in negative coverage across presidencies, and 3) an erosion of public support for the Office. Here I will present data that support these expectations.

To document these suggested patterns of coverage, I read and coded the transcripts to the CBS Evening News from January 1968 to January of 1985.[8] Approximately 5500 news stories concerning the president, the White House family, the president's staff, and the president's foreign and domestic policies are included in the sample. . . . Unfortunately, a full set of transcripts prior to January 1969 is not available. Therefore only three

Table 1   Story Tone by Administration

Administration	Positive	Neutral	Negative	Net Tone
All Administrations	18	55	27	−9
Nixon (first)	28	51	20	+8
Nixon (second)	10	50	39	−29
Ford	20	59	21	1
Carter	17	55	28	−11
Reagan	13	57	30	−17

of the presidents in the sample (Nixon, Carter, and Reagan) completed a full four year term. Nevertheless, I believe that this sample of presidents is a diverse one and that it will support a sufficient exploration of the thesis.[9] The president's examined differ in personality, party affiliation, and ideology. Most important, they achieved different levels of success while in Office. . . .

The results of this study show that the tone of the 55% of the 16 years of presidential news considered was neutral (Table 1). This finding is not completely surprising, however, because so much presidential news is the routine coverage of the institution. (Notice in Table 1 the consistency of the neutral coverage across the presidents.) Stories concerning presidential appointments and nominations and White House statements tend to have no evaluative dimension, yet they make up a great deal of White House coverage. Moreover, the conventions of modern journalism, which are strictly adhered to by CBS News, require news reports to be balanced, fair, and free from personal bias. Stories with a balance of positive and negative comments were coded neutral. Nevertheless, despite these conventions 27% of the coverage of the president was negative, compared to 18% positive. That is, 60% of the directional press was negative. This invites further investigation.

The measure "net tone" is used to pursue this investigation. It captures the net evaluative portrayal of the president. An example illustrates how this measure was computed: Suppose the evening news one night contained three stories about the president, and the first one was positive and was 100 transcript lines long, and the second was neutral and 80 lines long, and the third story was negative and 60 lines long. The total amount of presidential coverage in transcript lines for that show would be 240. Forty two percent (100/240) of this coverage was positive, 33% (80/240) was neutral, and 25% (60/240) was negative. The "net tone" as measured in lines of coverage was 17 (42% − 25% = 17). The net presentation of the president that evening therefore was positive. Similarly, if the first story was negative and the third story was positive, the "net tone" as

Figure 1 Net Tone Score Broken Down by Year

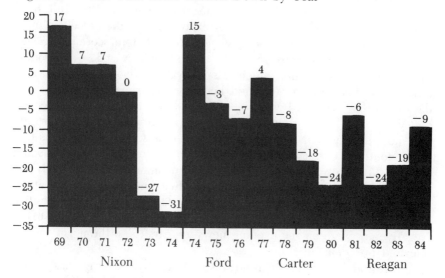

measured in lines of coverage would be −17, and the net presentation of the president that evening would have been negative. This measure assumes that neutral stories have no evaluative impact on public opinion. It also assumes that positive news stories and negative new stories in effect "cancel" one another. This measure allows us to capture the "net image" of the president portrayed on the evening news for a given period of time. For example, the "net tone" for the entire sample was −9. This means that the net evaluative portrayal of the presidency during the years considered was negative.

Main Patterns of Coverage

Figure 1 shows net tone scores broken down by year and contains the study's first finding: the net-portrayal of modern presidents on the evening news becomes more negative as their terms progress. This pattern holds for the Nixon, Ford, Carter and the first two years of the Reagan Administration. In only 5 of the 17 years studied (1974 is partitioned between Nixon and Ford) did the incumbent receive a net positive portrayal: 11 of the years were negative, with the bulk of the positive scores occurring in Nixon's first term. Nixon received a negative net portrayal on the evening news for one and a half of his five and a half year tenure. Net tone scores for two of Ford's approximately three year presidency were negative, while Carter received a negative score for three of his four years in Office. Surprisingly, in his first term Reagan received negative scores each of his four years as president.

My second major finding is that news coverage of the Office of the presidency has grown increasingly negative. Each of the full term presidents (i.e., Nixon—first term, Carter, Reagan) studied received more negative coverage than his predecessor. Nixon's net tone score for his first year in Office was 17; Ford, 15; Carter, 4; and Reagan, −6. . . . "[H]oneymoons" are also becoming much less enjoyable. Nixon's net tone score during his "honeymoon" (defined here as approximately the first 100 days in Office) was 30; Ford, 15; Carter, 28 and Reagan, 20. Moreover, honeymoons, at least with the electronic media, are ending more abruptly and more decisively. Nixon's first term net tone score following his first three months in Office drops 18 points (30−12), Ford, 15; Carter, 39 and Reagan, 38. Finally, the average post-honeymoon net tone score for Nixon was 5, for Ford −5; Carter −16 and Reagan, −17. Note that no president since Richard Nixon (first term) has received a net positive portrayal on the evening news after his first three months in Office. Negative coverage on the evening news appears to be the norm for the televised presidency.

The study's third expectation was that negative coverage has undercut public support for the president. Public approval influences the reception a President's proposals receive in Congress, his clout with foreign and domestic elites, and the boundaries of a President's Constitutional power. A president's approval rating, as measured by Gallup, has been shown to be a good predictor of the vote share received by incumbents running for reelection and of the success members of the president's party encounter in midterm elections.[10] Because the presidents need public support to govern effectively, political analysts are disturbed by the tendency for presidents to lose support as their terms progress. . . .

Citizens, it is assumed, monitor various performance dimensions of the presidency through the media, which disseminates information concerning the president and his policies. . . . [T]he strong positive correlation . . . between net tone scores and Gallup support ratings (averaged for corresponding periods), suggest that the president's portrayal on the evening news is one, albeit of several, determinates of public support.[11] The correlation coefficients for net tone score with Gallup approval ratings for each presidency were as follows: Nixon, .89; Ford, .54; Carter, .83 and Reagan, .72.

Ronald Reagan: The Great Communicator?

Contrary to his popular image as a "great communicator," his acting skills, his landslide defeat of Carter, the assassination attempt on his life; and despite his string of legislative victories, Ronald Reagan received more negative coverage than any of the presidents considered (See Table 1). Nevertheless, he has been able to transcend the consequences of this negative portrayal: he's maintained popular support; won the endorsement of his party and an overwhelming victory against Walter Mondale. Instead of contradicting the Six O'Clock presidency thesis, however, I believe the Reagan Administration may help confirm it.

To understand the Reagan presidency it is necessary to distinguish two forms of the electronic media, "controlled" and "uncontrolled." Controlled media is the form of electronic media over which the White House has the most influence. The tone of such coverage is generally positive, but this can vary depending on the personal attributes of the president and the skills of his staff. Examples of controlled media include presidential addresses and political advertisements. Toward the other end of the continuum is "uncontrolled" media, principally the evening news. The White House can exert some influence over the coverage the president receives on the evening news through its control over the president's schedule, access to the president and his aides, and the release of information. However, the White House cannot significantly influence the tone of the coverage the president receives on the evening news over an extended period of time.[12] Arrayed along the continuum lie the other forms of coverage, their position based on the level of control the White House has over the president's portrayal.

The Reagan Administration has been able to maintain public support despite its negative portrayal on the evening news by effectively using the controlled electronic media. Where once presidents used the press to "go over the heads of Congressmen," the Reagan Administration has used controlled electronic media (e.g., weekly radio broadcasts, political advertisements prior to the electoral season, and recently, the setting up of the White House News Service which will distribute the Reagan Administration's version of the news to radio stations and small newspapers) to transcend the pattern of network news coverage I have described. This unexcelled use of controlled television coupled with the public relations skills of the president's top aides has, for Reagan's first term, allowed Reagan to transcend the negative coverage he has received and has buttressed his political popularity.

Notes

1. Walter Cronkite, as quoted in Marvin Barrett, *Rich News, Poor News* (New York: Crowell, 1978): 10.
2. Dan Rather, as quoted in Hoyt Purvis, editor, *The Presidency and the Press* (Austin, Texas: The University of Texas Press, 1976), proceedings of a symposium on the presidency and the press, sponsored by the Lyndon B. Johnson School of Public Affairs. Also see, Ron Nessen, "The Washington You Can't See on Television" *TV Guide* (September 20, 1980): 9-12.

3. Interview with Rex Granum, ABC News.
4. Interview with Susan Zirinski, CBS Evening News producer.
5. As quoted in Edward J. Epstein, "The Selection of Reality" *The New Yorker* (March 3, 1973): 41.
6. Interview with Susan Zirinski, producer for CBS Evening News. Also, see "Fairness: Network Fear of Flacking" in Michael J. Robinson and Margaret A. Sheehan, *Over the Wire and on TV: CBS and UPI in Campaign '80.* (New York: Russell Sage Foundation, 1980): 91-139.
7. Robinson and Sheehan: 139. Also, James Fallows argues that reporters' lack of knowledge of history results in an insensitivity to the constraints which inhibit the exercise of presidential power[.] . . . Fallows believes that White House reporters feel confident in reporting five types of news stories: scandals or criminal activity, internal rivalries among administration aides, presidential politics, presidential gaffes, and fifth, the "business of winning elections and gaining points in the polls." See James Fallows, "The President and the Press," *The Washington Monthly* (October, 1979): 9-17.
8. . . . [T]he study's results are generalizable to ABC and NBC because the norms which guide the gathering and editing of news, and the constraints under which reporters and technicians work are fairly consistent across the three networks. See Epstein, 1973: xvi.
9. On average . . . the evening news was examined on pre-determined week-days, two days each week for each of the 832 weeks in the study. The sample was also stratified by day of the week to insure that variations in number and percentage of weekdays (that is, "Mondays," "Tuesdays," etc.) were kept to a minimum. . . .

All stories which referred directly to the president, the presidency, the president's family, friends, staff or references to the president's policies; the secretary of state and the vice president would be included in the analysis. Excluded were stories concerning Executive Branch departments (Office of Management and Budget, for example) which did not refer specifically to the president or the Administration; stories about a remote "presidential task force" or commission which have only a tangential relationship to the president and which are not discussed directly in terms of the president's policies; and network announcements of news coverage of the president or related programming, e.g., "CBS will present a special on President Reagan's first year in Office tonight at 10 pm." The unit of analysis is the news story. . . .

Positive Tone: Legislative success, public or private approval for the president's policies; reports which portray the president in a favorable light. Words used by anchors or correspondents to characterize president's behavior or policies—"bold adventure," "statesmanlike," "restrained during crisis"— that represent values which are associated with effective presidential performance. Stories which show the president endorsing values which are integral to American society, the so-called "motherhood" issues, were also coded positive. Finally, stories which show that the president's policies are working (troop withdrawals from Vietnam, positive economic reports) were coded positive.

Neutral Tone: balance of positive and negative coverage, or no evaluative tone whatsoever. For example, stories concerning the introduction of legislation, presidential appointments and nominations, were generally coded neutral.

Negative Tone: legislative setbacks or defeats, bad policy or personal evaluations (when they are the main emphasis of the story); disparaging remarks about the president or the president's policies (e.g., policies are unfair, vague, ineffective). Also coded negative were stories which show that the president's policies aren't effective or which portray the president in an unfavorable light.

10. See George C. Edwards, *Presidential Influence in Congress* (San Francisco: W. H. Freeman, 1980; Richard E. Neustadt, *Presidential Power* (New York: John Wiley, 1980); Louis Fisher, *The Constitution Between Friends* (New York: St. Martin's Press, 1978); Edward Tufte, "Determinants of the Outcomes of Midterm Congressional Elections," *American Political Science Review* 69 (September, 1975): 812-826.

11. Gallup support score averages were derived from the *The Gallup Opinion Index*, report No. 182, October-November, 1980. (Princeton, New Jersey: The Gallup Poll, 1980).

12. These results are particularly surprising given reports of the Reagan Administration's success at staging events, limiting access to the president, and otherwise managing the news so as to get a favorable portrayal. See Steven R. Weisman, "The President and the Press: the art of controlled access" (*The New York Times Magazine*, October 14, 1984): 34-83.

4.3 ▬

The Three Faces of Ronald Reagan

David L. Paletz and K. Kendall Guthrie

Editor's Note. Do events like President Reagan's push for a 25 percent cut in tax rates or his 1984 trip through Europe look substantially different when seen through the prism of diverse news sources? To find out, David L. Paletz and K. Kendall Guthrie compared stories about these two events in a local newspaper, in an elite newspaper, and on the nightly television news. They found that each source's treatment was quite distinctive and that it portrayed three substantially different Ronald Reagans.

The major lessons of the analysis are that newspeople have the power to shape the images of public officials by telling stories in their own way, that the choice of a particular version hinges, in part, on the resources available to the news source, and that the final product helps or hinders the objectives of the president. Smaller papers are likely to report the president's version of the story uncritically; major papers are apt to explore angles of their own choice, such as speculating about the president's political motives or soliciting views from presidential opponents. Network coverage is apt to typecast the president and structure the news to conform to the preordained image.

The essay also documents presidential maneuvers to control media coverage. It highlights the fact that presidents control their picture images far more than the text presented with the pictures. They can provide good pictures to soften or even override a story's negative verbal content.

Paletz is professor of political science at Duke University. He has made unique contributions to the field of political communication through his many books and articles on media power in politics. Guthrie, at the time of writing, was a doctoral candidate at the Annenberg School of Communications at the University of Southern California. The selection is from "The Three Faces of Ronald Reagan," *Journal of Communication* 37:4 (Autumn 1987): 7-23. One table and all notes have been omitted.

During his first term, Ronald Reagan traversed the potholes of politics, his sometimes unpopular policies, administration scandals, and a

---

Reprinted and abridged from *Journal of Communication* 37, no. 4 (1987): 7-23. Reprinted by permission of Oxford University Press.

recession to arrive, bedecked with popularity, at a landslide re-election triumph. In so doing, he defied the conventional wisdom of press, pundits, and scholars that a president's popularity inevitably, even inexorably, declines.

Unusual political circumstances partially account for Reagan's success. After a succession of failed presidents, the American public (including many journalists) wanted someone to demonstrate that the office was not unmanageable, that it could be a fount of action. Certainly, in his first term Reagan did not involve the country in military conflict, and he displayed skill in achieving the passage and implementation of much of his program. By 1984 people felt the flush of economic recovery and transferred their relief onto the incumbent.

Contributing mightily to Reagan's success, so it is claimed, was benign, often favorable, media coverage (2, 3, 4, 5). One critic even berated the White House press corps for acting "with unusual frequency during Reagan's first two years as a kind of *Pravda* of the Potomac, a conduit for White House utterances and official image mongering intended to sell Reaganomics" (10, p. 37; see also 12). Other journalists, angry with both the administration and their colleagues who apparently acquiesced in this media manipulation, wrote articles cataloguing some of Reagan's tactics and success. Most notable was *New York Times* White House correspondent Steven R. Weisman, who lamented that "Mr. Reagan has ignored some of the unstated ground rules under which reporters have traditionally covered the presidency. As a consequence, he has dramatically altered the kind of information the public receives about him and his administration" (24, p. 36).

But this chorus of complaint contradicts and defies the prevailing view of political communication researchers that, on balance, the media contribute to the decline and fall of presidents (8, 14, chap. 4). Moreover, one study contends that, rather than bolstering Reagan, "the nation's reporters have written or said that Reagan is dumb, lazy, out of touch with reality, cheap, senile, ruining NATO, tearing up his own safety net, even violating his constitutional oath" (17, p. 54).

In an attempt to illuminate, if not resolve, the questions about President Reagan's media coverage, we analyzed reporting of two quite disparate events—one domestic, the other international—that we expected to engender different coverage. We hypothesized that different media outlets, because of their varying audiences, norms, and resources, would react differently to Ronald Reagan's public relations efforts. We therefore analyzed our two events in three outlets—network news, a national elite newspaper, and a local newspaper that relies on wire service reports for national news.

The first event we tracked is President Reagan's push for a 25 percent cut in tax rates. By July 1981, Congress had passed the president's budget-cutting packages and had begun work on the kingpin of supply side economics, the tax cut. With Congress scheduled to vote at the end of the month, the president started to lobby wavering legislators. When passage of the bill still seemed uncertain, he unsheathed a nationally televised address to mobilize people into calling and writing to Congress.

Meanwhile, as Democrat leaders counter-lobbied, Reagan pressured legislators behind the scenes. The president won decisively on July 29. Democrats attempted postvote tactics to kill the bill but failed. The conference committee reconciled the differences and sent the tax cut plan for presidential signature on August 4, just as the Air Traffic Controllers began their strike.

During the key nine-day period (beginning on July 27, 1981, with the president's major promotional speech and ending August 4, 1981, when CBS News stopped its coverage of the issue), President Reagan appeared infrequently before the news media. He particularly avoided unscripted events and reporters' questions. When he did emerge in public it was to give speeches to friendly audiences or to television cameras that could not talk back. Thus, he addressed a trade lobbying group on July 27, presumably in part because the coverage would serve as a tantalizing preview to his televised address scheduled for that night. He then disappeared from media scrutiny while Congress bickered over the tax bill's details. The president's aides carefully parceled out a few quotes or activities to guide the press, but Reagan made no public comment until the tax bill passed and he could claim victory. He thus displayed himself as a cheerleader and victor, without publicly soiling his hands in the politics necessary to get the bill passed. Reagan then again vanished while Congress haggled over the politically touchy Social Security issue and the ramifications of the tax cut, deciding which programs to eliminate.

The second episode we examined is the president's June 1-10, 1984, European trip. During the winter and spring of 1984, Reagan presided as a serene statesman at the White House while his Democratic rivals criss-crossed the country wounding each other politically. As the long primary season ended, Reagan and his strategists launched his re-election cam-paign—not with traditional political stump speeches but with a presiden-tial trip to Europe full of picturesque and symbolic vignettes designed for the press, especially nightly television news.

Resplendent in academic robes, Reagan accepted a degree from the University College at Galway. At Ballyporeen, the president drank beer at a pub and prayed in the church where his Irish ancestors were baptized. Numerous scenes with world leaders displayed the president's statesman-ship and international clout. And he exhibited and evoked emotional patriotism at the fortieth anniversary of the D Day ceremonies.

As usual, the president was carefully shielded from interaction with the media. During the ten-day trip, which received constant press coverage, he directly answered reporters' questions only three times: getting into a helicopter as he departed Washington; once in a shouted exchange just after he arrived in London; and then at a press conference on the last day of the trip at which he recounted his accomplishments.

Neither the tax cut nor the European trip was guaranteed in advance to be counted a Reagan success. To the president's advantage, the tax cut fell within the end of what has been called the "alliance phase" of press-presidential relations (8). During this period news organizations supposedly "communicate the White House line and channel the ideas and image of the president to their audience. White House officials cooperate with reporters' objectives of obtaining access to everyone in the new administration" (8, p. 274). However, passage of the proposal was in doubt, forcing the president to use many political ploys. Furthermore, the event contained conflict—between the Democrats and Republicans as well as about who would benefit from the cuts—which journalists tend to highlight. Since reporters were on their home turf in Washington, they had easy access to both sides. We therefore expected more favorable coverage because of the honeymoon but more analysis, conflict, and politics because reporters had access to the opposition.

The European trip presented a similar balance of assets and liabilities for Reagan. Past presidential trips have generally received positive and abundant coverage. Severed from their outside sources when covering a foreign trip, reporters are constrained to accept the official White House description of events. However, this particular trip fell into the "detached phase" of press relations, during which White House officials are supposedly "more concerned about preventing reporters from seeing their flaws than in getting them to prepare stories that will be favorable to their policies" (8, p. 274). Furthermore, reporters covering Reagan had voiced frustration at and opposition to what they felt were the administration's manipulative tactics toward the media (see 9, 10). Thus, reporters might be wary and ill disposed to serve as a conduit for the White House version of events. We therefore expected the coverage to have less political content, since it was a policy and public relations trip, but to be more strident, because of reporters' objections to staged events and to being manipulated.

In devising our content analysis categories, we assumed that how President Reagan would be portrayed would depend upon the subjects that the media emphasized in their stories about him. The sentence was our basic unit of analysis. We coded a total of 5,422 sentences—792 in the *Durham Morning Herald*, 733 on the "CBS Evening News," and 3,897 in the *New York Times*. Each sentence was coded as follows: *policy* (allocation of goods or services; ideological statements; diplomatic goals or plans; standard operating procedures), *politics* (strategies to get policies passed into law; references to elections; deliberately vague sentences or those supporting or disfavoring an issue without explaining its substance, or giving political motives for supporting a policy), *patriotism* (references to national symbols, traditions, or values; sentences aimed at stirring national pride or sentiment), the president's *personality* (descriptions or displays of his character or emotions; also nonsubstantive quips or jokes), and *miscellaneous/color* (indisputable facts: description of a thing or person's appearance; description of a person's physical action). We also classified each sentence as either *description* (detailing only "objective" events or facts) or *analysis* (going beyond facts to draw inferences or conclusions or to speculate on motives or implications or causation).

Story content in part depends on the sources reporters use. So we cross-referenced each sentence as follows: *Reagan quoted* (exact words; in television coverage, sentences when the president is shown speaking only), *Reagan paraphrased* (by the reporter; also included a reporter reading a direct Reagan quote) or *discussed* (by the reporter or someone else), and *Reagan supporter* (a statement supporting Reagan or his policies, within the context of the story, including actions as well as words; also general references to U.S. policy), *critic* (statement of opposition to Reagan or his policies within the context of the story), and *neutral/uninvolved or no source.*

In examining television news stories, we cross-referenced the sentences for each subject category with their concurrent television image. The connections were: reporter or commentator speaking and simultaneously shown on the screen; the reporter's voice heard over visuals of the president (what we call "dub over Reagan"); and the president speaking and simultaneously shown.

After a month, we recoded a randomly selected 10 percent of the stories (4 on television and 17 in print, involving 233 and 1,063 decisions, respectively). The intracoder reliability was 92 percent for television and 90 percent for print; intercoder reliability was 86 and 83 percent.

Overall, press coverage reflects a successful White House strategy of providing a "theme of the day" approach, with one event to enhance the president's purposes and popularity. According to *Time* White House correspondent Laurence Barrett, whose observation reflects inside access to the Reagan presidency, "how events had played and would play on the air and in print" dominated every strategy session (1, p. 442). When possible, aides construct "news events" to elicit specific headlines. . . .

The *Durham Morning Herald's* lead story emphasized the peace initiatives. The Associated Press story began: "President Reagan, declaring 'America is prepared for peace,' announced Monday that he will consider a Soviet proposal to renounce the use of force in Europe if Moscow agrees to consider specific Western proposals to reduce the chance of war on the continent" (16, p. 1).

Dan Rather began the June 4 "CBS Evening News": "President

Reagan told the Irish Parliament today that the United States, for the first time, is now willing to consider a favorite Soviet arms proposal, a treaty that would ban the use of force in Europe." Although correspondent Bill Plante ended the segment by noting that "Mr. Reagan's speech was carefully planned to soften his image in Europe, where many believe he is dangerously trigger-happy," the story's overall thrust conveyed the president's desire for peace.

The *New York Times* led with Reagan's peace initiative on page 1: "President Reagan told the Irish Parliament today that he would be willing to discuss with the Soviet Union the possibility of a NATO renunciation of the use of force if Moscow would agree to a specific set of measures to limit the risk of military confrontation in Europe" (23, p. 1). The *Times* did print one story detailing Reagan's political motives and two stories discussing protestors—but on page 12.

So, by priming reporters, the president and his aides can frequently beguile the media into following his agenda and perspective, at least for that day. But already we see differences in the media's responses. As suggested by the *Herald* story, the AP wire service was essentially a conduit for the president's message, its coverage uncritical. "CBS Evening News" highlighted the president's message, but the reporter ascribed a political motive to it. And the *New York Times*, while treating the president's script as its main story, had enough staff following the trip to report his supposed motives and to provide coverage of dissenters, although relegating them to a less prominent page. Our content analysis suggests that this pattern of media variation holds for these three overlapping yet in many ways distinct faces of Ronald Reagan.

The wire reports about the president used in the *Durham Morning Herald* rarely went beyond what he said and did. At times, the coverage exhibited a celebrity syndrome, chronicling what Reagan wore and ate. Interpretation, ascription of motivation, or the infusion of politics into ceremonial appearances was infrequent. Thus the Ronald Reagan of the *Durham Morning Herald* appears as the dominant policy-maker and statesman in both the national and international spheres. This presidential focus, relative lack of politics (especially in the trip coverage), and scant amount of analysis unite to present the president favorably.

The most outstanding feature of the wire service coverage was the high amount of miscellaneous description and color material, almost twice the amount in other media (see Table 1). . . .

The wire service's dispatches were filled with description. The *Herald's* front-page story on the opening day of the summit was typical: "After the reception in the parkside palace, built in the 16th century by Henry VIII, a motorcade took the seven leaders down The Mall to 10 Downing St., the Prime Minister's official residence, where they posed for pictures in the ornate Yellow room, then sat down for a working dinner"

Table 1   Subjects of Sentences in Stories about Tax Cut and European Trip

Tax cut	Herald (N=438)		Times (N=1,555)		CBS (N=399)	
	N	%	N	%	N	%
Personality	9	2	78	5	12	3
Politics	110	25[d]	389	25	167	42
Policy	174	40	824	53[a]	167	42
Patriotism	9	2	31	2	21	5
Misc. color	136	31[c]	233	15	32	8
Average story length	19.89		43.2		19.95	
No. of stories	22		36		20	
European trip	(N=354)		(N=2,342)		(N=344)	
	N	%	N	%	N	%
Personality	40	11	177	8	34	10
Politics	46	4[c]	539	23	70	21
Policy	83	23	832	36[b]	100	30
Patriotism	15	4	255	11	20	6
Misc., color	200	56[c]	539	23	110	33
Average story length	15.4		38.4		19.65	
No. of stories	23		61		17	

[a] Differences between *Times* and both CBS and *Herald* significant at .01 (z test).
[b] Difference between *Times* and CBS significant at .05 and between *Times* and *Herald* at .01 (z test).
[c] Differences between *Herald* and both CBS and *Times* significant at .01 (z test).
[d] Difference between *Herald* and CBS significant at .01 (z test).

(15, p. 1). Similar descriptive passages abound through the wire service coverage. Especially during the European trip, the *Herald* ran such AP stories, replete with descriptions of photogenic events.

The *Herald* also de-emphasized politics compared to the other media, especially during the European trip when the political issues were more subtle than during the tax cut vote. While the *Herald* and the *New York Times* both devoted 25 percent of their coverage to the political aspects of the tax cut, this is far less than CBS's 42 percent. . . .

The abundant description also meant less analysis than in the *Times* (see Table 2). . . . During the European trip, the analysis dropped to 8 percent of the total coverage, substantially lower than the *Times's* 26 percent and CBS's 19 percent. Overall, the wire reporters seemed content simply to describe what happened and not ask why.

The *Herald* also had a much more presidential focus than the *New*

Table 2 Proportion of Content Description Versus Analysis in Stories About Tax Cut and European Trip

	Description		Analysis		Total
Tax cut	N	%	N	%	N
Herald	350	80	88	20	438
Times	995	64	560	36	1,555[a]
CBS	315	79	84	21	399
European trip					
Herald	326	92	28	8	354[a]
Times	1,733	74	609	26	2,342[a]
CBS	271	81	63	19	334

[a] Difference from other media significant at .01 (z test).

York Times although it was similar to CBS in this regard (see Table 3). It devoted 29 percent of its space to Reagan paraphrased or discussed during the tax cut and 38 percent during the European trip. This emphasis may be in part due to its more limited space. . . . Such a limited newshole for national and international events leaves little space for coverage of actors other than the president.

The Ronald Reagan of the *New York Times* is a man primarily concerned with policy; political dealings are secondary. Nor is Reagan the only policy-maker. The policy-making process is often protrayed as complex and the president is not always intimately involved. Consequently, he shares the limelight with critics, supporters, and uninvolved experts.

Our content analysis (see Table 1) shows that the *Times's* coverage centers substantially more on policy than either the *Herald's* or CBS's. . . . Table 2 shows that, in line with its greater policy emphasis, the *New York Times* also ran more analysis about the tax cut (36 percent, about 15 percent more than the other media); during the European trip, it again ran 36 percent analysis (7 percent more than CBS and 18 percent more than the *Herald*). In fact, the *Times* frequently ran separate stories marked "analysis"; the other media did not.

The *Times* portrayed the complexities of the policy process and the president's sometimes peripheral involvement in several ways. For instance, while all media quoted Reagan approximately the same percent of the time during the two events, the *Times* paraphrased or discussed Reagan only 20 percent of the time during the tax cut compared to 29 and 31 percent in the *Herald* and on CBS (see Table 3). The figures for

Table 3 Average Allocation of Sources in Stories About Tax Cut and European Trip

Tax cut	Herald (N=438)		Times (N=1,555)		CBS (N=399)	
	N	%	N	%	N	%
Reagan quoted	39	9	140	9	28	7
Reagan paraphrased or discussed	127	29	311	20[a]	124	31
Critic	106	24	295	19	84	21
Supporter	105	24	342	25	76	19
Neutral/uninvolved or no source	61	14	467	30	87	22
European trip	(N=354)		(N=2,342)		(N=344)	
	N	%	N	%	N	%
Reagan quoted	42	12	187	8	30	9
Reagan pharaphrased or discussed	135	38	632	27[a]	124	31
Critic	21	6	422	18	50	15
Supporter	50	14	515	22	33	10
Neutral/uninvolved or no source	106	30	586	25	87	26

[a] Difference between *Times* and both CBS and *Herald* significant at .01 (z test).

coverage of the European trip were 27 percent for the *Times*, 38 percent for the *Herald*, and 40 percent for CBS.

The *Times* also devoted more space than the *Herald* and CBS to policy-makers other than the president and to uninvolved or neutral experts. For example, it gave almost equal coverage to critics and supporters during the tax cut issue. Because of its extensive reporting of the parlaying on Capitol Hill and the views of neutral or uninvolved participants, the paper depicted Reagan as a foreground figure in a crowded landscape.

During the European Economic Summit, the *Times* portrayed the president as merely one of the world leaders. . . . Indeed, the *Times* frequently gave policy-making credit to aides, whereas CBS and the *Herald* tied it to the president.

Along with its policy emphasis, the *Times* did provide variegated reporting of Reagan. June 5 coverage of the European trip was typical, with stories previewing the policy issues expected to arise at the summit, describing the president's lunch with the queen and a dispute involving his secret service agents, and humorously describing the trip bureaucracy.

Moreover, *Times* reporters occasionally inserted language that undermined, or at least modified, the extent to which the stories served the president. Wrote one, "presidential aides have not even tried to conceal their delight over the resonance that today's visit is expected to have with millions of Irish-American voters at home." He described the day's events as "a carnival of nostalgia with heavy political overtones" and noted that Reagan sipped stout "as cameras whirred" (22, p. 8).

Indeed, in contrast to the *Herald*, which generally ignored the political dimensions of the trip and gave dissenters from the president's policies short shrift, the *Times* sometimes highlighted both. . . .

Nonetheless, the *Times* did not ignore the visual images flowing across the Atlantic. The White House publicity machine provided a plethora of photographs on the European trip, which the *Times* and *Herald* ran almost daily. These photographs nearly always showed the president as happy, reinforcing his public image of self-confidence and geniality. Moreover, print reporters often described the pictures, thus reinforcing their effects. . . .

At first blush, the "CBS Evening News" coverage seems to fit between that of the *Herald* and the *Times*. For example, CBS provided more policy coverage than the *Herald* but less than the *Times* (Table 1). Sometimes, as with its focus on the president as policy-maker, its coverage is close to the *Herald;* but its percentage of analytical reporting of Reagan's European trip is closer to the *Times* (Table 3).

But the CBS coverage stands out, as is clear from Table 1, in the high percentage of sentences we classified as "politics" in the tax cut episode and the substantial percentage, almost as much as the *Times's*, in the network's reporting of the European trip. The Reagan seen on CBS may be a preeminent leader and policy-maker, but he is one whose motives are frequently political.

This finding confirms a difference between CBS and UPI coverage of the 1980 presidential campaign identified by Robinson and Sheehan: that CBS was "more political" (18, p. 209). But they also described the network's coverage as "more critical" (18, p. 209). This gave us pause. Watching our videotapes we perceived the same intentions by some of the CBS reporters to infuse criticism or at least skepticism into their stories. Why, we wondered, did their efforts often seem unsuccessful?

The explanation, we believe, can be found in the relations between words and visuals in the CBS News stories. On the one hand, the CBS personnel involved in reporting, editing, and producing the evening news obviously seek to show the president in stories about or related to him. On the other hand, the president and his advisors limit his televisable public appearances (we call this "controlled exposure"). They also try to ensure that, when he does appear, he looks and acts in ways most advantageous to his political and policy interests.

Unlike the wire services, and for reasons considered by Robinson and Sheehan (18, pp. 217-239), CBS News is unwilling to serve as a mere conduit for the president's self-interest and self-serving appearance, yet it uses, if not relies on, visuals engineered by the White House. This subtle irony makes its coverage so intriguing.

Sometimes the White House image prevails. Indeed, when the president is shown speaking, policy and, to a lesser extent, patriotic sentences dominate; politics is banished. . . . Thus, the 8 out of 20 stories dealing with the tax cut on the "CBS Evening News" in which Reagan appeared centered on policy issues favorable to the president, such as cutting government waste or the merits of lowering taxes; politics, pressuring people to vote for those policies, was peripheral.

. . . When the president is not pictured, tax cut stories have an almost two-to-one politics-to-policy ratio, the reverse of the ratio when he is shown.

. . . [W]hen we analyze the television coverage closely, we uncover some intriguing data. The president was shown and heard simultaneously for just ten percent of CBS coverage of the European trip, a mere three percent more than the tax cut. He was, however, shown (but not heard) far more often during the trip; but with the voice of a network correspondent dubbed over his visuals 26 percent of the time, compared to 6 percent for the tax cut episode. In other words, reporters were unwilling to give the president's words, as contrasted to pictures of him, untrammelled access to the television audience. They insisted on orally framing European trip events for viewers.

Certainly the frame that television reporters applied was often consistent with the pictures of the president: reporters simply narrated the activities shown—they may have lacked time or inclination to do otherwise, considered it journalistically improper to intervene, etc. Thus the percentages of "miscellaneous, color" content are similar for the European trip irrespective of who appears on the screen and who speaks, the president or the reporter.

On occasion, however, television reporters transcended or contradicted the pictures, usually to insert into their stories the politics the president omitted. Even though the European trip lacked obvious political angles, the subject was politics 26 percent of the time when reporters were speaking over the president, 31 percent when other pictures provided the backdrop, and only 3 percent when the president was shown and heard.

. . . Research suggests, however, the primacy of the visual over the audio channels. . . . As a result, the pictorial messages portraying Reagan as a patriot and policy-maker may well be more strongly ingrained in the viewers' minds than the political and critical aspects of the story that reporters convey with their words (6). Viewers will likely associate reporters and anchors with the political issues and Reagan with policy, patriotism, and good will. . . .

The *New York Times*, AP, and "CBS Evening News" differ in their economic resources, their conceptions of their audiences' characteristics, interests, and needs, and their reporting norms, with two important effects. First, to some extent, they each focus on different aspects of the president and his conduct of the office. Second, and perhaps more significant, they differ in their vulnerability and resistance to the public relations techniques of the presidency, particularly as practiced by the Reagan White House (13, 19, 20). We believe that similar differences between media should be found in coverage of other high officials during other time periods. We will briefly describe the three faces we uncovered.

Facing severe deadline pressure and the need to provide a diversity of clients with acceptable service, AP reporters are essentially presidency body watchers. Relying extensively on the public record and publicly observed behavior, they speedily describe and transmit the president's official activities (7, 21). This often entails serving as conduit for his themes, ideas, and perspectives—for reality as the president defines it. Interpretation, ascriptions of motivation, and infusions of politics into ceremonial presidential appearances are infrequent.

Such coverage finds a comfortable and comforting home in the *Durham Morning Herald*. With its emphasis on local news, its limited space for national and international events, the paper does not publish a diversity of stories about the presidency. The ones printed derive from and often feature Reagan at the expense of other policy-makers; his opponents are relatively little noted. As a result, he appears as the dominant policy-maker and statesman in both the national and international spheres. This presidential focus, lack of politics, and absence of analysis combine to present Reagan most favorably.

The *New York Times* covers President Reagan diligently. As a result it often serves as a conduit for his vision and version of events. But the *Times* also devotes attention to policy issues and to the policy process. Policy-making and execution are often complex, and the president is not always intimately involved in the details. Consequently, other participants, including critics and dissenters, receive coverage. The Reagan portrayed by the *Times* is thus an important but not hegemonic national and international policy-maker who occasionally dabbles in politics.

Limited in time but not geographic space, "CBS Evening News" shows Reagan almost whenever he makes himself available. Other policy participants in executive branch decision making are relegated to relative obscurity. In the process, CBS visually transmits, however begrudgingly, the symbolic vignettes with which the president beguiles the public. But its reporters often verbally express skepticism about his intentions and interpret his behavior and actions politically. The "CBS Evening News"

Reagan is the powerful and important figure in national and international arenas, a man more statesmanlike and policy-minded than his counterparts, but one whose motives, CBS reporters tell us, are inescapably political.

There is another Reagan face that neither the *Herald,* nor CBS, nor even the *Times* fully reveals. It can be glimpsed in the pages of Barrett's exhaustive account of the first two years of the Reagan administration (1). It is fascinating: a president who like most people combines convictions and ignorance, determination and indecision, tough words with prudence. It is this apparent inability of the mass media to capture President Reagan beyond the clichés, in all his complexity and contradictions, that must be our abiding concern.

References

1. Barrett, Laurence I. *Gambling with History: Ronald Reagan in the White House.* Garden City, N.Y.: Doubleday, 1983.
2. Bonafede, Dom. "That's Mike Deaver at the Hub of Reagan's Presidential World." *National Journal* 12, August 15, 1981, pp. 1461-1465.
3. Bonafede, Dom. "The Washington Press—Competing for Power With the Federal Government." *National Journal* 14, April 17, 1982, pp. 664-674.
4. Bonafede, Dom. "The Washington Press—An Interpreter or a Participant in Policy Making." *National Journal* 14, April 24, 1982, pp. 716-721.
5. Bonafede, Dom. "The Washington Press—It Magnifies the President's Flaws and Blemishes." *National Journal* 14, May 1, 1982, pp. 767-771.
6. Booth, Alan. "The Recall of News Items." *Public Opinion Quarterly* 34, 1970-1971, pp. 604-610.
7. Fishman, Mark. *Manufacturing the News.* Austin: University of Texas Press, 1980.
8. Grossman, Michael B. and Martha Joynt Kumar. *Portraying the President: The White House and the News Media.* Baltimore: Johns Hopkins University Press, 1981.
9. Hamburger, Tom. "How the White House Cons the Press." *Washington Monthly* 12, January 1982, p. 22.
10. Hanson C. T. "Gunsmoke and Sleeping Dogs: The Prez's Press at Midterm. *Columbia Journalism Review* 6, May/June 1983, p. 27.
11. Hart, Roderick P. *Verbal Style and the Presidency: A Computer-Based Analysis.* Orlando, Fla.: Academic Press, 1984.
12. Hoffman, David. "At Home: The Candidate, Packaged and Protected." *Washington Journalism Review* 6, September 1984, pp. 37-41.
13. Locander, Robert. "Modern Presidential In-Office Communications: The National, Direct, Local, and Latent Strategies." *Presidential Studies Quarterly* 13, Spring 1983, pp. 242-254.
14. Paletz, David L. and Robert M. Entman. *Media Power Politics.* New York: Free Press. 1981.

15. "Reagan Asks Persian Gulf Joint Action." *Durham Morning Herald*, June 8, 1984, p. 1.
16. "Reagan Says He'll Consider Kremlin Offer." *Durham Morning Herald*, June 5, 1984, p. 1.
17. Robinson, Michael J., Maura Clancy, and Lisa Grand. "With Friends Like These. . . ." *Public Opinion* 6, June/July 1983, pp. 2-3, 52-54.
18. Robinson, Michael J. and Margaret A. Sheehan. *Over the Wire and on T.V.* New York: Russell Sage, 1983.
19. Rubin, Richard L. *Press, Party, and Presidency.* New York: W. W. Norton. 1981.
20. Seymour-Ure, Colin. *The American Presidency: Power and Communication.* New York: St. Martin's Press. 1982.
21. Tiffen, Rodney. *The News from Southeast Asia: The Sociology of Newsmaking.* Singapore: Institute of Southeast Asian Studies, 1978.
22. Weisman, Steven R. "Reagan Finds 'Contentment' in Ancestral Village." *New York Times*, June 4, 1984, p. 8.
23. Weisman, Steven R. "President Asserts He Would Discuss Non-Use of Force," *New York Times*, June 5, 1984, p. 1.
24. Weisman, Steven R. "The President and the Press: The Art of Controlled Access." *New York Times Magazine*, October 14, 1984, pp. 36ff.

4.4 ▬▬▬

Three Faces of Congressional Media

Michael J. Robinson

Editor's Note. Michael J. Robinson spotlights the changes that modern media coverage have brought about in Congress. He provides fascinating details about the manner in which Congress is covered by a variety of media. Each medium differs in impact from the others and even varies within itself at different times. Accurate assessments of the overall effects of all media singly or in combination remain elusive because there are no adequate weighting criteria.

Robinson outlines the major effects of media coverage. It produces telegenic candidates, safe House incumbents, vulnerable senators, and a Congress that lacks the public's confidence. By contrast, respect for the presidency as an institution remains high, in the wake of deferential news treatment. Incumbent presidents, however, generally receive rougher media treatment than do incumbent members of Congress. If Robinson is correct in his assessments, the media have indeed altered the face of U.S. politics.

Robinson, a political scientist trained at the University of Michigan, has devoted much of his career to the study of the media's influence on U.S. politics. At the time of writing, he was teaching at Catholic University and was directing the Media Analysis Project at The George Washington University. The selection is from Thomas E. Mann and Norman J. Ornstein, eds., *The New Congress* (Washington, D.C.: American Enterprise Institute, 1981), 55-96. Several tables have been omitted.

Ask anybody on Capitol Hill about the most basic change in the relationship between Congress and the media since 1960 and the response is practically catechistic—the media have become harder, tougher, more cynical. Committee chairmen, senior Republicans, press secretaries, aides in the press galleries and media studios at the Capitol, and members of the Washington press corps express what amounts to a consensus: the biggest change in the relationship between Congress and the media is that the

---

From *The New Congress*, ed. Thomas E. Mann and Norman J. Ornstein (1981). Reprinted with the permission of the American Enterprise Institute for Public Policy Research.

press has grown more hostile to Congress.

Having conducted almost fifty personal interviews and collected some sixty questionnaires from representatives, staff, and reporters between 1977 and 1980, I found that only one person in fifteen thought this toughening was not the major development.[1] One official in the House of Representatives, who has worked personally with congressional correspondents for almost thirty years, put it this way: "The biggest change has been readily discernible—the greater emphasis on the investigative approach. Years ago there was an occasional exposé, but the last six to eight years there has been a shift toward the Watergate approach."

Press secretaries seem particularly sensitive to the change in attitudes. One former reporter, who has now served almost twenty years as press secretary to a senior House Democrat, expressed his frustration with the "new journalism" he sees in and around the Capitol. The press, he says, has become "bloodthirsty." It has "developed a sickly preoccupation with the negative aspects of governmental operations, the presidency, the Congress, the administrative agencies." The media "think we're all crooks and it only remains for them to prove it." This man speaks for many of the staff who work directly with the press corps in Congress. . . .

Despite the prevailing view, this essay argues: that the mass media, in toto, have *not* hurt the membership electorally, especially in the House; that even the news media have *not* been of a piece in their relationship with Congress; that many of the major changes brought by the media to Congress have been brought *not* by a "new journalism" but by the campaign media or by practices associated with "old journalism"; that change has *not* been fundamental and continuity has *not* disappeared.

Combining these points with what I shall present later, . . . I offer these conclusions concerning the changing relationship between the in-house, campaign, and news media and the Congress over the last twenty years:

1. The in-house media in Congress have changed as fully as the news media since 1960, and they have tended to negate much of the effect that the new, hardened Washington press corps has had on incumbents.

2. The campaign media around Congress have grown at least as fast as the news media in Congress, and under most circumstances they still tend to benefit incumbents, especially in the House.

3. The new toughness of the national press corps is not much in evidence in the local press. In some respects, the local media may have actually become "softer" than they were in 1960.

4. The discrepancy between the "soft" local press and the "tough" national news media has grown wider since 1960, and this widening gap goes a long way toward explaining why people hate Congress but love their congressman.

5. The "media-mix" that has developed in Congress since 1960 helps explain both the increase in safety of House incumbents and the concomitant decline in the safety of incumbents in the Senate.

6. The greatest effect of the new media-mix on Congress as an institution has been to attract a new kind of congressman.

7. The new media-mix has continued the evolutionary process, begun with radio, through which the executive branch grows increasingly more important than Congress as a policy-making institution.

8. *The media, taken together, have not done much to damage the members of Congress* but have damaged the institution of Congress—at least a little.

This last point may be the most important of all. In fact, I believe that the membership has learned to cope very effectively with the modern congressional media—even if the institution and the leadership have not. So, while it may be true that the mass media have proved somewhat detrimental to the institution, their three faces have not looked unkindly on the members per se. The overall pattern is one of change much in keeping with David Mayhew's notions about Congress. One finds, as Mayhew might have guessed, resourceful members who have restricted the impact of the media and adapted beautifully to their new forms, but a disunified institution far less able to restrict or adapt to those very same forms.

To understand all of this, however, one must remember that the congressional media are a mixture of the national, local, and regional press, an in-house press, and an ever-growing campaign media. Any analysis that stresses only the so-called new journalism oversimplifies the changing relationship between Congress and the mass media. One must emphasize the pluralism of congressional media if one takes into account all the major dimensions of modern, mass, political communication.

"In-House" Media—Unambiguous Advantages

... The ability to communicate more often with more constituents directly through the mail has been one of the most important changes in the in-house media. In fact, much of the technology adorning the new congressional office either produces mail or can be used to facilitate mail. Mail—in its volume alone, which has increased over 300 percent— represents a revolutionary change in in-house communications over the last two decades.[2] Currently, the average American receives two pieces of mail every year from Congress.

The increase in congressional mail can be explained in part by population growth, in part by an increasing national politicization. But the major explanation is the coming of modern computer technology to

Congress. In 1960 nobody had a computerized mail system. As of 1979 almost every Senate office and, according to *Congressional Quarterly*, 300 House offices have computerized mailing facilities.[3] Younger members increasingly consider computerized mail a political necessity. The House itself found in a study conducted in 1977 that the freshman class was almost twice as likely to employ computerized correspondence as senior members.[4] One can expect "managed mail" to increase rapidly as the seniors leave.

But the new in-house correspondence systems mean more than a greater quantity of mail, and more than efficient mail. The new system can also mean "targeted" mail. Most mail from members is computerized, and most of it is sent in direct response to a constituent inquiry or problem. But more and more "personalized" mail is unsolicited and is sent to types of individuals who might be pleased by what it says: this is "targeted" mail, one of the big new phenomena on Capitol Hill.

. . . If the member wants to send letters to all Blackfoot Indians who have written to him on ERA and who live on a particular street or block, he can do it without much effort. . . .

. . . As early as 1956 the Senate and House began operating separate in-house recording studios for members and leaders. The studios in both houses have always been used for the same purposes—to provide members with convenient, cheap, and sympathetic programming that can be mailed home to broadcasters and used on local channels as news or public affairs presentations. . . . My interviews . . . indicate that members are using the studios more and more, especially the younger members. . . .

. . . The radio and TV studios are only part of the congressional in-house press. For over 120 years the House and Senate have maintained a network of auxiliary offices which aid the press as it covers the membership day to day. It all began in 1857 when the Senate and then the House opened their own Press Galleries. Following the establishment of the first two Press Galleries in the nineteenth century, Congress responded with five more in the twentieth—a Radio and Television Gallery and a Periodical Gallery for each house and a Photographers' Gallery for both, all of which existed by 1960. The staffs in all seven galleries work in a rather strange environment, servants of the media as well as of the Congress. While the correspondents are paid by their respective news organizations, the gallery employees are paid by the House or Senate. The galleries are there to help both the press and the Congress. . . .

Thus, in terms of in-house media, *Congress has expanded and adapted most in the areas that help members directly. It has done less in the areas that are general and institutional in emphasis.* Congress has adjusted to developments in the media . . . selectively, and "personally," with special concern for the electoral life of its individual members.

There is one final dimension, perhaps more important than the rest, which suggests how much the in-house media have grown in the last twenty years. . . . [P]ress secretaries labeled as such were few in number in the Senate and practically nonexistent in the House when Congress entered the 1960s. Because definitions change and press secretaries are often called something other than "press secretary," it is almost impossible to quantify precisely the growth of the congressional press secretariat, but the information that does exist indicates that that growth has been striking. . . .

The growth in the congressional press secretariat suggests again that the media-mix in Congress has not been so bad for the members. They hire press people, after all, to praise them, not to harm them. It is not possible to say which side started the escalation in personnel, the press or the Congress. But in either case the growth of the new journalism has probably been countered, or its effects at least diluted, by the growth in the press secretariat. . . .

. . . Nothing stands more visibly for change in the relationship between Congress and the media than the national televising of House floor proceedings. But along with change has been a commitment to continuity—House TV is another case study in how Congress has adapted to the media by looking out for number one, the membership. . . .

. . . [A]ll equipment and all personnel in the system are part of the House of Representatives. Control of the system is in the hands of the Speaker, who exercises that control through a Speaker's advisory Committee on Broadcasting and an advisory team working in the House Recording Studio.

In keeping with the tradition of adapting the media to their own needs, the members and the leadership have provided for themselves quite well. H. Res. 866 provides for in-house technicians with stationary cameras (nobody can be pictured falling asleep or inadvertently acting uncongressional under this system), blackened screens during roll-call votes (members cannot be caught changing their votes at the last moment, or even voting at all for that matter), and ready access to videotape files (members can, if they wish, send "news" clips to the stations back home at very low cost). Added to all that is continuous live coverage of all proceedings, broadcast by over 850 cable TV systems across the nation on C-SPAN (Cable Satellite Public Affairs Network).[5] . . .

Two factors confounding attempts to evaluate the impact on the public have been the lack of information on the size of the audience watching House proceedings on television and the lack of network (or station) utilization of the tapes themselves. The major audience for television would, of course, be the network audience—now estimated to be above 55 million viewers nightly. But the networks have tended not to use the tapes of floor proceedings, in part because they objected to the

House's decision to keep control of the cameras and in part because the networks still regard the House as less newsworthy than the Senate.

The only other news audience comes through C-SPAN, the 850 cable systems which tie directly into the Capitol telecasts. The potential audience for C-SPAN is, at present, 18 million viewers, but nobody knows who watches, or how often. The fact that the networks and C-SPAN only provide for a limited coverage or a small audience is a major reason for assuming that House TV has caused little public response. . . .

The Campaign Media: Potential Problems for Incumbents

Campaign media are those that candidates use to get elected. The major difference between campaign media and in-house media is who pays: Congress pays for in-house media out of general office accounts; candidates pay for campaign media out of private campaign funds. Since 1960 three basic changes have occurred in the relationship between Congress and its campaign media: (1) candidates now use the media more, (2) they use them more effectively, and (3) challengers find in the campaign media a new opportunity, but one still qualified by the old reality of incumbent advantage. . . .

While comparable and detailed figures on media expenditures are not available for the last twenty years, we know from the work of Edie Goldenberg and Michael Traugott that by 1978 congressional candidates were spending well over half (56 percent) of their total campaign budgets on all the mass media combined.[6] These authors estimate that in the six years between 1972 and 1978 the amount spent on broadcasting alone in House elections tripled.[7] . . .

. . . By spending so much more than ever before, congressional candidates have both created and understood a new electoral environment. The increasing use of the media is both cause and reflection of the growing impact of campaign dollars on electoral returns. . . .

. . . [A]s voters continue to grow less loyal to party and candidates continue to spend more money to attract votes, the campaign media become more influential. . . .

. . . [T]he campaign media remain for most members of Congress a *potential* threat. A serious attack that relies on campaign media *can* fatally damage an incumbent. But most often no such challenge materializes. For one thing, most challengers cannot compete in dollars and cents. . . . At least in the House, a case can be made for arguing: that the campaign media have not much redefined congressional electoral politics; that television advertising is still too expensive and too inefficient for most House campaigns, where TV dollars are largely wasted reaching people who live outside the district; that incumbents still make more use of the media than their challengers; and that, at best, the campaign media have made House campaigns a wee bit less certain than before. . . .

The News Media: Cynicism and Symbiosis
in the Two Worlds of [the] Press

The news media are what most of us think of as *the* media. But even the news media are less than monolithic in their relations with Congress. Television news differs from print, print differs from radio, radio differs from TV; and in each medium, local coverage differs from national. In terms of impact these differences are crucial.

... The intuition that the news media are increasingly hostile to Congress fits best the reality of the *national* press. The evidence abounds. ...

My own content analysis of network news coverage of Congress leads me to believe that this approach is not confined to the national print media. Back in 1976, after the Supreme Court in *Buckley* v. *Valeo* gave Congress thirty days to reconstitute the Federal Elections Commission or witness its demise, David Brinkley commented to an audience of 15 million, "It is widely believed in Washington that it would take Congress thirty days to make instant coffee." [8] The complete results of my analysis of network coverage of Congress suggest much the same thing—the national press is fairly tough on Congress. ABC, CBS, and NBC ran 263 "Congress stories" in January and February of 1976, according to my analysis, and among them I found not a single item that placed Congress or its members in a positive light. I did find 36 stories (14 percent) that tended to present Congress or its members in a negative light.[9] The fact that Congress received no good press on the evening news for a period spanning five weeks in 1976 suggests that the national press do not find much about Congress to their liking. ...

... In December 1969, Senator Daniel Brewster (Democrat, Maryland) was indicted in federal court on charges that included illegally accepting money for what amounted to legislative favors—bribery. Nine years later, Congressman Daniel Flood (Democrat, Pennsylvania) was indicted on federal charges of much the same sort. Though the two cases are not identical, it seems reasonable to compare the coverage given them in the press and to take that coverage as evidence of how the behavior of the press had changed.

Using the Vanderbilt *Television News Index and Abstracts,* I counted the stories that network television broadcast on the Brewster and Flood cases, including all network stories heard on the evening news in the year of the indictment or the year following—1969 and 1970 for Brewster, 1978 and 1979 for Flood.

... According to the *Index,* Flood was referred to in fifty-nine different news stories, while Brewster was mentioned in eight. More incredible, Flood was the principal news focus or a secondary news focus for 4,320 seconds of network time, while stories about Brewster amounted to only 170 seconds. Flood-related stories received twenty-five times as much network news attention as did Brewster-related items, even though Brewster was a senator and Flood "only" a representative.

Some of this difference is accounted for by the fact that Brewster stood alone in his scandal, while Flood had the misfortune of being implicated in a much broader scandal—along with then Congressman Joshua Eilberg and then U.S. Attorney David Marston. Marston in particular increased the newsworthiness of the Flood case because Marston was a Republican in a Democratic administration and was eventually fired by President Carter for reasons having more to do with "old politics" than incompetence. But these extraneous factors cannot easily account for all of the difference. The Flood coverage, so much more extensive than anything even dreamed of in the Brewster case, serves to corroborate the idea that the national press had changed during the 1970s—had become more "cannibal" in its congressional reporting.

. . . History, logic, and the evidence all indicate that the local media have not really been overcome by the Watergate syndrome, so conspicuous in the national media. . . . At least as late as 1974, critics of the press were still complaining about what one might best call a *symbiotic* relationship between the local media and incumbents in Congress— symbiotic not only because each "partner" profited from the continued relationship, but also because each clearly understood the other's mission and needs. . . .

What may be the best evidence for believing that the local press is not Woodstein—let alone Evans and Novak—comes from the Center for Political Studies (CPS) at the University of Michigan. . . . Using a sample of 216 newspapers, CPS found that in the last phase of the 1978 congressional campaign the average congressman received a score of 1.9 for his coverage in the local press, on a scale ranging from 1.0 (totally positive) through 3.0 (totally negative).[10] Incumbents fare well, getting positive attention, and lots of it. Incumbents receive twice the coverage their challengers get and, . . . more positive coverage than challengers or Congress as an institution or the government generally.[11] The differences are small, but they always favor incumbents. . . .

. . . One of the less conspicuous changes affecting press coverage of Congress has been the steady increase in the size of the Capitol Hill press corps. . . . Without doubt the greatest growth has come in radio . . . an increase of 175 percent in the number of both radio and TV correspondents admitted to the congressional press corps in a sixteen-year period. During the period, the number of print journalists increased by "only" 37 percent. The rate of increase for electronic news people has been precisely five times greater than for print, and the overwhelming majority of the new media people are in radio.

Radio and electronic news coverage of Congress has rendered the

Capitol Hill press corps more regional—hence, more local—in its behavior. This localizing of news through "regional" coverage of Congress has probably meant that the news about members comes out much "softer" than would have been the case without the explosion in radio. For two reasons, regional radio has probably worked to dilute the impact of the new journalism in Congress. First, regional electronic news people are, by definition, more local in outlook than the national press and, therefore, more dependent on access to members. Regional radio and local television people bring their local concerns with them to Congress, and they need to establish good relations with the new members who share those concerns. Second, the electronic media *generally* treat Congress "better" than the print media. . . .

. . . The local and national press are two separate worlds, and since 1960 they have grown more distinct. Why is this so, and what are the implications?

First, a qualification. The differences between the national and local press should not be exaggerated. The nationals do not often go out of their way to be tough when toughness is unwarranted; our analysis of congressional news in 1976 showed that eight out of ten stories on network news were *not* negative.[12]. . .

Moreover, locals can be tough when they have to be. Milton Hollstein describes, for example, the treatment Congressman Allan Howe received at the hands of the Salt Lake City media. The press, he said, served as "pillory" when Howe was caught with a decoy prostitute, and its "excessive," "gratuitous," "knee-jerk," and "questionable" coverage of the incident "made it impossible for [Howe] to be reelected" to Congress, even before the reported facts had been corroborated.[13]

Nonetheless, the basic differences in local and national coverage need some explanation. Most of those who have offered explanations have emphasized the variations between the local and national press in size and beat. A few others have dwelled on the economic self-interest of the local press; the theory holds that publishers urge editors to persuade journalists to treat the local congressman kindly in the hope that he may, at some point, vote for or amend legislation that will profit the newspaper. Another form of economic determinism has been used to explain the pleasant relationship between local broadcasters and congressmen. The theory here is that a contented congressman might go to bat for an FCC-licensed broadcaster if there were a licensing challenge. Both of these economic theories hinge on the owners' seeking to maximize their economic self-interest. The journalists are secondary.

But social psychology probably has as much to do with the relationship between the media and Congress as economics does, and the correspondents' behavior probably matters more than the interests of their capitalist publishers. At least half a dozen studies all make it clear that symbiosis emerges from a network of friendships and "mutual dependencies" between journalists and newsmakers. . . . But the representatives of local media are drawn in closer to the sources than the national press; mutual dependency is a larger ingredient in their friendships with the newsmakers. . . .

. . . [S]ize—especially the size of the networks—gives the national press a real advantage in dealing with members. The local media are still imprisoned by their smallness and weakness. . . . Nationals for the most part focus on the institution, not on individual members. . . . Focusing on institutions makes it easier to be tough. One does not have any particular pair of eyes to avoid when one attacks Congress. This is one reason why, as we have seen, Congress received more negative coverage than positive in 1978 but congressional *candidates* got more positive coverage than negative.

Add to all this the very real tendency for the national media to recruit the tougher journalists coming out of the local press and you get a fairly complete explanation for the hardness of the Washington press corps and the softness of the local news. The nationals look hard at the institution. The locals exchange glances with their representatives. This pattern holds unless the local member gets into trouble: then all the press—national, regional, local—glares. Such is the nature of the press in Congress.

Consequences

Now that we have considered the changes in the in-house, campaign, and news media as each relates to Congress, we must ask, So what? What has the new media-mix done to or for Congress? Let us consider this question along three dimensions: attitudinal, electoral, and institutional.

. . . Because the national news media have grown apart from the local media, and because the local media have probably been expanding more rapidly than the rest, the news media help explain a most interesting paradox in American public opinion—nationwide contempt for Congress and district-wide esteem for its members. The two types of media covering it coincide with the two sides of Congress's image. . . .

Of course, there are other interpretations of the paradox of opinion in Congress. Some authorities on Congress contend that members actually do a good job as representatives but that the institution actually fails to do its job as a legislature. Others . . . contend that members work the bureaucracy so effectively in the interests of their constituents that constituents learn to respect them but not the institution. Both of these interpretations seem ultimately too literal. Constituents simply do not deal enough with their congressmen to produce the paradox of congressional public image. Only the media are broad enough in reach and scope to account for the bulk of opinion toward Congress or its members. CPS congressional election studies in the 1970s indicate that 52 percent of all citizens read about their member in the newspapers; 14 percent had met the member personally. Fewer than one person in six ever deals with a member directly, even using a very loose definition of "direct" contact.[14]

Knowing what we do about local coverage, we may plausibly assume that the local press accounts for much of the favorable image that members enjoy.... [D]istricts with more negative press about Congress, the institution, hold more negative news of Congress—districts with more positive press go significantly in the other direction. The national media, which reach everyone with their critical coverage of the institution, and the local media, which reach constituents and accommodate members, *together* serve as the single best explanation for the paradox of public opinion toward Congress.

... The fact that the nationals relinquish to the locals the job of covering individual congressmen has direct implications for the members' safety at election time. Locals keep their readers relatively happy with their representatives by giving incumbents lots of coverage, most of it favorable. The result is safer incumbency. And when one factors in the growth of the in-house media, which inevitably serve to protect incumbents, the result is ever greater safety for those holding office—precisely the pattern that has prevailed among House membership since 1960....

... House members control much of their own press—much more than presidents, governors, or senators. Members control their press because they (1) make greater and more sophisticated use of in-house media, (2) attract, by and large, more money than challengers in ad campaigns, (3) maintain a closer relationship with the local press than senators, and (4) attract much less coverage from the nationals so long as they stay unindicted. House members have grown increasingly safe electorally as they have gained greater control of all the media at their disposal....

The Senate media-mix is very different. Senators' relationships with the local media are less intimate because senators deal with whole states, not with one or two papers as House members do. If propinquity explains cordiality, senators lose out because they simply cannot be as close to their press—or their constituents—as members of the House. The senator also attracts better financed challengers, who can buy TV time and who can use their resources more efficiently than practically any House member. The campaign media can hurt senators more because their challengers are more likely to be able to afford them. But most important, senators attract national coverage—a must for any potential presidential contender, but a potential disaster for an incumbent who comes out looking bad on the evening news.... Somewhat ironically, powerful senators are less able to control their images than "invisible" House members. In the Senate campaign of 1980, thirteen of twenty-nine incumbents went down to defeat, which approaches a 50 percent attrition rate. In 1980, as in the recent past, the House incumbents were four times safer than the Senate incumbents.

. . . Obviously, not everything has changed. Some of the most important aspects of the relationship between the mass media in Congress continue much as they were in 1960. One of these is the news media's preoccupation with the presidency. Although the data are inconclusive, it seems that Congress as an institution is still very subordinate to the executive in news attention and news manipulation.[15] The print media have been inching back toward a more equitable balance between presidency and Congress, but television has stayed with the executive. . . .

The presidential hegemony that is still felt in the press means a public that "thinks presidential" and relies on presidents to get us through, make things happen, control public policy. This is not simply a quantitative advantage that the presidency enjoys. The media have consistently treated the executive less negatively than the Congress. For reasons that follow rather closely those which explain the easier coverage given the membership than Congress per se, the executive generally gets better press than the legislative branch. Even in 1974—the year of Nixon's resignation—the press treated Congress more negatively. . . . [A]ccording to the Center for Political Studies at Michigan, the president received coverage that was 39 percent negative, but the Congress was saddled with negative press amounting to 42 percent of the total.[16]

The results of this continued assault on Congress have proven to be substantial. Whether the explanation is "reality" or "the media," Congress has not had a better public image than the president since 1960, except in some of the Watergate years. In fact, even in September 1979, when Jimmy Carter's public approval rating on the Associated Press/NBC poll plunged to 19 percent—the lowest level of public approval assigned to his or *any* presidency, ever—the Congress still did worse: the Congress stood at 13 percent—six points, or 30 percent, below Carter. Both the quality and quantity of national press coverage of Congress has hurt Congress in its competitive relations with the presidency. After Watergate, after Vietnam, after all of it, the media still help render us a "presidential nation"—while making us less "congressional."

There is perhaps a major lesson in all this concerning the media, our political institutions, and their respective roles. *The media, by focusing so fully on the office of president and then inevitably on the inadequacies of any person holding the job, may be producing an office that is more powerful but at the same time may be weakening the political power of each individual president.* On the other hand, *the media,* by treating Congress poorly but its incumbents relatively well, *may be strengthening incumbents but weakening their institution.* . . .

. . . [T]he most important institutional change to have occurred as a result of the new media-mix in Congress has been with the membership. The new media-mix, in and out of Congress, has manufactured a new kind of candidate, a new kind of nominee, and a new kind of incumbent. This is not simply a matter of looks or hair style, although clearly they are part of the change. It comes down to a question of style or legislative personality—what James David Barber might call "legislative character."

We have already seen evidence of how different the new generation in Congress is in its attitude toward the media. Compared with the class of 1958, the class of 1978 was three times more likely to make heavy use of the congressional recording studio, three times more likely to regard the House TV system as "very useful," three times more likely to have relied "a lot" on TV in the last election. Over 60 percent of the class of 1978 said "yes" when asked if they had used paid media consultants in their first successful campaign for Congress. Nobody in the class of 1958 answering my survey had used a media consultant to get elected the first time. Almost beyond doubt the media culture of the membership has changed.

Although these figures pertain to campaign style more than legislative character, one may infer that the increasingly greater reliance on the media for nomination, election, status in the Congress, and reelection is one sign of a new congressional character—one more dynamic, egocentric, immoderate, and, perhaps, intemperate. The evidence here is speculative and thin. But interviews and recent studies indicate that the media, intentionally or unintentionally, have recruited, maintained, and promoted a new legislative temperament.

One media consultant . . . believes that the media (plus the decision in *Buckley* v. *Valeo*, the case outlawing limits on a congressional candidate's spending) have changed the type of congressional candidate and officeholder.

> You look through . . . and you get the guys with the blow-dried hair who read the script well. That's not the kind of guy who'd been elected to Congress or Senate ten years ago. You've got a guy who is not concerned about issues; who isn't concerned about the mechanics of government; who doesn't attend committee meetings; who avoids taking positions at any opportunity and who yet is a master at getting his face in the newspapers and on television and all that. You get the modern media candidate which is, in a lot of ways, Senator [name], who has no objective right to be elected to public office.

The same consultant sees a new style of legislator:

> You get a lot of young guys particularly who do two things, sort of the typical young congressman these days. He gets elected, he hires a bunch of pros to run his office, sets up a sophisticated constituent contact operation through the mails and through other things and an actuality

service and all that kind of thing. Then he goes out and showboats to get more press so that he gets reelected and is considered for higher office. Those become of much more importance to him than the functioning as a national legislator or part of a branch of government. . . .

. . . In the final analysis the changes in congressional media over the last twenty years have produced mixed blessings and not just a few ironies—for Congress, for its members, and for us.

For the House membership the changes have meant greater safety but, at the same time, greater anxiety about getting reelected. . . .

For the senators, changes in the media-mix have meant less safety but, at the same time, greater opportunity for achieving national prominence. Network news coverage of the Senate can make an investigating senator a household word in a matter of days. Some senators have become nationally prominent through television almost overnight.

On both sides of the Capitol the changes in the media have given younger members and maverick members more political visibility—and consequently greater power—than ever before. But at the same time, modern news media have also meant that all the members of Congress work in an institution that has ever increasing image problems. In a final irony the modern media in Congress mean that although more policy information is directly available to members than ever before, the members themselves spend no more time with that information than they ever did. Public relations, after all, has become more and more demanding on the members' time. Policy can be more efficiently handled by staff or subcommittee.

The media generally benefit public people, not public institutions. For the most part the new media-mix has rendered Congress no less safe, but a little less serviceable—the members no less important, but the Congress a little less viable. The major impact of the modern media on Congress has not been the result of post-Watergate journalism but the inevitable consequence of focusing more public attention on elected officials, all of whom owe their jobs to local constituents. The media have made congressmen somewhat more anxious, somewhat more adept at media manipulation, and somewhat more responsive to local interests. But this merely shows us that Congress and its membership have a highly democratic base. What the news media have done to Congress is what one would expect when the level of information concerning an essentially democratic institution increases—greater responsiveness to the locals and greater concern about saving oneself. In all that, there is obviously good news, and bad.

Notes

1. Unless otherwise noted, the quotations in this chapter are from these interviews.
2. Figures supplied by the Senate Appropriations Committee.
3. Irwin B. Arieff, "Computers and Direct Mail Are Being Married on the Hill to Keep Incumbents in Office," *Congressional Quarterly Weekly Report*, July 21, 1979, p. 1451.
4. Dianne O'Shetski, "Analysis of Survey on Computer Support Provided to Member Offices, As of April 1977," House Administration Committee Report, August 1977, p. 10.
5. For a thorough discussion of the history and politics of House TV, see Donald Hirsch, "Televising the Chamber of the House of Representatives: The Politics of Mass Communication in a Democratic Institution," thesis, Oxford University, 1979.
6. Edie Goldenberg and Michael Traugott, "Resource Allocation and Broadcast Expenditures in Congressional Campaigns" (paper presented at the annual meeting of the American Political Science Association, Washington, D.C., September 1979), p. 7.
9. Michael J. Robinson and Kevin R. Appel, "Network News Coverage of Congress," *Political Science Quarterly* (Fall 1979), p. 412.
10. Arthur Miller, "The Institutional Focus of Political Distrust" (paper prepared for the American Political Science Association, Washington, D.C., September 1979), p. 39. . . .
11. Miller, "Institutional Focus," p. 39.
12. Robinson and Appel, "Network News."
13. Milton Hollstein, "Congressman Howe in the Salt Lake City Media: A Case Study of the Press as Pillory," *Journalism Quarterly*, vol. 54, no. 3 (Autumn 1977), p. 454.
14. Miller, "Institutional Focus," p. 37.
15. My own research shows practically no change in the level of presidential news on network evening news (all networks) between 1969 and 1977. . . . Susan Miller, using 1974—the year when impeachment proceedings were instituted against Nixon—reached very different results, with Congress getting slightly more print coverage than the president. See "News Coverage of Congress: The Search for the Ultimate Spokesman," *Journalism Quarterly*, vol. 54, no. 3 (Autumn 1977), p. 461.
16. Arthur Miller, Edie Goldenberg, and Lutz Erbring, "Type-Set Politics: The Impact of Newspapers on Public Confidence," *American Political Science Review*, vol. 73 (June 1979), p. 71.

4.5 ━━━

The Media and Watergate

Gladys Engel Lang and Kurt Lang

Editor's Note. This selection further illustrates how and why political leaders vie for media coverage during power struggles. Gladys Engel Lang and Kurt Lang assess the extent to which news stories affected the course of political events during the Watergate scandal that led to President Richard Nixon's resignation. They conclude that despite voluminous news stories, media influence was only peripheral to the outcome. Their analysis is important because it indicates the limitations, as well as the potency, of media coverage. Even peripheral media involvement, however, can be crucial. Would the Watergate affair have grown to major proportions without news coverage?

The selection also highlights how the media are used as a battleground in the fight to win public opinion support. The Langs call attention to the major role played by news stories in forming public opinion and in gauging and interpreting what the public thinks. These interpretations influence the conduct of politics because decision makers usually accept the media's assessment.

The authors have collaborated in numerous path-breaking studies of mass media images and their effects on public opinion. At the time of writing both were professors of sociology at the State University of New York at Stony Brook. The selection is from *The Battle for Public Opinion: The President, the Press, and the Polls During Watergate* (New York: Columbia University Press, 1983).

. . . What was the effect of the media on the creation, the course, and the resolution of Watergate? The answer is not as obvious as it may appear. Despite the heroic efforts of some journalists, Watergate had no visible effect on the 1972 presidential election. Yet six months later, even before the televised Senate Watergate hearings, the nation's attention had become riveted on the issue, and for more than a year thereafter, until

Richard Nixon's dramatic exit, Watergate dominated the headlines and the network news. . . .

Richard Nixon himself believed that public opinion was the critical factor in what he called the "overriding of my landslide mandate." For him, the struggle to stay in office, especially after the firing of Special Watergate Prosecutor Archibald Cox, when impeachment first became a real possibility, was a "race for public support." He called it his "last campaign," only this time it was not for political office but for his political life.[1]

As the President saw it, the main danger of being impeached resided in the public's becoming conditioned to the idea that he was going to be impeached. This was a good enough reason for Nixon's strategists to keep a close watch on all indicators of public sentiment—letters, telegrams, telephone calls, editorials, television commentaries, press reports, and, especially, what the polls showed. At the same time, the President developed a media strategy specifically and directly aimed at winning the battle of the polls. The media were the principal battlefields on which the major confrontations took place. Television, because of how it was used by all sides, played a most active role in the conflict.

Many observers of Watergate agree that it was Nixon's defeat in the battle for public opinion that forced him to retreat at crucial points when he failed to rally support for his stand to limit the scope of any probe into the Watergate break-in. Ultimately, it left him no alternative but to bow out. In this view, the way public opinion made itself felt exemplified "democracy at work," a favorite cliché of the news media. Ford lent it official sanction in his inaugural address when he told the nation, "Here the people rule." The view in the Nixon camp was less benign. Public opinion was seen as an ever-present danger. Stirred up by the media, deliberately manipulated by his enemies, and tracked by pollsters, public opinion was to become the hostile force that ultimately *drove* Nixon from office.

Not everyone believing that public opinion influenced the resolution of Watergate agrees that it hastened the end. In fact, an argument can be made that public opinion had exactly the opposite effect, that it slowed the process and prolonged the crisis. Some members of Congress, reluctant to move against the President unless assured that they had a majority solidly behind them, felt restrained by public opinion. Polls that continued to show most people opposed to Nixon's removal from office failed to provide this reassurance, though these same polls also showed large majorities believing that the President was somehow involved in a "serious" scandal and not just caught up in the usual politics. Critics of opinion research have gone so far as to argue, some most vociferously, that during most of Watergate the major polls, whether by inadvertence or design, exaggerated the extent of opposition to impeachment. Consequently, the media were slow to register the groundswell for impeachment.

A third group of political analysts regards this emphasis on public opinion as totally misplaced and the Nixon strategy as misdirected. To them the battle for public opinion was only a sideshow. The media, in treating the issue as a political struggle for public support, diverted attention from the one crucial element in the downfall of Richard Nixon: the accumulation of incriminating evidence. If Watergate was a political contest, as it obviously was, the stakes consisted of information. Those pressing the case on legal grounds had to be mindful of public reaction but only insofar as people had to have confidence in the fairness and objectivity of the process by which the President was being judged.

Clearly the nation had experienced a dramatic shift in public opinion during the more than two years of controversy, which began with a break-in and ended with Nixon's resignation. What could account for such a reversal? The first place to look for an explanation is in the behavior of the media. TV, radio, and print are essential to the formation of public opinion in the modern nation in two ways. They disseminate information that allows members of the public to form opinions and, just as important, they convey to politicians and to others an image of what public opinion is, thus giving it a force it would not otherwise have. . . .

Watergate had broken into public consciousness only after the coverage had created a sense of crisis. This is not to say that the Watergate issue was something that the electronic and print media had created out of whole cloth. The coverage, which had stirred interest in Watergate, was dictated by events but the media themselves had become part of the field of action. Political figures with a stake in the outcome were using whatever publicity they could attract to advance their own goals and interests, thereby providing grist for the media and adding to the number of Watergate-relevant events there to be covered. As a result, the coverage reached saturation levels with Watergate on the front page and on the evening news day after day after day as well as on early morning, late evening, and Sunday public affairs programs. But the headlines alone would not have sufficed to make a serious issue out of a problem so removed from most people's daily concerns. Continuity was necessary to rivet attention to new facts as they emerged. The process is circular. Media exposure and public attention generate responses at the elite level that produce still more news in a cycle of mutual reinforcement that continues until politicians and public tire of an issue or another issue moves into the center of the political stage.

. . . On matters of concern to people, because they fall within their direct experience, as is the case with various bread-and-butter, sickness-and-health, life-and-death issues, the media clearly lack power to suppress concern. But they can do more than stimulate interest. By directing attention to these concerns, they provide a context that influences *how* people will think about these matters—where they believe the fault lies and whether anything (and what) should be done. Publicity given to essentially private concerns transforms them into public concerns. Whether or not it increases the problem for those affected, it does increase morale and legitimates the will to protest.

With regard to high-threshold issues like Watergate, the media play an even more essential role. Had it not been for the news reports about Watergate, hardly anyone would have known about campaign finance violations, "dirty tricks," illegal surveillance by persons connected with the White House, and the lot. Media attention was necessary before Watergate could be considered a problem. Yet, in publicizing a high-threshold issue like Watergate, the media do more than direct attention to a problem; they influence how people will think about it. They supply the context that, by making the problem politically relevant, gives people reasons for taking sides and converts the problem into a serious political issue. In this sense the public agenda is not so much set by the media as built up through a cycle of media activity that transforms an elite issue into a public controversy.

None of this should be read to mean that the media, all on their own, dictate the public agenda. They cannot "teach" the public what the issues are. They certainly do not operate in total autonomy from the political system. The gradual saturation of news content with Watergate depended on political developments in which the press itself was only one of several movers. Agenda building—a more apt term than agenda setting—is a collective process in which media, government, and the citizenry reciprocally influence one another in at least some respects.

Let us . . . sketch out how the news media affect this agenda-building process.

First, they highlight some events or activities. They make them stand out from among the myriads of other contemporaneous events and activities that could equally have been selected out for publicity. Making something the center of interest affects how much people will think and talk about it. This much is only common sense.

But, second, being in the news is not enough to guarantee attention to an issue. The amount and kind of coverage required varies from issue to issue. Different kinds of issues require different amounts and kinds of coverage to gain attention. Where news focuses on a familiar concern likely to affect almost everyone, this almost guarantees instant attention. In the case of a high-threshold issue like Watergate, which also surfaced at the wrong time, it takes saturation coverage to achieve this result. Specifically, recognition by the "cosmopolitan" media was not enough. Only after the more locally oriented press had become saturated with news of Watergate developments did it emerge as an issue that would remain on the political and public agenda for nearly 16 months.

Third, the events and activities in the focus of attention still have to be framed, to be given a field of meanings within which they can be understood. They must come to stand for something, identify some problem, link up with some concern. The first exposé of the political fund used to finance the unit responsible for the break-in was publicized during a Presidential campaign. It was reported and interpreted within the context of that continuing contest. The Democrats' effort to change this context by interpreting Watergate as a symptom of widespread political corruption within the Administration was not very successful. Watergate remained, at least for a while, a partisan issue. The context had first to be changed.

Fourth, the language the media use to track events also affects the meaning imputed to them. Metaphors such as "Watergate caper" and "bugging incident," which belittled the issue, disappeared that spring under an avalanche of signs of a high-level political scandal. The press, along with politicians, adopted less deprecatory codewords. "Watergate" or "Watergate scandal" came to denote the various questionable activities now being disclosed. The words stood for nothing specific, yet for anything that could possibly happen.

Fifth, the media link the activities or events that have become the focus of attention to secondary symbols whose location on the political landscape is easily recognized. They also weave discrete events into a continuing political story, so that the lines of division on the issue as it develops tend to coincide with the cleavage between the organized political parties or between other sharply defined groups.... When Watergate first surfaced during the 1972 campaign, it was defined primarily as a partisan clash between Democrats and Republicans. By Spring 1973 opinion still divided along political lines, but a realignment was under way as the issue changed and sides began to shape up around the "need to get the facts out," over the public "right to know" vs. "executive privilege," and on the question of confidence in the integrity of the government.

Finally, there are the prestige and standing of the spokesmen who articulate these concerns and demands. Their effectiveness stems in good part from their ability to command media attention. Democratic politicians like Larry O'Brien and George McGovern had been lonely voices ... when, during the campaign, they pressed for a full investigation. Their demands, though publicized, were neither much heard nor much heeded. They were known as people with an axe to grind. But as the controversy escalated, the publicity given Judge Sirica's admonishment that the full truth had not been told led prestigious Republicans to call for explanations, and their various attempts to get at the facts put pressure on the White House. The bystander public was being wooed....

... Based on the evidence, we reject the paranoid version of Watergate propagated by the White House that the crisis was manufactured by a hostile press which finally drove Nixon from office. But we also reject the populist view that Nixon was forced to resign because he lost his battle for public opinion. The moving force behind the effort to get to the bottom of Watergate came neither from the media nor public opinion but from political insiders. The conflict pitted the White House against those who, for whatever reason, wanted full disclosure of the facts behind the illegal attempt to plant wiretaps in the national headquarters of the Democratic Party. . . .

The press was prime mover in the controversy only in its early phase, when the Woodward and Bernstein tandem first linked the Watergate burglars to the Nixon campaign committee and, during the campaign, uncovered other stories that hinted at the politically explosive potential of the "bugging" incident. But with Nixon's decisive electoral victory, the press came close to abandoning Watergate. Then, as the issue revived and conflict over the scope of the investigation intensified, the press mainly lived off information insiders were happy to furnish it. . . .

Had the news media, by their coverage of Watergate, directly persuaded the public of the seriousness of White House misdeeds, of Nixon's complicity, of a threat to basic values, and that impeachment might be warranted? Not directly, but by their reporting and their comments, by the way they highlighted some events, by the context within which they framed these events, by the language they used to track developments, by linking news they reported to symbols familiar to the audience, and by the persons they singled out (or who offered themselves) as spokesmen in the controversy, the media certainly influenced the way the public—and politicians as well—thought about and defined the underlying issue.

. . . [I]t is difficult to demonstrate, in the narrowly scientific way that has become the researcher's norm, that watching or listening to a particular Watergate speech, press conference, or televised testimony was what directly changed people's opinion. Many media effects remain elusive and can be understood only as the outcome of a cumulative process. Thus we have pointed to evidence that minor, incremental, and sometimes subtle changes sooner or later contributed to major shifts. For example, the most important effect of the televised Senate Watergate hearings was a "sleeper," not immediately noticeable. By subtly changing the issue, the televised hearings prepared the ground for the outburst that so instantaneously followed the firing of the Special Watergate Prosecutor. Similarly, it was the high regard in which the major spokesmen against impeachment were held as the result of the televised Judiciary Committee proceedings that made their subsequent defection so persuasive.

The charge that the Watergate coverage was unfair or somehow "distorted" remains basically unsubstantiated. Nixon was hardly at the mercy of the media. The same publicity that was effectively utilized by his opponents was available to Nixon whenever he chose to make use of it. And Watergate did yield the headlines to other news on several occasions—not only during the Middle East crisis in October 1973 but later when, shortly before the impeachment debate, Nixon traveled abroad in what he called his "search for peace." As President, it was easy for Nixon to command attention; as leader of his party, he was apt to be treated gingerly by Republican editors until his intransigence overtried their loyalties. There is no question that the media thrive on scandal, and they did thrive during Watergate; but by the yardstick of reporting during the impeachment and trial of Andrew Johnson or during the Dreyfus case, they more than adhered to the norms of journalistic objectivity.

The main contribution of the media to moving opinion along was their extensive and full coverage of critical events. The visibility of the controversy helped more than anything to legitimate the process by which Nixon was ousted. . . . Because the deliberations of the House Judiciary Committee were televised, they were cast into the mold of an adversary proceeding, with most arguments couched in legal rather than political language. The decision was depicted as compelled by the evidence, with members—regardless of personal conviction—accepting the majority decision. They saw themselves, as they had told the nation, as representatives of the impersonal authority embodied in the Constitution, the highest law of the land. . . .

Still another question is how much the public was reacting to the substance of the Watergate disclosures or to Nixon himself. After all, other Presidents had been guilty of acts whose constitutionality was questionable or of behavior that fell short of the expected high standards of personal or political propriety. Yet these others somehow managed to avoid Nixon's fate. They somehow managed to keep up appearances either by sacrificing subordinates, who took the blame, or making sure that nothing beyond unsubstantiated rumor ever got out. Why should Nixon have failed with a similar strategy, one that he had previously employed with striking success? For one thing Nixon by his behavior throughout his political career had made enemies within the working press. As President, however, he commanded deference and respect and was treated with caution. Yet, once insiders put him on the defensive, these reporters were astounded at how far Nixon had evidently been willing to go to assure his reelection and to punish his "enemies." Thereafter they were ready to resurrect the image of the "old Nixon" and were less willing to declare sensitive areas out-of-bounds. Nixon was to harm himself further with the press by a pretense of openness. When pressed on Watergate, he repeatedly assured his questioners that he would cooperate to clear up the scandal, yet always with a proviso that allowed him to renege at a later date. As a result, Nixon was to appear less and less ingenuous even to his own followers. It was not the abuse of power, revealed in the Senate hearings, as much [as] his obstruction of the legal process that in the last analysis cost him the most support. The constituency that in the early months backed him on Watergate became increasingly impatient to have the issue resolved. This included many people who were still confident that the evidence would show that Nixon had done nothing worse than had other Presidents.

In this climate the opposition to Nixon gradually gained strength. It became difficult to defend Nixon on any but the narrowly legal grounds staked out by Republicans on the Judiciary Committee. . . .

Be all this as it may, there could have been no real public opinion on Watergate without the media. They alone could have called into being the mass audience of "bystanders" whose opinion had to be taken into account. It was likewise the media which, by reporting and even sponsoring polls, presented the cast of political actors in Watergate with a measure of public response to their every move. . . . The impression of public support made it easier to move against Nixon simply because the bystander public withheld the vote of confidence the President had so eagerly sought in order to defeat impeachment politically. Only in this sense, and this sense alone, was Nixon "driven" from office by his loss of public support.

Note

1. Richard M. Nixon, *RN: The Memoirs of Richard Nixon* (New York: Grosset and Dunlap, 1978), pp. 971, 972.

4.6 ▬▬▬

Collective Political Action and
Media Strategy: The Case of Yamit

Gadi Wolfsfeld

Editor's Note. Among the various strategies that groups can use to bring their concerns to the attention of government, media publicity has become increasingly popular. This is especially true for poor and powerless groups who cannot afford expensive legal or lobbying strategies. Using a case study drawn from Israel as an example of a protest action by small groups with limited resources, Gadi Wolfsfeld describes how three groups employed a combination of strategies to protest action planned by the government.

Although media attention is useful to nearly all protest groups, the groups' characteristics and goals determine the type and extent of publicity likely to be most helpful as well as the diverse obstacles each group will face in gaining media attention. Among the obstacles is the fierce competition among groups for limited news space. In addition, as the selection by Todd Gitlin in this section also shows, the costs of attaining media coverage may be very high in terms of conflict escalation, opposition from friends and foes, and penalties for unlawful activities that may be necessary to gain access to the media. Unfortunately, powerless groups that normally would not receive media coverage often have to engage in disorder to attract attention. Wolfsfeld's study constitutes an important step in developing theories about the role the media play, combined with other social forces, in the successes and failures of social movements.

At the time of writing, Wolfsfeld held a joint appointment as lecturer in the Communications Institute and the Department of Political Science at the Hebrew University in Jerusalem, Israel. The selection is from "Collective Political Action and Media Strategy: The Case of Yamit," *Journal of Conflict Resolution* 28:3 (September 1984): 363-381.

Arenas of Conflict

The mass media can be usefully thought of as one of a number of overlapping arenas of conflict that serve as gateways to the government.

From *Journal of Conflict Resolution* 28, no. 3 (September 1984): 363-381. Reprinted by permission of Sage Publications, Inc.

Each arena has its own set of entrance fees, rules of the game, and associated risk/reward ratios. Entrance fees are equivalent to the amount of group resources needed in order to participate, while the rules establish role expectations for the contestants. . . .

Two of the cheapest arenas are, not surprisingly, the riskiest. In the physical arena even a relatively small group of individuals is able to carry out a great deal of violence, with significant amount of impact, especially when the act is executed in the section of the arena that overlaps with that of the media. Physical attacks however, carry the risk of personal injury, or even death. For less desperate groups who nevertheless cannot afford the entrance fees of the more institutional forms of action, the media arena seems to serve as an increasingly popular portal to the government. In the last two decades, direct action techniques—a mainstay of the media arena—have become increasingly popular forms of political action (Barnes, Kaase, et al., 1979).

Lipsky (1970) was one of the first to emphasize the importance of the mass media in protest strategy. Protest, he argued, was the only political resource at the disposal of the weak and powerless, and therefore action groups depend on the media to activate reference publics in "ways favourable to protest goals" (1970:181). As later studies (Gitlin, 1980; Bromley and Shupe, 1979; Molotch, 1979) also pointed out, protest leaders often find themselves paying a heavy price for such publicity, as they attempt to overcome the inherent conflict of carrying out actions that will be covered by the media without alienating supporters or the general public.

The costs of entering into the media arena are equivalent to the definition of newsworthiness (Tuchman, 1978). Groups must plan and execute protests to fit media "frames" (Gitlin, 1980), which serve as institutional filters designed to meet the structural and commercial needs of the press (Bromley and Shupe, 1979). While conflict is a central issue for the media, its prevalence in society demands that a group's actions exhibit unusual amounts of drama, violence (or potential violence), and/or novelty. Groups must compete with a wide assortment of other, often more powerful contestants in order to gain even a minimal amount of control over the scarce resource of media coverage. Other costs of media competition are related to risks such as conflict escalation, personal injury or prosecution, and the aforementioned delegitimizing in the eye of supporters and third parties.

The risk/reward ratios of the media arena depend, in part, on the nature of the participants. As referred to earlier, small unstructured groups have an especially great need for media attention, as such publicity offers the only real entrance to the public agenda of important issues (McCombs, 1981). The risk, however, is also especially great, for such groups lack the organization necessary for sustained political action.

Media fame tends to be particularly brief; and all must be gambled on one or two media events, after which such groups are forced to return to their former obscurity.

Wealthier groups, on the other hand, can afford the luxury of competing in several arenas at once, and the truly powerful can acquire media coverage for such actions at no additional charge. Leaders can hire professionals, such as lawyers and lobbyists to act for their cause. . . .

Group needs are not only a function of internal structure, the aims of a group also affect the place of the media in overall strategy. A social movement, for example, can afford to bypass the mass media in its initial stages of mobilization by using more direct methods of recruitment. A movement that aspires to change the values of a whole society, however, can little afford to remain out of the public eye. . . .

. . . [O]nce again however, access to the media is most expensive for those that need it most. Leaders find themselves unable to control the messages that they try to transmit through the media filter (Gitlin, 1980; Bromley and Shupe, 1979; Molotch, 1979). They become frustrated over the media's need to simplify, contrast, and exaggerate in the unending search for sensation; group image is both the reward they seek and the most serious risk they must endure. In addition, such groups inevitably find themselves in serious role conflicts when choosing between being true to their ideals and manipulating the media with publicity "events" (see Simons and Mechling, 1981).

Media strategies are related, then, to basic group needs.

. . . The greatest need for ad hoc groups is to achieve public exposure quickly, and their greatest risk lies in premature extinction. They are likely therefore, to use a great deal of force in order to compete with more powerful institutions for media space. The media needs of more organized groups are likely to be better related to providing support for more general strategies and actions. Thus a strategic use of the media will be characterized by a temporal and conceptual integration into an overall network of actions taking place in the political, economic, and/or legal arenas. . . . The greatest media need for such groups is persuasion, and thus their acts are likely to be highly symbolic in content. Although such symbolism may take on either expressive or strategic aspects, it should be distinguishable from those modes of protest in its emphasis on image enhancement, and by implication its focus on changing public opinion and recruitment.

The discussion up to this point may have left the reader with the impression that as group structure and goals determine media dependency and risk, protest leaders are mere pawns in structurally determined outcomes. Such is not the case. The role of action group planning sessions is to find a repertoire of political actions that will minimize the risk involved in entering the media arena and still achieve the collective aims of competition. Whether on the basis of trial and error (Jenkins, 1981) or shared experience (Tilly, 1978) leaders attempt to allocate group resources to achieve the maximum benefit with the minimum of collective cost.

A general theory about media repertoires would have to deal with such factors as historical precedent, level of government repression, and media norms for covering internal political conflict. The case study presented below is more modestly designed to show how leaders from three different types of action groups struggled to overcome their own particular media risks. Although each of the groups faced rather similar types of organizational and strategic dilemmas, their degree of innovation in risk reduction reminds one of the importan[ce] of understanding contextual factors better when dealing with collective action as a whole, and with media strategy in particular. . . .

The emphasis will be placed . . . on the differences between the groups in their efforts to lower costs and increase collective benefits in light of their particular set of internal and external circumstances.

Method

In a first attempt to examine the dynamics of the approach presented, a comparative case study seems the most appropriate. . . .

The signing of the Camp David accords in September 1978 between Israel and Egypt set the stage for just such a case study. Within the context of the overall withdrawal from Sinai, the Israeli government committed itself to an unprecedented act: the evacuation of the town of Yamit and the surrounding settlements. Yamit had been established by an earlier (Labour) government that intended to turn the area into a major population center and possibly a new border with Egypt. The town and the farms flourished and for those who lived there became a veritable tropical paradise, complete with beaches, palm trees, no crime, and a cheap local labor force. It was no surprise therefore, that the protests against the government were both long and bitter.

Three groups were active in protesting against the government. The farmers from the agricultural settlements surrounding Yamit were the first to become organized and active. Although some of their initial protests were against the withdrawal itself, they reluctantly accepted the inevitable, and thus the vast majority of actions were designed to ensure that the government grant them the maximum compensation for evacuation and resettlement.

The second group, business, was a relatively small group that was organized over the issue of compensation at a relatively late stage. It was a loosely structured group, brought together by mutual frustration over what its members termed the government's gross mishandling of the entire evacuation.

The third group, and by far the largest, was the Movement to Stop the Retreat in Sinai. It was in fact a coalition of religious Jews who believed that Yamit was part of the historical, and therefore holy, land of Israel, and of secular Israelis who were opposed to giving up Sinai for security reasons. The movement was distinguished from the other two groups not only by its ideological focus but also by the fact that its members came almost exclusively from outside of the Yamit area. . . .

The research methodology consisted of direct observation and in-depth interviews with the major actors involved in the Yamit story. This included virtually all of the action leaders and the members of the press who reported on Yamit.[1] The observations and interviews were carried out mostly during the major period of resistance—between December 1981 and April 1982. Several follow-up interviews with the informants were carried out during the month of May.

Business

Contrary to popular belief, the townspeople of Yamit never formally organized against the Sinai withdrawal. . . .

It was only in November of 1980, after hearing about the farmers' successes, and over two years after the signing of the Camp David accords, that a group of some sixty independent businesspersons formed an organization to represent themselves to the government. The only ties among the members were created by their mutual frustration over the previous negotiations and their collective surprise at the amount of money being offered to the farmers. Their resources were virtually nonexistent. They had no official headquarters, no office staff, no lawyers or professional advisors, and no collective funding. Their elected leadership lacked both negotiating experience and media sophistication.

The negotiations continued for over a year with no results. Fearing that time was running out, the business organization staged a series of "media events," most notable of which was closing the gates of the town to all traffic. Although several government offices were burned, the businesspersons were able to reduce the risk of government repression by concentrating their energies on well-publicized threats of violence that were never actualized. Thus leaders quickly learned that by using such phrases as "the final confrontation" and "the end of the line," they were guaranteed front page coverage. They also arranged for photo sessions of children (who left school for a few hours) filling sand bags, and bulldozers digging "anti-tank" ditches, which in reality were only several meters long. One of the reporters commented on the changing scene at Yamit:

> For months they ran around begging to get more coverage of their demands. The government was basically ignoring them and using the time [before the evacuation] to reduce their claims. As soon as they

closed the city and burned those houses, they were surrounded by reporters and cameras from all over the world. Now the press was running after them.

As an initial tactic for raising an issue on the Israeli public agenda, such media events serve as a relatively cheap entrance fee into the arena. They put pressure on the government to respond before the situation gets worse, with little risk of either personal injuries or legal repercussions. After dominating the headlines for several days, however, the business group soon found itself out of its own political depth. The strategy was one of brinkmanship: a show of force to scare the government into dealing with them. Quickly, however, they found that the game of pseudo-violence was not that simple. The leader of the business organization interviewed immediately after the city closing described his own dilemmas at the time:

> It's all very complicated. Every time you make a move you have to take into account how each element will respond. How will this or that Minister react, the farmers, the Movement, and even your own followers. Sharon [Defence Minister] says he wants to come into the city. Do you open the gate for him or not? You have to make a decision in five minutes, and the whole world is out there waiting. If you say you're going to open, all the extremists will start yelling, and demand a new vote. Always pressure and more pressure. . . .

The businesspersons had no trouble obtaining media *attention,* but they never attained media *control.* Perhaps the best indication of this factor was the leadership's agreement that they needed a media advisor in order to exploit better the publicity that they had obtained. A statement made by one of their "official spokesmen" is typical. When asked about how he felt a media specialist might help, he replied,

> He'd tell us to burn tires today, but not in two days, because the French Foreign Minister will be here . . . I don't know what. I know how to fly, another guy knows how to make cabinets, and a third compressors; we don't know how to write documents, to talk to the media. We're not politicians, and with the press you need professionals—just like every government office has. . . .

Media sophistication is an increasingly important resource for any collective action group to obtain, but that only a very few can afford to buy.

The business group began to pay the bill for their publicity very quickly. A massive backlash of citizen groups, politicians, and newspaper editorials united against the "extortionists" and severely weakened the group's bargaining position. After going to the edge of a physical confrontation with the army, they could either pass over their planned threshold of violence or back down. As many of the reporters pointed out to them, threats alone would no longer be considered news. After a token concession by the government, they chose the latter course. They closed the town a second time and carried out a few isolated incidents, but never regained the momentum they had lost.

. . . In resource mobilization terms, they were forced to demobilize, because of their inability to successfully compete for the resource of media attention and a lack of affordable alternative arenas.

Lacking the skills, or the alternative means for a sustained and systematic struggle, and unwilling to take the risks associated with serious political violence, brinkmanship provided their only real channel of influence. The strategy was, of necessity, [a] short-term one, and the business's illusion of power quickly faded.

The Farmers

. . . There were two kinds of agricultural settlements in the Yamit area: moshavim and kibbutzim. While the former is more individual-oriented than the latter (from the perspective of private property) both exist as closed communities where collective resources and collective decision making are a major part of both the ideology and the actual living experience. In addition, the connection between the various settlements was structured and regular.

It was no coincidence, therefore, that after the Camp David accords were signed the farmers were the first group to mobilize and act. A separate action committee was formed with a full-time chairman, whose sole responsibility was dealing with the issue of compensation. His office was already equipped with all of the necessary tools of administration and communication as well as a full-time secretary. In addition, the elected leadership had a good deal of negotiating experience with the government and the Jewish Agency in the establishment and maintenance of the settlements.

The farmers began their struggle immediately after the signing at Camp David. Some of the first acts took place in the legal and economic arena; they hired one of the most prestigious law firms in the country and withheld their produce shipment to the northern part of the country. Besides these acts they organized a great deal of public protest. From the time of Camp David until the final withdrawal they carried out four conventional demonstrations, eight acts of public disorder, as well as seven publicly declared threats of disorder and violence.

The farmers were much more selective in both the intensity and timing of their protest events than was the business group. For the most part their protests were relatively minor acts of disobedience designed to bring pressure on the government at certain critical junctures in the negotiations.

. . . [T]he farmers also went to the brink of serious violence on one occasion. The government had promised the Egyptians that they would turn over one of the local vegetable fields much earlier than the rest of Yamit, in May of 1979. The farmers held a confrontation with the army against the return of property; and while much of it was expertly staged for the media, there was a real danger of casualties. Unlike the business group, however, the farmers were able to return from the brink of violence and begin again, using alternative means of action.

Public protest, then, was one of many different weapons used by the farmers against the government. Their overall strategy combined techniques of persuasion, negotiation, and coercion (Turner, 1970), each being used at what was seen as the most opportune time. . . .

A strategic media strategy is possible only when group leaders have the organizational structure and resources necessary for planning long-term tactics. The farmers' flexible repertoire allowed for a lower level of constant pressure, combined with conventional political maneuvering. They used the media, but in a manner that allowed them a much greater degree of both quantitative and qualitative control, which therefore was a great deal less risky. The ability to pick and choose one's conflict arenas is a luxury reserved for the organizationally rich.

The Movement to Stop the Retreat in Sinai

The movement differed from the other two groups in two significant ways. First, its members came almost exclusively from outside the Yamit area. Secondly, both its goals and its *Weltanschauung* were ideological. Both of these factors had a clear effect on media strategy. The movement, therefore, offers an important contrast to the rather straightforward practices of the other two groups.

The level of organization in the movement can be described as being somewhat lower than that of the farmers' group but much higher than that of business. The main body of supporters came from Gush Emunim, a movement with many settlements on the West Bank and a rich experience of collective action. This core of members was extremely active and was able to mobilize a considerable amount of resources very quickly. . . .

The total movement, however, had members who came from a wide variety of both geographic and ideological sources: religious leaders, members of youth movements, students at religious schools, secularists living in Yamit, and even a few individuals who were previously unaffiliated. Throughout the struggle over the withdrawal these groups formed both formal and informal factions that pulled in every conceivable direction. Gamson (1975) was one of the first to systematically demonstrate how such factionalism severely weakens a movement. . . .

One is again reminded of the distinction between resources acquisition and control. The farmers had less manpower than the movement, but their better communal ties allowed them to mobilize their members more easily.

Nevertheless, the movement was also able to exploit its collective resources and compete in several different arenas. In the political arena, the movement established a political party, Tchiyah, which was able to obtain three seats in the Knesset. The members also hoped to block the withdrawal physically by bringing so many supporters to live in illegal settlements that the authorities could not possibly remove them all. As the withdrawal grew closer, however, the movement turned to more conventional and media dependent protests: sit-ins, hunger strikes, blocking roads, and occupying buildings.

The movement's approach to public opinion was quite different from those of the other two groups. The business group had hoped to use the public's fear of disaster as a weapon to pressure the government into concessions. The farmers often had the luxury of opting out of the battle over the hearts and minds of the Israeli public and negotiating with the government in private. The movement saw the "education" of the Israeli public as one of its primary goals. The name of the group was very consciously chosen (Retreat *in* Sinai, rather than *from* Sinai) in an attempt to show that the evacuation was only one element against a more general retreat in Israeli society. Yamit was therefore seen as a preliminary battle in a much larger campaign.

Movement leaders expressed a great deal of ambivalence about using the mass media. All of them realized the group's need for publicity, especially for persuasion and recruitment, but not all were willing to sacrifice ideological integrity. This role conflict (Lipsky, 1970) expressed itself in almost every area of media strategy. The leaders wanted both to feel and to appear genuine, while the media demanded publicity stunts; leaders were most interested in "teaching" people about their ideals, while the media was only concerned with events; the movement wanted to project the reasonableness of its cause, the news focused on the bizarre and the dangerous. In internal discussions this conflict was usually expressed in the distinction between "substantive" and "media" considerations. . . .

Perhaps, however, the conflict over using the media would not have been so severe had the issue of Yamit arisen in a different manner. Gush Emunim, for example, can in general be more selective in its use of the media with regard to the struggle over the West Bank. What distinguished the battle over Sinai from other political issues was the fact that the Camp David accords presented the believers in the "complete land of Israel" with a fait accompli. Instead of their usual proactive strategy, Gush Emunim found themselves in a reactive position with a scheduled date of defeat. Many of their conflicts over media use became much more pressing than usual as they attempted to maximize their effectiveness with regard to the immediate conflict without sacrificing their image for more long-term goals.

This conflict also put the movement at a distinct disadvantage to the other two groups in the early stages of the struggle. Establishing settlements, however ideologically satisfying, simply did not make good news copy. One of the leaders describes their dilemma in the competition over the resource of publicity.

> It's always a problem with any popular movement, and certainly a protest movement. On the one hand you want publicity, on the other, you don't want to create scandals—it's just not our way, and in any case it's not effective from a public relations point of view.... We, had a real problem when we wanted to transfer the public's attention from the compensation issue to the withdrawal. It was almost impossible.... They [the businesspersons] were threatening and getting coverage, and we were creating settlements and being ignored.

As the date of the withdrawal grew closer, and the need for new recruits more desperate, the movement developed a tactic that allowed it to achieve a maximum of publicity with a minimum amount of risk to their image: victimization. Provocative sit-ins and land grabs were carried out in a clear attempt to bring on a reaction by the army who was forced to be filmed dragging away protesters offering only "passive" resistance. Hunger strikes and threats of suicide (symbolically referred to as being done in the name of God) were never officially sanctioned by the movement executive, but spokespersons always stressed the sincerity of the victims. All threats of violence were internally directed, and, in direct contradiction to the other two groups, the leadership continually attempted to downplay the aggressive image presented in the media.

Throughout the struggle the movement continued to use a symbolic media strategy. In the final days, for example, when reporters had come from around the world to be a ready and willing audience, members were shown planting new fields and building hothouses in a collective denial that the evacuation would ever take place....

... The movement had failed in its attempts to bring tens of thousands of supporters to the area. In desperation, many of the followers in Yamit called for taking extreme measures such as the use of weapons against the soldiers. Although it had become clear to almost all of the members that the withdrawal itself could not be prevented, many considered any militant confrontation with the authorities as beneficial, as it would create a "national trauma" that would not be quickly forgotten. This backup position would serve well in future debates about territorial compromises in the West Bank. In the end however, despite a highly inflamed atmosphere and a great store of handmade weapons, the violence was sufficiently contained to prevent any major injuries. A member of the executive describes the final discussions:

> We decided that Yamit was lost and there was no point continuing the violence. Don't get me wrong, it wasn't out of the beauty of our souls. It's just that we saw that there would be other battles, and it wasn't worth the price in terms of our image without the benefit of saving Yamit.

Movement leaders, then, while forced to turn to the media arena, used a strategy which minimized their greatest risk (a damaged public image) so that they could continue to compete in the future. All of their various tactics were tied by symbolic and persuasive content through which the movement hoped to sway the public to its cause.

Conclusion

The theoretical model presented in this study offers a useful starting point for asking questions about the role of the mass media in political collective action. Alternative conceptualizations may consider the press merely as an additional resource that groups try to mobilize in their attempts to challenge the authorities. Considering the mass media as one of several conflict arenas has, it seems, several advantages. First, groups must carry out some type of collective action—*before* they can obtain access to the mass media—a fact that runs counter to the notion of mobilizing the resource of the media to be used for action. As Lipsky (1970) points out, groups must pass a certain threshold of organizational sophistication before they are ever "heard of" at all. Second, the conceptual framework emphasizes the importance of understanding the ways in which collective actions in different arenas demand different types of resources as well as very different types of behavior. Picketing is no more appropriate to a court room than reading a legal brief is to televised demonstrations.

Most important however, the framework presented offers a way of thinking about the relationship between direct action, violence, and the mass media. Direct action is seen as one of several alternative channels of access to influence the government, and one that is especially important to groups who cannot afford to reach officials through more conventional means. In this respect, it is more useful to think about the ways in which groups plan events in order to attract the media than about a press that is merely "reporting" ongoing events. Action group leaders plan out a media strategy that allows them to meet group needs at a minimum collective cost. It is perhaps unfortunate that the costs of such a transmission often involve some sort of disorder, and often violence.

Nevertheless, these are the rules of the news game, and those who refuse to play it will be replaced by more eager participants.

A truly powerful organization, on the other hand, can set its own rules. A labor union leader, for example, can obtain coverage for a mere speech, and an extremely large protest movement can obtain coverage for a peaceful demonstration. At the other end of the power continuum are the acts of a few terrorists who must threaten to, or actually do, kill people in order to obtain the attention of the press. What the model suggests is that in the same way that the media serves as an alternative channel of political influence, so disorder and violence often serve as alternative means of achieving access to the mass media. The rules of competition over the resource of publicity are far from equal. . . .

Note

1. Leaders were selected according to the degree to which they held central positions and the extent of their contact with the press. Twenty recorded interviews were carried out (in Hebrew), each about an hour and a half in length. Those who would be alarmed at such a small sample must keep in mind the size of the population considered. The number of protest leaders and Israeli reporters responsible for bringing the news to the rest of the country never exceeded thirty individuals. None of the individuals approached refused to be interviewed.

References

Barnes, S. and M. Kaase, (1979) *Political Action*. Beverly Hills, CA: Sage.

Bromley, D. G. and A. D. Shupe (1979) *"Moonies" in America: Cult, Church, and Crusade*. Beverly Hills, CA: Sage.

Eckstein, H. (1980) "Theoretical approaches to explaining collective political violence," in T. R. Gurr (ed.) *Handbook of Political Conflict*. New York: Free Press.

Gamson, W. A. (1975) *The Strategy of Social Protest*. Homewood, IL: Dorsey.

Gitlin, T. (1980) *The Whole World is Watching: Mass Media in the Making and Unmaking of the New Left*. Berkeley: Univ. of California Press.

Jenkins, J. C. (1981) "Sociopolitical movements," in S. Long (ed.) *The Handbook of Political Behavior*. New York: Plenum Press.

Lipsky, M. (1970) *Protest in City Politics*. Rand McNally.

McCombs, M. E. (1981) "The agenda setting approach," in D. D. Nimmo and K. R. Sanders (eds.) *Handbook of Political Communication*. Beverly Hills, CA: Sage.

Molotch, H. (1979) "Media and movements," in M. N. Zald and D. McCarthy (eds.) *The Dynamics of Social Movements*. Cambridge, MA: Plenum Press.

Oberschall, A. (1973) *Social Conflict and Social Movements*. Englewood Cliffs, NJ: Prentice-Hall.

Simons, H. W. and E. W. Mechling (1981) "The rhetoric of political movements," in D. D. Nimmo and K. R. Sanders (eds.) *Handbook of Political Communication*. Beverly Hills, CA: Sage.

Snyder, D. (1979) "Collective violence: a research agenda and some strategic considerations," *J. of Conflict Resolution* 22: 499-538.

Tilly, C. (1978) *From Mobilization to Revolution*. Reading, MA: Addison-Wesley.

Turner, R. H. (1970) "Determinants of social movement strategies," in T. Shibutani (ed.) *Human Nature and Collective Behavior*. Englewood Cliffs, NJ: Prentice-Hall.

Tuchman, G. (1978) *Making News*. New York: Free Press.

4.7 ■■■■■■

Making Protest Movements Newsworthy

Todd Gitlin

Editor's Note. Todd Gitlin studied how the desire for media attention and the resulting coverage affect the evolution of protest movements and the course of political change. In the essay presented here, he analyzes the media's role in the development and demise of Students for a Democratic Society (SDS). SDS was a major New Left protest movement on U.S. campuses in the 1960s. Gitlin bases his findings on stories from the *New York Times* and CBS news—sources deemed politically influential because they were widely used and respected by political elites. These sources also were monitored carefully by people within the protest movements.

Gitlin concludes that the New Left was forced to define itself in ways that made it newsworthy for the establishment media. In the process, it sowed the seeds of its own destruction. The major lesson for protest movements, Gitlin believes, is that they must learn to protect their identity in the face of media blandishments.

Gitlin has worked as a writer and as a teacher of politics and poetry. He has been particularly interested in studying counterculture movements. His writings have appeared in *The Nation, The New Republic, The Christian Century,* and *Commonweal.* The selection is from *The Whole World Is Watching* (Berkeley: University of California Press, 1980).

. . . In the late twentieth century, political movements feel called upon to rely on large-scale communications in order to *matter,* to say who they are and what they intend to publics they want to sway; but in the process they become "newsworthy" only by submitting to the implicit rules of newsmaking, by conforming to journalistic notions (themselves embedded in history) of what a "story" is, what an "event" is, what a "protest" is. The processed image then tends to *become* "the movement" for wider publics and institutions who have few alternative sources of

From Todd Gitlin, *The Whole World Is Watching: Mass Media in the Making and Unmaking of the New Left,* pp. 3-4, 21-31, 128-129, and 283-287. Copyright © 1980 by The Regents of the University of California.

information, or none at all, about it; that image has its impact on public policy, and when the movement is being opposed, what is being opposed is in large part a set of mass-mediated images. Mass media define the public significance of movement events or, by blanking them out, actively deprive them of larger significance. Media images also become implicated in a movement's self-image; media certify leaders and officially noteworthy "personalities"; indeed, they are able to convert leadership into *celebrity*, something quite different. The forms of coverage accrete into systematic framing, and this framing, much amplified, helps determine the movement's fate.

For what defines a movement as "good copy" is often flamboyance, often the presence of a media-certified celebrity-leader, and usually a certain fit with whatever frame the newsmakers have construed to be "the story" at a given time; but these qualities of the image are not what movements intend to be their projects, their identities, their goals. . . .

The year 1965 was a pivotal one in the history of SDS [Students for a Democratic Society], and in the student movement as a whole: pivotal both in reality and in the realm of publicity. SDS organized the first major national demonstration against the Vietnam war, and then failed to lead the antiwar movement that was burgeoning. Politically, SDS moved away from its social-democratic progenitors, eliminating its anti-Communist exclusion principle for members. Organizationally, SDS was tense with generational conflict as a new ideological and geographical wave began to displace the founding generation.

Also during 1965, SDS was discovered by the national media. As SDS became a famous and infamous national name and the germ of a national political force, publicity came to be a dimension of its identity, a component of its reality. By the end of that year, an SDS program that barely existed was front-page news all over the country, and SDS was being denounced by members of the Senate and by the attorney general of the United States. In 1965, SDS changed irreversibly from an organization that recruited its elites and communicated its ideas face to face, to an organization that lived in the glare of publicity and recruited both elites and members on the basis of reputations refracted in large part through the channels of mass media. The nature of that publicity changed too, over time; but the spotlight remained, an invariant fact that for the rest of the movement's life had to be taken into account. For the next several years, the student movement faded in and faded out—even the cinematic language seems appropriate—under the globular eye of the mass media. Its actions were shaped in part by the codes of mass media operations. It conducted its activities in a social world that recognized it, liked it, and disliked it through media images, media versions of its events and rhetoric. To some extent the movement even recognized *itself* through mass-mediated images. In 1965, then, the spotlight was turned on for good. As different filters were clamped onto the floodlamp, it changed colors; the movement tried, at times, to place its own filters onto the lamp or to set up its own; but the spotlight was there to stay. . . .

. . . As movement and media discovered and acted on each other, they worked out the terms with which they would recognize and work on the other; they developed a grammar of interaction. This grammar then shaped the way the movement-media history developed over the rest of the decade, opening certain possibilities and excluding others. As the movement developed, so did the media approaches to it, so that the media's structures of cognition and interpretation never stayed entirely fixed. . . .

It bears emphasis that the media treatment of the movement and the movement approach to the media were themselves *situated*, sewn into an historical context. Movements and media are not creatures of each other; they work on each other, but, as Marx said in another connection, not in conditions of their own making. . . .

The Struggle Over Images

What was the course of the media-movement relation in 1965?

For their different reasons, the media and the movement needed each other. The media needed stories, preferring the dramatic; the movement needed publicity for recruitment, for support, and for political effect. Each could be useful to the other; each had effects, intended and unintended, on the other. As Herbert Gans has written more generally: "In any modern society in which a number of classes, ethnic and religious groups, age groups and political interests struggle among each other for control over the society's resources, there is also a struggle for the power to determine or influence the society's values, myths, symbols, and information." [1] The struggle of movement groups with reporters and media institutions was one instance of a larger and constant struggle; so was, and is, the continual jockeying in which elements of the State intervene to shape or constrict media content. The interaction not only existed in history, it *had* a history. At times, movement and media were symbiotic, at times antagonistic. We can even detect distinct, though overlapping, phases. At first the mass media disregarded the movement; then media discovered the movement; the movement cooperated with media; media presented the movement in patterned ways; the quality and slant of these patterns changed; different parts of the movement responded in different ways; elements of the State intervened to shape this coverage. These were "moments" in a single, connected process, in which movement participants, media institutions and the State—themselves internally conflicted—struggled over the terms of coverage: struggled to define the movement and the nature of political reality around it. . . .

In the struggle over the right and the power to define the public images of the movement in 1965, one can discern five essential phases:

I. Starting in 1960, and up through the late winter of 1965, SDS was not covered by major news media. For its part, SDS did not actively, forcefully, or consistently seek major media coverage. That was not the way a political organization got started. As SDS's first president and national secretary Alan Haber says about the period 1960-62: "The coverage wasn't much and I didn't feel much about it. The kind of stuff we did wasn't organizing demonstrations where we'd look and see what they said about it. . . . SDS was not media-oriented." [2] And for their part, the media were simply not interested in an organization so small and tame. SDS had 19 chapters on paper (of which 6 were real) and 610 members in October 1963; 29 chapters and almost 1,000 members in June 1964; but 80 chapters and more than 2,000 members in June 1965; and 124 chapters and 4,300 members by the end of 1965.[3] . . .

To get its ideas across to a fragmented, scattered left and to left-liberal groups, "what SDS wanted was to get written up in left oriented small circulation things," not the mass press. If anything, the prevailing attitudes toward mass media were disdain and suspicion. Celebrities were distrusted. "We weren't even in that world," as Flacks says. "Why would any of the media be interested in SDS?" [4]

For their part, the media paid little attention. SDS did not perform photogenically; it did not mobilize large numbers of people; it did not undertake flamboyant actions. It was not, in a word, newsworthy.

II. In the late winter of 1965, after the independent upswelling of the Berkeley Free Speech Movement, the media discovered SDS. A few reporters took the initiative and SDS, for its part, cooperated actively. That winter, a sympathetic reporter, Fred Powledge of the *New York Times*, on his own initiative, wrote at length and respectfully about SDS's politics and approach, heralding the emergence of a "new student left." Powledge's article, published in the *Times* of March 15, 1965, certified student radicalism as a live national issue. The SDS leadership of 1964-65 showed a growing interest in large-scale student organization and in publicity, but was far from organizing actions or propounding slogans for the sake of "how they would look." Under National Secretary C. Clark Kissinger, the National Office began to send out press releases more regularly, and, especially after the steady bombing of North Vietnam started in February, members of the SDS elite began for the first time to entertain thoughts of a *mass* student movement.[5] Still, SDS did not envisage a central role for the press in the process. Indeed its own communications were scanty and improvised. The National Office published an irregular mimeographed monthly *Bulletin*, and sent newsy biweekly "Work List" mailings to key local and national activists; there were phone and mail contacts with chapters and individual members, and occasional visits by "campus travelers" and speechmakers; but SDS did not publish its own weekly newspaper until January 1966.

III. With the SDS March on Washington on April 17, 1965, student antiwar protest—and SDS activity in particular—became big news. Now reporters began to seek out SDS leaders and to cover protest events. That spring, major articles on the New Left appeared in newsmagazines (*Newsweek, Time, U.S. News & World Report*), large circulation weeklies (the *Saturday Evening Post*, the *New York Times Magazine*), and the liberal weeklies (the *Nation*, the *New Republic*, the *Reporter*); and television news produced its own survey pieces. The movement was amplified.

But which movement? The observer changed the position of the observed. The amplification was already selective: it emphasized certain themes and scanted others. Deprecatory themes began to emerge, then to recur and reverberate. The earliest framing[6] devices were these:

- *trivialization* (making light of movement language, dress, age, style, and goals);
- *polarization* (emphasizing *counter*demonstrations, and balancing the antiwar movement against ultra-Right and neo-Nazi groups as equivalent "extremists");
- *emphasis on internal dissension;*
- *marginalization* (showing demonstrators to be deviant or unrepresentative);
- *disparagement by numbers* (under-counting);
- *disparagement of the movement's effectiveness.*

In the fall, as parts of the antiwar movement turned to more militant tactics, new themes and devices were added to the first group:

- *reliance on statements by government officials and other authorities;*
- *emphasis on the presence of Communists;*
- *emphasis on the carrying of "Viet Cong" flags;*
- *emphasis on violence in demonstrations;*
- *delegitimizing use of quotation marks* around terms like "peace march";
- *considerable attention to right-wing opposition to the movement*, especially from the administration and other politicians.

Some of this framing can be attributed to traditional assumptions in news treatment: news concerns the *event*, not the underlying condition; the *person*, not the group; *conflict*, not consensus; the fact that "*advances the story*," not the one that explains it. Some of this treatment descends from norms for the coverage of deviance in general: the archetypical news story is a crime story, and an opposition movement is ordinarily, routinely, and unthinkingly treated as a sort of crime. Some of the treatment follows from organizational and technical features of news coverage—which in turn are not ideologically neutral. Editors assign reporters to beats where news is routinely framed by officials; the stories then absorb the officials' definitions of the situation.[7] And editors and reporters also adopt and reproduce the dominant ideological assumptions prevailing in the wider society. All these practices are anchored in organizational policy, in recruitment and promotion: that is to say, in the internal structure of institutional power and decision. And when all these sources are taken into account, some of the framing will still be explained unequivocally; some must be understood as the product of specifically political transactions, cases of editorial judgment and the interventions of political elites. The proportion of a given frame that emanates from each of these sources varies from story to story; that is why stories have to be scrutinized one by one, as concretely as possible, before we can begin to compose general theories.

. . . The overall effect of media coverage was blurred and contradictory; there was not a single voice. But increasingly the impression was conveyed that extremism was rampant and that the New Left was dangerous to the public good.

In short, the media were far from mirrors passively reflecting facts found in the real world. The facts reported were out there in the real world, true: out there *among others*. The media reflection was more the active, patterned remaking performed by mirrors in a fun house.

IV. As media actively engaged the movement, an adversary symbiosis developed. Within the movement, arguments emerged about how best to cope with the new situation. Some groupings within the movement stayed on the defensive; others turned to the offense. In neither case was it possible to ignore the media spotlight, or to turn it at will to the movement's own uses.

Some movement organizers responded casually, at first, to the media's attentions. Their commitment to face-to-face organization remained primary; in their view, the press would play a secondary role in transmitting news and images to uncommitted publics. They were working within a pre-spotlight organizational form; they were eager to maintain the movement's own distinct communication channels. But in the fall of 1965, media attention and right-wing attacks caught them by surprise. The strategy they improvised called for a sort of judo operation: using the weight of the adversary to bring him down. They would use the unsought media attention to amplify the antiwar message. They began to speak into the symbolic microphone.

Others, committed to an antiwar movement before all else, and operating mostly outside SDS, began to organize symbolic events deliberately to attract the media spotlight. Very small groups of draft-card burners could leap to national prominence. Three pacifists, trying to awaken a national conscience, immolated themselves and died. Some within SDS proposed attention-getting actions—later called "media events"—that would, they hoped, place the issue of the war at the focus of national politics. Galvanizing opposition, even repression, from the administration or from the political Right could be a means to that end.

V. As the spotlight kept on burning, media treatment entered into the movement's internal life. The media helped recruit into SDS new members and backers who expected to find there what they saw on television or read in the papers. The flood of new members tended to be different from the first SDS generation—less intellectual, more activist, more deeply estranged from the dominant institutions. Politically, many of them cared more about antiwar activity than about the broad-gauged, long-haul, multi-issued politics of the earlier SDS. They were only partially assimilated into the existing organization; they viewed the SDS leaders, the remnants of the founding generation, with suspicion. The newcomers overwhelmed SDS's fragile institutions, which had been created for a tiny organization, a network of so-called Old Guard elite clusters living in intense political and personal community. The fragile person-to-person net of organizational continuity was torn.

This new generation coursed into SDS in the wake of the April 1965 antiwar march, and by June 1966 they had moved into the key positions of leadership. They were known as the Prairie Power people, underscoring—and at times exaggerating—their non-Northeastern, non-elite origins. True, this generation *did* differ from the founders in many ways; the distinction cannot be laid purely and simply at the door of the media and their selectivities. For one thing, the Old Guard elite had already graduated from college, many from elite colleges at that; many had moved into Northern ghettoes as community organizers. Most of the new leaders, by contrast, were still students at state universities. Coming from more conservative regions, Texas and the Great Plains primarily, many of the new generation had become radical quickly, because even mild rebellion against right-wing authority—hair grown slightly long, language grown obscene, or the like—provoked repression. If one were to be punished for small things, it was only a small step to declaring oneself an outlaw in earnest, a communist, a revolutionary: as soon be hanged for a sheep as a goat. So, as cultural rebels, they tended to skip the stage of consciousness that marked the Old Guard generation and informed its politics: a *radical disappointment* with existing liberal institutions, liberal promises, and liberal hopes. In style, too, they declared their deep disaffection from the prevailing culture: many were shaggy in appearance, they smoked dope, they had read less, they went for broke. Even Northeastern members of the Prairie Power leadership shared the new style.

The media not only helped produce and characterize this sharp break within SDS, but they proceeded to play it up; in so doing, they magnified its importance—both to the outside world and inside the organization. When it happened that, as the former SDS National

Secretary wrote in December 1965, "chapters, regional offices, and members find out what the organization is doing by reading the newspapers," [8] mass-mediated images were fixing (in the photographic sense) the terms for internal debate; they were helping define the organization's situation for it. Again, none of this happened in a vacuum. The drastic escalation in the war was at the same time pushing many people, both in and out of SDS, toward greater militancy, greater estrangement from dominant American values. The default of liberal forces isolated the whole generation of radical youth, pushing them toward the left. Larger cultural forces were nourishing the possibility of a deviant counter-culture. But the media blitz, by amplifying and speeding all these processes, prevented SDS from assimilating them. The organization tried—and failed. Thus the internal frailties that were later to undo the organization were already built in at the moment of its greatest growth and vigor. In its beginning as a mass organization was its end. . . .

. . . Again, *I am not arguing that the mass media system in general, or its particular ways of covering the New Left, were responsible for the destruction of the movement.* The movement arose in a specific social situation: it emerged from a limited professional-managerial class base, it was socially and politically isolated, and at the same time it was committed to the vast and complex political ambition of organizing the radical transformation of the entire society. Not only that, it hurled itself against an enormously destructive war. Its class narrowness, its deformities and misapprehensions, and the power of the State all weighed on its fate and threw it back on its self-contradictions. . . . The important point is that the movement paid a high price for the publicity it claimed and needed. It entered into an unequal contest with the media: although it affected coverage, the movement was always the petitioner; the movement was more vulnerable, the media more determining. But the movement was never powerless, never without choices, never without responsibility within the limits of the media-movement system as a whole.

To paraphrase Marx: media treatments shape movements, but not in conditions of their own making. . . . [T]he media impact on the New Left depended heavily on the political situation as a whole, on the institutional world that the media inhabit, and on the social and ideological nature of the movement. For convenience's sake at the outset, I can stake out my argument . . . by saying that the media pressed on SDS and antiwar activity in these ways:[9] (1) generating a membership surge and, consequently, generational and geographical strain among both rank-and-file members and leaders . . . ; (2) certifying leaders and converting leadership to celebrity . . . ; (3) inflating rhetoric and militancy . . . ; (4) elevating a moderate alternative . . . ; (5) contracting the movement's experience of time, and helping encapsulate it . . . ; and finally, (6) amplifying and containing the movement's messages at the same time. . . .

Implications for Movements

... *The more closely the concerns and values of social movements
coincide with the concerns and values of elites in politics and in media, the
more likely they are to become incorporated in the prevailing news frames.*
Since the sixties, for example, consumer organizations have been elevated
to the status of regular news makers; they and their concerns are reported
with sympathy, sufficiently so as to inspire corporate complaints and
counter-propaganda in the form of paid, issue-centered advertising.
Ralph Nader and other public-interest lawyers have become respected
celebrities, often interviewed for response statements, photographed in
suits and ties and sitting squarely behind desks or in front of bookshelves,
embodying solid expertise and mainstream reliability. They have learned
to make the journalistic code work for them, while journalists have
extended them the privilege of legitimacy. At times, environmentalist
groups like the Sierra Club have been adept at using the media to
publicize particular issues and to campaign for particular reforms. In the
seventies, the prestigious media policymakers have legitimized some
political values of their ecologically-minded peers in class and culture.
These concerns have been institutionalized in government agencies like
the Environmental Protection Agency and the Council on Environmental
Quality, which now serve as legitimate news sources. The more radical
wings of the environmental movement—those which challenge the raison
d'être of centralized mass production and try to join the concerns of labor
and environmentalists—are scanted.

Indeed, the very concept of a *movement* has been certified; an *activist*,
left or right, is now a stereotyped persona accorded a right to parade
quickly through the pageant of the news. Consumer activists, environmentalists, gay activists, feminists, pro- and anti-busing people, as well as
anti-abortionists, Jarvis-Gann supporters, Laetrile legalizers, angry log-
gers, farmers, and truck drivers—many movements which can be presented as working for (or against) concrete assimilable reforms have
become regular, recognizable, even stock characters in newspapers and
news broadcasts. The media spread the news that alternative opinions
exist on virtually every issue. They create an impression that the society is
full of political vitality, that opinions and interests contend freely—that
the society, in a word, is pluralist. But in the process, they do extend the
reach of movements that agree, at least for working purposes, to accept
the same premise—and are willing to pay a price.

It is hard to know in advance what that price will be, hard to
generalize about the susceptibilities of movements to the publicity process
and its internal consequences. Of internal factors, two seem bound to
increase a movement's *dependency* on the mass media: (1) the narrowness
of its social base; and (2) its commitment to specific society-wide political

goals. And then two other factors, when added onto the first two, seem to produce the most destructive *consequences* of media dependency: (3) the movement's turn toward revolutionary desire and rhetoric in a nonrevolutionary situation; and (4) its unacknowledged political uncertainties, especially about the legitimacy of its own leaders. Thus, in the case of the New Left: (1) It was contained within a relatively narrow social base: students and the young intelligentsia. (2) It had a specific political purpose, to end the war. These two factors in combination were decisive in forcing the movement into dependency on the media, although they did not by themselves generate destructive consequences. Proceeding into national reform politics from its narrow social base, the movement could hope to end the war only by mobilizing wider constituencies. Attempting to affect government policy in a hurry, it was forced to rely upon the mass media to broadcast the simple fact that opposition existed. And then the other factors came into play. (3) The New Left, in its revolutionary moment, allowed itself to believe it was in a revolutionary situation. . . . And at the same time, (4) the New Left's ambivalence about criteria for leadership, especially when coupled with its inability to engender a coherent political ideology and organization, left all parties damaged: leaders were vulnerable to the temptations of celebrity, while the rank and file were stranded without means of keeping their leaders accountable. On the face of it, the black movement of the sixties and seventies shared these vulnerabilities, and for the same reasons. . . .

. . . If a movement is committed to working for specific political goals but refuses to devote itself to revolutionary politics, it may avoid the most severe dependency on the media; it is more likely, too, to be able to control the content of its publicity. The United Farm Workers, for example, are entrenched within a narrow social base and are committed to specific goals; but they have an undisputed leader whose media presence is (I am told) heralded with pride rather than envy; and by avoiding revolutionism, they have been able to occupy the media spotlight without subjecting themselves to its most destructive glare.

Reformist movements, then, are less vulnerable to structural deformation in the publicity process than are revolutionary ones. Reformists can achieve media standing by getting *their* experts legitimated; the standard frames are equipped to show them—and their class—to relatively good advantage. Revolutionaries, by contrast, can achieve media standing only as deviants; they become "good copy" as they become susceptible to derogatory framing devices; and past a certain point, precisely what made them "good copy" may make them dangerous to the State and subject, directly or indirectly, to blackout. But to say that reformist movements are less vulnerable to disparagement is not to say that they are immune. They too, must confront the spotlight's tendency to convert leadership to celebrity, to highlight extravagant rhetoric (if not action), and to help induce transitional crises of generations. Likewise, the standard journalistic frames persist in marginalizing the most radical aspects of movements and setting them against the more moderate. They cover single-issue movements, but frame them in opposition to others: feminists against blacks, blacks against chicanos. *The routine frames . . . endure for reformist as well as deeply oppositional movements.* Even reformist movements must work industriously to broadcast their messages without having them discounted, trivialized, fragmented, rendered incoherent. Awareness of the media's routines and frames is no guarantee that a movement will be able to achieve publicity for its analysis and program on its own terms; the frames remain powerful, processing opposition into hegemonic order. But surely ignorance of the media's codes condemns a movement to marginality. . . .

Notes

1. Herbert Gans, "The Politics of Culture in America: A Sociological Analysis," in Denis McQuail, ed., *Sociology of Mass Communications* (Harmondsworth, England: Penguin Books, 1972), p. 373.
2. Interview, Alan Haber, December 9, 1976.
3. These figures are taken from Kirkpatrick Sale's extraordinarily accurate *SDS* (New York: Random House, 1973), pp. 119, 122, 193, 246.
4. Interview, Richard Flacks, January 9, 1977.
5. Ibid.; and telephone interview, Mike Davis, February 15, 1977.
6. Gitlin (*The Whole World Is Watching*, p. 7) defines media frames as "persistent patterns of cognition, interpretation, and presentation, of selection, emphasis, and exclusion, by which symbol-handlers routinely organize discourse, whether verbal or visual."
7. See Leon V. Sigal, *Reporters and Officials: The Organization and Politics of Newsmaking* (Lexington, Mass.: D. C. Heath, 1973), p. 47 and chap. 6; Harvey Molotch and Marilyn Lester, "Accidental News: The Great Oil Spill as Local Occurrence and National Event," *American Journal of Sociology* 81 (September 1965): 235-260; and Herbert Gans, *Deciding What's News* (New York: Pantheon, 1979), chap. 4.
8. C. Clark Kissinger, quoted in Sale, *SDS*, p. 255.
9. A certain cautionary note is both banal and obligatory. It is only for analytic convenience, which requires sequence, that I construct categories and discuss them one at a time. Analytic categories are mutually exclusive where history is continuing, multi-stranded, borderless, and messy. . . .

5. GUIDING PUBLIC POLICIES

T he media affect public policies in a variety of ways. Publicity may narrow the policy choices available to public officials. It may engender governmental action when no action might have taken place otherwise. Alternatively, by mobilizing hostile public or interest group opinions, the media may force a halt to ongoing or projected policies. This section contains examples of policy impact studies involving all of these contingencies in both domestic and foreign policy domains.

The opening selection shows how media coverage may affect the decisions of public officials in the judicial branch. David Pritchard demonstrates that the decision to allow a serious criminal case to be settled through plea-bargaining, without a full trial, is strongly related to the amount of pretrial publicity given to that case. Investigations of media influence on judicial officials remain rare, but the impact of media images on foreign policy makers has been a relatively common topic of research. Thus James F. Larson is able to make a number of general statements about the effects of media coverage on foreign policy decisions. For example, media attention has made private or secret negotiations more difficult. It also has changed public perceptions about foreign policies, and it has sharpened conflict by heightening emotions through sensational pictures. Larson illustrates these and other propositions with examples drawn primarily from the Iran hostage crisis.

After the two opening selections point to major media effects, Robert G. Picard's essay sounds a much-needed note of caution. Claims that effects have occurred or are likely to occur must be scrutinized carefully to make sure that the evidence is sound. Picard contends that many of the claims made about the adverse effect of media coverage on terrorists, their supporters, and their victims lack adequate proof. He urges more research before public policies are based on current beliefs that media coverage encourages terrorism. In his view, the opposite is true.

American journalists usually disclaim any motivation to influence public policies through their news stories. Except for the editorial pages, their credo calls for objective, neutral reporting. Investigative stories are the only major exception to this rule. They are designed to probe important social and political problems and engender remedial action. Are these goals achieved? If they are, what is the sequence of events? David L. Protess and his colleagues provide surprising answers based on a series of unique studies of television investigative reports.

287

Political folklore pictures the media as adversaries of officialdom who alert Americans to governmental misdeeds or failures. In reality, there are many situations when officials and journalists work together to bring about needed action. Susan Heilmann Miller tells a fascinating tale of one such collaboration. When members of Congress and journalists joined forces, they were able to spur State Department action to bring about the release of U.S. prisoners held in Mexican jails for violating drug laws.

The final selection deals with the impact negative publicity has had on the American nuclear energy industry. Stanley Rothman and S. Robert Lichter examine the nature of the coverage, the reasons for the negative approach, and public opinion and public policy responses over a span of several decades. They conclude that the images held and projected by media elites have greater influence on public perceptions and policies than the images held by specialists in the nuclear energy field.

5.1 ▄▄▄

Homicide and Bargained Justice: The Agenda-Setting Effect of Crime News on Prosecutors

David Pritchard

Editor's Note. There has been a great deal of debate about the effect of pretrial publicity on juries. By contrast, the effect of pretrial publicity on other participants in the judicial process has been examined only rarely. David Pritchard focuses attention on the impact of pretrial publicity on the decision of prosecutors to let a case go to trial or to settle it through bargaining between the prosecution and the defense. The latter process, known as "plea-bargaining," avoids the expense of a full trial. Not surprisingly, Pritchard's findings indicate that pretrial publicity does affect prosecutors' willingness to plea bargain in criminal cases. When the amount of publicity differs in otherwise similar cases, the less well-publicized case is more likely to be settled without a full-fledged trial.

How do news stories covering the activities of other publicity-sensitive public officials affect their behavior? A great deal more research is needed to answer that question precisely. But it seems clear from the limited number of studies done thus far, many of them cited by Pritchard, that this is one important area of media impact that warrants further exploration. It is a particularly promising area of research because it is based on pre-existing records of the activities of public officials rather than on their possibly fallible recollections about media influence, a distinction that makes the findings more credible.

At the time of writing, Pritchard was assistant professor at the Indiana School of Journalism, Bloomington, Indiana. He previously has investigated the types of crimes that attract media attention, including a study of the charge that newspapers routinely downplay homicides involving minority suspects. The selection comes from "Homicide and Bargained Justice: The Agenda-Setting Effect of Crime News on Prosecutors," *Public Opinion Quarterly* 50 (1986): 143-159.

The effect of publicity upon the adversary system of criminal justice has received an enormous amount of attention in recent years. The

---

From *Public Opinion Quarterly* 50 (1986): 143-159. Reprinted by permission of The University of Chicago Press.

Supreme Court of the United States has addressed the fair trial/free press issue several times, and many social scientists have studied the effect of publicity on potential jurors (for reviews of the empirical research see Bush, 1970; Connors, 1975; Simon, 1977; Buddenbaum et al., 1981).

Generally overlooked in the fair trial/free press debate, however, is the fact that as many as 90 percent of all criminal convictions in the United States are the result of plea bargaining rather than full-blown adversary trials (Heumann, 1978; Brosi, 1979). The defendant admits guilt in return for some implicit or explicit concession from the prosecution. Because there is no jury, there is no chance that press coverage will prejudice the jury.

Nonetheless, it is possible that press coverage will taint the *process*. This study addresses that issue by examining the relationship between newspaper coverage of individual cases and whether prosecutors engage in plea bargaining in those cases.

It is an important issue to consider, because the results of the consensual process epitomized by plea bargaining are quite different from those of the adversarial process epitomized by jury trials. For example, defendants found guilty by a jury are more likely to be sentenced to a period of incarceration, and can expect to receive substantially longer sentences than those whose cases are plea bargained, everything else being equal (Uhlman and Walker, 1980; Shane-DuBow et al., 1981; Brereton and Casper, 1982; Pruitt and Wilson, 1983).

Previous Work

Prosecutors are avid readers of newspaper stories about their cases, and most say that the news media are good indicators of the public image of the criminal justice system (Drechsel, 1983). So it is not entirely surprising that some prosecutors acknowledge that they take press coverage of a case into consideration in deciding whether to engage in plea negotiations.

For example, a study of plea bargaining in two California jurisdictions found that prosecutors and defense lawyers were less likely to agree in negotiations if a case had received news coverage (Utz, 1976). Surveys of prosecutors and public defenders in Cook County, Illinois, also suggested that a substantial number of prosecutors would not plea bargain in cases that had received news coverage (Jones, 1978)....

Why might publicity make a prosecutor unwilling to plea bargain a case? Alschuler (1968) studied prosecutors in a dozen large American cities, and found that they were motivated more by what they perceived to be their self-interest than by considerations of justice or fairness for the defendant....

In other words, prosecution is a political process, and prosecutors have a political stake in how their actions are perceived. Maintaining a public image as a crime-fighter is important to the prosecutor, perhaps to the extent of stressing adversary dispositions in publicized cases, regardless of the strength of evidence against the defendant. That way, if something "good" (like a conviction) happens, the prosecutor can take the credit. If something "bad" (like an acquittal or dismissal of charges) happens, the prosecutor can implicitly or explicitly shift the responsibility to the judge or to the jury. The result is that the blame is transferred (Newman, 1966; Galanter, 1983). Prosecutors may be especially likely to act this way in homicide cases (Alschuler, 1968).

In some cases, however, prosecutorial self-interest can lead to negotiations. This is most likely to happen when the prosecutor feels a need to get a conviction—any kind of conviction—despite weak evidence against the defendant. Alschuler writes: "Political considerations may, on occasion, make it important for a prosecutor to secure a conviction for a particular crime, and plea negotiations may provide the only practical means of achieving this objective"(Alschuler, 1968: 109).

However, prosecutors' most common reaction to publicity, the existing research makes clear, is a desire to avoid being perceived as soft on criminals.

The notion that the press may influence prosecutorial decision making has clear parallels with the familiar agenda-setting hypothesis, which suggests that the relative prominence of an issue in the news media will influence how salient that issue is to members of the audience (McCombs and Shaw, 1972; McLeod et al., 1974; Becker et al., 1975; Shaw and McCombs, 1977).

Most agenda-setting research has focused on possible effects on ordinary citizens. Only a few studies have explicitly tested the hypothesis that the press may help set the agendas of public officials. Gormley (1975) found mixed evidence for an agenda-setting effect of newspapers on state legislators. Lambeth (1978) concluded that the press helped set energy policy makers' agendas. In a study notable for the fact that it used a direct, rather than a self-reported measure of public-official behavior, Gilberg et al. (1980) found that press content set the agenda for Jimmy Carter's 1978 State of the Union speech. Swank et al. (1982) suggested, but did not test, the hypothesis that newspapers contribute to the salience of crime on local political agendas. Cook et al. (1983) found that a televised investigative report changed the agenda not only of citizens but also of elected officials.

On the other hand, Walker (1977) concluded that for three safety-related issues, the agenda of the U.S. Senate set the agenda for the *New York Times*. And Protess et al. (1985) found that the only agenda affected by a newspaper investigative series was future press coverage of the subject of the series.

In addition to the agenda-setting literature, research into reporter-source interactions contains considerable speculation (and some anecdotal evidence) suggesting that journalists' decisions about which stories to play up can influence the behavior of public officials (see, e.g., Matthews, 1960; Cohen, 1963; Dunn, 1969; Sigal, 1973; Weiss, 1974; Miller, 1978; and Peters, 1980). . . .

The Context of the Study

This study focuses on prosecutors in the district attorney's office in Milwaukee County, Wisconsin. The basic business of prosecutorial organizations is prosecuting criminal cases. In Milwaukee, as elsewhere in the United States, such cases are processed primarily by plea bargaining, which serves the cause of conserving relatively scarce organizational resources (Brosi, 1979). At the same time, however, it is not a popular way of settling cases (Hearst Corporation, 1983). In Milwaukee, for example, less than a quarter of the population favors plea bargaining (Metropolitan Milwaukee Criminal Justice Council, 1980). In addition, one of the city's newspapers flatly opposes the practice (Wills, 1977), while the other is merely skeptical (Milwaukee Journal, 1981).

Although in theory defendants decide whether to plead guilty or to exercise their constitutional right to a jury trial, in practice the prosecutor generally controls whether a case is plea bargained (Blumberg, 1967; Alschuler, 1968; Casper, 1972; Alschuler, 1975; Heumann, 1978; Gifford, 1981; Gifford, 1983). . . .

This study hypothesizes that newspaper coverage of a criminal case influences whether prosecutors engage in plea bargaining in a given case, and that the more extensive the newspaper coverage of a case, the less likely the district attorney's office is to negotiate in the case.

Data

Data to test this study's hypothesis were extracted from police and court records and from news stories. Information was obtained on every nonvehicular homicide case presented to the district attorney's office for possible prosecution during the 18-month period between January 1, 1981 and June 30, 1982. The study focuses on homicides because lesser crimes seldom receive press coverage in a major metropolitan community like Milwaukee. Three homicides that had not been disposed of by May 31, 1983 were eliminated from the analysis. Prosecutors filed homicide charges against every suspect arrested for homicide during the study period. In all, the cases of 90 homicide defendants were included in this study.

To find out how the cases were processed, every publicly available document on each case was scrutinized. Included were the inmate registration log at the Milwaukee County Jail; case files at the office of the Milwaukee County Clerk of Courts, Felony Division, which contained copies of criminal complaints, autopsy reports and other pieces of documentary evidence, summaries (and sometimes transcripts) of hearings, and memos from the prosecution and defense; and all news items about the cases published by Milwaukee's daily newspapers, both owned by the Journal Company, which granted full access to its files of clippings. The editions of the morning *Sentinel* and the evening and Sunday *Journal* that circulate in Milwaukee County carried 744 staff-written items—news stories, editorials, and columns of staff opinion—about the homicides in this study.

Measures

The independent variable in this study is the level of newspaper interest in the defendant's case. The dependent variable is the behavior of the prosecutor's office with respect to the case.

Level of Newspaper Interest in a Case

. . . The amount of space a newspaper devotes to a case can be measured in a straightforward manner. The number of news items about a case is an interval-level variable. So is the number of paragraphs written about a case. This study divides total number of paragraphs by total number of stories to come up with a measure of the level of newspaper interest in the case: the average length of news items about the case, excluding editorials (which tend to be quite short) and excluding stories published after the prosecutor's discretionary period.

That discretionary period is defined as lasting from the date of the homicide until the mode of disposition was known, generally at the beginning of a trial or the acceptance of a guilty plea by a judge. Ending the discretionary period any earlier would skew the results of the analysis, because plea agreements can be—and in several cases were—made or unmade at the last minute. . . .

Average story length, rather than total number of stories or paragraphs, is used because average story length in theory is not a function of how long a case lingers in the felony disposition process. The total number of stories or paragraphs the press devotes to a case, on the other hand, can be more a function of how many pretrial hearings take place than of how interested the press is in the case.

Number of paragraphs, rather than number of column inches, is used to measure story length because varying column sizes in both newspapers made computing standardized column inches very difficult. Standardized column inches and number of paragraphs are highly correlated, however (Budd, 1964).

Both Milwaukee newspapers covered homicides similarly (Pritchard, 1985). For that reason, this study combines the newspapers' coverage to form a single variable: the average length of the stories the Milwaukee newspapers published about a defendant's case. Separate analyses were conducted for each newspaper's coverage, with results virtually identical to the result produced by the combined coverage variable.

The newspapers published no stories at all about 5 of the 90 homicide prosecutions in this study. Those cases are coded as having an average story length of 0.

The amount of newspaper staff effort devoted to a given case was measured by analyzing newspaper content. The typical piece of crime news comes directly from routine law enforcement or judicial sources, often documentary sources such as police blotters, jail logs, and criminal complaints (Stanga, 1971; Cohen, 1975; Sherizen, 1978; Drechsel et al., 1980). Reporters who cover police and court beats can gather such news with relatively little effort.

On some cases, however, reporters do more. The may use nonroutine sources such as witnesses to the crime, friends and relatives of the suspect and/or victim, or not-for-attribution comments from law enforcement officials. Editorials and staff-written columns of opinion also represent nonroutine kinds of coverage.

Accordingly, stories about homicide cases can be categorized either as "routine" (if only routine sources were used) or "nonroutine" (if at least one nonroutine source was used). Of the 744 news items in this study, 13.4 percent were nonroutine by this definition.[1] . . .

Prosecutor's Plea Bargaining Behavior

Plea bargaining in this study is measured not by whether a case was settled consensually, but by whether the prosecutor actually engaged in plea negotiations. This "negotiated/did-not-negotiate" variable measures the prosecutor's actual behavior, not whether that behavior led to a consensual outcome. . . .

Court records and/or news items contained explicit evidence that prosecutors engaged in negotiations in 45 of the 90 cases in this study. In 35 of the cases in which prosecutors negotiated, the result was a consensual settlement, in which the prosecutor and the defense agreed on the appropriate disposition of the case. In the remaining 10 cases, defendants refused plea bargains offered by prosecutors. Those cases either went to jury trial or were dismissed over the objection of the prosecution.

Control Variables

One of the most challenging tasks in a study of this nature is to hold constant factors that may affect both the independent and the dependent variables. In an attempt to achieve that goal, this study uses an extensive set of control variables. Much of the variation in crime seriousness, a factor that could influence both newspaper interest and prosecutors' plea bargaining behavior, is implicitly controlled by this study's exclusive focus on homicides.

Homicides themselves can vary in a number of ways, however, so additional control variables are used. They include personal attributes (race, age, and sex) of the homicide suspect and victim; whether the suspect and the victim knew each other; the suspect's prior record; the initial charge against the defendant (first-degree murder or a lesser homicide charge, such as manslaughter); whether the defendant was charged with crimes beyond the first homicide count; and the number of suspects alleged to have been involved in the homicide.

Some factors, such as the prominence of the homicide suspect and victim or the bizarreness of the incident, are difficult to quantify. In most cases, however, court records and news stories contain enough details of the incident and of the people involved in it to permit a qualitative evaluation of such aspects of the case.

Results

Discriminant analysis (Cohen and Cohen, 1975; Klecka, 1975) was used to test the hypothesis concerning the influence of newspaper coverage on plea bargaining behavior. The analysis supported the hypothesis: press behavior—specifically, the average length of stories about a case—was the strongest predictor of whether prosecutors engaged in negotiations. The proportion of stories about a case that relied partly or entirely on nonroutine sources, however, was not a significant predictor of negotiations.

Table 1 shows the results of the analysis. Of all the variables, five proved to be statistically significant (at p=.05) predictors; average story length (the shorter the average story, the more likely the prosecutor would negotiate); whether the defendant and the victim knew each other (negotiations were more likely if the defendant and victim had been acquainted); the defendant's prior record (negotiations were more likely if the defendant had no prior record); the seriousness of the initial charge (negotiations were more likely when charges were less serious); and whether the defendant faced multiple charges stemming from the incident (negotiations were more likely when there was only one charge).

. . . [The discriminating] variables . . . account for 23.8 percent of the

Table 1   Results of Discriminant Analysis, with Whether the Prosecution
Negotiated as the Dependent Variable

Canonical correlation squared	.238
Improvement in ability to predict	53.3%
Relative contribution of significant discriminating variables:	
Average story length	34.8%
Suspect knew victim	26.9%
Prior record	· 19.5%
Initial charge	12.4%
Multiple charges	6.5%

total variance in whether the prosecution engaged in plea negotiations.
Average story length is the strongest predictor of prosecutorial behavior,
contributing more than a third of the variance accounted for by the
[discriminant analysis], 34.8 percent, which is 8.3 percent of the entire
variance.

Easier to understand, perhaps, is the fact that the discriminant
function correctly predicts the prosecutor's negotiating behavior in 69 of
the 90 cases (76.7 percent). Without the information contributed by the
variables in the function, successful predictions could be made only half
of the time. In other words, knowing the values of the variables in the
function provides a 53.3 percent improvement in predictive ability over
chance guessing. The function is statistically significant at the .0003 level.

Discussion

This study's findings suggest that newspapers help set the plea
bargaining agendas of Milwaukee prosecutors, at least in homicide cases.
The amount of space newspapers were willing to devote to the typical
story about a case was a stronger predictor than any other variable in this
study of whether the prosecutor would negotiate.

. . . Most other research in this area has relied on public officials' own
estimations of whether they have been influenced by the media
(Gormley, 1975; Lambeth, 1978; Cook et al., 1983; Protess et al., 1985).
Virtually all the measures of prosecutorial behavior used in this study,
however, came directly from court records. The data came from cases
that were already completed, ensuring that the participants were not
aware that their behavior would become part of a research project. In
addition, the data were recorded by court employees as part of the normal
routine of the criminal courts, with no hint that the data would provide
the raw material for an academic study. Unless the raw data contain a
systematic bias that is not immediately apparent, they are unobtrusive
measures (Webb, et al., 1966), unlike the self-reported data used as
dependent measures in much of the research into the possibility that the

news media may set the agenda for public officials.

That said, it must be acknowledged that documentary records are far from perfect. The facts of certain cases ... strongly imply that the prosecution offered a deal that was turned down, despite the fact that court records and newspaper coverage contain no explicit evidence of negotiations.

Similarly ... the strength of evidence against a defendant (or a defendant's accomplice) could influence whether the prosecution negotiated a case. Evidence strength was not included as a quantitative variable in this study because it is extremely difficult to measure in any systematic way (Eisenstein and Jacob, 1977:182-183). In addition, evidence strength may well be a socially defined construct greatly dependent upon attributes of the relationships between the prosecutor and the defense lawyer, and between the defense lawyer and the defendant.

Finally, it is difficult to predict what effect a strength-of-evidence variable would have on plea bargaining. If evidence is weak, the prosecutor has an incentive not only to negotiate but to offer a good deal. If the evidence is strong, however, the defendant has an incentive to plead guilty even if not offered a good deal to avoid the so-called trial penalty (Uhlman and Walker, 1980; Shane-DuBow et al., 1981; Brereton and Casper, 1982; Pruitt and Wilson, 1983). Guilty pleas in cases where there is no evidence of negotiations often are implicit plea bargains (Heumann, 1978).

Related to the issue of evidence strength are questions involving the content of negotiations. . . .

This study did not have access to information about the offers and counter-offers that are a normal part of negotiations, but researchers should attempt to gain access to such information (see, e.g., Maynard, 1984).

Future research should also examine in detail the extent to which prosecutors (or other law-enforcement personnel) influence newspapers' decisions about which cases to cover and how to cover them (see, e.g., Drechsel, 1983). This study found no evidence of such an influence, but then court records and news coverage are not the best places to look for such an effect. Researchers need to get into newsrooms, prosecutors' offices, courthouse hallways, and courtrooms to find the answers to such questions. . . .

Note

1. All coding was done by the author. To test intercoder reliability, a colleague coded a 10 percent sample of the 744 news items. There was agreement on 96 percent of the items, resulting in a reliability coefficient (Scott's pi) of .85 (Scott, 1955).

References

Alschuler, A. 1968. "The prosecutor's role in plea bargaining." *University of Chicago Law Review* 36:50-112.

————.1975. "The defense attorney's role in plea bargaining." *Yale Law Journal* 84:1179-1314.

Becker, L. B., M. E. McCombs, and J. M. McLeod. 1975. "The development of political cognitions." In S. H. Chaffee, ed., *Political Communication: Issues and Strategies for Research.* Beverly Hills, Calif.: Sage Publications.

Blumberg, A. 1967. *Criminal Justice.* Chicago: Quadrangle Books.

Brereton, D. and J. D. Casper. 1982. "Does it pay to plead guilty? Differential sentencing and the functioning of criminal courts." *Law and Society Review* 16:45-70.

Brosi, K. B. 1979. *A Cross-City Comparison of Felony Case Processing.* Washington, D.C.: U.S. Department of Justice.

Budd, R. 1964. "Attention score: a device for measuring news 'play'." *Journalism Quarterly* 41:259-262.

Buddenbaum, J. M., D. H. Weaver, R. L. Holsinger, and C. J. Brown. 1981. *Pretrial Publicity and Juries: A Review of Research.* Bloomington, Ind.: Indiana University School of Journalism.

Bush, C. R. 1970. *Free Press and Fair Trial: Some Dimensions of the Problem.* Athens, Ga.: University of Georgia Press.

Casper J. 1972. *American Criminal Justice: The Defendant's Perspective.* Englewood Cliffs, N.J.: Prentice-Hall.

Cohen, B. C. 1963. *The Press and Foreign Policy.* Princeton, N.J.: Princeton University Press.

Cohen, J., and P. Cohen. 1975. *Applied Multiple Regression/Correlation Analysis for the Behavioral Sciences.* New York: John Wiley & Sons.

Cohen, S. 1975. "A comparison of crime coverage in Detroit and Atlanta newspapers." *Journalism Quarterly* 52:726-730.

Connors, M. M. 1975. "Prejudicial publicity: an assessment." *Journalism Monographs* 41.

Cook, F. L., et al. 1983. "Media and agenda setting: effects on the public, interest group leaders, policy makers, and policy." *Public Opinion Quarterly* 47:16-35.

Drechsel, R. E. 1983. *News Making in the Trial Courts.* New York: Longman.

Drechsel, R. E., K. Netteburg, and B. Aborisade. 1980. "Community size and newspaper reporting of local courts." *Journalism Quarterly* 57:71-78.

Dunn, D. 1969. *Public Officials and the Press.* Reading, Mass.: Addison-Wesley.

Eisenstein, J., and H. Jacob. 1977. *Felony Justice: An Organizational Analysis of Criminal Courts.* Boston: Little, Brown and Co.

Galanter, M. 1983. "Reading the landscape of disputes: what we know and don't know (and think we know) about our allegedly contentious and litigious society." *UCLA Law Review* 31:4-71.

Gifford, D. G. 1981. "Equal protection and the prosecutor's charging decision: enforcing an ideal." *George Washington Law Review* 49:659-719.

————. 1983. "Meaningful reform of plea bargaining: control of prosecutorial discretion." *University of Illinois Law Review* 1983:37-98.

Gilberg, S., C. Eyal, M. McCombs, and D. Nicholas. 1980. "The State of the Union Address and the press agenda." *Journalism Quarterly* 57:584-588.

Gormley, W. T., Jr. 1975. "Newspaper agendas and political elites." *Journalism Quarterly* 52:304-308.

Hearst Corporation. 1983. *The American Public, the Media & the Judicial System: A National Survey on Public Awareness and Personal Experience.* New York: The Hearst Corporation.

Heumann, M. 1978. *Plea Bargaining: The Experiences of Prosecutors, Judges, and Defense Attorneys.* Chicago: University of Chicago Press.

Jones, J. B. 1978. "Prosecutors and the disposition of criminal cases: an analysis of plea bargaining rates." *Journal of Criminal Law & Criminology* 69:402-412.

Klecka, W. R. 1975. "Discriminant analysis." In Nie, N., et al. *Statistical Package for the Social Sciences,* second ed. New York: McGraw-Hill.

Lambeth, E. B. 1978. "Perceived influence of the press on energy policy making." *Journalism Quarterly* 55:11-18, 72.

Matthews, D. R. 1960. *U.S. Senators and Their World.* Chapel Hill: University of North Carolina Press.

Maynard, D. W. 1984. "The structure of discourse in misdemeanor plea bargaining." *Law & Society Review* 18:75-104.

McCombs, M., and D. L. Shaw. 1972. "The agenda-setting function of mass media." *Public Opinion Quarterly* 36:176-187.

McLeod, J. M., L. B. Becker, and J. E. Byrnes. 1974. "Another look at the agenda-setting function of the press." *Communication Research* 1:131-166.

Metropolitan Milwaukee Criminal Justice Council. 1980. Public Opinion Survey 600.

Miller, S. 1978. "Reporters and congressmen: living in symbiosis." *Journalism Monographs* 53.

Milwaukee Journal. 1981. "A deeper look at plea bargains." Editorial, January 11.

Newman, D. J. 1966. *Conviction: The Determination of Guilt or Innocence Without Trial.* Boston: Little, Brown and Co.

Peters, C. 1980. *How Washington Really Works.* Reading, Mass.: Addison-Wesley.

Pritchard, D. 1985. "Race, homicide and newspapers." *Journalism Quarterly* 62:500-7.

Protess, D. L., D. R. Leff, S. C. Brooks, and M. T. Gordon. 1985. "Uncovering rape: the watchdog press and the limits of agenda setting." *Public Opinion Quarterly* 49:19-37.

Pruitt, C. R., and J. Q. Wilson. 1983. " A longitudinal study of the effect of race on sentencing." *Law & Society Review* 17:613-635.

Shane-DuBow, S., et al. 1981. *Wisconsin Felony Sentencing Guidelines: Phase 1 of Research and Development.* Madison: Wisconsin Center for Public Policy.

Shaw, D. L., and M. E. McCombs. 1977. *The Emergence of American Political Issues: The Agenda-Setting Function of the Press.* St. Paul: West Publishing.

Sherizen, S. 1978. "Social creation of crime news: all the news fitted to print." In C. Winick, ed., *Deviance and Mass Media.* Beverly Hills, Calif.: Sage Publications.

Sigal, L. V. 1973. *Reporters and Officials: The Organization and Politics of Newsmaking.* Lexington, Mass.: D.C. Heath.

Simon, R. 1977. "Does the court's decision in Nebraska Press Association fit the research evidence on the impact on jurors of news coverage?" *Stanford Law Review* 29:515-528.

Stanga, J. E. 1971. "The press and the criminal defendant: newsmen and criminal justice in three Wisconsin cities." Unpublished Ph.D. dissertation, University of Wisconsin.

Swank, D. H., H. Jacob, and J. Moran. 1982. " Newspaper attentiveness to crime." In H. Jacob and R. L. Lineberry, eds., *Governmental Responses to Crime: Crime on Urban Agendas.* Washington, D.C.: National Institute of Justice.

Uhlman, T. M., and N. D. Walker. 1980. "'He takes some of my time, I take some of his': an analysis of sentencing patterns in jury cases." *Law & Society Review* 14:323-341.

Utz, P. J. 1976. *Settling the Facts: Discretion and Negotiation in Criminal Court.* Lexington, Mass.: Lexington Books.

Walker, J. 1977. "Setting the agenda in the U.S. Senate: a theory of problem selection." *British Journal of Political Science* 7:423-445.

Webb, E. J., D. T. Campbell, R. D. Schwartz, and L. Sechrest. 1966. *Unobtrusive Measures: Nonreactive Research in the Social Sciences.* Chicago: Rand McNally & Co.

Weiss, C. H. 1974. "What America's leaders read." *Public Opinion Quarterly* 38:1-22.

Wills, R. H. 1977. Milwaukee *Sentinel* Editorial Policy.

5.2 ▬▬▬

Television and U.S. Foreign Policy:
The Case of the Iran Hostage Crisis

James F. Larson

Editor's Note. Press influence on foreign policies of major nations has been growing by leaps and bounds in recent decades. Policy makers pay close attention to news stories, watching for events that might have escaped normal diplomatic observations, as well as for the opinion-shaping images that might be conveyed. Alexander Haig alleges that review of the previous night's newscasts was his first order of business when he served as White House chief of staff, deputy national security adviser, commander of NATO, and secretary of state. Through its image-making power, television especially has become a catalyst for policy making; often it acts even as a participant.

This essay by James F. Larson sets forth nine major features that characterize the interaction between news and policy making and illustrates them with data drawn from coverage of Iran by U.S. television from 1972 to 1981. Particularly striking is the fact that the extent of coverage is strongly related to the availability of exciting pictures. When governments restrain access to pictures, television news coverage shrivels. When ample pictures are available, especially emotionally stirring ones, television news is saturated with them, often to the exclusion of most other stories. Larson points out that television news coverage makes private or secret negotiations more difficult. It can, however, also ease negotiations by serving as a communications channel linking political elites across national boundaries.

Larson, at the time of writing, was assistant professor in the School of Communications, University of Washington. He has worked for the Voice of America and is the author of *Television's Window on the World: International Affairs Coverage on the U.S. Networks* (1984). The selection comes from "Television and U.S. Foreign Policy: The Case of the Iran Hostage Crisis," *Journal of Communication* 36:4 (Autumn 1986): 108-130.

. . . Iran is both a compelling case study and a major landmark in our understanding of the structural relationship between television news and

Reprinted and abridged from *Journal of Communication* 36, no. 4 (Autumn 1986): 108-130. Reprinted by permission of Oxford University Press.

U.S. foreign policy. One focal point of such a study is the 444-day crisis involving U.S. hostages in Teheran, beginning with their seizure on November 4, 1979.

The Iran hostage crisis was quintessentially visual in nature. It evokes visual memories of angry crowds outside the U.S. embassy in Teheran, armed 'students" who overran the embassy and seized hostages, the bearded Ayatollah Khomeini surrounded by followers, clergy visits to the hostages at Easter and Christmas, and charred bodies of U.S. servicemen left in the desert after an abortive rescue mission. Additional imagery emanated from the United States: repeated briefings by State Department press spokesman Hodding Carter, comments from the White House by President Carter's press secretary, Jody Powell, the statements and activities of hostage wives and families. ABC's creation and promotion of an evening news special called "America Held Hostage," and, not least, Walter Cronkite's weeknight newscast reminders of the duration of the hostages' captivity.

Reflecting on its visual character, Lang and Lang (3) called the hostage crisis an occasion in which the televised event, regardless of how authentic or revealing of the real thing, became shared experience: "The reality that lives on is the reality etched in the memories of the millions who watched rather than the few who were actually there" (p. 213).

Lloyd Cutler (2), who served in the Carter White House during the Iran crisis, argues that the large, immediate reach of television is an important factor in its influence on the timing and substance of foreign policy decisions. As communication researchers have long known, that reach increases greatly in times of crisis. In a nationwide Roper survey conducted in early 1980, 77 percent of the respondents indicated they had been getting most of their news "about the crisis regarding the U.S. hostages being held in Iran" from television, compared with only 26 percent[1] who cited newspapers as the major source (7). In similar Roper surveys conducted during noncrisis circumstances, about 65 percent of the public indicate that they get most of their news about "what's going on in the world today" from television, compared to approximately 47 percent who cite newspapers (6).

The Iran experience stretched and challenged past conceptions about the news media and foreign policy, stimulating a public debate over acceptable norms for both television and government in a novel situation. Out of the controversy grew a consensus among scholars, government officials, and journalists that the Iran hostage crisis was a watershed event deserving special scrutiny.

This study explores what the Iran experience either modifies or confirms about our knowledge of the relationship between television and U.S. foreign policy. Its focus on that relationship in a single nation is primarily a limitation of the research design and should not obscure the international or transnational import of any findings. The global scope of changes in both television and foreign policy is ever more widely acknowledged by policy-makers, media professionals, and scholars.

In this study the Iran case is used to evaluate a set of nine propositions about television and U.S. foreign policy. These propositions are developed through a selective review of the existing literature on media and foreign policy and organized according to some key concepts in that literature. These propositions will then be applied to content data on newscasts between 1972 and 1981. . . .

. . . The data come principally from the *Television News Index and Abstract*, published as a guide to the videotaped early evening news broadcasts contained in the Vanderbilt Television News Archive. . . . Data were collected for an alternate network's news telecast on every fourth evening. This procedure assumes a high degree of similarity in the amount and nature of coverage on the three networks and provides a large sample of data representing ABC, CBS, and NBC in equal proportions.

Television's relationship to U.S. foreign policy toward Iran may be examined according to five major phases in network news coverage of that nation: Iran before the revolution (January 1972-October 1977), demystification of the Shah and the revolution (November 1977-January 1979), Iran drops from view (February 1979-October 1979), the hostage crisis itself (November 1979-January 1981), and the immediate aftermath of the hostage captivity (February 1981-December 1981). . . .

Content analyses of weeknight news broadcasts from 1972 through 1977 confirm the paucity of television coverage of Iran before the revolution, a period when the Vietnam war and the 1973 Middle East war received some saturation coverage. Table 1 shows that Iran appeared in only about one percent of all international news items from 1972 through 1977. . . .

Despite the relative lack of attention to Iran during this period of almost six years, three aspects of the coverage define television's role as an observer. First, there was heavy reliance on the wire services for news from Iran. A count of all stories broadcast by the three networks from 1972 through October 1977 shows that 48 percent were anchor reports (without film or video and read or voiced by an anchor correspondent). Second, only one-quarter of all stories involving Iran were foreign video reports, originating with overseas correspondents and containing filmed or videotaped visuals. However, fewer than half of these or only ten percent of all reports involving Iran, originated from that nation itself. The others were filed from such locations as OPEC meetings in Austria, Algiers, and Vienna or a meeting between the Shah of Iran and Henry Kissinger in Zurich. Finally, there were two dominant and interrelated themes in network coverage of Iran from 1972 through October 1977—oil

Table 1   Amount of Coverage of Iran on Network Television Early Evening News, 1972-1981

Year	Minutes per Week on the "Average" Network	Iran Stories as a Percent of all International News
1972	.8	1.2
1973	.6	1.2
1974	1.2	1.1
1975	.8	.7
1976	.9	1.1
1977	1.1	.6
1978	2.7	1.6
1979	20.0	26.3
1980	26.6	32.0
1981	7.0	8.8
N (stories)	433	7,054

and arms sales. Taken together, well over half of reporting on Iran dealt with these two topics.

In its role as a participant in foreign policy, network television covered the activities of government. As usual, state visits, presidential travel, and activities of the secretary of state all received coverage. President Nixon visited Iran in May 1972, the Shah visited the United States in July 1973 and May 1975, Henry Kissinger met the Shah in Zurich in February 1975, Secretary of State Vance met the Shah in Iran in May 1977, and Empress Farah visited the United States in July of that year. For the most part, coverage of such events followed the norm of coverage of diplomatic activity with an ally in an important area of the world.

Network coverage also contained hints but no sustained attention to events indicating that all was not well within Iran. For example, there were bombings at the Shah memorial and United States Information Service during President Nixon's May 1972 visit to Iran, attributed by at least one network to "Marxist guerrillas." In 1975, U.S. Air Force personnel and a U.S. embassy employee were killed in Iran, with the former action attributed to an "anti-Shah" group. . . .

. . . However, all of these reports on bombings, killings, potential danger to Americans in Iran, and demonstrations by Iranians in the United States received minuscule attention when compared to network coverage of oil and arms.

Both the amount of coverage given to Iran during the 1972-1978 period and the nature of such coverage suggest that television news predominantly reflected the activities of the White House State Department and other U.S. policy officials during this period. Mowlana and colleagues (4) examined all content of the *Middle East Journal, Foreign Affairs*, and *Foreign Policy* from 1970 through the summer of 1978 to see whether foreign policy experts had noted signs of internal instability in Iran that might not have been picked up by the media. Their analysis showed that few if any of the experts writing for these journals detected the massive grass roots anti-Shah sentiment building in Iran. However, Mowlana notes that the "most serious misunderstandings of the Iranian situation in terms of their effect on public opinion were promulgated by the media. The communication media rarely strayed from the administration's official line, in either their perceptions or coverage of the Iranian political upheaval"(4).

Network television in the early 1970s portrayed a story that depicted Iran as a strong ally and supplier of oil, needing support principally in the form of U.S. arms. Although the Shah may have had his internal problems, their depth was never apparent and hence the storyline did not lead adequately into the events that followed. For U.S. television audiences trying to understand why Iranian students would be demonstrating in the United States and "terrorists" killing Americans in Iran, there was relatively little context or background. That circumstance began to change in November 1977.

For sheer public reach and political impact, the Shah's November visit to the White House might be described as a turning point in network coverage of his government. While state visits are a common occurrence at the White House, often with ceremonies on the South Lawn, this visit produced a politically devastating visual scene. Tear gas used to quell demonstrations outside the White House floated across the South Lawn as President Carter was greeting the Shah. A nationwide television audience witnessed the president and the Shah, not to mention assembled dignitaries and the press, dealing as best they could with the effects of tear gas.

The effect on subsequent television coverage of the event was dramatic in tone if not in quantity. From that point on, the Shah himself and the activities of Savak (the Iranian secret police) and the military became a more dominant theme in network coverage of Iran. While the Shah continued to receive some "favorable" coverage consonant with his past characterization as a staunch friend and ally of the United States, the U.S. visit marked the clear beginning of a gradual change in network coverage that showed some flaws in the man and the nature of his regime. Still, there was no dramatic increase in the amount of coverage of Iran on the network nightly news broadcasts during most of this fifteen-week period. As evidence, Table 1 shows that Iran was involved in only 1.6 percent of all international news stories broadcast during 1978.

... In August and September of 1978, Chinese leader Hua Kuo Feng visited Iran, and antigovernment violence also escalated. In response, all three networks dispatched their own correspondents to Iran. This move not only changed the observer role of television in the foreign policy process from that time on but also made television a more active participant in the events that transpired.

During the last half of 1978, well over half of all reporting originated with network correspondents in Iran. The dominant theme during this period was antigovernment marches, strikes, and protests, leading inexorably toward the downfall of the Shah early in 1979.

In late 1978, demonstrators in the city of Qum called for the establishment of a new government led by the exiled Ayatollah Khomeini. For a brief period of several months, beginning in November 1978, the networks reported from Paris on Khomeini's activities and served as a channel linking him with Iran and the rest of the world. During January 1979, after the Shah left Iran, television served as a channel for messages between Khomeini and the shaky government of Prime Minister Shapour Bakhtiar. . . .

Upon his departure from Iran, the Shah himself and his health condition became one center of network television attention. The other focus of attention during February and March became the interpretation to U.S. television audiences of the new and largely unforeseen political situation in Iran, especially its implications for the United States. Topics covered during February and March included loss of U.S. military equipment in Iran, contingency plans to evacuate Americans from Iran; the impact of the Iran situation on OPEC and rising oil prices; an attack on the U.S. embassy in which a Marine sergeant was captured and returned; pro-Shah soldiers continuing to fight; the Ayatollah Khomeini's inability to control revolutionaries; secret trials and firing squads; and Iran's censorship of U.S. television reporting.

During the next seven months, April through October, coverage of Iran dropped to a very low level. . . .

. . . This period could aptly be called the calm before the storm in television coverage of Iran. For all practical purposes, there was an eight-month hiatus in direct network television coverage of news from Iran, right up to the cataclysmic event that marked the beginning of a sustained period of intensive coverage of that country: the takeover of the U.S. embassy in Teheran and seizure of embassy personnel as hostages during the first week of November 1979.

In summary, network television's role as an observer of events in Iran declined noticeably during the nine months between the arrival of the Ayatollah Khomeini in Iran and the seizure of U.S. hostages. As a consequence, its role as a participant in foreign policy was also greatly diminished during this period of time. Its reporting on actions of U.S. policymakers was minimal, as were its contributions to those policy-makers.

The actual seizure of U.S. hostages and their 444-day period of captivity sustained high levels of network news attention, accounting for approximately three-quarters of all news stories from Iran during the entire 1972-1981 decade. As shown in Table 1, Iran accounted for 26.3 percent of all international news broadcast by the networks in 1979 and 32 percent, or nearly a third, of such news during 1980. As an alternative measure, Table 1 shows the average length of time devoted to Iran stories by a network. In 1980, for example, each network averaged close to 27 minutes, or more than an entire nightly news broadcast each week devoted to Iran. . . .

During the captivity of the hostages, 49.5 percent of all network stories on Iran were domestic video reports, principally by correspondents in Washington, D.C., with some originating from the United Nations and other U.S. locations. Only 14.4 percent of all stories were anchor reports, which is largely indicative of active network coverage throughout the hostage ordeal. The remaining 36.1 percent of stories were visual reports originating in Iran and other nations.

. . . [A]ttempts at diplomatic communication between Iran and the United States accounted for the bulk of coverage. Taken together, statements by the White House, State Department, and the Ayatollah Khomeini or representatives of clergy in Iran, along with more general reports concerning U.S. or Iranian government policies, accounted for 47.4 percent of all stories broadcast during the period of captivity. . . .

The hostage seizure on November 4, 1979, thrust U.S. television into unchartered territory by greatly expanding its role as a participant and potential catalyst in the foreign policy process. . . . Television news became a principal channel of communication between the two governments. . . .

Both governments very quickly expressed concern and some frustration with the performance of television (1). Within a week of the hostage seizure, White House press spokesman Jody Powell had met with representatives of the three television networks to request restraint in coverage of the Iran situation. The meeting coincided with NBC's airing of an interview with one of the hostages, Marine Corporal William Gallegos. Because of certain conditions agreed to by NBC and the Iranian captors in Teheran, the Gallegos interview sparked a public debate among the television networks and public officials concerning the role and responsibility of the network news medium.

On November 18, the Iranian government took out a full-page advertisement in the *New York Times* in order to print the 3,500-word text of a one-hour Iranian television address delivered by the Ayatollah Khomeini. In the speech, the Ayatollah had rejected the plea of a papal representative in Iran for the release of the U.S. hostages. A message at the top of the advertisement read: "Ayatollah Khomeini's statement has been only briefly and very selectively referred to by the media. Therefore, we print his message here for his intended audience, the people of the United States of America."

U.S. government representatives were also displeased with television reporting of Khomeini's statement but for different reasons. In the December 11 *New York Times*, Hodding Carter, speaking personally and "off the record," expressed his view that television interviews might well have "rhetorically boxed the revolutionary leader into a corner on the subject of possible trials of the hostages held in Teheran." Pressed by interviewers the Ayatollah had indicated that the hostages definitely would go on trial. Those interviews, Carter said, "put into concrete what could have been dismissed as muttering behind closed walls." In the same article, Carter's views were disputed by the chief executives of all three television networks.

Iranian displeasure with the reporting of U.S. television networks also took other forms. Quint (5) reports that in early 1980 all three networks were first deprived of satellite facilities and then, on January 14 ordered out of the country with other U.S. reporters and photographers. However, Iran permitted them to return in early March. . . .

. . . In the spring of 1980, as part of his sanctions package against Iran, President Carter proposed an interruption in Iranian use of communication satellites through the INTELSAT system. Within a short time, the president's proposal was quietly shelved over concerns about using a commercial satellite for political purposes. In effect, the U.S. government acknowledged the overriding importance of INTELSAT as a transnational corporate entity.

. . . All three networks made interviews with wives, mothers, or other relatives of the hostages part of the story within a day or two of the embassy seizure. This strong element of human drama, having been injected at the very beginning of the story, would be difficult to ignore later. The story of human separation was reinforced by the early release of some black and women hostages and the later release of hostage Richard Queen, who suffered from an undisclosed illness. Their reunion with families and friends tapped television's power to convey emotion and intimacy.

Network attention to the human drama of the hostages' situation, coinciding with the presidential election of 1980, accented the domestic side of this particular international news story. . . .

Analysis of the content of network coverage shows clearly that no political candidate made it a major issue, either before the nominating conventions or during the actual campaign. Instead, the issue was tacit and pervasive, recognized by all the candidates and brought home in a powerful way by network television's attention to the human impact of the Iran crisis within the United States.

Following saturation coverage of the return of the hostages on the day of President Reagan's inauguration in January 1981, levels of coverage began to drop. As shown in Table 1, coverage of Iran during 1981 accounted for only 8.8 percent of all international news, compared with 32 percent the preceding year. Furthermore, two-thirds of the coverage accorded Iran was concentrated during the first six months of 1981. By the last quarter of 1981, attention to Iran had come full circle, falling to the low levels shown in the 1972-1977 period. . . .

The contribution of the Iran case to an overall understanding of the television-foreign policy relationship may be summarized by recounting the evidence it provides for each of the general propositions stated at the outset.

1. *The technology and organizational structures for gathering and disseminating international television news are inherently transnational in nature.* The Iran case illustrated the transnational character of television news as well as any event to that date. Iranian and U.S. leaders, as well as other groups in both nations, repeatedly used television to address public audiences, often across national boundaries. The U.S. government's decision not to seek interruption of satellite communication to and from Iran as part of a package of sanctions underscores this characteristic.

2. *The presence of television news makes private or secret negotiations between governments more difficult.* During the several weeks immediately following seizure of the hostages, television was a preferred medium for communication between governments in Iran and the United States. Given U.S. uncertainty about the locus of power and leadership control in Iran and probable Iranian suspicions concerning U.S. behavior in any secret negotiations, the initial preference for a public exchange through television is understandable. However, both governments eventually expressed public frustration with television coverage, and this sense of frustration is probably the best indication of support for this proposition.

3. *Access to appropriate pictures heavily influences current television news gathering practices.* The presence or absence of network correspondents in Iran directly affected the amount if not the nature of coverage. During most of the prolonged crisis, access to U.S. television was a major goal of the militants who held the hostages and of the Iranian government. As noted by Adams and Heyl (1), provision of such access bolstered the story's visibility on television news.

During other phases of the 1972-1981 decade, U.S. television correspondents were not present in Iran of their own accord. Most notable were the seven months, April through October 1979, directly preceding the hostage seizure, characterized by television's heavy reliance on wire service reports and an almost total lack of visual news from Iran. During this period the networks themselves had determined that no *appropriate* (conflictual or telegenic) pictures were accessible. Television is a greater force in foreign policy when there is direct and immediate visual coverage than it is during those periods of reliance on wire service or other nonvisual reporting.

4. *Television news provides episodic accounts often focusing satura-tion coverage on a "big story" and resulting, over the long run, in an ahistorical account.* Television coverage of Iran in the early 1970s, along with most print media coverage, ignored a body of history from the 1950s and 1960s that might have helped place the current developments in context. Instead, three-quarters of all coverage in a decade came during the 444 days of the hostage crisis, and a great deal of that consisted of saturation coverage of selected episodes. Little attention was devoted to the causes and precedents of the hostage crisis.

5. *Television network news usually follows or reinforces U.S. government policy.* In the case of Iran, television shared this propensity with most of the print media, especially prior to the revolution, when the major policy concerns of OPEC oil prices and U.S. arms sales, along with travel by the President or the Shah, accounted for much of the low-level coverage. During this initial period, the networks showed little deviation from the official U.S. government stance. Although in late 1977 the networks began to examine charges against the Shah and his government, such reporting was well within the purview of the broad Carter adminis-tration emphasis on human rights. The basic pattern of government-press cooperation continued through the hostage crisis itself, with approxi-mately half of all coverage reporting various attempts at diplomatic communication between Iran and the United States. . . .

6. *Television news sometimes participates in foreign policy by serving as a direct channel of communication between government officials or policy elites in one nation and those in others.* At least as early as 1978, television served as a channel to convey the Ayatollah Khomeini's activities and ideas from Paris to Iran and the rest of the world. For a short period during November 1979, both Iran and the United States used television as a direct means of communication while representatives of both nations were groping to establish informal, more secretive channels. On other occasions during the 444-day hostage crisis, television was an important channel for messages from one government to another.

7. *Policy problems may be created or exacerbated by lack of media attention to basic processes of social and cultural change in developing nations.* In this respect, Iran was a particular instance of the more general problem of world communication imbalance between developed and developing nations. Both policy-makers and television journalists appear to have missed a major part of the story leading up to the hostage crisis. In the case of Iran, the lack of an appropriate long-term policy by the U.S.

government and the absence of serious attention by network television news to underlying processes of cultural, religious, and economic change went hand in hand.

8. *Television's power to convey emotions and a sense of intimacy can be a factor in foreign policy.* Network television attention to hostage families in the United States, visits or interviews with the hostages in Iran, and the return of the hostages constituted major ongoing themes of coverage during the crisis. Such attention provides a gripping story line of human drama. The visual coverage of hostages and their families helped to sustain audience interest in the crisis and simultaneously created a climate or set of pressures within which the president and other U.S. officials conducted foreign policy.

9. *Television can change public perceptions about foreign affairs, particularly when it conveys new visual information and when such information is repeatedly presented over a long period of time.* In that role, network television helped to change the image of the Shah for the U.S. public beginning in 1977 and 1978 through increased reporting on the Shah himself and the activities of Savak and the military. Televised scenes of the Shah's White House visit in November 1977, with the accompanying demonstrations and tear gas, provided a supportive context.

Although the above propositions concerning television and foreign policy may be far from exhaustive or conclusive, they underscore the increasing importance of the problem. Television news can participate in foreign policy as well as simply observe it. In the case of dramatic events, television can actually serve as a catalyst to foreign policy initiatives. These roles of television news have implications for, first, the manner in which scholars conceptualize the relationship of news media to foreign policy; second, policies and practices of television news organizations; and third, the conduct of foreign policy and international diplomacy. Analysis of certain critical events can help to illuminate each of these areas. To date, Iran is an exemplary case in point.

Note

1. The percentages sum to more than 100 because the Roper surveys allowed multiple responses to this question.

References

1. Adams, William and Phillip Heyl. "From Cairo to Kabul with the Networks, 1972-1980." In William C. Adams (Ed.), *Television Coverage of the Middle East*. Norwood, N.J.: Ablex, 1981. pp. 1-39.

2. Cutler, Lloyd N. "Foreign Policy on Deadline." *Foreign Policy 56*, Fall 1984, pp. 113-128.
3. Lang, Gladys Engel and Kurt Lang. *Politics and Television Re-Viewed.* Beverly Hills, Cal.: Sage, 1984.
4. Mowlana, Hamid, "The Role of the Media in the U.S.-Iranian Conflict." In Andrew Arno and Wimal Dissanayake (Eds.), *The News Media in National and International Conflict.* Boulder, Colo.: Westview Press, 1984, pp.71-99.
5. Quint, Bert. "Dateline Tehran: There Was a Touch of Fear." *TV Guide*, April 5, 1980, pp. 6-12.
6. Roper, Burns W. "Trends in Attitudes toward Television and Other Media: A Twenty-Two Year Review." Report for the Television Information Office, New York, April 1981.
7. Television Information Office. "Public Finds Television News Is Presenting Iran Crisis Objectively, Coping Well with Manipulation Efforts." News release, New York, March 13, 1980.

5.3 ■■■■■■

News Coverage as the Contagion of Terrorism: Dangerous Charges Backed by Dubious Science

Robert G. Picard

Editor's Note. People and their governments throughout the world are greatly concerned about the many incidents of terrorism. Most agree that terrorists are primarily interested in attracting media attention as a way to publicize their grievances and generate pressures to accede to their demands. Accordingly, there has been much concern that media coverage of terrorism may become an incentive for terrorists to commit violent acts. Media executives have been uncertain about proper coverage of terrorism, and governments have weighed the possibility of legislating curbs on terrorism stories.

Robert G. Picard's essay runs counter to this protective trend. He argues that there is inadequate scientific proof that media coverage does, indeed, spur terrorism; he also suggests that increased publicity might actually lessen terrorism. He urges more research to settle the controversy and suggests ways to do it.

Picard's study is one of many examples where the belief that the media influence a particular political situation is strongly buttressed by the logic of the situation but where incontrovertible scientific proof is lacking and would be difficult to produce. Unpublicized terrorist acts, which would establish that terrorism can thrive without publicity, are hard to identify. It is equally difficult to get believable testimony from terrorists about whether publicity motivated their actions. As usual, this uncertainty about media effects poses serious dilemmas for policy makers. To act or not to act becomes, indeed, the question.

Picard received his Ph.D. from the University of Missouri and has worked as a newspaper editor. At the time of writing, he was teaching at the Louisiana State University School of Journalism. The selection is from "News Coverage as the Contagion of Terrorism: Dangerous Charges Backed by Dubious Science," *Political Communication and Persuasion* 3:4 (1986): 385-400.

From *Political Communication and Persuasion* 3, no. 4 (1986): 385-400. Reprinted by permission of Taylor & Francis.

Introduction

When NBC News broadcast a three-and-a-half minute interview in May with Abul (Mohammed) Abbas, head of the Palestine Liberation Front that hijacked the *Achille Lauro* last year, the news organization was subjected to swift and pointed criticism.

"Terrorism thrives on this kind of publicity," charged State Department spokesman Charles Redman; he said it "encourages the terrorist activities we're all seeking to deter." [1]

A similar response was seen in Great Britain when the British government attacked the BBC for its plans to broadcast the documentary "Real Lives: At the Edge of the Union," which included an interview with Martin McGuinness, a spokesman for the legal political wing of the Irish Republican Army who is accused of being a top-ranking official in the outlawed paramilitary group.

Home Secretary Leon Brittan asked the BBC not to air the program saying it was "wholly contrary to the public interest." [2]

Such incidents have led to calls for more control over what is broadcast and printed about terrorism and those who engage in such political violence. At the American Bar Association Meeting in London this past year [1985], Prime Minister Margaret Thatcher told the gathered attorneys that democracies "must find a way to starve the terrorists and hijackers of the oxygen of publicity on which they depend." [3] Her statement met with support from U.S. Attorney General Edwin Meese and other U.S. officials.

While these efforts primarily have been aimed at getting media to adhere to voluntary guidelines, other individuals have suggested that legal restraints be imposed. Imposition of such restraints would face greater difficulty in the United States than abroad, due to the First Amendment, but many argue that they are necessary to control terrorism and protect public safety.

Behind the efforts to induce self-restraints or impose government restraints on the media is the belief that coverage of terrorism and terrorists creates more terrorism and terrorists. The idea that media are the contagion of terrorism has been widely heralded and is repeatedly used to justify efforts to alter media coverage.

This has occurred despite the fact that there is no significant evidence that media act as a contagion.

This paper will review the argument that media coverage spreads terrorism by giving encouragement to those who engage in such violence and it will explore the literature upon which it is based. It will also suggest paradigms within which to view and explore media effects on terrorists that offer a variety of important research opportunities.

The Contagion Literature

During the past two decades the literature associating media with terrorism and implicating media as a contagion of such violence has grown rapidly. When carefully dissecting that literature, however, one finds it contains no credible evidence that media are an important factor in inducing and diffusing terrorist acts.

Most books, articles, essays, and speeches on the topic are comprised of sweeping generalities, conjecture, supposition, anecdotal evidence based on dubious correlations, and endless repetition of equally weak arguments and nonscientific evidence offered by other writers on the subject of terrorism.

As one reviews the literature it becomes shockingly clear that not a single study based on accepted social science research methods has established a cause-effect relationship between media coverage and the spread of terrorism. Yet public officials, scholars, editors, reporters, and columnists continually link the two elements and present their relationship as proven.

The dearth of evidence associating the two variables is not the result of conflicting studies or arguments over interpretation of evidence, but rather the absence of research on the subject. At times some scholars have attempted to overcome that problem or to place the pallor of respectability over their opinions by "borrowing" conclusions from the literature of the effects of televised violence and crime on viewers and then projecting similar effects to coverage of terrorism.

The use of this questionable tactic is disquieting to anyone who ascribes to social science research philosophy. It is especially disturbing when one considers the potential abrogation of civil liberties that could result and the unsettled state of knowledge about the effects of televised violence and crime.

Without wishing to cast aspersions on mediated violence research, it is safe to say that, in the aggregate, the thousands of studies on the subject are contradictory, inconclusive, and based on widely differing definitions, methods, and assumptions. The literature has been the subject of some of the most heated debates in the social sciences.

Social learning, arousal, and disinhibition theories on the effects of media portrayals of violence and crime have nevertheless been transferred to the issue of terrorism portrayal. The results of studies supporting the views of terrorism researchers have been accepted in the face of conflicting evidence.

This has occurred despite the fact that studies on the effects of portrayals of violence and crime have yielded no cause-effect relationship. At best, it can be said that media portrayals do not cause the audience to become violent but *may* affect *some* media users who have antisocial tendencies and may spread uncertainty and fear among others.

While these violence research findings suggest reasonable hypotheses for terrorism research, no research along those lines has been conducted. Instead, what should only be hypotheses about media and terrorism have been accepted as fact.

Other fascinating pseudoscientific types of evidence offered in support of the notion that media are the contagion, reported in some of the most important sources on media and terrorism, are public opinion polls of political and law enforcement officials, as well as members of the public, about the relationship between media and terrorism.

While the polls present interesting insights into the perceptions of these individuals at given times, and add something to the understanding of how terrorism affects people, they are used by some writers as evidence that media are indeed the contagion of terrorism. Because the public and officials believe them to be the contagion, media must be the culprit, we are told.

Because the opinion of these groups of people is presumably affected by the agenda set by past statements of government officials, media critics, and terrorism control researchers—all of whom have repeatedly alleged the link between media and terrorism— it is not surprising that other officials and the public should parrot their views.

Despite such problems, the contagion argument is continually used against media. Rudolf Levy, a Defense Department expert on terrorism who has taught at the U.S. Army Intelligence Center and School, recently conveyed the media as contagion view throughout the military community in the publication *Military Intelligence*, saying that experts believe that this type of coverage often has adverse effects, such as:

- Encouraging the formation of new groups. Tactical successes and successful exploitation of the media lead to terrorists taking advantage of the momentum of previous actions and, thus, to an increase in terrorist acts.
- Keeping the terrorist organization's name before the public and "the masses" on whose behalf the terrorists supposedly act.
- Leading other less successful groups or individuals to commit more daring acts of terrorist violence.
- Tempting terrorists, who have received favorable media coverage in the past, to attempt to seize control of the media.[4]

A similar view has been expressed by the American Legal Foundation, a right-wing group that recently urged the government to restrict media coverage. The group argues that "because they give the terrorists a convenient stage to vent their political grievances, the media actually encourage terrorism and may promote the increasing violence and drama of terrorist attacks." [5]

Some of the most recognizable names in terrorism research are less sanguine about the accuracy of the contagion hypothesis, but they have nevertheless embraced and/or diffused it widely.

M. Cherif Bassiouni, who has written widely on the subject and taught many who are carrying on research and activities aimed at preventing or controlling political violence through legal means, recognizes the problems with the contagion idea but nevertheless does not reject it.

"Although this hypothesis would not appear entirely susceptible to empirical verification, at least with respect to ideologically motivated individuals, concern over this contagion effect has been repeatedly expressed, and the theory retains a certain intuitive reasonableness," he wrote.[6]

Other experts such as Alex Schmid and Janny de Graaf at the Centre for the Study of Social Conflicts in The Netherlands are willing to accept the contagion effect despite the lack of empirical evidence that it exists or that it would not exist if the media coverage were removed. Although admitting gaps in knowledge about the contagion effect they still argue:

> The most serious effect of media reporting on insurgent terrorism, however, is the likely increase in terroristic activities. The media can provide the potential terrorist with all the ingredients that are necessary to engage in this type of violence. They can reduce inhibitions against the use of violence, they can offer models and know-how to potential terrorists and they can motivate them in various ways.[7]

Robert L. Rabe, assistant chief of police for the Metropolitan Police Department in Washington, D.C., promoted the view that there may be value in the hypotheses as well. In his address at a terrorism conference, he stated:

> And what of the contagion of such detailed coverage of a terrorist incident? By glorifying terrorist activities with extensive news coverage, the event is projected as an attraction for others to emulate. If such is the case, terrorism has truly made the television media a pawn in the great game of propaganda.[8]

Even members of the media have accepted the contagion idea. NBC News President Larry Grossman recently presented that view in a more popular form to a Society of Professional Journalists' meeting.

"Does television allow itself to be 'used' by terrorists and does television coverage, therefore, encourage terrorist acts? The answer is yes to both," he said. "The very existence of television undoubtedly bears some responsibility for the 'copycat' syndrome of terrorism today." [9]

But not all terrorism scholars fully embrace the view. Brian Jenkins, director of the Rand Corporation's terrorism research, has argued that the media cannot be solely blamed for the spread of terrorism. "(T)he news media are responsible for terrorism to about the same extent that commercial aviation is responsible for airline hijackings," he says. "The vast communications network that makes up the news media is simply another vulnerability in a technologically advanced and free society. . . ." [10]

Rand Corporation studies have found some evidence of contagion in the diffusion process of terrorist activity types. Jenkins, although unwilling to completely damn news coverage as the culprit, has noted clusters of occurrences in airline hijackings and embassy sieges and indicated media *might* have played a role in those occurrences.[11] The inference, however, is based on no scientific evidence.

Other research on terrorism has noted that in the case of many airline hijackings in the 1970s, for example, terrorist hijackers often had specific knowledge of radio, navigation, and operating equipment on aircraft and of commercial aviation practices, suggesting they had specialized training and that extensive planning of campaigns of hijacking had occurred. These factors tend to indicate that some of the multiple hijackings were planned well in advance and that the "clustering" of hijackings may not necessarily be blamed on media coverage alone.

Diffusion Theory Possibilities

General conclusions that can be drawn from studies of diffusion of innovations in other situations do not provide much support for the view that media are crucial elements as a contagion. Mass media have been found to be best at assisting diffusion when combined with interpersonal channels and when used in reinforcing rather than persuasive roles. . . .

If one accepts general diffusion theory as having relevance to the spread of terrorism one would have to hypothesize that media may play a role in the awareness aspect of the adoption process of terrorism, but only a minor part—at best—in the evaluative, acceptance, and adoption portions of the diffusion of terrorist techniques.

Diffusion principles also provide a testable explanation for the increasing number of acts of political violence. Because they provide an established normal S-curve of cumulative adoption of innovations, researchers on terrorism could develop methods to analyze adoption of various techniques and practices to determine whether the adoption followed normal patterns or was unusual. . . .

The diffusion principles suggest hypotheses that are well suited for testing in the realm of terrorism, although no such studies exist today that add evidence to the discussion of media and terrorism.[12]

It is clear, then, that no causal link has been established using any acceptable social science research methods between media coverage and the spread of terrorism. Without such a link, media are being unjustifiably blamed for the increasing acts of violence throughout the world.

I do not wish to be interpreted, however, as taking the position that no link can ever be established, only that one cannot do so with the state of knowledge today.

The fact that media cannot be shown to be the contagion of terrorism does not exonerate it from excesses in coverage that have been shown to harm authorities' ability to cope with specific incidents of violence, have endangered the lives of victims and authorities, have been unduly sensational, and have spread fear among the public. For such errors in judgment and violations of existing industry standards, the offending media must bear the responsibility. One would hope that such problems will diminish as journalists become more acquainted with the techniques of terrorists and discuss the problems and implications of their coverage.

Coverage as a Preventative of Terrorism

If media cannot be shown as the cause of the spread of terrorism, can they be shown to be useful in preventing or reducing the scale of violence in terrorist attacks?

One important school of thought suggests coverage may actually reduce the possibility of future violent action on the part of those who engage in terroristic violence by removing the need for individuals and groups to resort to violence in order to gain coverage.

The view that some coverage may reduce terrorism is not held solely at the fringes of the terrorism research community, although it receives little support among the government officials and those to whom they most often turn for advice in combating terrorism.

Abraham H. Miller, who has written extensively on legal issues involving media during terrorist incidents, notes that major elements of the view: "If terrorism is a means of reaching the public forum, violence can be defused by providing accessibility to the media without the necessity of an entry fee of blood and agony," he writes.[13] Indeed, that was a conclusion reached at a conference on terrorism at Ditchley Castle in Oxfordshire, England, in 1978.

Another conclusion urging full, complete, and serious media coverage of such violence was reached by the Task Force on Terrorism and Disorders, which noted that

> The media can be most influential in setting the tone for a proper response by the civil authorities to disorders, acts of terrorism, and political violence. It can provide an outlet for the expression of legitimate public concern on important issues so as to act as a safety valve, and it can bring pressure to bear in response to public sentiment in an effective manner to redress grievances and to change official policies.[14]

The response to the problem of terrorism should be *more* not *less* news coverage, the task force argued: "The news media should devote more, rather than less, space and attention to the phenomena of extraordinary violence."[15] If such coverage avoids glamorizing the perpetrators of violence, provides reliable information, and gives appropriate emphasis to the consequences of violence, it will increase public understanding, reduce public fear, and assist in reducing violence, the report indicated.

These conclusions were reached by the task force despite the fact that it generally accepted a stimulus—response view of media effects. While admitting that no authoritative evidence directly linked media and violence, the group accepted the premises that media directly or indirectly influence potential perpetrators of violence and potential victims and that coverage of such violence affects the ability of authorities to respond. . . .

The provision-of-forums-as-a-means-of-combatting terrorism view holds that reasonable provision of forums in noncoerced environments may help reduce the frustration that leads to such violent acts and lead to an understanding of the issues or points of view of the dissidents.

Two psychologists who conduct research in the area of terrorism, Jeffrey Rubin of Tufts University and Nehemia Friedland of Tel Aviv University and the Project on Terrorism at the Jaffee Center for Strategic Studies, recently argued that governments should help provide access, which would be necessary in most nations where broadcasting is government operated or government related. The two argued:

> Governments should also try to reduce the destructiveness of terrorism by making it clear that a less dramatic performance will suffice to get the desired audience attention. . . . Imagine that Yasir Arafat or George Habash were to be invited to meet the press on Israeli television to express their views on what they consider to be political reality in the Middle East. Such an arrangement would provide these actors with the element of legitimacy they seek and would air issues without resorting to anything more violent than the savagery of the Israeli news media.[16]

As with most of the theories surrounding the role of media in terrorism, there is little supporting evidence—only intuition—bolstering this free-expression as-a-means-of-controlling-violence theory. The theory has merit and deserves to be studied closely, however, as do the principles from the diffusion approach.

Several possible studies come to mind here, including behavioral analyses of groups whose views have been carried by media without coercion. In recent times, IRA, Palestinian, Basque, Red Army Faction, and other groups have received platforms to express their views through interviews and other forums. A study of the behavior of these groups in the periods after their interviews would be enlightening. One would hypothesize that the behavior would become less spectacularly violent after the forums are provided—a hypothesis borne out by casual observation in the case of Yasir Arafat's supporters since international forums were provided the PLO in the 1970s.

It would appear to be inappropriate for journalists to interview members of groups taking part in terrorist acts while such acts are underway. This type of interview has occurred during the course of hijackings, building sieges, kidnappings, and other prolonged acts of terrorism.

Interviews under such conditions are a direct reward for the specific act of terrorism underway and can interfere with efforts to resolve the crisis. There is also some evidence that such coverage can prolong crises. In addition, such interviews all too often increase the spectacle of the event, spread fear, and provide a coerced platform for the views of the groups involved.

I do not believe, however, that interviews not conducted during a specific event need be treated in the same manner, despite protestations to the contrary by government officials. . . . If the coverage-as-a-preventative-measure theory is correct, such interviews should be helpful.

When such coverage is provided, however, journalists should not allow their media to become mere propaganda vehicles for those who engage in violence. Such occasions should be used as a means of exploring the causes and factors that led to violence, of discussing policy options, and of encouraging nonviolent alternatives. . . . [T]he journalist must truly *question* the interviewee, not merely provide a forum.

. . . The idea of opening media to alienated and disenfranchised persons and groups as a means of reducing violence seems preferable to nearly any other option for controlling violence, but the chances of the idea being widely accepted are very slim. The media themselves would be reluctant to do so out of fear of offending audiences and experiencing revenue losses, as well as fears of being accused of supporting terrorists. . . .

In addition, media are not likely to convey much information conflicting with the views of the government in the nation in which they operate or that is likely to create a conflict between the media and the government. . . .

Because there will be continuing terrorism in the years to come and no projected decline in such activity, there is great danger ahead for media in all nations that suffer from terrorist attacks. Movement toward restricting the flow of information through media is gaining momentum, backed by dubious studies couched in the scientific jargon of the social sciences. Most officials and members of the public do not know enough to be able to question that evidence.

Those of us in the social sciences who appreciate and understand the contributions of media to society have a duty to help the public and officials part the veil of ignorance that shrouds the subject of terrorism and the media. . . . [W]e do need to set out to find out just what the reality is. I suspect we will find that the media are a contributing factor in the spread of terrorism, just as easy international transportation, the easy availability of weapons and explosives, the intransigence of some governments' policies, the provision of funds to terrorists by a variety of supportive governments, and a host of other factors are to blame.

Whatever the results of our research, it will move us closer to reality than the views offered by those who argue that the media are wholly at fault and those who argue that the media are blameless. The resulting knowledge will make it less likely that governments will act precipitously to control media coverage and that journalists will gain a better understanding of terrorism that will leave them less open to manipulation and more aware of the consequences of their actions.

Notes

1. Peter J. Boyer, "Arab's Interview Stirs News Debate," *New York Times*, May 7, 1986, p. A7.
2. Joel Bellman, "BBC: Clearing the Air," *The Journalist*, January 1986, p. 20.
3. "Thatcher urges the Press to Help 'Starve' Terrorists," *New York Times*, July 16, 1985, p. A3.
4. Rudolf Levy, "Terrorism and the Mass Media," *Military Intelligence*, October-December, 1985, p. 35.
5. *Terrorism and the Media* (Washington, D.C.: American Legal Foundation), p. 24.
6. M. Cherif Bassiouni, "Problems of Media Coverage of Nonstate-Sponsored Terror-Violence Incidents," in Lawrence Z. Freedman and Yonah Alexander, eds., *Perspectives on Terrorism* (Wilmington, DE: Scholarly Resources, 1983), p. 184.
7. Alex P. Schmid and Janny de Graaf, *Violence as Communication: Insurgent Terrorism and the Western News Media* (Beverly Hills, CA: Sage Publications, 1982), p. 142.
8. Robert L. Rabe in Yonah Alexander and Seymour M. Finger, eds., "Terrorism and the Media," *Terrorism*, 1979, p. 69.
9. Larry Grossman, "The Face of Terrorism," *The Quill*, June 1986, p. 38.
10. Quoted in Schmid and de Graaf, op. cit., p. 143.
11. Brian M. Jenkins, "The Psychological Implications of Media-Covered Terrorism," *The Rand Paper Series* P-6627, June 1981.
12. An excellent volume drawing together the results of hundreds of diffusion studies throughout the world is Everett M. Rogers, *Communication of Innovations: A Cross-Cultural Approach*, 3rd ed. (New York: Free Press, 1983).

13. Abraham H. Miller, *Terrorism: The Media and the Law* (Dobbs Ferry, NY: Transnational Publishers, 1982), p. 24.
14. National Advisory Committee on Criminal Justice Standards and Goals, *Disorders and Terrorism: Report of the Task Force on Disorders and Terrorism* (Washington, D.C.: Law Enforcement Assistance Administration, 1977), p. 65.
15. Ibid., p. 368.
16. Jeffrey Z. Rubin and Nehemia Friedland, "Theater of Terror," *Psychology Today*, March 1986, p. 28.

5.4 ▆▆▆▆▆

The Impact of Investigative Reporting on Public Opinion and Policymaking: Targeting Toxic Waste

David L. Protess, Fay Lomax Cook, Thomas R. Curtin, Margaret T. Gordon, Donna R. Leff, Maxwell E. McCombs, and Peter Miller

Editor's Note. The case presented in this selection is part of a continuing series of studies that analyze the impact of investigative news stories on public policy, policy makers, and the general public. Through close ties with the media, the authors knew when investigative stories would be published. This enabled them to measure audience attitudes before as well as after the stories appeared. Some case studies revealed that the investigative stories had substantial influence on public policies; others did not. Comparison of the types of effects that were produced, as well as those that did not materialize, permits the authors to theorize about the conditions under which investigative stories influence public opinion and policy agendas.

Although many aspects of the cause and effect sequence remain to be clarified, one thing is clear: it is not true, as traditionally believed, that investigative journalism works primarily by mobilizing public opinion, which then pressures public officials to act. Instead, effects were produced most consistently when reporters and policy makers collaborated to produce policy changes. Unambiguous reports about new issues, which surfaced for a limited time only, were most likely to produce policy responses.

Maxwell E. McCombs is professor and chairman of the Department of Journalism at the University of Texas at Austin. All other authors are affiliated with Northwestern University's Center for Urban Affairs and Policy Research, then directed by Professor Margaret T. Gordon. David L. Protess and Donna R. Leff are also associate professors of journalism in the Medill School of Journalism; Fay Lomax Cook is associate professor in the School of Education, Peter Miller is associate professor in the School of Speech, and Thomas R. Curtin is a doctoral student in the School of Education. The selection comes from "The Impact of Investigative Reporting on Public Opinion and Policymaking: Targeting Toxic Waste," *Public Opinion Quarterly* 51 (1987): 166-185. Several tables have been omitted.

From *Public Opinion Quarterly* 51 (1987): 166-185. Reprinted by permission of The University of Chicago Press.

This article reports the fourth in a series of field experiments that test the agenda-setting hypothesis (McCombs and Shaw, 1972) for news media investigative reports. Our goal is to treat these field experiments as case studies from which we can develop empirically grounded theory that specifies the conditions under which investigative reports influence public agendas and policy-making priorities. Unique to studies of agenda-setting is our use of pretest-posttest research designs, made possible by journalists' disclosure of forthcoming investigative stories to the research team with adequate time for pre- and postpublication survey interviewing. A further distinctive feature is our concern with detailed tracing of the life course of a media report from an examination of the initial investigation by journalists, to the publication of the report, the effects on the general public and policymakers, and eventual policy outcomes.

The first of these studies (Cook et al., 1983) found that a nationally televised investigative news report on fraud and abuse in the federally funded home health care program had significant effects on the agendas of both the public and policymakers. The study found that home health care-related issues (and not unrelated issues) became significantly more important to citizens and policymakers exposed to the televised report than to nonviewers. Yet, actual policy changes after the report's publication resulted more from direct pressure for change by the journalists themselves than from demands by the general public or political constituencies.

The second study (Protess et al., 1985) measured the impact of a *Chicago Sun-Times* investigative series disclosing government improprieties in the reporting and handling of rape against Chicago area women. The effects of the newspaper series were considerably more limited than in the first study, in part because the pretest disclosed an already high level of awareness and concern about the problem. The most striking result was a sharp increase in the number, length, and prominence of stories about rape in the *Sun-Times*—that is, the largest measurable effect was on the medium itself rather than on its audience. However, as in the home health care study, policymaking effects included legislative hearings and related "symbolic" political actions (Edelman, 1964).[1]

The effects of the third investigative report, a five-part local television series about repeatedly brutal Chicago police officers, provided an "in-between" case (Leff, Protess, and Brooks, 1986). The series had significant effects on viewer attitudes about police brutality but not on their assessment of the priority or salience of the problem in comparison with other social concerns. Nonetheless, the series resulted in major policy changes within the Chicago Police Department, in part because its publication coincided with a hotly contested Chicago mayoral election in which mayoral challenger Harold Washington used the series to help make the Department an issue.

Why is it that some investigative reports "catch on" and affect the views of members of the public and policy elites, while others do not? Why is it that all three investigative reports had some form of policy impact, despite the fact that they did not all have effects on the public and policymakers? In answer to the first question, several explanations have tentatively been suggested in our earlier work: the nature of the medium of presentation (print versus television); the style of presentation (unambiguous, with clear villains and heroes, versus ambiguous, where fault is not clear and where solutions seem difficult to find); the "age" of the issue on the media's agenda (a new issue that has infrequently been presented in the past and about which the public has little knowledge versus an old issue that has recurred over time on the media's agenda and about which the public is aware).

None of these explanations provides a possible answer to the second question concerning the investigative reports' impact on policy. Regardless of the above factors, some form of policy impact occurred in all the cases we have examined to date. In the home health care and rape cases, the impact was symbolic with legislative hearings and proposals for policy changes. In the police brutality case, the impact was substantive with actual, major policy changes occurring. Clearly, more case studies are needed before we can develop an empirically grounded theory that specifies under what conditions and with what kinds of issues media investigations influence public agendas and policymaking processes.

The current study examines the public opinion and policymaking impact of a local television investigative series concerning the toxic waste disposal practices of a major Chicago university. In this case, the publication format was virtually identical to the earlier police brutality study; a multipart television report, aired during a "ratings sweeps" period, by the same correspondent on the same local television station. Further, one of the primary "targets" of the series was also a city regulatory agency, the Chicago Fire Department, which was accused of failing to enforce its environmental safety regulations. However, here we examine a different kind of issue—i.e., toxic waste disposal—at a different point in the city's political history—i.e., a year into Mayor Harold Washington's first term, when he was locked in a struggle with the City Council over control of Chicago's city government.

This article first will discuss the attitudinal impact of the toxic waste series on the general public and policy elites. Next, we trace the effects of the series on public policymaking in Chicago, focusing on the Fire Department's response to disclosures about its shortcomings. Finally, we analyze the findings of the four studies and try to identify and explain emerging patterns.

Research Design

The pretest, posttest experimental design is highly appropriate, but not traditionally utilized, in research involving nonlaboratory studies of media effects (Cook and Campbell, 1979). More typical in such research endeavors is the use of cross-sectional (McCombs and Shaw, 1972; McLeod, Becker, and Byrnes, 1974; Erbring, Goldenberg, and Miller, 1980) or panel study designs (Tipton, Haney, and Baseheart, 1975; Shaw and McCombs, 1977; MacKuen, 1981). In this study, however, two factors made field experimentation practicable: the reporters' cooperation with researchers and the lengthy preparation time of the report, which made advance planning by the researchers possible. Thus, researchers were able to obtain prepublication measurements of public and policymaker attitudes about the precise subject matter of the forthcoming television series. Survey questions about unrelated matters were used to obtain control data.

The resulting television series, "Wasted Time," was broadcast on three successive nights beginning 13 May 1984 on WMAQ-TV, Channel 5, a Chicago-based station owned and operated by the National Broadcasting Company (NBC). The reporter was Peter Karl, a well-known local investigative journalist who also served as correspondent on the police brutality series that was the subject of our third study. The series was promoted heavily by the television station, since it was broadcast in the middle of a highly important ratings period.

The series disclosed that the University of Chicago was storing potentially hazardous toxic chemical and radioactive wastes beneath several of its buildings, including some classrooms. Stories alleged that the storage violated Chicago Fire Department regulations, as well as the environmental standards of several state and federal agencies, including the U.S. Environmental Protection Agency (EPA), the U.S. Occupational Safety and Health Administration (OSHA), and the U.S. Department of Energy. Each night, the broadcast described an assortment of delays by the University in constructing relatively inexpensive facilities to ameliorate the waste disposal problem, thus giving the investigative report its title "Wasted Time." At no time did the series state that anyone at the University was in immediate danger, but the use of pictures of chemical explosions and fires that had occurred on the campus a decade earlier suggested the potential harm involved. One implication of the series was that the violations would not have persisted over time if certain federal, state, and local agencies were doing their jobs properly (i.e., the EPA, OSHA, the U.S. Department of Energy and the Chicago Fire Department).

General Public

Through random-digit dialing techniques, 395 respondents from the Chicago Metropolitan area were contacted two weeks before the television series aired. . . .

The telephone sample was then stratified by the respondents' self-reported television viewing habits into regular watchers of Channel 5 news (N = 208), and watchers of other evening newscasts or nonwatchers of any television news (N = 186). We expected that Channel 5 newswatchers were likely to be exposed to the investigative series, while others would constitute a quasi-experimental comparison group. One week after the broadcast of the series, researchers recontacted the entire sample. . . . 235 persons agreed to be reinterviewed, comprising the general public sample in this study. The respondents in this sample, though proportionately more female than the pretest respondents, did not differ significantly in educational level, age, or ethnic or racial background from the individuals who refused to be reinterviewed or who could not be recontacted after the pretest.

Since general viewing habits are not perfect predictors of the public's actual *exposure* to a specific television series, respondents were asked at the conclusion of the posttest interview whether they had "seen, read, or heard anything about recent news media investigative stories about toxic waste disposal problems at the University of Chicago." Follow-up questions were then asked about the source and extent of the exposure. Those responding "yes" to the question were considered "series-aware" group members, while those responding "no" were defined as a comparison group. Respondents in these two groups did not differ significantly in gender, educational level, age, or ethnic or racial background. . . .

To avoid sensitizing respondents to the subject of the investigative series, researchers embedded questions related to toxic waste disposal and other environmental problems among questions about crime, unemployment, police brutality, child abuse, and governmental corruption. Of the forty separate items in the questionnaire, twelve were related to general environmental issues and six to chemical or radioactive waste disposal problems. We hypothesized that change would occur among the Channel 5 viewers on questions about the environment and toxic waste, while responses to other questions would remain constant from pre- to posttest. We expected the comparison groups' responses to remain constant on all questions. . . .

Policymakers and Policymaking

A purposive sample of forty policy elites was selected for their interest and potential influence on environmental policymaking. Those surveyed included public administrators from Illinois and federal environmental protection agencies, state legislators, members of the Chicago City Council, University officials, and lobbyists from public interest groups and private waste disposal companies. Persons who were considered likely to know about the investigative series prior to pretest interviewing were excluded from the sample. Interviews were conducted by telephone; 31 of the 40 respondents were reinterviewed after the television broadcast.

As in our previous studies, we made no attempt to establish a group of nonexposed elite respondents. We expected that persons with significant interest in the subject of an investigative report would almost certainly hear about it, even if they failed to view the particular stories. Indeed, 23 of the 31 respondents indicated in posttest interviews that they "saw, read, or heard" something about the series. Statistical analyses were performed on the self-defined "exposed" and "unexposed" groups.

The policymakers were asked a series of questions that were identical to those in the survey of the general public. The questions included items both related and unrelated to the subject of the investigative series. In addition, the elite respondents were asked about their past, present, and anticipated future policymaking activities related to toxic waste disposal problems.

After the series, researchers tracked policy developments that might be attributable to the Channel 5 investigation by interviewing an expanded sample of policymakers and conducting analyses of related budgets, legislation, and regulatory and administrative initiatives. Content analyses of local media coverage of environmental issues were also performed both as an additional indicator of the level of governmental response to the series and as a measure of its impact on the news media's agendas.

Impact of the Investigative Report on the General Public

In examining public attitudes before and after the broadcast of the Channel 5 investigation, we wanted to determine whether changes occurred on questionnaire items related to the subject of the series. To test whether the changes between the pretest and posttest were different for the exposed group from the nonexposed group, we used analysis of covariance (ANCOVA), employing the pretest score as the covariate. . . .

The data show no effects of the series, as measured by the ANCOVA analysis. Some items bordered on significant change, however, giving slight indications of change in perception due to the series. In particular, compared to those unaware of the series, those exposed to the reports were slightly more likely to say that environmental news stories cause confusion. Both series-aware and unaware respondents reported worrying somewhat less about improper storage and disposal of chemical waste at the posttest. Both groups of respondents tended to decrease their evaluation of the Chicago Fire Department, which suggests that other stimuli produced a small judgmental change. Evaluation of environmental agencies other than the Fire Department remained constant, as did measures of respondent's behavior concerning environmental problems.

In short, the agenda-setting hypothesis was not supported by the findings. Responses to questions about the importance of toxic waste disposal in relation to other issues did not change significantly. In comparison with other problems, toxic chemical and radioactive waste disposal was consistently at or near the bottom of their reported agendas.

Impact of the Investigative Report on Policymakers and Policymaking

... [T]he mean responses of policymakers to the surveys before and after the investigative report ... indicate stronger support for the hypotheses than do the survey results for the general public.

Policy elites were asked to evaluate the performance of eleven government agencies. We expected that the investigative report would result in policy elites' lowering their assessments of the jobs done by four agencies—the Chicago Fire Department, the U.S. Department of Energy, the EPA, and OSHA. The changes were statistically significant ($p < .05$) for the performance evaluations of three of the four government agencies targeted by Channel 5 as bearing responsibility for the problems disclosed. Change in the evaluation of the fourth agency, the Chicago Fire Department, was in the expected downward direction ($p < .10$). Change was also significant for one of the seven unrelated agencies added as controls—the U.S. Social Security Commission—but this appears to be a chance change by the unexposed policy elites whose evaluations increased to more positive ones while the series-exposed elites' evaluations did not change.

Marked changes also occurred on one of the questions designed to measure the behavior of policymakers. When asked, "In the coming months, how much of your time do you think *will* be spent on toxic waste disposal problems?" the group exposed to the series changed significantly in the direction of "more" time. This finding is consistent with our analysis of the actual policymaking consequences of the investigative series. Since the series aired, each of the governmental agencies named by Channel 5 initiated actions to monitor the University's compliance with toxic waste disposal regulations.

Perhaps the most dramatic of these enforcement efforts was made by the Chicago Fire Department. On the morning after the first broadcast, a team of high-ranking Department officials inspected the buildings where chemical wastes were stored, and cited the University for failing to comply with 20 of the City's safety regulations. The Department gave the University 30 days to comply with its standards and threatened publicly to initiate criminal proceedings if it failed to do so.

Media coverage of the Fire Department's initiative was swift. A *Chicago Tribune* headline in newspaper's next edition read: "City Faults U of C on Fire Safety," and the *Sun-Times* reported that the "U of C Is Cited as Fire Violator." The *Hyde Park Herald*, a weekly newspaper serving the community surrounding the University, headlined: "UC Responds to Hazard Charge" and called editorially for a study of the problem. All three newspapers credited the Channel 5 investigation as the catalyst for the governmental actions.

Channel 5 itself reported the "Fire Department crackdown" on its evening newscast later the same day. (The station's television competitors ignored the story, however.) Pictures of the Department's inspections were shown, and the story was repeated in the remaining two segments of the investigative series. The television station claimed that the action was taken "in response to our series on hazardous waste disposal problems at the University." In fact, however, Channel 5 correspondent Peter Karl had discussed the possibility of an inspection in several telephone conversations with Fire Department officials two days *before* the first part of the series was aired. The officials had agreed both that the inspection would occur and that it would not take place until the morning *after* the airing of the initial broadcast. Channel 5, in turn, covered the inspection as if it occurred at the initiative of the Fire Department, i.e., without direct prodding by its investigative reporter.

This form of journalist-policymaker collaboration has been described in our earlier studies (Cook et al., 1983; Molotch, Protess, and Gordon, 1987). What is significant here is that general public and policymaker respondents were exposed to news media stories about governmental "reforms" before the allegations in Channel 5's three-part series had been completely aired. Thus, the public's perceptions of the series may have been colored somewhat by media reports that included the presentation of both a problem and its "solution."

Interviews by researchers with Fire Department officials at the end of the 30-day compliance period indicated that the University had, in fact, corrected the fire hazard aspect of its waste disposal problem. The University also was implementing plans for the much-delayed facility to provide a more permanent solution to its environmental difficulties. However, content analyses of Channel 5 and other media revealed that the media did not cover these *post*series developments. Unlike our study of the *Sun-Times* rape series, the issues of toxic waste disposal at the University of Chicago or elsewhere did not rise on the news media's agenda of concerns. Content analysis of the *Chicago Tribune* for 3-month periods both before and after the publication of the Channel 5 series showed a slight *decline* in column inches of news stories and editorials on toxic waste disposal problems. A review of the assignment log at Channel 5 for the same periods showed only a minor increase in the frequency of such stories.

. . . Similarly, policymakers' assessments of the importance of toxic waste disposal as an issue did not change significantly after the broadcast of the series. Perhaps this was because by the end of the series and the time of the posttest interview, the problems were being eliminated. There is no indication that the series produced any substantive initiatives (i.e., legislative, regulative, or budgetary) to deal with larger questions of toxic waste disposal, either on college campuses or elsewhere in the U.S. society. Thus, we call its policy impact "individualistic" because it was specific only to the particular problem documented at the University of Chicago.

Discussion of Findings

With the completion of this fourth study, we are somewhat better able to compare the varying impacts of the different investigative reports. Table 1 summarizes the results of the four case studies. Both the home health care broadcast and the police brutality television series were found to have greater *public* impact than either the toxic waste or the rape series. Nonetheless, like the police brutality series, the toxic waste investigation resulted in significant changes in the attitudes and actions of *policymakers*. The policymaking impact of the current case is the most focused. It appears to be attributable more to journalistic lobbying with Fire Department officials than to published investigative reports themselves. This is similar to the developments that occurred in the home health care investigation, where we found that it was not the members of the public who were so aroused by the report that they pressured their representatives to act. Rather, it was the active collaboration between journalists and policymakers during the prepublication phase of investigation that generated the policy outcome. In the two other cases that we studied, no such collaboration occurred, but policy changes nonetheless resulted.

What factors account for these similarities and differences? This question probably has a different answer depending on the target of impact that one wishes to understand—on the public, on elites, or on policy itself. For public attitudes to change, two factors seem to be important—the nature of the media portrayal and the frequency of attention by the media to the issue in the past. When the media portray an issue in an unambiguous way with dramatic, convincing, and clear evidence, public attitudes are more likely to change (see also Tyler and Cook, 1984:706). For example, the police brutality series documented the seriousness of the problem thoroughly, including a statistical analysis of

Table 1 Summary of Four Case Study Findings of the Impact of Investigative Reports on the Public, Policy Elites, and Policy

Subject of Case Study	Medium	Format	Journalists' involvement with policymakers	General public impact	Elite impact	Policymaking impact
1. Home health care fraud and abuse ("The Home Health Hustle")	Network television	Single report	Extensive	Yes	Yes	Yes (symbolic)
2. Assaults against women ("Rape: Every Woman's Nightmare")	Local newspaper	5-part series	Minimal	No	No	Yes (symbolic)
3. Police brutality ("Beating Justice")	Local television	5-part series	Minimal	Yes	No	Yes (substantive)
4. Toxic waste disposal ("Wasted Time")	Local television	3-part series	Extensive	No	Yes	Yes (individualistic)

brutality cases against the police and a 5-year review of all lawsuits filed against police in federal courts in Chicago. Its interviews with brutalized victims and action shots of identified "villains" made for powerful drama. In all these respects, the series was most similar to the home health care television report. Both investigations had significant impacts on the public.

On the other hand, like the *Sun-Times* rape series, Channel 5's "Wasted Time" investigation was stylistically ambiguous. Villains and victims were not well-defined. Rather, the television station attributed the problem to "bureaucratic delays," not venal conduct. The harm alleged was more *potential* than actual, and the presentation of the findings contained frequent exceptions and caveats. For example, the second part of the series began with the statement by correspondent Karl that "this is not a scare story of radioactive contamination on the campus of the University of Chicago."

Moreover, the edge of the toxic waste series' potential impact may have been dulled by the simultaneous presentation of problems and their solution, which created the impression that the danger was under control. The repeated mention that a permanent solution would result from the University's construction of an inexpensive facility (which had already been planned) further circumscribed the scope of the problem.

The equivocal nature of the presentation may help to explain why there was a tendency for posttest anxiety about the problem to be reduced. It may also help to explain why respondents in the exposed groups were somewhat more likely to be " 'confused' [about] news stories about environmental problems, like chemical or toxic wastes.... " In sum, the actual importance or seriousness of a problem may be less significant for influencing public attitudes than its "mediated reality" (Nimmo and Combs, 1983).

The second factor that seems important for influencing general public attitudes is the nature of the issue that the media are addressing. Certain issues receive fairly consistent treatment by journalists. Their place on the news media's agenda of interests may be higher or lower at different times, but they regularly tend to be the object of reportorial scrutiny. Examples include news about crime, governmental waste and corruption, and corporate windfall profit making. Borrowing from terminology used in a somewhat different context, we call these topics "recurring issues" in the news (Walker, 1977). Investigative stories about recurring issues have lower impact potential. Media effects are limited by the routine discussion of such issues in news stories, creating an information blur that may obscure the transmission of even unique disclosures. Further, as information is accumulated about a particular issue over time, the effect of subsequent communication tends to diminish (Saltiel and Woelfel, 1975; Downs, 1972). Thus, the impact of investigative reports about rape, toxic waste, and police brutality in Chicago may have been circumscribed by their appearance in the midst of a recurring stream of news events on these subjects.

On the other hand, issues that become subject to breakthrough news reports have a greater opportunity to produce effects. The home health care report provides an example of a "nonrecurring issue" in the news, one that has received infrequent or no prior attention from journalists. Investigative news stories about such issues have higher impact potential because they reveal matters that may be relatively unknown before their publication. The public's lack of accumulated information on these issues may increase its susceptibility to investigative media messages (Cook et al., 1983), although the effects may not be long-lasting (Watt and van den Berg, 1981; Saltiel and Woelfel, 1975; Downs, 1972).

We would suggest that news media investigative reports with the maximum ability to produce attitude change are those that involve unambiguous presentations of nonrecurring issues. This may explain why the home health care investigation, which spotlighted an "undiscovered" problem by showing greedy agency directors victimizing the elderly and handicapped, had the strongest public impact of the four case studies. Conversely, ambiguously presented reports on recurring issues, like the rape series and toxic waste investigation, have the least opportunity to change public attitudes. . . .

Explanations for the effects of news media investigations on policy elites and on policy are more complex and less well understood. Two of the four cases showed effects on elites, and in all four cases, policymaking effects occurred. A review of the four case studies suggests that many factors may influence the nature and extent of governmental responses to investigative reporting. These factors include the timing of the publication in relation to political exigencies, the extent of journalistic collaboration with policymakers, the level of general public and interest group pressures, and the availability of cost-effective solutions to the problems disclosed.

In the toxic waste series, the proximate cause of the initial governmental response was the involvement in the policymaking process of the Channel 5 correspondent. The level of involvement was sufficient to prompt an immediate effort to correct the specific problem at the University of Chicago. Likewise in the home health care case, the policy impact (legislation hearings and proposals for change) resulted from the active collaboration between journalists and policymakers (i.e., high-level staff members of the Senate Permanent Investigations Subcommittee).

In the other two cases, journalists did not orchestrate the policy impacts. In the rape study, we found that the series provided a platform for those already pushing for reform of rape legislation. Policymakers who already had proposals and programs to recommend before the series made their announcements soon after publication of the series, using the investigative report as a backdrop for their announcements.

In the police brutality study, the series also provided a platform but in a different way from that described above. The investigative report's results were used by Chicago mayoral challenger Harold Washington as ammunition against incumbent Mayor Jane Byrne, who had appointed the police superintendent. When elected, Washington was responsible for many of the policy changes in the police department.

Do investigative reports always result in some form of policy response? Investigative reports uncover problems in the social fabric of society. Officials directly responsible for the particular domain in which a problem is uncovered may feel obligated to take some action to show they are "responsive" and "responsible." Since our cases are small in number and are not necessarily representative of all investigative reports, we cannot generalize. However, the results to date suggest that investigative reports may have more influence than previously thought. The evidence that such reports present about social conditions serves to put policymakers on the defensive. They must either attempt to justify the problem or act to solve it. Actions—symbolic, individualistic, or substantive—are the responses seen in the cases analyzed here.

Note

1. Symbolic acts have been described as "dramatic in outline and empty of realistic detail" (Edelman, 1964:9). Here we use the term to describe policy "changes" that are largely rhetorical. Thus, when a public official responds to a media exposé by making speeches about the problem, by convening governmental hearings, or by announcing as news previously approved legislation, we call these acts symbolic. Conversely, "substantive" reforms are tangible regulatory, legislative, or administrative changes that occur after an investigative story is published. In making this distinction, we do not mean to suggest that substantive reforms are necessarily more likely than symbolic reforms to lead in the long run to the *correction* of the problem disclosed by the media.

References

Cook, F. L., T. R. Tyler, E. G. Goetz, M. T. Gordon, D. Leff, and H. L. Molotch (1983). "Media and agenda-setting: Effects on the public, interest group leaders, policy makers, and policy." *Public Opinion Quarterly* 47:16-35.

Cook, T. D., and D. T. Campbell 1979). *Quasi-Experimentation: Design and Analysis Issues for Field Settings.* Chicago: Rand McNally.

Downs, A. (1972). "Up and down with ecology: The 'issue attention cycle.'" *Public Interest* 28:38-50.

Edelman, M. (1964). *The Symbolic Uses of Politics.* Urbana: University of Illinois Press.

Erbring, L., E. Goldenberg, and A. Miller (1980). "Front-page news and real-world cues: A new look at agenda-setting by the media." *American Journal of Political Science* 24:16-49.

Leff, D., D. Protess, and S. Brooks (1986). "Changing public attitudes and policymaking agendas." *Public Opinion Quarterly* 50:300-314.

MacKuen, M. B. (1981). "Social communication and the mass policy agenda." In M. B. MacKuen and S. L. Coombs, *More Than News; Media Power in Public Affairs.* Beverly Hills: Sage.

McCombs, M., and D. L. Shaw (1972). "The agenda-setting functions of the mass media." *Public Opinion Quarterly* 36:176-187.

McLeod, J. M., L. B. Becker, and J. E. Byrnes (1974). "Another look at the agenda-setting function of the press." *Communication Research* 1:131-166.

Molotch, H., D. Protess, and M. T. Gordon (1987). "The media-policy connection: Ecologies of news." In D. Paletz (ed.), *Political Communication: Theories, Cases, and Assessments.* New Jersey: Ablex.

Nimmo, D., and J. Combs (1983). *Mediated Political Realities.* New York: Longman.

Protess, D. L., D. R. Leff, S. C. Brooks, and M. T. Gordon (1985). "Uncovering Rape: The watchdog press and the limits of agenda-setting." *Public Opinion Quarterly* 49:19-37.

Saltiel, J., and J. Woelfel (1975). "Inertia in cognitive processes: The role of accumulated information in attitude change." *Human Communication Research* 1:333-344.

Shaw, D. L., and M. E. McCombs (eds.) (1977). *The Emergence of American Political Issues: The Agenda-Setting Function of the Press.* St. Paul: West Publishing Company.

Tipton, L., R. Haney, and J. Baseheart (1975). "Media agenda-setting in city and state election campaigns." *Journalism Quarterly* 52:15-22.

Tyler, T. R., and F. L. Cook (1984). "The mass media and judgments of risk: Distinguishing impact on personal and societal level judgments." *Journal of Personality and Social Psychology* 47:693-708.

Walker, J. L. (1977). "Setting the agenda in the U.S. Senate: A theory of problem selection." *British Journal of Political Science* 7:423-445.

Watt, J. H., Jr., and S. van den Berg (1981). "How time dependency influences media effects in a community controversy." *Journalism Quarterly* 58:43-50.

5.5 ▬▬

Reporters and Congressmen: Living in Symbiosis

Susan Heilmann Miller

Editor's Note. Conflict usually makes more exciting news than cooperation. But not always. Susan Heilmann Miller's essay presents a case study of
close cooperation between a member of Congress and reporters who worked
together so that each could achieve a major purpose. The member needed
publicity for the problems of several constituents to arouse pressure for
congressional hearings that might lead to action by the executive branch.
The reporters were eager for tip-offs on governmental wrongdoing so that
they could write exciting investigative stories and claim credit for engender-
ing appropriate remedies. Ultimately, through a combination of luck and
clever planning, the venture attracted substantial attention from television.
With wide media coverage the barrier of obscurity was broken, and this
along with several other favorable factors put the issue on the congressional
agenda.

 The data for the case study come from interviews conducted in 1975
with sixty-five reporters from newspapers, news magazines, television, and
news services; twenty-five members of Congress; ninety-seven congressional
aides; and five other observers. The author also monitored relevant congressional hearings as well as media coverage of the story in the *Washington
Post*, the *Los Angeles Times*, the *Chicago Tribune*, and the *New Orleans
Times-Picayune*.

 Miller is a Stanford Ph.D. who has applied her journalism training by
working for newspapers and journalism publications. This essay is excerpted
from her doctoral dissertation,"Congress and the News Media." The selection is reprinted from *Journalism Monographs*, no. 53 (January 1978).

 A good example of the extent to which cooperation [between
members of Congress and reporters] can be carried was an investigation
that eventually led to a series of hearings on the plight of U.S. citizens
serving time in Mexican jails.

From Susan Heilmann Miller, "Reporters and Congressmen: Living in Symbiosis," *Journalism
Monographs* No. 53 (January 1978). Reprinted by permission of the Association for Education in
Journalism and Mass Communication.

It began with a letter that arrived in the Washington office of California Congressman Fortney "Pete" Stark in the spring of 1974. The letter, from the family of an American being held in a Mexican jail, told of torture and extortion, and charged that personnel at the U.S. embassy in Mexico City had been less than responsive about investigating the situation. . . .

David Julyan, at that time a special assistant to Congressman Stark, told the families he would look into the matter, and he soon found other families with similar complaints. Prisoners were expected to pay for food, showers and toilet paper, costing up to $100 per month, and there was also an initial "lodging" fee of $800 to $2,000. All prisoners had to pay, but the fees for Americans appeared to be higher. Some families had also been victimized by lawyers who promised reduced or suspended sentences and then absconded with thousands of dollars more. Some prisoners said they had been sexually abused, tortured, forced to sign confessions they didn't understand, and otherwise denied legal rights and due process as provided by Mexican law and international accords. . . .

Once Stark decided to take on the prisoners' cause, the challenge was to gather enough information to demonstrate the need for a Congressional inquiry. As a junior member of Congress, Stark didn't have chairmanship of a committee with proper jurisdiction. He would have to convince his Congressional colleagues that the topic warranted their attention. The best way to do this, in the minds of Stark and his staff, was to collaborate with an investigative reporter. Stark explained, "We've done other things that way, too. . . . You go to an investigative reporter if you think he'll put some effort into it. . . . Sometimes you play boy editor—try to guess where a story fits, and who might be interested in it."

In this case, the obvious first choice was the Washington bureau of the Los Angeles *Times*. First of all, many of the families of prisoners lived in Southern California. The *Times* has a solid national reputation for investigative reporting. The news service it provides jointly with the Washington *Post* reaches hundreds of newspapers all over the country. Hundreds of copies of the *Times* itself are flown in each day from Los Angeles for distribution to Washington officialdom. Furthermore, the Washington bureau makes a point of staying in close contact with the entire California delegation. . . .

. . . [B]ureau chief Jack Nelson was available—and interested. . . . He and Julyan struck a bargain. As Julyan explained, "I said we'd like to share the story with them if they'd agree to go big. . . . Or, if they didn't go, we wanted their word they'd not disclose anything if they decided to drop it." There was also a confidentiality clause. . . .

Nelson looked at what they had, and liked it. He notified *Times* editors in Los Angeles, and they agreed to put both a reporter in Los Angeles and the *Times* reporter in Mexico City on the story. . . .

Pete Stark pointed out that a big advantage of working with the Los Angeles *Times* was that the paper had a reporter based in Mexico City. "It wasn't feasible for us to go to Mexico at that time," he said, adding, "One of our big concerns at that point was: What if we're wrong? What if these people are making up this stuff? We'd look pretty silly. The information from the Los Angeles *Times* was our first independent, unbiased review, and verified that the problems were real."

Nelson added that there were advantages to the *Times* to working with Stark.

> They had a lot of information volunteered to them—because they were part of Congress—that probably wouldn't have been volunteered to us, or that we would have had to work so hard to get that it wouldn't have been worthwhile. We wouldn't have had the time or the resources to pursue the story without their information. People were less reluctant to talk to them than they would have been to talk to a reporter. On the other hand, I interviewed the head of DEA [Drug Enforcement Agency] and got information and things they had no way to get—or, they wouldn't have gotten the same reaction, because we're reporters and they aren't.

In summary, each side had certain sources, skills or assets that the other lacked. By putting their heads and their information together, the Los Angeles *Times* and Stark's staff were able to come up with a more complete picture than either could have gotten on its own.

The cooperation went even further than the sharing of information and sources. Julyan and Nelson also coordinated the timing of the release of their information. There was nothing in the press from mid-September to the first week in December. Both were working as quietly as possible until there were enough data for Congressman Stark to make public allegations about embassy insensitivity and perhaps criminal culpability to support his call for a thorough investigation, plus enough data for a six-part series in the Los Angeles *Times*. Just as the series began to appear, Stark released a copy of a letter he had sent to President Ford and Secretary of State Kissinger, outlining the situation, and suggesting a course of action. The *Times* ran a separate story about Stark's letter on the second day of the series.

Explained Julyan, "Of course they knew it was being written, and when it would be released. We wanted to feed one off the other. It was a good handle for a story for them, and it was good for us to get the publicity for our letter and for the issue." He added, "It was a natural outgrowth of the confidence and cooperation built up over that eight-week period that we plan the timing. Besides, we had so much lead time. We knew three weeks ahead when their series would run, and we had a tacit agreement to coincide." . . .

In the second article, Jack Nelson described the hesitancy of U.S.

embassy officials to deal with the prisoners' charges of torture and other forms of mistreatment. He noted they evidently did not want to offend the Mexican government and observed they tended to play down or deny accusations. He also noted, "If embassy personnel have difficulty in finding out about arrests, Mexican lawyers have no such difficulty." Nelson then detailed complaints by American parents that a lawyer to whom they had paid thousands of dollars and gotten no assistance had been recommended by U.S. consular official Danny Root. Root denied the charges. U.S. counsel general Peter Peterson said that he couldn't believe that Root would have done such a thing and the parents must have misunderstood what Root was saying.

The third story, again . . . from Mexico City, carried other comments by Peterson. He denied that the U.S. government was pressuring Mexico to keep the Americans in prison. . . . The fourth story . . . was based on interviews with State Department officials in Washington. Joseph Livornese, acting director of the State Department office of special consular affairs, stated that U.S. embassies were limited in what they were able to do for Americans arrested in foreign countries. He noted that the State Department had sent a protest note to the Mexican government in July after receiving numerous reports of brutality and extortion against American prisoners. Although the note and several others had not been answered formally, Livornese pointed to fewer arrests of Americans at the Mexico City airport in recent weeks as evidence that the Mexican government was responding to the complaint. . . .

The fifth story . . . described the "appallingly similar" stories of the heavy-handed techniques Mexican prison officials used to extort money and the high-pressure techniques of Mexican attorneys, one of whom contacted families through a cousin in Los Angeles. It was headlined, "Mexican Drug Busts: The Families Also Pay." The final story . . . pointed out that although Mexico was believed to supply 60 per cent of the heroin reaching the U.S.—and that U.S. officials were praising Mexico's recently stepped up efforts to stem the influx—heroin was not much of a problem in Mexico. Ironically, the number one drug problem there was glue sniffing. The implication was that the drug arrests of Americans in Mexico were being carried out as a courtesy to the U.S.

The primary interest of the Los Angeles *Times* in working with Stark and his aides had been to gather enough information to produce a series of articles. Their daily contact ended with the running of the series.

However, for the people in Congress, the work was just beginning. A few weeks after Stark's letter and press release, some State Department personnel visited his office, talked with Julyan and agreed to launch an investigation. There were a few stories about the investigation during the first few months of 1975, but relatively little media interest in the issue and few efforts by Stark or Julyan to push it. Then, in March, Stark became dissatisfied with what he considered a lack of action—even interest. Said Julyan, "We came out of low profile. We started beating the drum—saying that State was doing a whitewash, and we didn't trust their investigation, and it should be given to the House."

Julyan drafted a resolution of inquiry—a privileged motion that calls for the gathering of information. Once referred to a Congressional committee, it must be acted on within a specified period of time. Explained Julyan, "It's very difficult to get a hearing in Congress. You've got to figure out how to get your issue to the front of the hearing list." . . .

. . . The first of what was to be a series of hearings on U.S. citizens imprisoned in Mexico was held at the end of April. It was largely based on information that Congressman Stark and the Los Angeles *Times* had gathered, and both Stark and David Julyan were invited to testify. The committee [International Policy and Military Affairs subcommittee] also heard from numerous State Department officials.

The outcome was that the subcommittee asked Stark to select 15 test cases. It then asked the State Department to prepare an extensive report on the allegations these prisoners were making and on what the State Department could do about them. . . . When the State Department reported back to the subcommittee in July, it was once again pointed out that the department's authority in a foreign country was limited and suggested that many of the charges voiced by Stark and the prisoners had been exaggerated.

This time the subcommittee was skeptical. The hearing was closed, and the written transcripts of all such hearings are edited before they are published to avoid not only security leaks and diplomatic blunders, but also minor embarrassments. . . .

Even though the hearing was closed, there was a lot about it in the press. Congressmen Stark and [Dante] Fascell had an impromptu press conference afterwards, releasing a copy of Stark's testimony and others' comments. Reporters got wind of everything else from the various "principals" or their aides.

By this time press interest in the topic was beginning to mount. No more than a month later, the August 14 issue of *Rolling Stone* magazine carried an article entitled "The Black Palace and the Women of Santa Marta: Tales of Torture, Extortion and Abandonment by the U.S. Embassy from Americans Currently Imprisoned on Drug Charges in Mexico." The Black Palace and Santa Marta are two of the many men's and women's prisons where Americans are being held. . . . Essentially, it was the same story that the Los Angeles *Times* had told six months earlier, even down to some of the same examples. And, like the *Times*' stories, it referred to the efforts being made by Pete Stark.

The difference was that, for reasons peculiar to journalism, this story triggered interest in the rest of the nation's news media. Some people call it agenda-setting: the ability of some media to define which topics their readers talk about and other media carry. Various media are recognized as having preeminence in particular subject areas. For international news it's the New York *Times;* for Washington news, the wire service daybooks; for national domestic issues, the Washington *Post;* and for anything that might be considered "anti-establishment" or "counter culture," the agenda-setting publication is *Rolling Stone.* Thus it was that, shortly after the August 14 story appeared, Stark's office began getting phone calls from reporters. . . .

In addition to the various newspaper stories, there was a piece on NBC News and a ten-minute spot on the "Today" show. Both were tied to the third hearing, in October, 1975. Explained Julyan, "We suggested they tie it to the hearings for a news peg. That's true of a lot of people. We'll suggest they may want to wait a day or two to tie their story to something coming up." . . .

The October hearing was open to the press, and the news media were there in force. Once again the State Department representatives indicated that there was a limit to what they could do, and in any case their investigation of prisoners' complaints was being hampered by the sheer number of cases. By now there were 550 Americans in Mexican jails—most of them on drug offenses. . . .

A few days later the committee sent a letter of protest to Secretary of State Kissinger and released a copy to the media. By now, the committee had become impatient with both the U.S. government and the Mexican government and felt that media publicity was its best hope of getting changes in the treatment of Americans arrested in Mexico. Shortly after the October hearing subcommittee staffer Mike Finley explained:

> The Mexican case has gotten to a certain point where it's my opinion and I think it's also Mr. Fascell's that we need to change the attitude of the Mexican government by getting our own executive branch to say something—or by getting the American people so upset that it makes an impression on the Mexican government regardless of what the executive branch is doing. We're now trying deliberately to get publicity. Trying to spark interest with publicity. Trying to get the word to the Mexican government that the U.S. Congress is not going to forget about the issue.
>
> Here, the press has involvement, a role to play—if we can assume the press were a passive instrument, and that's not quite the case. But we realize that if they report something it can help our cause and we can use that for our ends. What can we do to get publicity? We can ask a prisoner to take off his clothes and show us his scars in front of the glowing TV lights. That's what I mean by the press having a role to play in what we do. We might get total cooperation of the executive branch and still not get anywhere with the Mexican government. But if we get people so upset that it cuts down on tourism, now *that* will make an impression. If we get Walter Cronkite saying Mexico is a lousy place,

that will have an impact on the Mexican government with or without anything our government does.

He added, "We're seriously considering bringing in prisoners to testify. We may do that in January. There are different ways to use the press."

Explained Congressman Stark:

The problem with dealing with a bureaucracy is that the people seem to be incapable of changing. They keep saying, "We've done nothing wrong. . . .

We've done everything according to our regulations." There's no way to get them to try something different. The only thing they understand is that you can ridicule them in the media. Make them look silly. They respond then, because they don't like to be laughed at.

A few days after the October hearing, the Washington *Star* ran an extensive front-page story outlining the positions of Stark, the subcommittee, the State Department and the Mexican government. . . .

What began with a letter from two families to their Congressman eventually became an issue that dozens of Congressmen were hearing from constituents about, that a Congressional subcommittee was investigating and that the State Department was being forced to reconsider. It would later lead to efforts to arrange a prisoner exchange. When the first American prisoners returned to the U.S. in December, 1977, Congressman Stark and the news media were conspicuously present.

The news media functioned in a variety of ways to make the prisoners an issue. Stark believes that one of the most important functions in the early stages was to establish the validity of the prisoners' complaints. Said Stark, "The Los Angeles *Times* series gave us a certain legitimacy. There's always a question in Congress of raising hell, demanding an investigation, and then not having anything to back it up. . . . The press did two things: It provided information and legitimized the issue."

However, the Los Angeles *Times* series apparently played only a minor part in actually bringing about the hearings. People associated with the subcommittee insisted they would have responded regardless of whether there had been prior publicity in the press. . . . David Julyan explained, "We wanted a Congressional forum . . . and we used both the resolution of inquiry and press interest as an argument to Congressman Fascell. . . . Our argument was that it was a good issue and that the press had generated a lot of public interest. "But," said Julyan, "the press by itself wouldn't have been sufficient." Nor did the investigative reporting itself bring about any immediate response from the State Department. . . .

However, press coverage did get television into the act. Said Stark:

When the press gets the electronic media interested, two things happen. You get far broader coverage. Ten minutes on the "Today" show gets interest all over the country, and the electorate hears about the issue. Secondly, when the electronic media come to a hearing, you get all the members there. They start to demagogue and become more attentive and assertive. Witnesses from the State Department start to act and sound much more concerned. So, what happens is that TV at a hearing gets *everybody* sounding more concerned about the issue—and that gets a certain sense of importance for the issue.

Of course, TV coverage also broadened the mail, and then other Congressmen referred their complaints to us.

In other words, coverage of the issue served two different but complementary functions. It directly changed the public behavior of State Department officials. It also generated interest among the electorate. This, in turn, increased the interest of members of Congress in getting further modifications in State Department policies and routines.

Finally, coverage of both the hearings and the general topic served still another function. It put the Mexican government on notice that U.S. citizens, Congress and the State Department were pressuring for a change. . . . Mexican officials—like their U.S. counterparts—are conscious of their public images and anxious to avoid unfavorable publicity. Thus, the fact that the U.S. news media were now championing the prisoners' plight may have been as potent a political force as anything Congress itself could do.

5.6 ■■■■■

Elite Ideology and Risk Perception
in Nuclear Energy Policy

Stanley Rothman and S. Robert Lichter

Editor's Note. Stanley Rothman and S. Robert Lichter's book, *The Media Elite: America's New Powerbrokers*, published in 1986, stirred much debate in the scholarly community because the authors claim that the media elites' very liberal orientation on many controversial social and political issues are reflected in their stories. One of these issues is nuclear energy generation. In the essay presented here, Rothman and Lichter discuss why news stories have described nuclear energy as far more risky than have the reports by health and physical scientists. The authors explain this discrepancy by pointing to the predispositions and ideologies of media elites and their reliance on sources that share their pessimistic views.

Rothman and Lichter attribute the decline in public and governmental support for nuclear ventures to negative media stories. Given the climate of apprehension about the safety of nuclear energy, the industry has withered in the United States, while it remains vital in Europe and other foreign sites. Rothman and Lichter's views provide an interesting contrast to Timothy W. Luke's argument in Part 6. Luke contends that government sources, rather than media elites, shaped the images of the Chernobyl nuclear disaster, thereby ensuring the survival of the nuclear power industry.

Rothman is Mary Huggins Gamble Professor of Government at Smith College and director of its Center for the Study of Social and Political Change. Lichter is co-director of the Center for Media and Public Affairs and teaches at The George Washington University. The selection comes from "Elite Ideology and Risk Perception in Nuclear Energy Policy," *American Political Science Review* 81:2 (June 1987): 383-404. Several tables and all notes have been omitted.

Nuclear Energy, Ideology, and the Perception of Risk

In the 1950s, the vast majority of U.S. citizens supported the development of nuclear energy ("Opinion Roundup" 1979, 23). Today a

---

Reprinted by permission of the authors and the American Political Science Association.

substantial majority opposes the building of new nuclear plants. More-over, opposition is strongest among the most articulate and politically active segments of the population. Cost overruns and the abandonment of many partially completed nuclear facilities in the United States have probably played a role in the development of negative attitudes among various leadership groups. Nevertheless, for the average person, fears about the safety are far more important (Inglehart 1984). The meltdown at Chernobyl in the Soviet Union has accentuated such fears to the point where nuclear development is not, at this time, a viable energy option in the United States.

The view that nuclear plants are unsafe is shared by a significant number of citizens in positions of social influence or responsibility. For the past several years, we have been surveying various leadership groups in the United States, including national-media journalists, science journal-ists, military leaders, congressional staff, partners in top corporate-law firms, creators of television and motion picture entertainment, high-level government bureaucrats, and public-interest-group leaders. The journal-ists were surveyed in 1979, although the follow-up questions on nuclear energy were administered in 1982. The remaining groups were sampled in 1982. The overall sample size for this analysis is 1,136 individuals. The samples were generally drawn randomly from each targeted group.

Respondents rated the safety of nuclear plants on a seven-point scale ranging from 1 (very unsafe) to 7 (very safe). We characterized scores of 5 or higher as exhibiting relative confidence in the safety of nuclear plants. The results (see Table 1) indicate considerable variation among the groups sampled. Thirty-seven percent of the journalists interviewed consider nuclear plants to be safe, as do only 13% of the television-entertainment elite, 14% of the motion-picture elite, and 6% of public-interest-group leaders. By contrast, 49% of the corporate lawyers believe nuclear plants are safe, as do 52% of top-level federal bureaucrats and 86% of military leaders.

How do these diverse estimates of nuclear safety accord with the scientific community's own evaluations? To find out, we sampled, in 1980, one thousand scientists drawn randomly from *American Men and Women of Science (AMWS)* supplemented by another sample of three hundred scientists who work in energy-related fields. We defined the latter group broadly, including persons in fields such as atmospheric chemistry, solar energy, conservation, and ecology. In all, we included 71 disciplines in our energy-expert subsample. In our smaller nuclear-energy-expert sample, we included experts working in such nuclear-related fields as radiological health and radiation genetics, as well as nuclear engineers and physicists. Seventy-four percent of the scientists sampled returned usable questionnaires.

Scientists, especially those in energy-related fields, regard nuclear

Table 1 Are Nuclear Plants Safe?

Sample Groups	Percentage Rating Nuclear Plant Safety 5 or Higher	Sample Size
Total leadership sample	36.8	1,203
Bureaucrats	52.0	199
Congressional aides	39.1	132
Lawyers	48.6	149
Media	36.5	156
Journalists at *NY Times* and *Washington Post*	29.4	51
Journalists at TV networks	30.6	49
Military	86.0	152
Movies	14.3	90
Public interest	6.4	154
TV, Hollywood	12.5	103
Total scientists sample	60.2	925
Energy experts	75.8	279
Nuclear-energy experts	98.7	72

energy as a necessary and relatively benign source of energy. Ninety percent of the random sample and 95% of the energy-expert sample believe that we should proceed with the development of nuclear energy. Seventy-six percent of the energy-expert sample and 99% of the nuclear-energy-expert sample believe nuclear plants to be safe. . . .

We administered a short form of the survey to the same respondents in 1985 with almost exactly the same results. A second replication of our study in Germany [1986] reveals that German scientists agree with their U.S. counterparts (Institut fur Demoskopie 1985). Engineers in energy-related fields are even more supportive of nuclear energy than are scientists (Lichter et al. 1986). . . .

How does one explain the wide differences in safety estimates among the various nonscientific leadership groups we have studied? . . .

Nuclear Energy: Scientists Versus the Media

. . . One would, . . . expect the public and various leadership groups to follow the lead of the scientific community on this issue. In fact the public is relatively unaware of the views of the scientific community. In a 1984 national poll, almost 6 out of 10 respondents expressed the belief that those scientists who are energy experts are evenly split as to the safety of nuclear energy or consider nuclear energy unsafe (Unpublished Cambridge Reports, February 1984).

The general public is not alone in these views. Most of the elite groups in our sample seriously underestimate scientific support for nuclear energy. For example, 70% of television producers, writers, and directors believe that fewer than 65% of those scientists who are energy experts support the further development of nuclear energy. Indeed, like the general public, most of the leadership groups we studied perceive energy experts as sharply divided on the issues of nuclear energy. And this belief is associated with their views of nuclear safety. . . .

. . . Part of the reason for erroneous public perceptions of the views of the scientific community on nuclear energy lies with the manner in which information about those views is communicated to the public by scientists themselves. The scientific community as a whole does not communicate with the general public. Rather, a somewhat smaller group of more visible scientists does most of the communicating (Goodell 1977), and this group seems skewed toward the antinuclear argument.

Our survey asked scientists both how many articles they had published in professional peer-reviewed journals and how many articles they had published on science policy questions for the more general public. . . .

On the one hand, 57% of our entire sample and 59% of our pronuclear sample had published more than 10 articles in academic or professional journals, compared to only 41% of the very antinuclear scientists. On the other hand, while only 11% of all scientists and 13% of highly pronuclear scientists have published articles on science policy in popular journals, the figure for antinuclear scientists is 36%.

More significantly, among scientists who have published on nuclear energy in professional journals, only 1 out of 10 believes that the possibility of an accidental release of radioactivity from reactors is a very serious problem. In contrast, among those who have published on nuclear energy only in popular journals, 4 out of 10 hold this view. Only 1.5 out of 10 in the professional-journal group believe that there are serious problems with the safety systems of nuclear plants, compared with 7 out of 10 in the popular-journal group. Lastly, more than 9 out of 10 in the professional-journal group are reasonably or very sure that we now possess the knowledge to solve the problems of nuclear energy, as against only 6 out of 10 in the popular-journal group. All these differences are statistically significant.

The publicly oriented group is small. One hundred and twenty scientists in our sample have published on nuclear energy. Of these, only 10 have written solely for popular journals. However, this suggests that between one and two thousand scientists listed in AMWS had written articles on nuclear energy for the general public without ever submitting their ideas to review by professional peers.

The relative skepticism toward nuclear energy of scientists who write

Table 2   Support for Nuclear Energy Among Scientists and Leading Journals

Leadership Groups	Score on Nuclear Support Scale	Number of Cases
Nuclear experts	7.86	72
Energy experts	5.10	279
All scientists	3.34	741
Science journalists	1.30	42
Prestige-press journalists	1.16	150
Science journalists at *New York Times*, *Washington Post*, TV networks	.47	15
TV reporters and producers	−1.89	18
Public television journalists	−3.25	24

only in popular journals may help explain why the public has a distorted view of the attitudes of the scientific community. However, this cannot be the full story. Given the absolute numbers, many more pronuclear than antinuclear scientists have published articles in popular journals. It is possible that antinuclear scientists publish in larger circulation periodicals, but our data point to another factor.

Elite journalists, including leading science journalists, are skeptical of nuclear energy. The most skeptical journalists of all are television commentators. On a "nuclear-support" scale, constructed from several survey items whose scores range from -9 to +9, scientists in energy-related fields score 5.10, while television reporters and commentators score -1.89 (see Table 2). Journalists employed by the national media are politically liberal, and, as with other groups, their political ideology correlates with skepticism about the safety of nuclear energy. Most importantly, these attitudes seem to be reflected in news coverage. We analyzed news coverage of nuclear safety from 1970 through 1983 in the *New York Times*, the three major news magazines (*Time, Newsweek,* and *U.S. News*), and the three commercial television networks (ABC, NBC, and CBS).

This content analysis of national media coverage found that a distinct antinuclear tilt started in the early 1970s on television and the late 1970s in print. Overall, the major print and broadcast outlets analyzed failed to report the views of the scientific community accurately. Antinuclear stories outnumbered pronuclear stories by two to one on television and in news magazines. Judgments of particular safety issues were primarily negative at all outlets, reaching a two to one margin on television. Among nuclear experts cited in news stories, critics outnumbered supporters by

Table 3 Media Coverage of Nuclear Safety, 1970-1983
(in Percentages)

Content	New York Times	News Magazines	Television
Story slant			
Pronuclear	7	25	17
Antinuclear	10	46	42
Neutral/balanced	83	29	41
Safety judgement			
Positive	45	45	34
Negative	55	55	66
Expert sources cited			
Pronuclear	9	17	11
Antinuclear	7	40	62
Neutral/balanced	84	43	27
Number of stories	486	213	582

Note: Ten-percent random sample for *New York Times*, full universe for magazines, 50% sample for television.

more than two to one in news magazines and five to one on television (see Table 3 and Lichter, Rothman, and Lichter 1986).

Additional evidence is available from other sources. The Media Institute found that antinuclear experts and groups appeared on prime-time TV newscasts during the 1970s about twice as often as pronuclear sources (Media Institute 1979). By far the most widely quoted "independent expert" source on nuclear energy on television newscasts during the period of the study was the Union of Concerned Scientists (UCS). The UCS has been very critical of nuclear energy.

The individual "expert" who received the most television exposure during the period of the Media Institute study was Ralph Nader, and the only academic scientific expert quoted in the aftermath of Three Mile Island was Dr. Ernest Sternglass, a strongly antinuclear radiologist. Neither in the eleven-year period before Three Mile Island nor during the month after were pronuclear outside experts among the 10 top-quoted sources. The only pronuclear sources in the top 10 were spokesmen for utility companies and the nuclear industry. . . . [T]he public credibility of such organizations is quite low.

As our data indicate, many independent pronuclear scientists are available. Some of them, like Hans Bethe, are both well known and active in their support of nuclear energy. The views of such people would have been far more representative of the scientific community than those of Dr. Sternglass.

Physicist Bernard Cohen recently conducted a poll of academics in the radiation health field. He found that 91% believe that public fears of radiation are excessive, and about the same proportion believe that television and the press exaggerate its dangers. When asked to evaluate the scientific credibility of 19 scientists who write or speak about radiation, these experts gave Dr. Sternglass their lowest rating (14 on a scale ranging from 1 to 100) (Cohen 1983, 258-62).

It is conceivable that antinuclear scientists are more likely to seek out the media than are pronuclear scientists. However, we found that pronuclear scientists are no more likely to refuse to be interviewed by journalists than are their antinuclear counterparts. It seems equally likely, therefore, that journalists tend to seek out antinuclear scientists. Indeed, the elite journalists we surveyed were asked to list information sources they considered reliable on nuclear energy. They selected more antinuclear than pronuclear sources by a margin of over three to two (Lichter, Rothman, and Lichter 1986).

. . . [J]ournalists are probably no different from anyone else in that, to help them understand issues that are both controversial and highly technical, they seek out sources they trust. And people tend to trust "experts" who share their own social outlooks.

During the 1950s' fluoridation controversy, the leading national media deferred to the views of the scientific establishment in ways that they no longer do. Certainly, reporters then were just as interested in disaster as they are now, and the science staffs of television or newspapers were neither larger nor better-trained than they are today. Today, however, journalists regard "antiestablishment" scientists as rather more trustworthy than mainstream scientists (Goodfield 1981).

It is hard to know to what extent media coverage actually influences the views of the larger public. In the recent past, most academic commentators have suggested that this influence is minimal. However, more recently, scholars such as Elizabeth Noelle-Neumann (1973) in Germany and Michael Robinson (1976) and Benjamin Page (Page, Shapiro, and Dempsey 1984) in the United States, have begun to build an impressive case on the other side.

It is not unreasonable to ascribe erroneous elite and popular perceptions of scientists' nuclear-energy views at least partly to media coverage, and other evidence adds to the plausibility of this conjecture.

References

Cohen, Bernard. 1983. *Before It's Too Late: A Scientist's Case for Nuclear Energy.* New York: Plenum Press.

Goodell, Rae. 1977. *The Visible Scientists.* Boston: Little, Brown.

Goodfield, June. 1981. *Reflections on Science and the Media.* New York: American Association for the Advancement of Science.

Inglehart, Ronald. 1984. The Fear of Living Dangerously: Public Attitudes toward Nuclear Power. *Public Opinion* 6:41-44.

Lichter, S. Robert, Stanley Rothman, and Linda Lichter. 1986. *The Media Elite.* Bethesda, MD: Adler and Adler.

Lichter, S. Robert, Stanley Rothman, Robert Rycroft, and Linda Lichter. *Nuclear News.* 1986. Washington, D.C.: Center for Media and Public Affairs.

Noelle-Neumann, Elizabeth. 1973. Return of the Concept of a Powerful Mass Media. *Studies of Broadcasting* 9:67-112.

Opinion Roundup. 1979. *Public Opinion* 2:23-24.

Page, Benjamin I., Robert Y. Shapiro, and Glen R. Dempsey. 1984. Television News and Changes in Americans' Policy Preferences. Paper presented at the annual meeting of the Midwest Political Science Association, Chicago.

Robinson, Michael. 1976. Public Affairs Television and the Growth of Political Malaise. *American Political Science Review* 70:409-32.

6. CONTROLLING MEDIA EFFECTS

A lthough the scholarly community remains engaged in lively debate about the potency of mass media, governments and people everywhere treat the media as powerful political actors. Governments try to regulate them so that news stories will not endanger national interests or work at cross-purposes with established authorities. Additionally, public and private officials try to manipulate the news so that stories favor their causes.

This section begins with a look at the political forces that come to play in the United States when policies for the control of media power are made. Since the First Amendment to the U.S. Constitution prohibits Congress from making any "law abridging the freedom of the press," many people wrongly believe that U.S. media are free from government control. It is true that print media enjoy ample, although not unlimited, freedom to support or sabotage governmental policies and philosophies. They also can grant or deny publicity to various interest groups and viewpoints as they see fit.

The situation is quite different for the electronic media, however. Government regulations substantially curtail the freedom of entrepreneurs in electronic media enterprises to run their businesses as they please, although legislators and regulatory commissions explicitly deny the intent to control news content. Erwin G. Krasnow, Lawrence D. Longley, and Herbert A. Terry describe how government control invariably has thrust the electronic media into the thick of political controversy. Their essay includes a model providing an exceptionally clear overview of the patterns of interaction among the various participants in broadcast policy making.

The next two essays detail how government officials try to manipulate the media. Martin Linsky describes the successful efforts of the U.S. Postal Service to generate news stories in support of postal reforms that powerful interest groups opposed. Linsky's research has convinced him that efforts to win favorable publicity are absolutely essential to effective governance. Timothy W. Luke analyzes the equally successful efforts of the United States, the Soviet Union, several European countries, and several nuclear power interest groups to influence the media images about a major nuclear disaster in the Soviet Union. His essay illustrates how political reality, more often than not, is created by public officials rather than by newspeople.

Manipulating images in the news is not the only way to exercise control. When avoiding bad images is the goal, it may be most effective to withhold information entirely. The usual justification is that disclosure would harm national security. John Downing discusses how this tactic is used in Britain and the United States. Although national security certainly must be protected from harmful media disclosures, government officials often seek protection unnecessarily. Governments, eager to hide their activities, may deliberately exaggerate security risks. This dilemma, as Downing suggests, requires further study.

The final selections deal with issues of media control that are of particular concern to third world nations. René Jean Ravault addresses the claims of third world governments that controls are needed to curb the deleterious influence of Western media on third world people and politics. Ravault's essay undermines the plea for controls by arguing that third world complaints are unjustified because they are based on the unscientific assumption of automatic media effects.

The third world's unhappiness with images projected by Western media is not limited to news reaching their countries. Third world nations are also unhappy with much of the news about them published in the West. A few nations are trying to change these images by hiring public relations firms. Robert B. Albritton and Jarol B. Manheim describe the tactics available for such efforts and assess the chances for success. Their findings indicate that news media, eager for good story material, are quite susceptible to the blandishments of public relations professionals.

6.1 ■■■■■■

The Politics of Broadcast Regulation

Erwin G. Krasnow, Lawrence D. Longley, and Herbert A. Terry

Editor's Note. The authors of this selection discuss the major factors that
have shaped and continue to shape broadcast regulation and now deregulation. Technological changes are occurring at a dizzying pace, but in Congress
and the executive branch it is still "politics as usual." Despite mounting
pressures to scrap the Federal Communications Act of 1934, several recent
efforts have failed to win passage for a new act more suitable for modern
technology and developments.

One major policy issue that has made passage of a new act difficult is
electronic media regulation. Television and radio have been regulated in the
past because it was feared that a scarcity of broadcast channels would
prevent vigorous competition. Technology has changed so that there is now
more competition among electronic media than among daily newspapers,
which are unregulated. Still, pressure to continue television regulation
remains strong because the power of the medium over the public's thinking
seems awesome to many people.

If regulation continues, several existing rules will need reexamination
because they have proved unworkable or because they have had highly
undesirable side effects. The controversy surrounding these changes ensures
that the politics of broadcast regulation will continue to be exciting.
The political battles yet to come will continue to provide excellent insights into the interaction of media institutions with their political
environment.

At the time of writing, Erwin G. Krasnow was a communications lawyer
serving the National Association of Broadcasters as senior vice president and
general counsel. Lawrence D. Longley was a professor of government at
Lawrence University, specializing in interest group politics. Herbert A.
Terry, who has been affiliated with the National Citizens Committee on
Broadcasting, was teaching telecommunications at Indiana University. The
selection is from *The Politics of Broadcast Regulation*, 3d ed. (New York: St.
Martin's Press, 1982).

The Historical Context of Broadcast Regulation

Broadcast regulation, like broadcasting itself, has a history spanning just over a half-century. There is more constancy, both substantively and structurally, to that history than one might expect for so dynamic a field. For example, the basic statute under which the FCC currently operates, the Communications Act of 1934, is fundamentally identical to the legislative charter given to the Federal Radio Commission in 1927. The process that produced the 1927 and 1934 acts in fact displayed many features that characterize the regulatory process today. Just like today, the creation of the legislative framework involved many parties—indeed, almost the same parties as those of the 1980s. Like today, the result was compromise—compromise that continued to be susceptible to reconsideration and reinterpretation. . . .

Several aspects of the early history of broadcast regulation deserve emphasis. Five key participants emerged, themselves giving rise to a sixth, the Federal Radio Commission and its successor, the FCC. The broadcast industry was involved in the genesis of broadcast regulation. Self-regulation was attempted but proved inadequate. After that, the industry worked actively with the executive and legislative branches of government to shape what was viewed as legislation required to eliminate audio chaos. Also involved from the beginning were the courts. . . . The public was involved as well, its complaints about deteriorating radio service helping advance radio legislation on Congress's agenda by 1927.

Congress and the executive branch of government are the two remaining participant groups. . . . Disputes between the president and Congress are reflected in the "temporary" nature of the FRC and the continuing interaction today between the president and Congress whenever an FCC member is nominated and subjected to the confirmation process. When Secretary of Commerce Hoover's regulatory activities were blocked by the courts, the salvation of American broadcasting lay with Congress. When Congress *did* act to establish a regulatory agency, the agency's existence and financing were subjected to yearly congressional consideration.[1] By giving the FRC limited financial and technical resources, Congress effectively ensured the Commission's dependence on congressional good will and kept a firm grip on this "independent" regulatory agency.

A final distinctive feature of the federal government's early regulation of broadcast stations was the focus on licensing as a primary regulatory tool. . . . The strong emphasis on the FCC's licensing role results in part from the fact that Congress did not expressly give the Commission the power to regulate the rates or profits of broadcast stations.[2] It predetermined that there would be strongly fought battles over several aspects of licensing in the future: Should the "traffic cop" review such things as choices of content in making licensing decisions? What, in general, would be both the process and standards for getting licenses renewed? . . .

Taylor Branch has divided government agencies into two categories: "deliver the mail" and "Holy Grail." "Deliver the mail" agencies perform neutral, mechanical, logistical functions; they send out Social Security checks, procure supplies—or deliver the mail. "Holy Grail" agencies, on the other hand, are given the more controversial and difficult role of achieving some grand, moral, civilizing goal. The Federal Radio Commission came into being primarily to "deliver the mail"—to act as a traffic cop of the airwaves. But both the FRC and the FCC had a vague Holy Grail clause written into their charters: the requirement that they uphold the "public interest, convenience and necessity." This vague but also often useful congressional mandate is key to understanding today's conflicts over broadcast regulation. . . .

Former FCC Chairman Newton Minow has commented that, starting with the Radio Act of 1927, the phrase "public interest, convenience and necessity" has provided the battleground for broadcasting's regulatory debate.[3] Congress's reason for including such a phrase was clear: the courts, interpreting the Radio Act of 1912 as a narrow statute, had said that the secretary of commerce could not create additional rules or regulations beyond that act's terms. This left Hoover unable to control rapidly changing technologies. The public interest notion in the 1927 and 1934 acts was intended to let the regulatory agency create new rules, regulations, and standards as required to meet new conditions. Congress clearly hoped to create an act more durable than the Radio Act of 1912. That plan has been at least somewhat successful as it was not until about 1976 that Congress seriously began to consider a major change in its 1934 handiwork. . . .

The meaning of the phrase, however, is extremely elusive. Although many scholars have attempted to define the public interest in normative or empirical terms, their definitions have added little to an understanding of the real relevance of this concept to the regulatory process. One scholar, after analyzing the literature on the public interest, created a typology for varying definitions of the term, but in the end he decided not to "argue for adoption of a single definition, preferring instead to categorize ways in which the phrase may be used. Different circumstances . . . may employ different usages."[4] . . .

Besides providing flexibility to adapt to changing conditions, the concept of the public interest is important to the regulation of broadcasting in another sense. A generalized public belief even in an undefined public interest increases the likelihood that policies will be accepted as authoritative. The acceptance of a concept of the public interest may thus become an important support for the regulation of broadcasting and for the making of authoritative rules and policies toward this end.[5] For this reason the courts traditionally have given the FCC wide latitude in determining what constitutes the public interest. As the U.S. Supreme Court noted in 1981:

> Our opinions have repeatedly emphasized that the Commission's judgment regarding how the public interest is best served is entitled to substantial judicial deference. . . . The Commission's implementation of the public interest standard, when based on a rational weighing of competing policies, is not to be set aside . . . for "the weighing of policies under the public interest standard is a task that Congress has delegated to the Commission in the first instance." [6]

Judge E. Barrett Prettyman once expanded upon the reasons for such deference:

> It is also true that the Commission's view of what is best may change from time to time. Commissions themselves change, underlying philosophies differ, and experience often dictates change. Two diametrically opposite schools of thought in respect to the public welfare may both be rational; e.g., both free trade and protective tariff are rational positions. All such matters are for the Congress and the executive and their agencies. They are political in the high sense of that abused term.[7]

Despite the usefulness of the public interest concept in keeping up with changing means of communications and the general tendency of the courts to defer to the FCC's decisions, conflicts over the meaning of the public interest have been recurrent in broadcast history. On occasion, the vague statutory mandate to look out for the public interest has hampered the development of coherent public policy since Congress (or influential members of Congress) can always declare, "That is not what we meant by the public interest." [8] Few independent regulatory commissions have had to operate under such a broad grant of power with so few substantive guidelines. Rather than encouraging greater freedom of action, vagueness in delegated power may serve to limit an agency's independence and freedom to act as it sees fit. As Pendleton Herring put it, "Administrators cannot be given the responsibilities of statesmen without incurring likewise the tribulations of politicians." [9] . . .

Unresolved Regulatory Problems

. . . Disputes concerning legal prescriptions imposed by the Communications Act often have centered on recurring value conflicts—assumptions about what ought or ought not to be done. One such question is the extent to which broadcasting should pursue social as well as economic and technical goals. The emphasis on the social responsibilities of licensees rests on the view that "the air belongs to the public, not to the industry" since Congress provided in Section 301 of the Communications Act that "no . . . license shall be construed to create any right, beyond the terms, conditions, and periods of the license." . . . Some of these rules and policies require broadcasters to present, or refrain from presenting, content contrary to what they would choose to do on their own. How far the FCC may go in the direct, or indirect, regulation of content without violating either the Communications Act's own prohibition in Section 326 against censorship or the First Amendment to the U.S. Constitution remains unsettled. Section 326 of the Communications Act states:

> Nothing in this Act shall be understood or construed to give the Commission the power of censorship over the radio communications or signals transmitted by any radio station, and no regulation or condition shall be promulgated or fixed by the Commission which shall interfere with the right of free speech by means of radio communications.

However, as we noted above, in the same act Congress also directs the Commission to regulate "in the public interest, convenience and necessity." [10] Using that standard, the Commission has promulgated many rules and policies governing broadcast programming that would be regarded by the courts as unlawful censorship of the print media. Early court cases, however, determined that the FCC did not have to ignore content, that it could consider it without necessarily engaging in censorship;[11] later court cases have perpetuated the view that government supervision of broadcast content is somehow more acceptable than review of print.[12] Clearly broadcasting continues to be plagued by divergent views of how to balance freedom with achieving socially desired and responsible service, while still not engaging in censorship.

Complicating this controversy is the conflict between First Amendment provisions guaranteeing the right of broadcasters, like other media owners and operators, to be free of government control over the content of programming and First Amendment theories that have been developed exclusively for broadcasting and that hold the rights of listeners and viewers to receive information to be "paramount" over the rights of broadcasters.[13] The theory is that in the "scarce" medium of broadcasting, some affirmative government intervention concerning content may be needed to ensure that the public hears diverse ideas and viewpoints. J. Skelly Wright, a judge of the U.S. Court of Appeals, has commented:

> [In] some areas of the law it is easy to tell the good guys from the bad guys. . . . In the current debate over the broadcast media and the First Amendment . . . each debater claims to be the real protector of the First Amendment, and the analytical problems are much more difficult than in ordinary constitutional adjudication. . . . The answers are not easy.[14]

These colliding statutory ground rules governing the freedom and obligations of broadcasters have been melded into one of the law's most elastic conceptions—the notion of a "public trustee." [15] The FCC views a broadcast license as a "trust," with the public as "beneficiary" and the broadcaster as "public trustee." The public trustee concept is a natural consequence of the conflicting statutory goals of private use and regulated allocation of spectrum space. Congress gave the FCC the right to choose among various candidates for commercial broadcast licenses and left it up to the Commission to find a justification for providing a fortunate few with the use of a valuable scarce resource at no cost. Legal scholar Benno Schmidt, Jr., thinks the public trustee concept was designed to dull the horns of the FCC's dilemma: to give away valuable spectrum space, with no strings attached, would pose stubborn problems of justification.

. . . One option exercised by the FCC to reduce controversy over its activities has been to substitute "content-neutral" or "structural" policies for policies that involve direct review of content. . . . As an alternative to . . . content regulation the FCC can attempt to structure the broadcast marketplace so that there are many stations with different owners and assume thereby that diversity of opinion will result naturally and without direct government review. Many FCC rules and policies—for example, the regulation of station ownership patterns—have been of this type. They do not, on their surface, look normative but are in fact examples of content-neutral means of achieving social objectives. . . .

. . . Throughout its history the FCC has had to wrestle with new problems brought about by such technical developments as network broadcasting, FM broadcasting, VHF and UHF telecasting, color television, cable television, direct broadcast satellites (DBS), multipoint distribution services (MDS), and other new or modified systems. The making of public policy in each of these areas goes far beyond resolving technical issues. Technical issues frequently disguise what actually are economic interests vying for control of some segment of broadcasting and related markets. The politics of broadcasting are thus present in technical as well as social controversies.

. . . [T]he FCC, like other regulatory bodies, has been subjected to considerable criticism concerning its inability to cope with change—the most common charge being that it is concerned mainly with preserving the status quo and with favoring the well-established broadcast services. . . .

An agency's ability to respond to and foster technological change is largely a matter of how dependent the agency is on dominant industry factions—the "haves" as opposed to the "have nots." Throughout its history the FCC has lacked sufficient skilled personnel and funds to weigh the merits of new technology and has been forced to rely on outside advice and technical opinion. When faced with complex technical questions, the Commission often has taken the easy road of finding in favor of the "haves" over the "have nots." Frequently, the result is delay in the development of these technologies. . . . Throughout most of its history, the Commission (usually with the support of the "haves") sought to limit the growth of technology rather than use technological innovations as correctives to problems. Beginning in the late 1970s, however, the FCC has adopted policies designed to foster technological growth as a way of promoting greater competition in the marketplace and a greater diversity of services.

The ability of a regulatory commission to inhibit or to promote a technical innovation that challenges the regulated (and sometimes sheltered) industry is a measure of the vitality and strength of that agency. . . . [T]he FCC has not been highly successful at giving birth to new communications services. At times, in fact, it has almost destroyed them. These failures result, at least in part, from the highly political environment in which the FCC operates. . . .

Broadcast Regulation: An Analytic Review

Broadcast regulation . . . is shaped by six primary determiners—the FCC, the industry, citizen groups, the courts, the White House, and Congress. In addition there are miscellaneous participants—the Federal Trade Commission or the Commission on Civil Rights, for example— sometimes involved in specific broadcast-related issues but whose participation in the regulatory process, while important, is less constant. . . . [T]he six primary determiners rarely can accomplish much by unilateral action. The president, for example, names members of the FCC but checks out potential appointees in advance with significant interest groups (the industry and, infrequently, citizen groups). In the end, the Senate must formally approve nominations. The determiners, in other words, interact with each other in a complex fashion. Often those interactions are as important as, or more important than, what the determiners do on their own. Any attempt to understand what goes on in broadcast regulation must explain regulation as the outcome of complex interaction patterns within a dynamic system. . . .

The politics of broadcast regulation can be seen in terms of an analytical framework or model we term the "broadcast policy-making system." Such a framework can be used both to understand the regulatory process and to suggest to scholars a conceptual orientation for work in this area.

As is the case with any model, the one we are suggesting is a simplification of reality. Yet to simplify is to streamline, to strip off surface complexities in order to show the essential elements of a system. . . .

Figure 1 represents the broadcast policy-making system. The six recurring participants in the regulatory process . . . are the authoritative

Figure 1   The Broadcast Policy-Making System

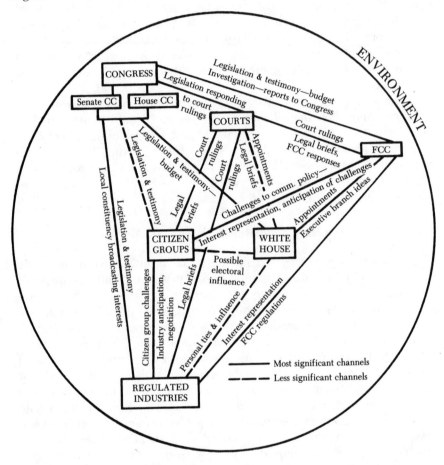

decision-making agencies at the heart of the model. The figure also charts various channels of influence among these six participants. It is significant that there is no one pathway through the core of the broadcast policy-making system, and any one of the various routes necessarily involves many participants. The key to understanding the politics of broadcast regulation lies in simultaneously analyzing the individual participants and their interactions. ... Although outside pressure, or "inputs," and the internal politics of each of the decision-making bodies can raise issues and define alternatives, it is the political relationships of, and interactions among, the six key determiners that are truly crucial to broadcast regulation.

Three of the principals (the White House, the courts, and citizen groups) usually play a less immediate, sustained, and direct role than the other three (the FCC, Congress, and the regulated industries). Thus, the primary channels of influence, information, and contact are traced among these three most significant determiners as the outer triangle in Figure 1.

The system produces policy dynamically. Policy decisions—which might be called "outputs"—emerge from the interaction of some or all of the participants. Although the need for policy decisions may sometimes be stimulated by parties outside the system—for example, by an action of the Federal Trade Commission—in most instances, the functioning of the system itself generates the need for still more policy decisions. In other words, although some policy decisions may have long lives, many remain accepted and unchanged only briefly: one day's policy outputs in this system commonly become the inputs for the next day's policy making.

The policy outputs of this system are varied. They include "public" policies such as FCC rules and regulations, final court actions, laws enacted by Congress, and executive orders. An example of legislation would be the statutory requirement . . . that all television sets sold after a certain date have UHF as well as VHF receiving capacity; an example of an agency decision would be the FCC's desire that incumbent broadcast station licensees should have preferred status, in renewal proceedings, over challengers for their licenses. . . . Outputs may even take the form of decisions not to do something, exemplified by recent trends in "deregulation" such as the FCC decision not to supervise the number of commercials radio stations carry. . . , or its decision not to concern itself with the entertainment programming format those stations use. . . . In our model, policy outputs may even include many of the actions of the regulated industries, whose implementation of or operation under FCC rules and regulations or the Communications Act of 1934 is, in many instances, authoritative because it is unchallenged.

In most instances, such policy outputs (or authoritative decisions) bestow rewards or impose penalties on other affected interests. Reactions of those interests—or, occasionally, outside interests—stimulate the system to generate further policy output. They become, in effect, input back into the system. Some inputs are specific, such as a demand by a citizen group that a broadcast station not be permitted to change its format. Other inputs are exceedingly general, such as the mood that can be cast over an independent regulatory commission by a president or by the current public image of the agency. It is important to realize, too, that the system does more than merely respond to demands; it also molds political demands and policy preferences.

The system, of course, does not function in a vacuum. It operates in the context of an environment consisting of many factors . . . including the historical element of broadcast regulation, the basic technical and economic characteristics of broadcasting, and broad legal prescriptions. The environment outside the system also encompasses other factors, such as public attitudes toward broadcasting and government regulation and the actions of related systems—the Federal Trade Commission, for example—which may at times inspire and influence the broadcast policy-making system. It even includes actions and groups beyond the United States, for the spectrum is an international resource and U.S. broadcast networks and programs have a worldwide effect. In recent years, for example, U.S. policies toward spectrum allocation for radio and toward the location and function of communications satellites have had to be reconciled with the desires of our international neighbors. The United Nations Educational, Scientific and Cultural Organization (UNESCO) has debated policies toward a "new world information order" that, although perceived by third world nations to be important to their development, are seen by Western nations as antithetical to notions of press freedom. The major demands and supports—outputs and inputs—that determine what the system does, however, generally originate from within. . . .

One important feature of the broadcast policy-making system is that it is highly turbulent. Largely because communications is influenced by rapidly changing technology, few specific policy decisions are stable and long-lasting. The system is always responding to new or changed conditions, with consequent incessant interaction among its participants. The operation of the policy-making system in specific instances is inherently unique; each policy-making problem is likely to differ in important respects from all others. However, certain recurring patterns about the politics of broadcast regulation can be identified.[16]

1. *Participants seek conflicting goals from the process.* Pluralism and dispersion of power in policy making do not by themselves suggest that the process is inevitably a struggle for control or influence. Conceivably the participants in such a process could share certain perspectives concerning what is to be done. Such is rarely the case, however, in the broadcast policy-making process. . . . [T]he gains of one set of participants are usually made at the cost of the interests of another. The policy demands of different groups often conflict; they must usually compete for scarce rewards.

2. *Participants have limited resources insufficient to continually dominate the policy-making process.* In a pluralistic complex such as that outlined in Figure 1, policy-making power tends to be divided. Although the FCC frequently initiates policy proposals, it lacks the ability to implement most of them single-handedly. To prevail, it must win significant support from other participants. Similarly, none of the other five participants has hierarchical control over the policy-making process, which is simply to say that nobody dominates the process consistently. In such a system policy making results from the agreement—or at least the acquiescence—of multiple participants, not from the domination of one. Coalitions of diverse participants work together and reward those belonging to them.

3. *Participants have unequal strengths in the struggle for control or influence.* Inequality among participants can arise because one party is inherently strong, cares more, or develops its potential more effectively. In the 1970s, for example, citizen groups had considerably less strength than the Federal Communications Commission and the broadcast industry in their ability to influence policy concerning radio station format changes. Even when one federal court agreed with the views of a citizen group, another federal court—supported by the FCC and by broadcasters—prevailed. Favorable public opinion, legal symbols, congressional allies, and the like are all potential sources of strength that participants have access to in differing degrees and that they may use with varying success on different issues.

4. *The component subgroups of participant groups do not automatically agree on policy options.* Each of the six groups we have identified consists of many subgroups: citizen groups range from liberal to conservative; the FCC is organized into bureaus representing interests that may conflict, such as cable television and broadcasting; there is not one single court but, instead, a hierarchy of courts, and it is common for a superior court to overturn the actions of an inferior court; radio broadcasters may sometimes view issues differently than television broadcasters. Thus, while it is useful to refer to the six principal participants as if each was one, it is important to recognize that each group may be unable—or find it very difficult—to agree on a common objective or course of action.

5. *The process tends toward policy progression by small or incremental steps rather than massive change.* One means of minimizing opposition to a policy initiative is to show its close relationship to existing and generally accepted policy. Frequently, earlier actions are cited to prove that the desired change is not unprecedented but only a logical continuation of past concerns and policies. One of the beauties of administrative law is that precedents usually can be found for almost any initiative. Although agencies are not as bound by precedent as are courts, they still hesitate to turn their backs on the past when it is pointed out to them. Such slow and gradual shifts in policy are not only strategic but probably inevitable, given the multiplicity of participants with conflicting goals, unequal strengths, and limited resources. Incrementalism tends to be at least a safe, if not necessarily the safest, course of action. As a result, however, the system is rarely bold or innovative and has a hard time responding to environmental pressures for massive change. . . .

6. *Legal and ideological symbols play a significant role in the process.* Throughout the evolution of policy a recurring theme of participants is the legal and ideological symbolism they may attach to a discussion of alternatives. In many instances policies are seen as threatening or protecting the "rights" of broadcasters or the "rights" of listeners and viewers, without refined and, most importantly, commonly agreed

upon specification of the meaning of those concepts. Broadcast policy-making discussions can also become embroiled in arguments over stock, symbolic rhetoric such as "localism," the "public interest," "access to broadcasting," or "free broadcasting." The terms become symbols cherished by participants in and of themselves without careful thought, or they are not commonly understood, so that ideological rhetoric sometimes supersedes real issues and actions in importance.

7. *The process is usually characterized by mutual accommodation among participants.* Customarily, participants in broadcast policy making do not attempt to destroy one or more of their opponents. Rather, the process is characterized by consensual, majority-seeking activities. Mutual adjustment among participants may occur in a variety of ways, including negotiation, the creation and discharge of obligations, direct manipulation of the immediate circumstances in which events are occurring, the use of third parties or political brokers capable of developing consensual solutions, or partial deferral to others in order to effect a compromise. To some participants, on some issues, however, accommodation is difficult if not impossible, and on these issues policy debate is intense and the perceived stakes the greatest. . . .

Notes

1. Congress followed a similar approach with the Corporation for Public Broadcasting, which initially received funding and authorization only on an annual basis, although it eventually received some advance, multiyear support.
2. See Roger G. Noll, Merton J. Peck, and John J. McGowan, *Economic Aspects of Television Regulation* (Washington, D.C.: Brookings Institution, 1973), p. 98. Section 153(h) of the Communications Act provides that "a person engaged in radio broadcasting shall not, insofar as such a person is so engaged, be deemed a common carrier."
3. Newton N. Minow, *Equal Time: The Private Broadcaster and the Public Interest* (New York: Atheneum, 1964), p. 8.
4. Barry M. Mitnick, *The Political Economy of Regulation: Creating, Designing and Removing Regulatory Forms* (New York: Columbia University Press, 1980), pp. 278-279. See, in general, Mitnick's chapter IV, "The Concept of the Public Interest."
5. See Virginia Held, *The Public Interest and Individual Interests* (New York: Basic Books, 1970), pp. 163-202.
6. *FCC v. WNCN Listeners Guild,*—U.S.—, 101 S. Ct. 1266, 67 L.Ed.2d 521, 535, (1981).
7. *Pinellas Broadcasting Co. v. FCC,* 230 F.2d 204, 206 (D.C. Cir. 1956), *certiorari denied,* 350 U.S. 1007 (1956).

8. [An] example ... [is] a Commission initiative to control advertising "in the public interest," which led to a stern rebuke from the House of Representatives.
9. Pendleton Herring, *Public Administration and the Public Interest* (New York: McGraw-Hill, 1936), p. 138. Vagueness, however, may also serve to protect the agency when its decisions are challenged in the courts, since the judiciary may be loath to overturn actions protected by a broad statutory mandate.
10. Congress did not uniformly use the phrase "public interest" in the Communications Act. For example, the standard of "public interest" is specified in Sections 201(b), 215(a), 221(a), 222(c)(1), 415(a)(4), 319(i) and 315; "public convenience and necessity" in Section 314(f); "interest of public convenience and necessity," Section 214(a); "public interest, convenience and necessity," Sections 307(d), 309(a), and 319(a); and "public interest, convenience or necessity," Sections 307(d), 311(b), and 311(c)(3). On September 17, 1981, the FCC recommended that Congress drop all broadcast-related mentions of "convenience" or "necessity." It called the words "superfluous. ... To the extent the issues embodied in these terms are relevant to radio regulation, they are subsumed under Commission review of the 'public interest.'" *FCC Legislative Proposal, Track I*, September 17, 1981, p. 25 [mimeo.].
11. See *KFKB Broadcasting Association, Inc.* v. *Federal Radio Commission*, 47 F.2d 670 (D.C. Cir. 1931) and *Trinity Methodist Church, South* v. *Federal Radio Commission*, 62 F.2d 850 (D.C. Cir. 1932).
12. See *Red Lion Broadcasting Co., Inc.* v. *Federal Communications Commission*, 395 U.S. 367, 89 S.Ct. 1794, 23 L.Ed.2d 371 (1969) and *Federal Communications Commission* v. *Pacifica Foundation*, 438 U.S. 726, 98 S.Ct. 3026, 57 L.Ed.2d 1073 (1978). In *Pacifica*, at 746, the court stated: "We have long recognized that each medium of expression presents special First Amendment problems. ... And of all forms of communications, it is broadcasting that has received the most limited First Amendment protection."
13. *Red Lion Broadcasting Co.* v. *FCC*, 395 U.S. 367, 390, 89 S.Ct. 1794, 23 L.Ed.2d 371 (1969). See also *CBS* v. *FCC*, ... 101 S.Ct. 2813, 69 L.Ed.2d 706 (1981).
14. Quoted in Fred W. Friendly, *The Good Guys, the Bad Guys and the First Amendment: Free Speech vs. Fairness in Broadcasting* (New York: Random House, 1975), p. ix.
15. This discussion is based on a theme developed by Benno C. Schmidt, Jr., *Freedom of the Press vs. Public Access* (New York: Praeger, 1976), pp. 157-158.
16. The generalizations that follow were suggested in part by Charles E. Lindblom, *The Policy-Making Process* (Englewood Cliffs, N.J.: Prentice-Hall, 1968).

6.2 ■■■■■

How Policymakers Deal with the Press

Martin Linsky

Editor's Note. The book from which this selection is taken was based on a three-year study done under the aegis of Harvard University's Center on the Press, Politics, and Public Policy. The author and his associates investigated six federal policy decisions during the Nixon, Ford, Carter, and Reagan presidencies to ascertain the interplay between press and government. All senior federal policy makers during the twenty-year span encompassed by the study were surveyed by mail to discover their perceptions of government-press interactions in policy making. In addition, twenty policy makers and sixteen journalists who had been identified by their piers as particularly successful were interviewed at length.

Based on this evidence, Linsky concludes that effective government requires that policy makers understand how media operate so that they can use media power to enhance important policy goals. If they fail to consider communications aspects of policy or if they mismanage them, policies are more likely to fail. The case study presented here, originally researched and written by David Whitman, involved reforms in the Postal Service and is an example of highly effective use of the media. It brought policy success when failure seemed to be in the cards. As is always true in complex situations, however, it is difficult to pinpoint the precise contribution made by the media campaign. All that can be said with certainty is that the reformers were convinced that their case would not have carried without a favorable press and an advertising blitz.

Linsky is a lecturer in public policy at the John F. Kennedy School of Government at Harvard University. He has had experience in government as a three-term member of the Massachusetts House of Representatives and assistant attorney general for the Commonwealth of Massachusetts. His journalism experience includes editorship of Cambridge's *Real Paper* and editorial writing and reporting for the *Boston Globe*. The selection comes from "How Policy Makers Deal with the Press," in *Impact: How the Press Affects Federal Policymaking* (New York: Norton, 1986), 148-168. Several footnotes have been omitted.

... Postal reform began to emerge as a concern for federal officials in the late 1960s. The volume of mail had just about tripled since World War II, the deficit from operations had increased to $1.1 billion, and systems and equipment were antiquated. If anyone needed tangible evidence of a problem, they got it when the Chicago Post Office nearly shut down in October 1966.

[Larry] O'Brien was postmaster general at the time, and he tried to take advantage of the Chicago crisis by warning that a "catastrophe" was approaching.[1] In April 1967, he told a stunned audience from the Magazine Publishers Association that he favored turning the Post Office Department into a nonprofit (and nonpolitical) government corporation. When O'Brien left the government to work for Robert Kennedy in his campaign for president, whatever momentum there was for postal reorganization went with him.

However dismal the prospects seemed, Nixon had made postal reform a campaign promise and he began to make good on his commitment early into his administration. The first step was a dramatic and unpopular one: Nixon and [Postmaster General Winton] Blount eliminated Post Office political patronage by ending the practice of allowing congressmen to name the postmasters. Republican congressmen, contemplating the fruits of recapturing the White House, were furious, but Nixon and Blount knew that with both the House and Senate controlled by Democrats, there would be no postal reform without Democratic support. If they waited until after filling available postal jobs with friends of Republican congressmen before moving on reform, they knew that the Democrats would never have taken them seriously. The second step, eventually more important but less visible for the time being, was to develop a strategy for convincing the public, and through them the Congress, of the benefits of reorganization. It was really a two-stage process: first the case had to be made that there was a serious and important problem at the Post Office; then, reorganization had to become the solution.

Blount knew that reorganization would not come about without going outside Washington: "Congress owned the Post Office and they liked that old baby just the way it was. We needed the newspaper pressure in the members' districts to shake up things." [2] He decided to set up what POD [Post Office Department] memos referred to as a "front organization" to push for reform. The idea had three enormous advantages: it provided a way to create a lobbying campaign that federal personnel were prohibited from doing directly or allocating funds for; it created a funding channel to allow those who favored reform to offset the efforts of the unions; and, most important, it permitted the public effort on behalf of the Nixon-Blount bill to be bipartisan.

The key to bipartisanship was O'Brien, the former postmaster general and former Democratic Party chairman who was already on record as favoring both reorganization and a grassroots lobbying approach. After some persuading, O'Brien agreed to co-chair the operation, to be called the Citizens Committee for Postal Reform (CCPR). The Republican half of the team was to be Thruston Morton, retired US senator and also a former national party chairman. The final step at the preliminary stage was to hire a marketing expert; Blount settled on William Dunlap, who did marketing for Procter & Gamble.

Dunlap was given an office at the POD, and two weeks to develop a full-scale plan. He remanded his public salary; P&G continued to pay him while he worked on the reorganization during 1969 and 1970. Dunlap wrote a marketing plan, he recalled, "just the way I would at Procter & Gamble. Essentially I took a packaging goods approach that you use to market a product, and applied it to the government sector." His approach was explicit, thorough, and very sophisticated. The purpose was to "stimulate the maximum amount of active support . . . and to utilize this favorable public reaction as a positive force that could be directed toward the members of Congress." [3] In the twenty-eight-page document he prepared, he laid out plans to utilize all the available media, national and local, print and electronic, in all their available slots: letters to the editor, editorials, news stories, feature articles by the postmaster general, and even appearances on entertainment television such as *The Tonight Show* and *The Joey Bishop Show*. The appeal to the media was to be based on their role as opinion makers, their self-interest as mail users, and their commitment to keep their readers and viewers abreast of the news, namely the news about postal reform. It was a saturation strategy in which press support, or at least press cooperation, was crucial.

Kick-off was set for May 27, 1969. During the preceding week, Blount and a handful of his aides gave background briefings to the editorial boards of papers in six major cities to ensure that all the coverage around the announcement was not from the highly political Washington press corps. On May 27, the president sent the reorganization message to the Congress. Nixon read a statement at the White House and Blount followed with a press briefing and a twenty-two-page press packet outlining the legislation. POD designed a special packet for editorial writers. There was a POD headquarters briefing for staff which was wired directly to three hundred top postmasters around the country. A POD publication called *Postal Life*, sent to every postal employee, explained the legislation in great detail. The Mail Users Council sent a "Memo to Mailers" presenting the reorganization proposal to sixty thousand business executives. CCPR, whose formation had been announced on May 26, issued a press release hailing the bill.

Editorial reaction to the reorganization was enthusiastic. Congressional reaction was cool in general, and absolutely frosty among the senior members of the House Post Office Committee (HPOC). Chairman Thaddeus Dulski (D-NY) had his own modest reform bill which stopped far short of establishing a government corporation to replace the Post Office Department. Senior Republicans on the committee were upset because the White House had eliminated congressional patronage in Post Office jobs. The administration had to reach all the way down to the fourth-ranking Republican Edward Derwinski (R-IL) and Democrat Mo Udall (D-AR) to find co-sponsors.

A confidential recap of a June 10 senior POD staff meeting indicated that reaching the postal employees was to be the number one short-run priority of the public relations campaign. Number two was producing favorable editorials in the home districts of congressmen on the Post Office Committee. Specific efforts toward these objectives were to be supported by continuing national coverage. During June and July, Blount appeared on *Meet the Press, Today,* and two nationally distributed radio programs; plus, he gave several dozen interviews to editorial boards, national reporters, and syndicated columnists. O'Brien and Morton testified together before Congress and appeared together before the National Press Club, drawing editorial praise for CCPR and postal reform as being "above politics." Ads soliciting support for CCPR were taken in the *New York Times* and the *Washington Post* in late June. Blount and other top officials at POD began giving background briefings for editorial boards at key papers around the country. POD press kits were mailed to virtually all of the nation's newspapers. Many newspapers used large parts of the press releases and editorials supplied by POD and CCPR. Some prestigious newspapers, such as the *Denver Post* and the *Milwaukee Journal,* were almost in front of the bandwagon, writing editorials urging Blount and CCPR to keep up the good fight against, as the *Journal* said, "the traditionalists in Congress." [4]

The activity produced coverage. As early as June 16, Dunlap counted 194 news stories, 232 editorials, 27 op-ed pieces, and 39 cartoons on the reorganization bill. At the end of June, Blount reported that 88 percent of the editorials favored the bill, now numbered H.R. 11750, with 9 percent undecided and only 3 percent opposed.

The pressure from the coverage was beginning to be felt where it counted—in the Congress. At a HPOC hearing near the end of July, Congressman Robert Tiernan (D-RI), originally opposed but thought to be wavering, refered to the "tidal wave" of local press support generated by CCPR. Testimony to Congress by union officials during the summer reflected their frustration at the success of CCPR in building support for the reorganization; they used words like "brainwashing" to describe what was happening.

By the time HPOC took its first vote in early October, there was as much support on the committee for the administration's bill as for

Dulski's. In six months, Blount and his friends had taken a solution that almost no one supported to a problem that few people took seriously and made it politically salient and even compelling.

Soon after the committee vote, postal reform became intertwined with another issue dear to the hearts of postal employees: a pay raise. Udall agreed to support a pay raise bill which was far in excess of what the administration said it would accept, and the Udall pay raise bill was rushed through the House on October 14, despite the threat of a presidential veto. . . .

While the president and the unions were facing each other in this stand-off during the fall, CCPR went back to the streets. The press campaign was more or less put on hold; something of a saturation point had been reached and there was no coming event to provide hard news coverage. . . .

CCPR began to gear up the media campaign as the Senate began its hearings on postal reform in November. The unions attacked CCPR: "One of the smoothest and most massive attempts at public brainwashing since the German glory days of Joseph Paul Goebbels," said NALC [National Association of Letter Carriers] President James Rademacher on November 25,[5] while simultaneously taking a page out of the CCPR success story and starting a media campaign of his own.

The objectives of the NALC campaign were to break the connection between reorganization and the pay raise, and to pressure the president into signing the pay raise bill when it reached his desk. It was a three-part initiative. First, ads were run in four hundred newspapers and on three hundred radio stations seeking support for the pay raise bill, and urging people to write to the president. Second, just to make sure the message was received, letter carriers, the ladies' auxiliary, and several unions distributed a total of six million pre-addressed cards with requests that they be filled out and sent to the White House. If Nixon still vetoed the bill, part three of the plan would be implemented: a march on Washington by 15,000 letter carriers, and a television broadcast responding to the veto message. Within a week of the beginning of the NALC marketing blitz the White House received three million pieces of mail in support of the pay raise. . . .

With the assistance of Udall, Colson and Rademacher hammered out a compromise in early December, trading substantial collective bargaining provisions and pay raise support, for ending union opposition to the government corporation concept. Rademacher says that he made the deal because he "saw the handwriting on the wall,"[6] but he had made a huge tactical error in not involving the rival postal union, the UFPC [United Federation of Postal Clerks], in the White House negotiations. As a result, Rademacher's union was the only one to support the compromise. . . .

Rademacher and Blount met the press and tried to claim that the victory was in everyone's interest, but the New York postal union locals were not convinced. A strike vote was taken on March 17, and on the next day all mail service was halted in New York City as the first postal strike in the nation's history was underway. . . .

Finally, after several weeks of hard bargaining, a package was worked out which provided for an immediate and retroactive pay hike, with a larger hike to take effect when reorganization was signed into law. The reorganization agreed to was in all essential respects the same as the one reported by HPOC. George Meany, who was by then speaking for the unions, hailed it as "a tremendous step forward" because postal employees had won the right to collective bargaining.[7]

The bill passed the House overwhelmingly on June 18. On the Senate side, eight of the twelve members of the Senate Post Office Committee were up for re-election in the fall and didn't want the blood of another postal strike on their hands. David Minton, then counsel to the committee, says that "reform was a high visibility item in the media following the strike and that had a very influential role in pushing reorganization through."[8] The Senate passed the bill in essentially the same form as it had come over from the House. When the House approved the conference committee report on August 6, reorganization was on its way to the White House, where, not surprisingly, the information folks at POD had prepared an elaborate bill-signing ceremony that received enormous and favorable press coverage.

The Impact of the Press

Assessing the impact of the press in the enactment of postal reorganization is complicated. What was produced in the media by the POD and CCPR press strategies went far beyond news coverage, and included commentary, editorials, and advertisements. In addition, there were other elements which played important roles, such as the grassroots organizing and the pressure it generated on members of Congress and the strike. White House support was obviously important. Winton Blount's tenacity was crucial. In the view of Congressman Derwinski, "What got postal reform through was that Blount was an unusually determined, able man who just bulldogged it."[9] Blount himself sees the campaign to win the support of the public and the local media as central to their success, although not solely responsible for it. "There is no key force or event that created postal reform; it was a lot of forces and events working together. . . . The campaign to draw media support was enormously important; that's the way you move the Congress and if we had not had the media support we would have had a bad time. I don't remember specific incidents where a Congressman would cite editorial support in his home district as his reason for changing his position, but you could see that their changes corresponded to periods when public support for reorganization was voiced. . . . If the public had been 'ho-hum,' fifty-fifty, I don't think we would have reorganized the Post Office." [10]

Assessing the impact of the press is further complicated by the understandable tendency to separate news coverage from editorials and both of them from paid advertisements. One of the insights behind the Blount strategy is that all those pieces of the media play a role and have an effect. Advertisements are public relations, not press coverage, but Blount and his allies understood that each element of the media has its own constituency and influence, and that all were important in putting reorganization on the agenda, framing the issue, putting pressure on the Congress, and eventually passing the bill. When it comes to advertising, the press is just a conduit. In the Post Office case, officials were able to get news coverage and editorial support for reorganization that was almost as unfiltered as their ads. It is challenging enough to examine what role in general the press played. The task becomes impossible if it has to include distinguishing impacts among different types of newspaper copy. It also becomes irrelevant, because the point is that the POD and CCPR set out to use the mass media, in all its formats, to help achieve their policy goals and they succeeded. The question is how much credit does the entire media campaign deserve for their success.

When the bill was filed in May 1979, the outlook for its passage was bleak. Postal reform was not a salient issue for the editorial writers, never mind the general public. It was a priority for the Nixon administration, but there was strong opposition from powerful unions, a Democratic Congress, Republicans angered by the patronage shutoff, and those beloved letter carriers who delivered the mail.

Then for a few months, the pro-reorganization forces had the field to themselves. The opposition was there, but asleep. During that period, most of whatever appeared in the newspapers about reform was there at the initiative of CCPR and the POD. When the opposition awoke in September, their advantage had been almost completely dissipated. What looked almost impossible in May now appeared to be about to happen. The unions had wanted a pay raise and wanted to keep their future in the friendly hands of the Congress. By mid-September, it appeared that they might get the worse of both possible worlds, no pay raise and a reorganization bill out of their beloved House Post Office Committee. During the interim, the POD and CCPR had been able to achieve two huge objectives. First, they had taken an issue, postal reform, and put it on the national political agenda. That was no mean feat, and it was aided enormously by the willingness of the president to climb aboard and stay there. Without the press strategy it seems very unlikely that, absent an unforeseen external intervening event such as another Chicago-type crisis, reorganization would have ever gained its momentum in the Congress in general or in HPOC in particular. The second great achievement during that period, besides putting reorganization on the front burner, was to frame the administration's bill in such a way as to give it the best shot at success. The framing had three pieces to it: whatever were the grievances with the Post Office, whether they be late mail or underpaid letter carriers, reorganization was an answer, if not *the* answer; support for the proposal was bipartisan; and the administration bill was the only real reform. While the unions and their supporters in the Congress were talking with each other, these three messages were being systematically trumpeted all over the land in a multimedia spectacular aimed directly at the press and the public, and only indirectly to the legislators themselves. When the music stopped, there was a sense out there that the problems in the POD were real, that the Nixon bill was a positive response to them, and that this was an issue above partisanship.

The unions recognized this and responded with their own press campaign, which stemmed the tide, not by directly countering any of those three messages, but by adding two of their own. The first was the CCPR, which was not what it appeared to be; the second was that the only real issue for the postal employees was pay. The unions appear to have understood that the clear field had given the POD and CCPR the opportunity to put reorganization on the political agenda and to frame it in a way that made the union opposition rhetoric on the merits no longer credible to journalists and editorial writers following the issue. By their own positive campaign, the unions were able to salvage the most they could: reviving the pay raise issue as a high congressional priority, and putting the CCPR and its campaign for reorganization temporarily on the defensive.

There was a third great press campaign in this story: the effort of the White House to try to create a climate during the strike which would help to ensure that whatever happened, reorganization would not be hurt by the walkout. As the strike spread, the White House developed a strategy with four objectives, as recalled by Ehrlichman: "Nixon . . . wanted us to paint the strikers as outlaws who were doing something illegal; . . . to convey to the American public how to use the post office during the strike; . . . to use the strike to sell postal reform; and finally, he wanted to make sure that he came out of this looking like a strong leader." [11]

The program was straightforward and well executed. Under the direction of H. R. Haldeman, a game plan was prepared to convey these messages through a variety of means, including saturating television talk and news shows with administration spokespeople and friendly members of Congress. Herb Klein sent fact sheets to three hundred editorial writers and nine hundred radio and television news directors. Handling the combination of messages was tricky; too much strong leadership and strike-baiting might backfire. Letter carriers were generally among the most popular of public employees, and the polls showed that there was substantial sympathy for the postal workers and their specific grievances. The administration did not want to encourage other unions to join the postal workers, or to encourage the most militant among their number to take control.

This campaign, too, was successful, although once again helped significantly by the firm commitment in the White House to sticking with the issue during the hard bargaining which produced the combined pay-and-reform package that eventually was enacted.

The press campaigns played a major role in the outcome of this policymaking. Campaign is not used casually here; these were not one-time efforts, such as a single press conference or individual leak. They were well planned, complicated, continuing, multifaceted, and well executed. Most important, they worked. One moral of the tale is that Ronald Reagan did not invent the concept of press management, but anyone who remembers Franklin Delano Roosevelt's fireside chats knows that anyway.

References

1. David Whitman, "Selling the Reorganization of the Post Office (A)," Kennedy School of Government, case C14-84-610, pp. 2-4.
2. Ibid., p. 9.
3. Ibid., pp. 11-12.
4. Ibid., p. 20.
5. Senate Post Office and Civil Service Committee, Postal Modernization, Hearings, 91st Congress, 1st session, 1969, page 800.
6. Ibid., p. 38.
7. Post Office Department transcript of Winton M. Blount/George Meany press conference, August 5, 1970, pp. 1 and 2.
8. Whitman, Post Office Sequel case, p. 7.
9. Ibid, pp. 7-8.
10. Ibid, pp. 8-9
11. Ibid, p. 4.

6.3 ▬▬▬▬

Chernobyl: The Packaging of
Transnational Ecological Disaster

Timothy W. Luke

Editor's Note. All governments seek to control media images, hoping that their policies and actions will create favorable impressions among the public. When a disaster strikes, like the 1986 explosion at Chernobyl in the Soviet Ukraine, government officials try hard to control damaging publicity. By taking an exceptionally broad sweep through news stories from the Soviet Union, the United States, and several European countries, Timothy W. Luke is able to demonstrate that control efforts are universal. In fact, the efforts of governments to interpret the story so that it supports their ideological stances are supplemented by similar efforts by private groups, such as nuclear power firms and the antinuclear movement.

Luke claims that damage control was effective. By depicting Chernobyl's problems as an isolated instance, occurring in a climate of bureaucratic inefficiency in an obsolete nuclear power plant, it was possible to convince much of the public that the disaster did not reflect on the safety of nuclear power. Hence nuclear power generation could proceed unhampered. Luke's conclusion appears to conflict with Rothman and Lichter's view in Part 5 that media coverage has seriously damaged the nuclear power industry. It should be kept in mind, however, that Luke deals with governmental efforts to control coverage of a single dramatic disaster whereas Rothman and Lichter discuss long-range coverage of the nuclear power industry under normal conditions.

Luke has published widely in the areas of political thought, international relations, and comparative politics. He is associate professor of political science at Virginia Polytechnic Institute and State University. The selection comes from "Chernobyl: The Packaging of Transnational Ecological Disaster," *Critical Studies in Mass Communication* 4 (1987): 351-375.

On Saturday April 26, 1986, an unprecedented event happened. At 1:24 a.m., two large explosions tore apart nuclear reactor No. 4 at the

---

From *Critical Studies in Mass Communication* 4 (1987): 351-375. Reprinted by permission of the Speech Communication Association.

Chernobyl atomic power station in the Ukraine, killing two people and releasing fissionable materials into the environment. Chernobyl is so shocking because it is that unlikely statistical improbability suddenly become an immediately real, transnational, ecological disaster. It starkly contradicts images of technical precision and positive cost-benefit comparisons with coal, oil, or gas consumption that the nuclear power industry usually packages into its image advertising. The catastrophic meltdown that experts had predicted could happen only once in 10,000 years took place less than 10 years after the first unit at the Chernobyl power station went on line. . . .

. . . The Soviet and American governments used the Chernobyl accident to forestall new criticisms of their commitment to nuclear energy. Anti-nuclear activists in contrast played upon Chernobyl to demystify the serious risks involved in nuclear power as well as its intrinsic ties to nuclear weaponry. None of Chernobyl's many meanings, then, exists as such. Instead, they have had to be manufactured in both the East and West to define the experience of Chernobyl for a diverse range of mass publics. As they are produced, the broader reception of such meanings is rarely clean, clear, or complete.

Against the backdrop of the events in the reactor itself, and their ongoing secondary implications on the economies and ecologies of Western and Eastern Europe, the meaning of Chernobyl has been remanufactured by Moscow, the news media, the nuclear power industry, anti-nuclear activists, and the OECD (Organization for Economic Co-operation and Development) nations to convey many ideological meanings. In this regard, Chernobyl is an excellent example of how spectacles develop and are managed in advanced industrial societies. . . .

The news of Chernobyl has fit well within the ideological mechanisms in both the East and the West. State agencies and technocratic experts have drawn on widely available cultural stories such as Faust, the sorcerer's apprentice, and Frankenstein to transform a specific social and historical event into a tale of technological inevitability. . . .

. . . *Newsweek*'s issue on Chernobyl, for example, stated, "so nuclear power turns out to be a bargain with the Devil," and "the Devil always sets his own fee" (Martz, Miller, Greenberg, & Springen, 1986, pp. 40, 49). According to one version of these official fables, post-Hiroshima humanity has made a fateful wager. In order to enjoy the immense but dark powers of the atom, nuclear society either has made a pact with Mephisto for its soul or has created an evermore threatening servant that can easily evade human control. Even General Secretary Mikhail Gorbachev felt the need to repeat these myths. During his May 14 television address to the Soviet Union, he implied that humanity directly confronted the nuclear power monsters it has created as an afterthought from the larger monster of nuclear arms. "For the first time ever, we have confronted in reality [at

Chernobyl] the sinister power of uncontrolled nuclear energy" (Greenwald, Jackson, & Traver, 1986, p. 32). Therefore, as Weinberg (1986, p. 57) claims, "in this Faustian bargain, humans in opting for nuclear energy, must pay the price of extraordinary technical vigilance if they are to avoid serious trouble."

Such mythologies stress the strengths of the status quo, glossing over the accident that has torn only a small, temporary hole in the conventional order. These stories represent realities and forces that are beyond the control of ordinary individuals. By reducing the Chernobyl disaster to the work of "alien, reified forces," the media presentations of Chernobyl reveal what Tuchman (1978, p. 214) sees as two familiar effects of the news. First, they affirm "that the individual is powerless to battle either the forces of nature or the forces of the economy." Second, they "soothe the news consumers even as they reify social forces. . . . If experts look into a 'freak accident,' it is to ensure that a similar disaster could never happen again." As a freak mishap, any failure easily can be assigned to the Chernobyl reactor operators' or designers' technical blunders. As a result, the nuclear magic basically remains sound; the disaster came only from inept magicians, and they rightly paid their price in serious trouble for lacking technical vigilance. On April 30, 1986, for example, a *New York Times* editorial reaffirmed the myths: "The accident may reveal more about the Soviet Union than the hazards of nuclear power. . . . Behind the Chernobyl setback may lie deeper faults of a weak technology and industrial base" ("Chernobyl's Other Cloud," 1986, p. A17, A19). When presented in these terms, the immediately visible images of Chernobyl can be taken as meaning something in themselves without contradictions, because they reassuringly link up with existing Western mythologies about the Soviet Union as an industrial power. Given this ideological spin in the West, all the correct myths thereby are revalidated: the nuclear bargain was not flawed, the Soviet Union simply was too weak for Mephisto; Chernobyl was merely a setback, revealing nothing about the growing hazards of atomic energy; the deeper fault was in Soviets, who lack a firm industrial base and strong technology; or, Soviet nuclear sorcerers lack adequate magic, so their atomic apprentice ran amok. Moreover, the atomic Frankenstein monster was unleashed *only* in the Soviet Union. Western nuclear sorcerers are much more crafty, just as a *Los Angeles Times* story on April 30, 1986 claimed: "Minimum safety standards . . . clearly have not been met in the Soviet Union, where most nuclear reactors—apparently including the ill-fated plant at Chernobyl—do not have containment structures of the sort that are almost universal outside Russia" (Dorman & Hirsch, 1986, p. 56).

When deployed in this context, such mythologies usually acquire an ugly ideological cast. As Alan Krass, an analyst with the Union of Concerned Scientists, noted, American officials "have an incentive for making the accident worse than it is—just as the Soviets have an incentive to make it better. There's no way to keep these things out of the propaganda war" (Levin, Charles, Winslow, Burton, Austen, & McKenzie, 1986, p. 26). . . .

The East

In the Soviet Union, on one level, Chernobyl enabled Moscow to reiterate the common Faustian mythologies of "Humanity Tragically Trapped by its Own Runaway Technology." General Secretary Gorbachev's May 14, 1986 address clearly was guided by such myths in explaining to the world and the Soviet Union one meaning of Chernobyl. On another level, however, Chernobyl served Gorbachev by expressing his personal break with the cultural and political stagnation of the Brezhnev era. It is unclear if Gorbachev chose this *glasnost* for himself or if the crisis forced *glasnost* upon him. Still, Chernobyl eventually was packaged in Moscow, first, as a subtle sign of Gorbachev's goal of cleaning out the Brezhnev era bureaucracy in the national and union republic bureaucracies and, second, as an indicator of Gorbachev's commitment to frankness, openness, and effective publicity. . . .

Although Gorbachev did not directly criticize Chernobyl's management of local officials in his May 14 address, *Pravda* reported on June 15 that the party organization at the Chernobyl site was "sharply condemned" by the local territorial apparatus (Hoffman, 1986, p. 35; Marples, 1986, pp. 32-35). The plant director and chief engineer were discharged for irresponsibility, inefficiency, poor discipline, and inadequate leadership, while the shift supervisors and plant foremen were described as still being on the defensive. Moscow, therefore, shifted the blame for the accident, the delay in evacuations, inefficient relief reports, and tardiness in reporting the accident for three days on to the Brezhnev appointees in the local and regional party apparatus. . . .

This concern with cleaning house and punishing lax workers was affirmed in March 1987, and the policy of *glasnost*, or the new openness of the Soviet state to popular opinion and the use of modern publicity techniques, has continued since the accident. In March 1987, the chairman of the State Committee for Atomic Energy told a visiting Nuclear Regulatory Commission (NRC) delegation that the persons responsible for Chernobyl would be put on trial soon in Kiev (Bohlen, 1987a, pp. A17, A19). Members of the delegation also visited the Chernobyl power station and were shown its operating units and the two under construction or development. But *glasnost* was not total. The team learned some minor details, but basically the NRC was told "nothing really new since Vienna" (Bohlen, 1987a, p. A19). Since the accident, many people inside and outside of the Soviet Union have complained that *glasnost* has not gone nearly far enough. In March 1987, Viktor Afanasyev, the editor of *Pravda*, complained that many state agencies still were giving his reporters scanty information and then only reluctantly ("Soviet Editor," 1987, p. A27). The Soviet press, however, continued to expose official blunders during the Chernobyl crisis, charging local officials with most of the blame (Bohlen, 1987c, pp. A1, A38)....

In seeking to package Chernobyl at home and abroad in the new look of *glasnost*, Gorbachev has been somewhat more successful (Bohlen, 1987b, pp. A21, A26). During his May 14 speech, he stressed the "accuracy" of Soviet accident reports versus the "veritable pack of lies" in the Western press and official commentary. Whereas he portrayed his regime's more open press policies on the Chernobyl disaster as frank and truthful, Gorbachev noted how it was overshadowed by false Western reports of "thousands of casualties, mass graves of the dead, desolate Kiev, [and] that the entire land of the Ukraine has been poisoned" (*Daily Report: Soviet Union*, 1986, p. L1-L4). At the same time, he linked Chernobyl to the danger of nuclear arms, calling for a summit with President Reagan to negotiate a test moratorium and announcing a continuation of suspended Soviet nuclear testing (Greenwald, Jackson, & Traver, 1986, pp. 32-33). By lashing back at overdrawn Western criticism, Gorbachev sought to cast the Soviet Union in the most favorable light as an honest, open, great power wrestling with the unknown mysteries and sinister forces of nuclear energy. He recounted why the accident happened, admitting to 13 deaths and 299 hospitalized casualties. He also emphasized that Soviet scientists had contained the threat and were capable of meeting the formidable technical challenges ahead. To prove he was serious about *glasnost*, Gorbachev apparently approved greater access to Chernobyl for the Soviet press, permitting unprecedented on-site interviews, dramatic close-up television footage of reactor No. 4, and critical reporting on the local authorities' response to the crisis....

In repackaging Chernobyl, the Soviet Union stressed its progressiveness as a nation fearlessly facing new technological frontiers with a new international openness. Even though it failed miserably to warn or assist its Eastern European allies and Western European neighbors in coping with Chernobyl's nuclear and economic fallout, the Soviet Union has gotten away with such negligence, perhaps because these behaviors were almost expected from Moscow. Gorbachev's packaging, to a degree, has pinned this aspect of Chernobyl on "the old regime" of Brezhnev appointees, while he holds out a promising image of himself and Raisa spurring the Soviet Union toward a more open future of prosperity, reform, and peace....

... Despite the negative aftershocks from the crisis, Chernobyl clearly has produced some positive fallout for the international image makers in Moscow.

The West

In the OECD nations, Chernobyl also soon acquired mythic dimensions.

. . . [T]he Chernobyl accident was used to assign fresh sources of meaning to the commonly circulated images of the Soviet Union as, first, a barbaric slave state with little regard for human life, and, second, as new evidence of the Soviet Union's continuing backwardness as an industrial power.

. . . Secretary of State George Shultz " 'bet $10' that the deaths were 'far in excess' " of the two initially reported by Moscow. Kenneth Adelman, head of the U.S. Arms Control and Disarmament Agency, also decried Soviet casualty reports as "frankly preposterous" (Dorman & Hirsch, 1986, p. 54). In the seesaw of superpower arms negotiations, the accident also was portrayed as meaning Washington could not trust Moscow to verify nuclear treaties because of the Soviets' inadequate disclosure about Chernobyl. A May 1 *New York Times* editorial argued, "Gorbachev cannot win confidence in his pledges to reduce nuclear weapons if he forfeits his neighbor's trust over the peaceful uses of nuclear energy" ("Mayday! and May Day," 1986, p. A26). President Reagan also used Chernobyl to cast doubt on Soviet credibility at the Tokyo economic summit, while *Time* (Greenwald, Aikman, & Traver, 1986, p. 46) reported one American official as saying, "Imagine what they do to national security items if they handle themselves like this with just a civilian power plant." In a similar vein, *The Times* of London stated editorially, "Soviet standards in nuclear power are lower and the risks of disaster consequently higher. . . . Plain self-interest may persuade the Soviet rulers to insulate nuclear energy policy from general Soviet paranoia and open its plants to international inspection" ("The Soviet Interest in Cooperation," 1986, p. 13). Thus the image of the Soviet Union as a totalitarian monolith with little regard for individual human life gained new meaning in the Chernobyl afterglow. Although Soviet government, military, and party leaders displayed great concern for the local citizens of Pripyat and Chernobyl and although individual firemen, technicians, and helicopter pilots displayed incredible personal sacrifice in containing the reactor fire, the bureaucratic confusion between Kiev and Moscow practically verified such cynical Western packaging of Chernobyl.

The Soviet Union clearly deserves no credit and little praise for its handling of Chernobyl. As Hoffman (1986, p. 36) concludes, "Any government, socialist or capitalist, that withholds from its citizens information about the dangers of nuclear energy or fails to help citizens protect themselves . . . before and after a nuclear accident at home or abroad diminishes its legitimacy and effectiveness." Nevertheless, as Bernstein (1986, p. 40) states of American nuclear information policies from the Manhattan Project to Three Mile Island, Americans must recognize that "their own government, at various levels, has sometimes suppressed information and deceived its own citizens about the safety and purposes of the U.S. nuclear program."

Chernobyl also was employed as a fresh citation to the Soviet Union's deepening technological backwardness. . . . White House Press Spokesman Larry Speakes announced that poor Soviet design and engineering were at fault in the crisis. To forestall comparisons with U.S. reactors, he assured the world that "ours are quite different from the Soviet system and have a number of redundant safety systems built in" (Greenwald, Aikman, Duffy, & McGeary, 1986, p. 43). Even though such claims were somewhat false, numerous Western experts came forward to assure the public that the Soviet reactor was antiquated, poorly designed, and lacked a containment structure. In Donald Regan's assessment, Soviet industrial backwardness was to blame, *not* atomic energy itself: "Nuclear power is a good thing for the future of many nations, including our own—we shouldn't throw out the baby with the bath water and condemn all nuclear power plants because of this" (Hawkes et al., 1986, p. 161).

To reinforce this picture of Soviet industrial inefficiency and incompetence, the Nuclear Energy Agency (NEA) of the OECD met 12 days after Chernobyl to assess the accident's meaning for the West. The NEA decided it should study how to improve cooperation in future nuclear accidents. It concluded, however, that because Western reactor types were quite superior to Soviet designs (Soviet reactors could not even be licensed in the West), no reconsideration of OECD nuclear energy programs was necessary. Since 30% of Western Europe's, 16% of the United States', and 20% of Japan's electricity is nuclear generated, the Tokyo economic summit affirmed the OECD's joint support of "properly managed" Western nuclear power (Fischer, 1986, pp. 47-48). . . .

The American media, in particular, actively participated in packaging Chernobyl in terms of Soviet callousness and backwardness. In its typical style, the *New York Post* ran headlines, lifted from a New Jersey Ukrainian weekly, that bellowed "MASS GRAVE—15,000 reported buried in Nuke Disposal Site" (McGrath, 1986, p. 31). More reputable news operations did not do much better. For days, on the basis of an unconfirmed report from Kiev, UPI, AP, NBC, ABC, CBS, *The New York Times*, and *The Washington Post* used the figure 2,000 deaths with varying degrees of qualification in reporting on Chernobyl. When put in context with official Soviet reports of 2 to 31 deaths, these news reports implicitly exposed the Soviet Union as the lying, untrustworthy dictatorship it always was. For most of the week following the accident, news reports consistently overestimated casualties, claimed two or even more reactors might be on fire, and suggested the rescue and cleanup were going very slowly. Reports of Western aid, like the West German robots, Swedish technical consultants, and the American bone marrow transplant team, also were highlighted to stress the Soviet Union's technical inabilities in coping with the disaster. Yet, beyond buying SPOT or LANDSAT photos for visual confirmation of their dire dispatches, most news organizations relied on Western officials and handouts for most of their copy rather than any on-the-spot reporting.

This tendency undoubtedly was accentuated by the unusual press access to officials afforded by President Reagan's Far East tour leading into the Tokyo summit. Overall, as Dorman and Hirsch (1986, p. 55) observe:

> The initial Soviet statements turned out to be largely correct on a number of significant concerns—for example, the number of casualties, the number of reactors on fire, and whether or not the fire had been contained—while those of the Reagan administration, which were taken by journalists at face value, proved not to be.

The American press also was remarkably slow about correcting its earlier sensational and inaccurate packaging of Chernobyl. By May 19, 1986, *The New York Times* and *The Wall Street Journal* ran stories reporting that the Soviet Union had built substantial containment structures in its reactors after Three Mile Island and that American complacency about U.S. reactor designs was unwarranted (Diamond, 1986, pp. A1, A6; Taylor, 1986, p. 4). Yet these insights were mainly drawn from an NRC briefing nearly two weeks earlier on May 8 and NRC Commissioner James Asseltine's testimony before the House on May 5. While titillating inaccuracies were given front-page first column spreads in late April, the sober realities were tabled for two or three weeks only to end up later as minor sidebars or back-page, second section fillers. In the end, both the Western press and Washington flatly claimed that if some media reports were inaccurate, "this was the inevitable result of the extreme secrecy with which the Soviet authorities dealt with the accident in the days following it" (Greenwald, Jackson, & Traver, 1986, p. 32).

Beyond the Western nations, the most highly motivated Western group, working to redefine the meaning of Chernobyl, was the American nuclear power industry. A White House official echoed their interests in *Time*: "we don't want the hysteria building around the Soviet accident transferring over to the American power industry" (Greenwald, Aikman, Duffy, & McGeary, 1986, p. 43). Given the American nuclear power industry's political problems at Indian Point, Seabrook, Shoreham, Browns Ferry, Zion, Diablo Canyon, Palo Verde, Three Mile Island, as well as the TVA and WPPSS (Washington Public Power Supply System) reactor programs, such concerns were quite significant.

. . . Chernobyl's meaning in the packaging of the Western nuclear power industry was simple: it had "no meaning" because the RBMK

[Russian Graphite-Moderated Channel tube] reactor was so radically different from all Western reactors. The Atomic Industrial Forum (1986, pp. 1-3) sent out mailings claiming that Chernobyl had no containment structure and that all American reactors had the extensive steel and concrete protective barriers that most Soviet units lacked. A public relations blitz mounted by the Electrical Power Research Institute also claimed that Chernobyl was poorly designed because it lacked steel and concrete containments common in the United States (Dorman & Hirsh, 1986, p.55). The Edison Electric Institute simply stated, "We have not and will not have a Chernobyl-type plant accident here" (Hawkes et al., 1986, p. 16). With no orders for new plants since 1978, the American nuclear companies were correctly worried. Before the accident, some experts foresaw offers for new plants by 1991 or 1996, but Chernobyl threatened to pull the plug on America's dying nuclear technology industry.

Subsequent revelations about Chernobyl's design, as well as those of American reactors, underscored the importance of assigning a negative, irrelevant meaning to the Soviet accident when it was headline material in the United States (Paul, 1987, p. 63). By May 1986, it was revealed that the United States was operating two graphite-moderated reactors, one water cooled and one gas cooled, in Washington and Colorado (Stoler, 1986, p. 59). Contrary to the Edison Electric Institute's claims, a Chernobyl-type graphite-fire accident theoretically could occur in either trouble-plagued unit. Moreover, the graphite-moderated N-reactor in Hanford, Washington as well as four other units in Savannah, Georgia, which are producing plutonium and tritium for the Department of Energy's nuclear weapons program, lack adequate containment structures (Hawkes et al., 1986, pp. 163-164). . . .

Conclusion

In the last analysis, the packaging of Chernobyl in both the East and the West basically has proven effective. Within days after the accident, it was clear that many of its threatening meanings had been contained. Even though they were not entirely neutralized, Chernobyl really has not called the future of nuclear power into question. Instead, the mythologies of advanced industrial ideology used Chernobyl to reaffirm the impossibility of future human progress without *more* nuclear power.

. . . In certain respects, the ideological reprocessing of Chernobyl by the Soviet Union, the Western media, the leadership of the OECD nations, and the Western nuclear power industry was interconnected. Each of them, working in its own fashion, sought to reaffirm the legitimacy of high technology and the authority of technological competence from an episode of high-tech disaster and clear technological incompetence. Otherwise, the anti-nuclear, ecological opposition might gain more ground in its struggle against nuclearization. Chernobyl flashed "transmission interruption," "technical difficulties," or "broadcast interference" across the screens of scientific-technological power. It had to be repackaged as a warning to everyone "not to adjust your sets." Those powerful elites with access, competence, and control of the technological codes were stalling the mass publics without access, competence, or scientific code command, reassuring them "to remain calm and await further instructions" rather than increase their growing resistance to the dominant ideology's endorsement of nuclear energy.

Despite these elites' best efforts, however, the nature of these images' reception is open to question, given the growing popular resistance to nuclear power and nuclear weaponry. In some smaller nations, such as Sweden, New Zealand, Australia, Denmark, Austria, Greece, and Luxembourg, an anti-nuclear consensus already has taken hold. For the ecological opposition, Chernobyl served well as its dire prophecies of nuclear disaster fulfilled in deadly fact. . . .

. . . Apparently, the ideological repackaging of Chernobyl, like many costly advertising campaigns, simply reinforced already existing attitudes, providing new reasons for individuals to continue holding on to their anti-nuclear or pro-nuclear stances.

References

Atomic Industrial Forum, Inc. (1986, May). *Multiple barrier containment: Significant differences between U.S.-Soviet reactors: AIF background info* [Publicity leaflet].

Bernstein, B. (1986). Nuclear deception: The U.S. record. *Bulletin of the Atomic Scientists*, 42 (7), 40-43.

Bohlen, C. (1987a, March 14). Chernobyl personnel to go on trial, U.S. delegation visits plants, finds radiation level "very low." *The Washington Post*, pp. A17, A19.

Bohlen, C. (1987b, April 26). Chernobyl was first test of Gorbachev's policy of openness. *The Washington Post*, pp. A21, A26.

Bohlen, C. (1987c, June 11). Soviet article charges local officials hid Chernobyl risks. *The Washington Post*, pp. A1, A38.

Chernobyl's other cloud. (1986, April 30). *The New York Times*, p. A17, A19.

Daily Report: Soviet Union. (1986, May 15). Text of 14 May Gorbachev television address. III, No. 94 Supp. 95 pp. L1-L4. Foreign Broadcast Information Service, Springfield, VA.

Diamond, S. (1986, May 19). Chernobyl design found to include safety plans. *The New York Times*, pp. A1, A6.

Dorman, W. A., & Hirsch, D. (1986). The U.S. media's slant. *Bulletin of the Atomic Scientists*, 42 (7), 54-56.

Fischer, D. A. V. (1986). The international response. *Bulletin of the Atomic Scientists*, 42 (7), 46-48.

Greenwald, J., Aikman, D., Duffy, M., & McGeary, J. (1986, May 12). Deadly meltdown. *Time*, pp. 39-44, 49-50, 52.

Greenwald, J., Aikman, D., & Traver, N. (1986, May 19). More fallout from Chernobyl. *Time*, pp. 44-46.

Greenwald, J., Jackson, J. O., & Traver, N. (1986, May 26). Gorbachev goes on the offensive. *Time*, pp. 32-33.

Hawkes, N., Lean, G., Leigh, D., McKie, R., Pringle, P., & Wilson, A. (1986). *Chernobyl: The end of the nuclear dream*. New York: Vintage Books.

Hoffman, E.P. (1986). Nuclear deception: Soviet information policy. *Bulletin of the Atomic Scientists*, 42 (7), 32-37.

Levin, B., Charles, K., Winslow, P., Burton, J., Austen, I., & McKenzie, H. (1986, May 12). The fear of nuclear chaos. *Macleans*, pp. 26-34.

Marples, D. R. (1986). *Chernobyl and nuclear power in the USSR*. New York: St. Martin's Press.

Martz, L., Miller, M., Greenberg, N. F., & Springen, K. (1986, May 12). There's a price to be paid for atomic energy, and it could be a high one. *Newsweek*, pp. 40-41, 44, 49.

Mayday! and May Day. (1986, May 1). *The New York Times*, p. A26.

McGrath, P. (1986, May 26). Did the media hype Chernobyl? *Newsweek*, p. 31.

Paul, B. (1987, March 18). Electric utility analysts almost never discuss financial impact of accidents at nuclear plants. *The Wall Street Journal*, p. 63.

Soviet editor tells reporters to change. (1987, March 15). *The Washington Post*, p. A27.

Stoler, P. (1986, May 12). Bracing for the fallout. *Time*, p. 59.

Taylor, R. E. (1986, May 12). Soviet workers trying to seal reactor's core. *The Wall Street Journal*, p. 4.

The Soviet interest in cooperation. (1986, May 2). *The Times*, p. 13.

Tuchman, G. (1978). *Making news: A study in the construction of reality*. New York: Free Press.

Weinberg, A. M. (1986). A nuclear power advocate reflects on Chernobyl. *Bulletin of the Atomic Scientists*, 42 (7), 57-60.

6.4 ■

Government Secrecy and the Media
in the United States and Britain

John Downing

Editor's Note. The freedom of expression that democratic societies prize
comes under severest attack when it conflicts with the right and duty of
democratic governments to protect the country's national security. There is a
perennial power struggle between government leaders who seek to control
the flow of communication and to conceal sensitive information in the name
of national security and the press and its allies who try to prevent allegedly
undue and harmful restraints on the flow of information. In this struggle, the
deck is stacked far more against the British media than their U.S. counterparts.

Nonetheless, as John Downing points out, government security censorship has kept many important policy issues from the public in both countries,
despite the numerous and inevitable cases of "leaks" and "whistle-blowing"
by government insiders. Because the absence of public dialogue about major
controversial issues can have dire consequences, Downing urges greater care
in defining the groundrules by which the needs for government censorship
are judged. This is a sound recommendation, but it founders on the near
impossibility of determining what does and does not imperil national
security when knowledgeable observers disagree vigorously and often violently.

Downing has been in close touch with the two countries whose systems
of government secrecy he compares. He was head of the Sociology Division
of Thames Polytechnic in London and, at the time of writing, chaired the
Communications Department at Hunter College in New York. He is
pursuing his interest in comparative communication policies by researching
Soviet international satellite communications and Spanish-language media in
the New York area. The selection comes from "Governmental Secrecy and
the Media in the United States and Britain," in *Communicating Politics:
Mass Communications and the Political Process*, ed. Peter Golding, Graham Murdock, and Philip Schlesinger (New York: Holmes and Meier,
Leicester University Press, 1986), 153-170.

Reprinted from Peter Golding, Graham Murdock, and Philip Schlesinger, eds., *Communicating
Politics: Mass Communication and the Political Process*, selected sections of pp. 153-170.
Copyright © 1986 by Holmes & Meier Publishers, Inc.

In 1984 Senator Barry Goldwater, conservative Republican chairman of the Senate Intelligence Committee, made public a letter he had just written to the Director of the Central Intelligence Agency. In it he asked the director: 'What the hell is going on?' He was referring to the CIA's secret decision to mine Nicaraguan ports. Senator Moynihan, vice-chairman, threatened resignation over the issue. In the same year, a junior British civil servant, Sarah Tisdall, was sacked and gaoled for six months for divulging to the *Guardian* the plans of the then Defence Minister Michael Heseltine to make a deliberately confusing statement to the House of Commons concerning the arrival of US cruise missiles at Greenham Common.

Secrecy was not total. Both cases were widely reported in the respective countries. After an international outcry, the CIA desisted from this form of subversion against Nicaragua. In Britain Ms. Tisdall served her sentence, despite the national outcry. The US case was only the latest in a twenty-year series of clashes between Congress and executive agencies over the waging of undeclared war. The British case was a classic of the UK's omnibus definition of secrecy rights, even to the point of effective judicial endorsement of a government minister's right to deceive the House of Commons. Neither case should be taken to summarize the entire character of government secrecy in the country concerned.

British debate over the comparison of government secrecy and the media in the USA and the UK is usually framed around the prior positions of reformers and traditionalists. Reformers point triumphantly to aspects of the US system to underpin their claim that openness in government is not tantamount to social revolution. Traditionalists look sniffily at the appearances — for example, the US Freedom of Information Act (1974) and the Government in the Sunshine Act (1977) — and insist that everyday information realities are much the same in both nations. In the USA, whilst one wing of opinion would regard Britain as politically immature in this area, another would envy its quaintly charming stability, its heartwarming trust in government's 'knowing what is best,' its small volume of infuriating leaks.

Only one sure conclusion can be drawn from these long-standing *prises de position*, namely that the British traditionalists — rightly or wrongly — are quite alone in awarding equal force to government secrecy in both nations. . . .

Secrecy or Selective Communication

. . . Secrecy in both nations is not used as an impermeable shield blotting out all communication, but as a device to allow the pinnacle of the power-structure to communicate how and when it prefers. It is a mechanism of control over all the other echelons of government — or of attempted control, at least. Concretely speaking, this means there are two types of 'leak': those favoured by the executive branch leadership, and those infuriating to it (see Toinet 1983). The first type, together with official pronouncements, constitutes the selective communication which secrecy rules are designed to promote.

In Britain this system is formalized in ways different from the USA. The classic case is the lobby system in Parliament (Tunstall 1970), where journalists are accredited as a bloc to hear off-the-record briefings by senior ministers on a regular basis. Thus this elite corps is flattered to be privy to government confidences, but is bound by the rules of the game to censor itself when communicating many specific aspects of what it hears. Even this understates the muffling effect of the institution, for parliamentary correspondents are rarely adept at handling the specifics of the military or the economy, for instance, and thus can easily be fed comfortable generalities.

In Washington, DC, the comparable nerve-centre of US government despite the diffusion of the federal bureaucracy over the country, and despite the weighty roles of a number of state and metropolitan governments, the operation of selective communication is more complex. A frequent British image is one of tough, insistent reporters, fed with great meaty chunks of delicious, hot information by civic-minded civil servants anxious to ensure open government. The FOIA is seen as the investigative journalist's charter, and a large proportion of journalists as 'investigative'.

. . . [L]eaks — selective communication — in the federal capital mostly derive from quite different dynamics. . . .

[L]eaks are not normally whistle-blowing to the general public in the USA. Indeed, there is a whole series of reasons why this is a misconception. Most important of these is the fact that journalists rely on official sources for their information just as much as in Britain (Sigal 1973: ch. 6; Wilson 1982). Secondly, few media have the resources to pay a sufficiently large staff to do the necessary ferreting. . . .

Thirdly, whilst US civil servant whistle-blowers may not face jail for leaks, this is far from the only effective sanction: 'In the Soviet Union, whistle-blowers are sent directly to criminal psychiatric wards. In this country, we drive our whistle-blowers to the borders of insanity and sometimes over the edge by humiliating them, taking their jobs, demoting them, or forcing them to do non-work; slander and character assassination are frequently used' (Ball 1984: 307-10). The British campaigns to abolish the Official Secrets Act often seem to forget that it is only the most provocative measure in a whole armoury of reprisals.

. . . [M]uch of the ferreting is not policy related at all, but personality related: an assault on privacy, not a dismantling of government secrecy. It means that in nations with the absurdly puritanical public codes of both Britain and the USA, the easiest way to sink any public figure not backed by a Kennedy-type machine is to publicize a so-called sexual or personal irregularity. . . . We may conclude for the moment that while there is a greater openness in government in the USA (and thus the *possibility* of greater public awareness) than in Britain, the situation is not as open as some British reformers would often suppose.

National Security and Government Secrecy:
The Sacred Cow

. . . [T]he risk of nuclear war has been a linchpin argument by state authorities in Britain and the USA in favour of retaining secrecy about all nuclear matters, whether strategic or energy-related. The argument for government secrecy to protect national security against nuclear catastrophe appears unassailable: only an extremely naive pacifist, it seems, could pursue the anti-secrecy case beyond this juncture.

Yet it is always when faced with such seamless, glittering unassailabilities that we need to be most on our guard. The fear of nuclear destruction can terrorize us into ceasing to think. I would contend that at this juncture, the 'national security' juncture, people have often switched off their minds. Ideologies are at their most penetrative when in part they ring true to a major reality. Let us examine some cases of government secrecy on nuclear topics to illustrate the argument.

The only two nuclear bombs so far to be dropped on a human target were those unleashed on Hiroshima and Nagasaki in August 1945. Argument about their use has mostly been based on the rightness or wrongness of terrorism against a civilian population. From this perspective, the main differences between their use and the almost equally murderous assaults on Tokyo in March 1945, and on Dresden and Hamburg, consist in the long-term genetic effects of nuclear weapons, and the fact that these have developed from kiloton to megaton level in the years since.

There has been little public argument as to why they were dropped. Yet there is a current among contemporary historians which would question whether, covertly, the purpose in dropping them was not primarily to intimidate the Soviet leadership, rather than to bring the war with Japan to a speedy end and so to save US lives (see Alperovitz 1965; Maddox 1973: 63-78). They would dispute that an effective surrender by Japan was unobtainable by other, less violent means. If this contention is accurate, its implications for the present argument are considerable. It means that *from the outset* the uses of nuclear power have been shrouded in secrecy and thus have been able to be other than they were claimed to be. The sacrificial victims of this strategic decision were at least those Japanese against whom the bombs were unleashed. And since the Western powers were in error when they assumed the Soviet Union was not already developing its own nuclear weapons (Holloway 1983: ch. 2), it seems clear that, far from frightening the world into a Pax Americana, these secret decisions actually triggered an arms race which could end by destroying the planet.

A further example, this time from the world of strategic nuclear war planning, is the secrecy of the Rand Corporation during the 1950s and 1960s (Kaplan 1983). Time and again the varied policies generated in this prototype think-tank can be seen to have been based on the most partial and empirically flawed assumptions. Nonetheless, it took itself, and more particularly was taken by the USAF high command, with intense seriousness, as offering the last word in wisdom for nuclear war. Yet, crucially absent from Rand's war-games was the consideration that nuclear war was unwinnable because some counterstrike missiles would be sure to create unimaginable destruction for the 'victor'. Secrecy led to lack of self-criticism; such lack of scrutiny might have led to nuclear disaster.

The situation in Britain was little different. The War Cabinet never discussed the atomic bomb in the period leading up to 1945; the (Labour) Deputy Prime Minister was told nothing about it; and the Labour Cabinet as a whole, after the 1945 election, never discussed Britain's own bomb. From then until now, every effort has been made to discountenance public debate on the subject.

The seriousness of the secrecy clamp has not been limited to nuclear weapons. Nuclear energy — repeatedly touted as the peaceful opposite to missiles, but directly linked to them by technology and by menace to safety — has also been the subject of extraordinary government secrecy in both countries (Hilgartner et al. 1983). Information about nuclear accidents, about fall-out effects, about environmental contamination, about profitability, about safety for nuclear plant workers, about safety measures against meltdowns, has been fiercely guarded and managed. Despite the dramatization of the issue in films such as *The China Syndrome* and *Silkwood*, as well as in a small flood of independently produced anti-nuclear documentaries in the USA, the powers that be have not willingly relinquished one iota of control over information in this area. Slowly, however, popular scientific education on this topic, at least, is beginning to make headway through anti-nuclear media and through intermittent information in the major media. Peace researchers in and out of universities have succeeded in piecing together a large amount of information on nuclear topics, both strategic and energy related. Once again, secrecy is a battleground, not a given.

There are still other developments which have taken place under the heading of nuclear-secrecy-for-security which also threaten our real security. In Britain, a 1976 law set up an armed police force, practically immune from government control, in order to defend — nuclear installations! To US readers this development might seem of minor significance, a curious topic for anxiety, since they have learned to live with armed police and security guards. But then they have also learned to live with, at some cost, a murder-rate 35 times higher per head for New York alone than for Britain as a whole. The development by piecemeal methods of an armed, irresponsible police force in Britain has not been a simple 'coming into line': it has represented the disappearance of an alternative, more civilized method of policing from the debate about social self-defence. This has not enhanced citizen security.

Yet the insecurities into which nuclear secrecy has led us are deeper still than these. Tightly restricted scrutiny and oversight have permitted the covert diffusion of nuclear technology and therefore bombmaking capacity to South Africa, Brazil and Argentina via West German sources, themselves still banned from making nuclear weapons, though not from a say over their use (Jungk 1979: ch. 5). It has also enabled Israel to acquire stolen plutonium for its weapons in the USA (Jungk 1979: 124; Hilgartner 1983: 172) — plutonium losses are a problem the US nuclear industry does not submit to public scrutiny. Nuclear proliferation, given the very large number of unaccountable governments and militarized states in the world, is hardly a security measure.

It seems, then, that the argument for secrecy from national security is less unassailable than it at first appears. The history of nuclear activity is littered with tragedies, menace, waste, and has been stamped with secretiveness. It is very hard to maintain that this secrecy has been in the public interest. The argument from national security is seductive *only* because it touches a nerve of fear.

The Secrecy Tug-of-War

Throughout, it has been argued that government secrecy is not a fixed category. It may well be a permanent tendency in government, at least in the type of governments we currently enjoy, but it can be rolled back or it can be allowed to flourish. (The former is much harder work.)

The problem of rolling it back is that government secrecy only tends to become an issue in the course of some major symbolic crisis. In the USA, Watergate became such an issue, which could be exploited to reveal covert and illegal action by the FBI and the CIA, as well as by the President. The Freedom of Information Act 1974 was the high-water mark of this movement. Yet as Demac [1984] has demonstrated in detail, the Reagan administration has worked exceptionally hard to subvert that achievement. One key area in which media freedom was increasingly being threatened during 1984 was through stricter applications of the libel laws, long a familiar mechanism for muzzling the media in Britain through the crippling costs of an unsuccessful suit. The Burger Supreme

Court — Burger was appointed Chief Justice by Nixon in 1969 — has never found in favour of the media in libel cases, and was taking active measures in 1984 to restrict appeal courts' capacity to find for the media in them. The $120 million suit brought against CBS by ex-General Westmoreland for their portrayal of his role in Vietnam was the most public instance in 1984 of the attempt to use libel laws against the media (see Friedman 1984; Garbus 1984).

In Britain, the Thatcher administration's first attempt to tighten the reins of secrecy still further (the Protection of Government Information Bill 1980) foundered in the exceptional publicity suddenly given to Sir Anthony Blunt, the protected fourth mole in the Philby spy case of the 1950s. The bill would have kept Blunt protected, and so Thatcher had to retreat — a nice irony. However, when 'video-nasties' came up for agitated public discussion in the early 1980s, the Thatcher administration was able to recoup some of its ground by stimulating a wave of revulsion against these loathsome but practically unavailable and unseen products, to push a censorship law through Parliament (Barker 1984).

Conclusions

. . . We have seen that for both Britain and the United States, the notion that the more economically advanced the country the more liberal and open its government is a nineteenth-century nonsense. We are faced with a persistent attempt to reduce the free flow of information and to buttress government and corporate secrecy, in the interests of business rights and supposed national security. How public commentators can simultaneously speak of the coming of the information society is difficult to grasp, unless we are to assume that life is completely reducible to bytes, that one unit of information is as useful to democracy as another.

Yet both Britain and the United States have deeply rooted cultural traditions in favour of political liberties. The question for the 1980s and to the end of the century is how many people in each country have forgotten their value, and what experiences will be lived through to revive and enact a fundamental commitment to open government. . . .

At the same time, there is a key legitimacy problem for both regimes to handle. If they are to continue to preen themselves in public on the comparison of their secrecy records with the Soviet bloc's, then their strategy for information control must diverge from that model. The art in their strategy must be exercised in picking precise areas for secrecy, delicate mechanisms for controlling the media, reserve powers 'for emergencies only'. . . . Yet, like tax laws, the more complex the apparatus, often the greater is its potential disarray. The campaign against the secrecy of power and for media responsive to the majority is in no respect already foreclosed.

References

Alperovitz, G. 1965. *Atomic Diplomacy.* New York: Simon and Schuster.

Ball, H. (ed.), 1984. *Federal Administrative Agencies: Essays on Power and Politics.* Englewood Cliffs, N.J.: Prentice-Hall.

Barker, M. (ed.), 1984. *The Video Nasties: Freedom and Censorship in the Media.* London: Pluto Press.

Demac, D., 1984. *Keeping America Uninformed.* New York: Pilgrim Press.

Friedman, R., 1984. "All-out battle: Westmorland's suit against CBS raises unusual libel issues," *Wall Street Journal,* 1 October.

Garbus, M., 1984. "New challenge to press freedom," *New York Times Magazine,* January 29.

Hilgartner, S. et al., 1983. *Nukespeak: The Selling of Nuclear Technology in America.* New York: Penguin Books.

Holloway, D., 1983. *The Soviet Union and the Arms Race.* New Haven, Conn.: Yale University Press.

Jungk, R., 1979. *The Nuclear State.* London: Calder.

Kaplan, F., 1983. *The Wizards of Armageddon.* New York: Simon and Schuster.

Maddox, R. J., 1973. *The New Left and the Origins of the Cold War.* Princeton, N.J.: Princeton University Press.

Sigal, L., 1973. *Reporters and Officials.* Lexington, Mass.: D. C. Heath.

Toinet, M. F., 1983. "L'Amerique de M Reagan part en croisade pour la democratie," *Le Monde Diplomatique,* July.

Tunstall, J., 1970. *The Westminster Lobby Correspondents: A Sociological Study of National Political Journalism.* London: Routledge and Kegan Paul.

Wilson, A., 1982. "The defence correspondent," in Aubrey, C. (ed.), 1982. *Nukespeak: The Media and the Bomb.* London: Comedia Publishing.

6.5 ▬▬▬

International Information:
Bullet or Boomerang?

René Jean Ravault

Editor's Note. In 1977 the UNESCO-sponsored McBride Commission, named after its chairman Sean McBride, investigated ways to create a New World Information Order to protect third world mass communication systems from domination by major Western powers. Third world nations had complained that Western news agencies, with the blessing of their governments, use their virtual monopoly on news dissemination to vilify the third world, ignoring positive developments. Western newspeople were accused of swamping the third world with information supporting Western imperialism and raising false expectations and dangerous demands among the peoples of the less developed world. Accordingly, the McBride Commission recommended curbs on the uncontrolled flow of information from the West to the third world and greater government control over the activities of the press.

The passage of time has done little to abate the controversy. Most Western observers refute the charges and denounce the proposed remedies as muzzles on a free press; observers in the third world, joined by socialist critics elsewhere, hold to the contrary, asserting that liberty without restraint amounts to license, damaging the third world.

René Jean Ravault approaches the controversy from an empirical basis. He argues that current research indicates that news does not have the hypodermic effects claimed by the proponents of the New World Information Order. Audiences transform the meaning of the news to suit their own purposes. Ravault also contends that Western news benefits the third world. Conceding a point to third world critics, he urges Western media to focus more on economic and political development issues.

Trained in sociology at the Sorbonne (Paris) and in mass communication at the University of Iowa, Ravault at the time of writing was a professor in the Communications Department at the University of Quebec (Montreal). The selection is from "International Information: Bullet or Boomerang?" in *Political Communication Research: Approaches, Studies, Assessments*, ed. David L. Paletz (Norwood, N.J.: Ablex, 1987), 246-265.

From *Political Communication Research: Approaches, Studies, Assessments*, ed. David L. Paletz, pp. 246-265. Reprinted with permission of Ablex Publishing Corporation.

During the last 10 years, international communication has more and more captivated the attention of a growing number of social scientists throughout the world. This increased interest in the subject seems to parallel the appearance, growth, and expansion of the demand from Third World countries, especially the non-aligned nations, for a *New World Information Order*. This demand has been progressively shaped and articulated at UNESCO meetings dealing with either transnational cultural problems or international information issues including, more recently, the implantation of new transborder telecommunication technologies (Hamelink, 1983, pp. 56-72).

While this demand for a *New World Information Order* has been the source of tumultuous debates both within UNESCO and in the industrialized Western World, especially by the commercial media which firmly oppose it, most scholars and researchers seem to support it, document it, reinforce it, and do their best to publicize it to a large educated audience.

. . . [C]ritics seem to agree on the necessity to denounce and debunk the reigning international information structure. To them, this structure is grossly imbalanced and benefits only the multinational corporations and transnational banks of the Western World, instead of contributing to the socio-economic and cultural development of the Third World countries.

Their analysis, paralleling, inspiring, and reflecting the analyses made by the spokespersons of the non-aligned countries, suggests that there is a strong relationship between the economic domination of the North over the South and the cultural domination of the First World over the Third World. According to them, as well as many spokespersons of the developing countries, the implementation of the *New World Information Order* should go along with the implementation of the *New World Economic Order*. Often getting more radical then most Third World's spokespersons, these researchers are proposing a *New World Information Order* in which economic and cultural dissociation of the developing countries from the West seems to be the ultimate solution or panacea.

Taking issue against this extremely radical solution . . . this paper contends that the cultural dissociation proposal is based upon a victimizing view of the communication process in which the receiver is considered to be passive and totally receptive to the "messages" broadcast or diffused by powerful producers or senders.

This victimizing view of the communication process has been notoriously referred to by Wilbur Schramm as the "Bullet Theory."

. . . During the last 30 years, the "Bullet Theory" has progressively been considered as ill-founded and abandoned by communication researchers, as Schramm (1971, pp. 6-11; emphasis added) puts it:

> . . . Communication was seen as a magic bullet that transferred ideas or feelings or knowledge or motivations almost automatically from one mind to another. . . . In the early days of communication study, the

audience was considered relatively passive and defenseless, and communication could *shoot something into them* . . . But scholars began very soon to modify the Bullet Theory. It did not square with the facts. The audience, when it was hit by the Bullet, refused to fall over. *Sometimes, the Bullet had an effect that was completely unintended.* . . .

Contrary to the obsolete "Bullet Theory," the "Boomerang Theory" does not consider the receiver as a passive target, but gives him or her a power to respond to one-way communications in stronger and more efficient ways. According to the "Boomerang Theory," the receivers, even deprived of diffusion means, can use information provided by the "cultural dominator" to their own advantage. They can even use this information in order to make decisions and elaborate military, diplomatic, political, and economic strategies totally unintended by the sender and sometimes quite detrimental to the "dominating sender."

Dissociating Third World countries from transnational communication networks would put them in the situation of their "dominators" who, while talking instead of listening, have not been able to foresee and react properly to decolonization, the uprise of national and ethnic minorities all over the world, the growing economic competition of newly industrialized countries, and almost all of the geopolitical and economic changes which have been taking place lately. . . .

Amazingly enough, excellent illustrations of the "Boomerang Theory" are provided by several of the experts and critical researchers whose postures were questioned in the preceding part of this article.

Eudes' argumentation in the last two chapters of his book [The Conquest of Minds] concludes in a way which strongly contradicts the general impression of effectiveness of the U.S. cultural export machinery:

> In most situations, poverty and oppression, tend to generate a systematic rejection of the ruling elites who, then, are considered as "denationalized" through their consumption of foreign cultural products. In such situations the practice of the American culture is mainly perceived as a sign of treason. Conversely, the national culture becomes a strategic agent in the resistance to the implantation of "interdependence" (Eudes, 1982, p. 252).

The contribution of the media and advertising to this "Boomerang" process is further emphasized by Hamelink who suggests that: "As a result of this bombardment by advertising, the elite sectors, with higher incomes, tend to be integrated increasingly into the international economy, while the poor, spending scarce resources on unneeded things, lag farther behind in essentials such as health and education. This creates a widening gap between the rich and poor and contributes to an explosive social disintegration" (Hamelink, 1983, p. 16).

In such situations, one could wonder what happens to the cultural "integration," "homogenization," and "synchronization" that the present international information structure is supposed to generate? In fact, instances of this kind of situation can be found in many places during this century of decolonization and national as well as ethnic revival. The most striking and recent case is certainly Iran. "There, an indigenous information system, Shi'ite Islam, discovered itself intact at the end of a decade or more of vigorous importation of Western culture and on the crest of a wave of oil prosperity. The whole quest for modernization was rejected along with the Shah and the electronic culture, technically advanced though it was, was suddenly seen to have been an excrescence, an imposition, a conflict-bearing overseas culture which appealed to a particular Western-leaning elite, but which had not and could not penetrate the entire culture" (Smith, 1980, p. 59).

Similar backlash or "Boomerang" situations seem to be present in many countries of Latin America and more especially, Central America. While Cuba and Nicaragua have expelled their Americanized or "Gringoized" urban elites and middle classes, conflicts between these classes seem to rage in other countries where American culture is omnipresent within the local media. . . .

In many instances, mass media have provided colonized audiences with a clear understanding of their dominator's views of the world. This knowledge of their enemy's expectations and values helped them to elaborate shrewd strategies of resistance which successfully led them to independence.

> . . . [D]evices introduced by the French, such as the radio, were adapted as a means of internal communication in the movement of independence from France. A similar phenomenon occurred [in Chile] during the rule of Allende. In the working class district of Santiago, North American television series were viewed with close attention; the symbols, however, were interpreted in accord with the prevalent resistance to North American influences (Hamelink, 1983, p. 31).

This awareness of the possibility for exported cultural products to generate a backlash against the exporting country rather than supporting it is not so new.

> In the early days of Hollywood exporting there was some anxiety in Washington as to its possible unfortunate consequences for the American reputation abroad. From time to time such anxieties have again surfaced; some surveys have shown that familiarity with Hollywood products does not necessarily induce love of the United States. Occasionally foreign regimes—including those of Hitler and Stalin—have used careful selections of especially unsavoury Hollywood films, deliberately to reflect discredit on the USA (Tunstall, 1977, pp. 271-272). . . .

Many other examples could be mentioned to point out that, indeed, the "Bullet Theory" is "full of holes." In many instances, the receiver using his or her own cultural and experimental background can, to a large extent, control the meaning that a foreign message has for him or her. Through the "Boomerang Theory" the function of communication can no longer be limited to the function intended by the producer or sender, it can have an adverse or perverse effect. As in the case of Iran, foreign cultural imports can contribute to the revival of a cultural and ethnocentric background, according to which, eventually, international communications are interpreted and evaluated. . . .

What, then, seems to be most needed for all countries involved in a world in which "escaping interdependence" seems to be a genuine utopia is not a return to pre-World War II economic and cultural dissociation of the have-not countries, which may very well lead us back precisely to what the United Nations Organization and UNESCO have been established to stand against; but rather a genuine opening of Western countries that, so far, have been legally and, worse, psychosociologically closed to most foreign (and more especially Third World) culture and communication products.

Indeed, because of the fact, briefly noted by Hamelink (1983, p. 81) that "the Federal Communications Commission in the United States has placed severe restrictions on the entry of foreign broadcasting into its territory," as well as the self censoring behavior of American audiences who seem to believe that America is the "top Banana" country in the industrialized and technologized world and consequently believe that they do not have anything to learn from foreign cultures. . . .

America is suffering from "linguistic and cultural myopia," which "is losing" her "friends, business and respect in the world" (Fulbright, 1979, p. 15).

The core countries of capitalism are seriously disadvantaged by their inability to comprehend adequately, not only what is going on in the world, but, most important, how foreign decision-makers perceive and make sense out of what is going on in the world and, consequently, will act or react to it. Then, being almost always "taken by surprise," the core countries of capitalism seem to demonstrate an increasingly dangerous tendency to overreact in a rather brutal fashion. These reactions having often taken the form of direct or disguised military interventions, they, sometimes, manifest themselves through unilaterally decided financial reforms or monetary measures which may very well end up jeopardizing the whole, so painfully elaborated, international monetary order, as we are witnessing nowadays.

If the *New World Information Order* based upon a balanced communication traffic (instead of cultural dissociation), as originally proposed and supported by a good number of Third World countries, were implemented, it would be able to make the core countries of the industrialized and technologized world better informed about how different social and ethnic strata of different nations in the world do perceive and make sense out of what is going on. Then, tremendous progress in the wisdom and welfare of all the people involved in this new and balanced communication process could be accomplished. . . .

References

Eudes, Y. (1982). *La Conquête des Espirits, l'appareil d'exportation culturelle americain.* Paris: Maspero.

Fulbright, J. W. (1979). "We're Tongue-Tied." *Newsweek* (July 30), 15.

Hamelink, C. J. (1983). *Cultural Autonomy in Global Communications.* New York: Longman.

Schramm, W. (1971). "The Nature of Communication Between Humans." In W. Schramm and D. Roberts (Eds.), *The Process and Effects of Mass Communication* (Revised ed.). Urbana, IL: University of Illinois Press.

Smith, A. D. (1980). *The Geopolitics of Information.* New York: Oxford University Press.

Tunstall, J. (1977). *The Media Are American, Anglo-American Media in the World.* London: Constable.

6.6 ▬▬▬

Public Relations Efforts for the Third World:
Images in the News

Robert B. Albritton and Jarol B. Manheim

Editor's Note. The power of newspeople rests largely in their ability to select news for publication and feature it as they choose. The many people in and out of government who want and need media publicity try to influence these media choices. A new profession—public relations counseling—has emerged to help publicity seekers reach their goals. Representatives of major interests in the public and private sectors routinely employ public relations staffs to gain access to the media for their employers' messages.

In recent years, foreign countries, especially third world nations, have joined the crowds of publicity seekers and image doctors. Robert B. Albritton and Jarol B. Manheim explain the motivations behind these efforts, discuss commonly used tactics, and assess the results. Their work is based on systematic comparative analysis of a large sample of nations that have public relations contracts with U.S. firms. Their study shows that it is indeed possible for countries to control the flow of news about them. Third world nations that have complained often and loudly about the adverse publicity they receive are able to reduce the number of potentially harmful stories and to increase the amount of favorable coverage. Nonetheless, complaints about unfavorable coverage and coverage imbalances persist.

At the time of writing, Albritton was associate professor of political science at Northern Illinois University; Manheim was associate professor of political science at Virginia Polytechnic Institute and State University. This article is part of a larger investigation of the patterns and slants of news coverage produced by public relations activities and the political consequences of public relations efforts. The selection is from "Public Relations Efforts for the Third World: Images in the News," *Journal of Communication* 35:1 (Winter 1985): 43-59. Several tables have been omitted.

During the 1970s, countries of the Third World embarked on a concerted program to overcome what they perceived to be the informa-

Reprinted and abridged from *Journal of Communication* 35, no. 1 (Winter 1985): 43-59. Reprinted by permission of Oxford University Press.

tional colonialism of the industrialized nations. The cornerstone of this effort, the so-called New World Information Order, was perhaps best summarized by Masmoudi (12), who identified two principal dimensions of concern.

The first of these dimensions, the technological, encompasses a concern that the sovereignty of Third World nations is threatened or subverted through the control exercised by the industrialized nations over the development, allocation, and use of telecommunications technology (8). The second, dealing with news flows and media operations, emphasizes software—what messages are conveyed and the process by which they are carried. Third World countries worry that they lack control over in-flows of information (news of the outside world, especially the selection of which stories and which aspects of those stories are salient, and all variety of entertainment media; see 20); out-flows of information (news of the Third World reaching other nations and the criteria that are applied to select it); and the communications infrastructure (news agencies, news wires, and the professional norms and behaviors of journalists). A central problem here is the operation of the major international wire services, which, it is contended, provide what many Third World countries perceive as an unflattering or otherwise inappropriate portrayal of their activities to audiences in the industrialized nations. Due to the inherent circularity of the process and to Western dominance, much of what the Third World learns of itself is focused through a Western lens (2, 10, 17).

The amounts of rhetoric, diplomatic effort, and, to a lesser extent, economic resources that various countries have applied to these activities for the past decade attest to the depth of their concern over images of the Third World that reach other nations. No doubt central to this concern is the realization that, through their effects on both the public and the policy agendas in countries like the United States, these images can influence policy making on issues of interest to the Third World (9; 13, pp. 7-14; 15).

A number of Third World nations have worked to gain control of their images on a more direct front—by contracting with U.S. public relations firms. In addition to some direct lobbying with officials of the U.S. government, these firms have provided such services as the preparing of press kits and other similar materials, counseling embassy personnel regarding how to phrase discussions of such topics as terrorism or human rights, organizing field trips for the press, conducting meetings and programs highlighting economic or other resources of the client country, establishing personal contact between client-government officials and influential U.S. officials or journalists, and providing advice as to specific policies or approaches to policy that could favorably affect the image of the client government (3, 5, 19). An examination of the mandatory foreign agent registration records of the U.S. Department of Justice shows, for example, that of the 25 countries whose governments contracted for services during the period 1974-1978, nineteen (76 percent) would be classified as Third World countries by one definition or another. This five-year period corresponds to that during which the issues raised under the rubric of the New World Information Order rose to prominence.

. . . [C]lear congruence between the goals of such attempts at image manipulation and the expressed desire to gain control of the flow of information from and about such countries, suggests that public relations activities have indeed been employed as a third dimension of the international struggle over information flows.

In this article we examine the effectiveness of several of these efforts by analyzing the coverage of five Third World nations—Argentina, Indonesia, the Republic of Korea, the Philippines, and Turkey—in the *New York Times*, each during a two-year period associated with a professional public relations effort. The *Times* was selected for analysis because it is the most widely read newspaper among elites both within and outside the U.S. government (21) and among the most widely cited by policy-makers (7), has been shown to have a strong agenda-setting effect on public opinion (22), is regarded as a benchmark of U.S. news coverage by foreign governments (see, for example, 4, p. 38), and carries a greater volume of foreign news than other major U.S. newspapers (16, 23). For these reasons, the *Times* represents a primary target for public relations efforts undertaken in behalf of Third World governments.

Using U.S. Department of Justice records, we identified the starting date of the public relations contract signed by each nation under review. For purposes of analysis, we defined the first day of the following month as the point of intervention in each instance. We then determined for each country a unique 24-month period consisting of the twelve months immediately before and after the intervention, and gathered serial data on several qualitative and quantitative indicators of news coverage of that country in the *Times*. Our data were drawn from the summaries of all *Times* articles provided in the *New York Times Index*.

Treating each insertion in the index as a unit of analysis and the aggregates for each month as a single observation, we coded news coverage of each country on several variables, including (but not limited to) the number of articles pertaining to the country, the number that could be judged as portraying either a positive or a negative image, and the number that referred to either cooperation or noncooperation between the country in question and the United States. Positive references included such topics as the country's progress, advances, resources, assets, strengths, continuity, stability, reliability, or dependability. Negative references included any mention of decline, weakness, poverty, liabilities lack of progress, instability, or unreliability. References to cooperation were defined to include friendly behavior toward, agreement with, or behavior in accordance with the policies or expressed preferences of the United States on the part of the contracting country. References to noncooperation included unfriendly behavior toward, disagreement with, or behavior in opposition to the policies or the expressed preferences of the United States.

Although we have in hand a number of materials distributed by public relations counselors in behalf of foreign government clients, we cannot at present claim to know what specific advice regarding image management was provided in any particular instance. And it is this private advice, much more than the slick published materials, that is central to the phenomenon in question. What we can state with both certainty and precision, however, is (a) *that* such advice was provided and (b) *when* it was provided. Because our purpose here is to assess not the components of the various public relations campaigns but rather their overall effect on news images, this limited information is quite sufficient.

Accordingly, our approach is simply to identify any change in the behavior or news coverage of a given client nation that is associated in time with the signing of a public relations contract. That change, in our view, when adjusted for such contributory factors as trend, represents the impact of the public relations efforts. For any given country, idiosyncratic events coinciding with the signing of a public relations contract might offer a plausible alternative explanation of these effects. But when changes associated with the signing of public relations contracts occur consistently across a variety of continents and time periods, as they do among the nations examined here, we believe that such rival interpretations of the data become increasingly implausible. . . .

A review of events in each country during its pre- and post-test period puts the subsequent data in perspective and highlights certain patterns of behavior that, at least superficially, seem to be associated in time with and to reflect the public relations activities. These patterns include exchanges of visits between foreign heads of state (or their surrogates) and high-ranking U.S. officials, the ending of political arrests and/or the freeing of dissidents, cosmetic redistributions of power within a client country, and new or renewed participation in various types of negotiations, among others. Two classes of information have been included in this review. The first comprises summaries (drawn from news accounts) of those events or activities during each two-year period judged by us to be most significant to the respective countries themselves, either on their own merit or as components of longer-term chains of events. Where such long-term chains were in evidence, most continued through both the pre- and post-test periods and were seemingly unaffected by the public relations activity. The second class of information consists of generally lesser notices or events judged by us to relate either directly or potentially to the public relations effort and especially to the patterns of image-sensitive behavior just noted. Most of these occurred during the post-test periods, but we have taken care to point out any connections to pretest activities (e.g., the *continuation* of releases of political prisoners in South Korea) and any directly counterproductive post-test activities (e.g., the press ban in Indonesia) as well.

Argentina.[1]   The period of analysis began in June 1975. During the two years under review, the Argentine economy was plagued by strikes, inflation, and government deficits. Terrorists and guerrillas threatened the stability of the Perón regime, and the president herself took a leave of absence to avert a military coup. An investigation was begun into charges of government corruption, Perón announced that she would not seek reelection and later withstood an attempt at impeachment, cabinet changes were commonplace, Perón was arrested in a military takeover (month 10) and Videla was elected president, Videla narrowly escaped two assassination attempts, and the government was repeatedly criticized for its human rights policies. During the post-intervention period, the military government released political prisoners, reopened a leading university, imposed a ban on anti-Semitic and pro-Nazi literature, and frequently announced that foreign debt and other economic problems were being resolved. Several generals were replaced in the government with moderate civilians, and President Videla called for a rapid return to democracy.

Indonesia.   Here the review period commenced in July 1976. Major events included bribery scandals involving international oil companies and the country's military leaders, a foiled coup attempt, the banning of *Newsweek* magazine, charges of human rights violations, an electoral victory by President Suharto, reductions in U.S. military assistance, a kidnapping incident in the Netherlands involving an Indonesian ethnic group, and a crackdown on the press. During the post-intervention period, the government granted amnesty to and released political dissidents, opened talks with the United States regarding its human rights policies, hosted a visit by Walter Mondale, reopened the nation's newspapers (the ban, too, had come after the intervention), and began talks on a new constitution.

Republic of Korea.   The analysis period includes the two years beginning in April 1977. During this time, the United States gave extended consideration to reducing its forces stationed in the country, the government sparred publicly with the Catholic church, the United States was accused of spying on Korean leaders and Korean bribery of members of the U.S. Congress was under investigation, and opposition leader Kim Dae Jong was placed under arrest. During the post-intervention period there was a visit by Soviet leader Leonid Brezhnev (a reminder of the potential dangers of a U.S. military withdrawal), resumption of reunification talks with the North, a meeting between Presidents Park and Carter, continuation of an earlier pattern of prisoner release, a U.S. Senate "study tour" of the country, and the development into a major tourist attraction of a newly discovered North Korean infiltration tunnel. In addition, some two months after the intervention, the *Times* reported that the Korean government had become noticeably more sensitive to its image abroad.

The Philippines. Our analysis began in February 1977. Events during this period included a continuing Moslem rebellion in the south, imposition of martial law, detention of journalists, discussion of continuing leases for U.S. military bases, and several incidents of political violence. During the year following the intervention, Vice-President Mondale visited, a new pro-Marcos political party was formed and elections were held, President Marcos promised to grant new authority to the legislature, a leading dissident was reluctantly freed and other political prisoners were pardoned, granted amnesty, and released, signals were put out of an improving relationship with China (a reminder of the country's strategic importance), and the discovery (or rediscovery) of a primitive tribe in a remote area was publicized.

Turkey. Here the analysis period began with the formation of a new government in March 1975. It was a time of high inflation and general political instability that was dominated by a bitter squabble with Greece over the fate of Cypress. A U.S. arms embargo was in force at the outset, and the military alliance between the two countries was strained. During the pretest period, Prime Minister Demirel survived an assassination attempt, relations with the Soviet Union softened noticeably (including an agreement on a large loan, the signing of a friendship document, and a visit to Turkey by a delegation of Soviet officials), Greek nationals attacked Turkish diplomats around the world, and a scheduled state visit to the United States was postponed. During the post-intervention period, Greece and Turkey agreed to negotiate the Cypress question, but tension continued. The Soviet Union claimed Turkey was acting in an unfriendly manner, the previously scheduled visit to the United States of a former prime minister took place (though he was assaulted by a Greek national during the visit), and President Carter sent a delegation to Greece, Turkey, and Cyprus. In month 14, the *Times* opined that many of Turkey's problems in the United States were really the work of the Greek lobby; in month 20, the paper noted the improvements in the country under the Demirel government; and in month 23, Turkey's movement away from the Soviet Union was reported.

Although there does seem to be some correspondence between certain of these events and behaviors and the signing of the respective public relations contracts, we do not find this anecdotal evidence in itself persuasive of the effects of public relations efforts. After all, many of these events may have taken place for other, less image-related reasons as well, and a mere recounting cannot establish clearly any underlying relationships. But we find these bits of evidence suggestive of behavioral tendencies on the part of both political actors and journalists that we believe to be associated with the public relations intervention, tendencies that are substantially apparent in a more rigorous, quantitative examination of the various experimental periods. . . .

As a glance at Table 1 will indicate, all five nations under review here had negative pre-intervention images. The table reports pre-intervention means for eleven indicators of news image. Elsewhere (11) we have identified two dimensions of such images, valence and visibility, which help to determine an appropriate public relations strategy for countries seeking improvement to pursue. In the present instance, such a strategy, based on an analysis of the first seven items in the table, would lead each of our countries to seek to (a) reduce their visibility (i.e., the amount of coverage they receive) and (b) improve their valence (i.e., the positive-negative balance of coverage) during the post-intervention period. An additional strategy would be to assume a more cooperative pose vis-à-vis the United States by eliminating, or at least masking, any apparent conflict between the two countries.

The final four indicators in Table 1 summarize pretest means on indicators related to this approach. Together, these strategies suggest that the effectiveness of public relations activities in altering the news images of these five countries can be assessed by examining separately three components of those images, with three very particular questions in mind. These pertain to reductions in visibility, improvements in valence, and improvements in the image of compatibility with the United States.

While the desirability of reducing news coverage may initially seem counterintuitive, given the complaint of some Third World nations that they receive too little attention in the Western press already, it is, in fact, quite consistent with the goal of gaining control over outflows of information that is explicit in both the calls for a New World Information Order and the broad conceptualization of public relations activities we employ here.

A case in point is provided by Rhodesia (now Zimbabwe), where the Smith government contracted for public relations advice during the period of civil war. During the year preceding this contract, *New York Times* coverage was replete with government-announced casualty counts whose collective effect was to portray an extremely violent society. Almost immediately upon the signing of the contract, and despite the continuation of the conflict itself, these government-controlled reports virtually disappeared from the *Times*. Partly as a result, although coverage of Rhodesia still reflected the violent nature of events in that country, the news was significantly less violent in its content than had earlier been the case (1).

Of the five countries under review, four demonstrate significant

Table 1   Average Monthly Scores of Five Nations on Selected Indicators of Image Visibility and Valence, Pre-contract Period

Indicator	Argentina	Indo-nesia	Republic of Korea	Philip-pines	Turkey
Total number of articles	21.6	5.1	18.3	10.3	17.5
Number of articles characterized by negative valence	16.1	1.3	9.8	7.2	11.7
Number of articles characterized by positive valence	1.9	0.7	2.8	2.7	3.0
Percent of total articles characterized by negative valence	75.0	46.4	56.1	68.2	64.1
Percent of total articles characterized by positive valence	8.0	33.1	14.8	30.2	23.1
Percent positive of all valenced articles	10.0	34.2	23.0	29.9	25.0
Net of positive-negative articles	−14.1	−0.6	−7.0	−4.5	−8.7
Number of articles indicating cooperation with U.S.	0.3	0.3	3.7	1.2	2.2
Number of articles indicating noncoopera-tion with U.S.	0.0	0.2	4.8	0.8	8.6
Percent of articles indicating cooperation with U.S.	1.1	10.8	18.4	11.9	15.8
Percent of articles indicating noncoopera-tion with U.S.	0.0	4.6	27.4	7.6	39.8

reductions in visibility during the post-intervention period. In the case of Argentina, the reduction was on the order of 50 percent (from 21.6 articles per month to 10.9); for Korea, the Philippines, and Turkey, it was greater still. The fifth contracting country, Indonesia, shows no such reduction associated with the public relations contract, but it is important to note that Indonesia had far and away the lowest pre-intervention level of visibility (see Table 1) and hence the least need for further reductions. Indeed, when news coverage of a country reaches such a low level (five articles per month), further systematic reductions may not only be especially difficult to achieve, but they may not even serve any practical purpose, since the country's news image is unlikely to be actively in the minds of those whom the public relations consultants seek to influence. Indonesia, in other words, probably started this period with precisely the level of anonymity that the four other nations in question were purposefully seeking. Thus, we may conclude that in all those cases where they were most necessary to achieve the requisite effect, substantial reductions in visibility did occur associated in time with the public relations effort.

. . . Our other work also suggests that, for countries whose initial images are of the type reported here, successful public relations efforts can bring about improvements in valence, though not necessarily to the point at which a country could be said to have a "positive" image. Rather, as visibility is reduced, opportunities are presented to introduce marginal, incremental shifts in a generally positive direction, so that at some later time, as news consumers begin to see more news of the country in question, the underlying setting will be much more favorable. In the present instance, then, we should expect to see the valence of each country improve during the post-intervention period. . . .

Each of our five countries demonstrates an improvement in valence on at least one of our summary indicators associated with the intervention. In the case of Indonesia, where visibility was essentially unchanged, ... this shift derives entirely from an increase in positive coverage. This, again, is consistent with the advantaged position provided by Indonesia's initially low visibility. Improved valence in Turkey, . . . a country with much higher initial visibility (see Table 1, Indicator 1), the change traces exclusively to reductions in negative coverage. In the Philippines, significant valence reduction is apparent. . . . much of the improvement is attributable to the reduction of visibility noted above. Consistent with this explanation, note that both positive and negative coverage decreased in association with the public relations effort, but that negative coverage decreased to a much greater extent. Finally, in Argentina and Korea . . . improvements derive from reductions in negative coverage and increases in positive coverage. In each country, then, image valence does change in the predicted direction during the post-intervention period. . . .

Clearly associated with the valence of an image, but substantively worthy of consideration in its own right, is a third component of news images of Third World nations in the U.S. press: the degree of cooperativeness that they are shown to manifest toward U.S. interests. Because the number of coded references to cooperation/noncooperation is relatively small, . . . the results here are tentative at best. Still, we believe they deserve some attention.

Clearly, to the extent that a public relations campaign focuses on these themes, its goal must be to reduce references to noncooperation (or outright conflict) between the client and target states and either at the same time or subsequently to increase references in the press to cooperation between the two. Our results here are rather more mixed than those reported above, with only three countries—Indonesia, Korea, and Turkey—showing significant change associated with the signing of their respective contracts. In the case of Indonesia, where positive enhancement of the valence is the locus of attention, references to cooperation with the United States increase significantly following the signing. Conversely, in Korea, where the emphasis is more on reducing visibility, contract-related change takes the form of reduced references to noncooperation. And in Turkey, which should show a pattern similar to that in Korea, references to noncooperation are in fact reduced significantly, but so, to a lesser extent, are those to cooperation.

Thus, in these three countries we find some evidence suggestive of intervention-related changes in the cooperation component of image, but the evidence is neither as consistent nor as persuasive as that relating to visibility and valence.

We began with the premise that systematic public relations activities directed at manipulation of national images as portrayed in the U.S. press represented a third dimension of the New World Information Order, one that was used by a large number of Third World nations during the middle and late 1970s. Based on an examination of five such contracting nations, we can now conclude that not only were such manipulative efforts undertaken, but they were in large measure successful. In every instance, the client nation was able to improve at least one component of its news image during the year following the signing of its contract, and in most instances the improvements were more extensive still.

Although such image improvements are unlikely to translate immediately into political advantage or policy gain within the U.S. arena, there is reason to believe that, over time, the creation and manipulation of informational settings can exert a positive influence on public opinion and political outcomes (6, 14, 15, 18). To the extent that Third World nations seek such advantage, then—and it is clear that each of the countries reported upon here did so actively—public relations campaigns of the type we have analyzed can be a useful instrument of policy. And to the extent that gaining such advantage by controlling outflows of information is a goal of the New World Information Order per se, such activities, which draw upon the peculiar vulnerabilities of the Western press, have been shown to be effective devices in attaining that end.

Note

1. The anecdotal summaries of events in Argentina, Indonesia, Republic of Korea, and the Philippines presented here first appeared in Manheim and Albritton (11). The summary of events in Turkey has not been reported previously.

References

1. Albritton, Robert B. and Jarol B. Manheim: "News of Rhodesia: The Impact of a Public Relations Campaign," *Journalism Quarterly* 60, 1983, pp. 622-628.
2. Ansah, Paul A. V."International News: Mutual Responsibilities of Developed and Developing Nations." In George Gerbner and Marsha Siefert (Eds.) *World Communications: A Handbook.* New York: Longman, 1983, pp. 83-91.
3. Cooney, John E. "Public Relations Firms Draw Fire for Aiding Repressive Countries." *Wall Street Journal* 193, January 3, 1979, pp. 1, 30.
4. Curtis, Bill. *On Assignment with Bill Curtis.* Chicago: Rand McNally, 1983.
5. Davis, Morris. *Interpreters for Nigeria: The Third World and International Public Relations.* Urbana, Ill.: University of Illinois Press, 1977.
6. Eyal, Chaim H. Unpublished doctoral dissertation. Syracuse University, 1980, as cited in Maxwell E. McCombs, "The Agenda-Setting Approach." In Dan D. Nimmo and Keith R. Sanders (Eds.) *Handbook of Political Communication.* Beverly Hills, Cal.: Sage, 1981, pp. 121-140, passim.
7. Grau, Craig H. "What Publications are Most Frequently Quoted in the *Congressional Record?*" *Journalism Quarterly* 53, 1976, pp. 716-719.
8. Hamelink, Cees J. "Informatics: Third World Call for New Order." *Journal of Communication* 29(3). Summer 1979, pp. 144-148.
9. Iyengar, Shanto, Mark D. Peters, and Donald R. Kinder. "Experimental Demonstrations of the 'Not-so-Minimal' Consequences of Television News Programs." *American Political Science Review* 76, 1982, pp. 848-858.
10. López-Escobar, E. *Análisis del "Nuevo Orden" Internacional de la Información.* Pamplona, Spain: Ediciones Universidad de Navarra, 1978.
11. Manheim, Jarol B, and Robert B. Albritton. "Changing National Images: International Public Relations and Media Agenda-Setting." *American Political Science Review* 78, 1984, pp. 641-657.
12. Masmoudi, Mustapha. "The New World Information Order." *Journal of Communication* 29(2), Spring 1979, pp. 172-179.
13. Merrill, John C. *Global Journalism: A Survey of the World's Mass Media.* New York: Longman, 1983.
14. Merritt, Richard L. "Transforming International Communications Strategies." *Political Communication and Persuasion* 1, 1980, pp. 5-42.
15. Page, Benjamin I. and Robert Y. Shapiro. "Effects of Public Opinion on Policy." *American Political Science Review* 77, 1983, pp. 175-190.
16. Semmel, Andrew K. "Foreign News in Four U.S. Elite Dailies: Some Comparisons." *Journalism Quarterly* 53, 1976, pp. 732-736.
17. Smith, Anthony. *The Geopolitics of Information: How Western Culture Dominates the World.* New York: Oxford University Press, 1980.
18. Stone, Gerald C. and Maxwell E. McCombs. "Tracing the Time-Lag in Agenda Setting." *Journalism Quarterly* 58, 1981, pp. 51-55.
19. Tedlow, Richard S. and John A. Quelch. "Communications for the Nation-State." *Public Relations Journal* 37, June 1981, pp. 22-25.
20. Tunstall, Jeremy. *The Media are American: Anglo-American Media in the World.* New York: Columbia University Press, 1977.

21. Weiss, Carol H. "What America's Leaders Read." *Public Opinion Quarterly* 38, 1974, pp. 1-22.
22. Winter, James P. and Chaim H. Eyal. "Agenda Setting for the Civil Rights Issue." *Public Opinion Quarterly* 45, 1981, pp. 376-383.
23. Womack, Brantly. "Attention Maps of 10 Major Newspapers." *Journalism Quarterly* 58, 1981, pp. 260-265.